Big Idea,

The making of cre...

JW COLLEGE ...NTR...

...HE-H...

HARROW COLLEGE
HH Learning Centre
Lowlands Road, Harrow
Middx HA1 3AQ
020 8909 6520

Big Idea, Small Steps
The making of credit-based qualifications

Peter Wilson

niace
promoting adult learning

© 2010 National Institute of Adult Continuing Education

Published by **niace**
promoting adult learning

21 De Montfort Street
Leicester LE1 7GE

Company registration no. 2603322
Charity registration no. 1002775

www.niace.org.uk

NIACE has a broad remit to promote lifelong learning opportunities for adults.
NIACE works to develop increased participation in education and training,
particularly for those who do not have easy access because of class, gender,
age, race, language and culture, learning difficulties or disabilities, or insufficient financial resources.

For a full listing of all NIACE's publications visit
http://shop.niace.org.uk

Cataloguing in Publications Data
A CIP record for this title is available from the British Library

ISBN 978-1-86201-439-8

Designed and typeset by 4word Ltd, Bristol, UK

For Mary

Contents

Preface

In November 2008 the relevant government departments of England, Wales and Northern Ireland announced the setting up of the new Qualifications and Credit Framework (QCF). The QCF marks a significant and potentially radical change from the previous National Qualifications Framework (NQF) in these countries. This is an account of where the QCF came from, how it was made, and where it might go in the future.

Although this account takes note of the formal process of development that preceded the launch of the new Framework, it is an explicitly personal view of how the QCF came into being. It is written from the perspective of someone involved in the process of developing the QCF from inception to implementation, as well as in what might be termed the 'pre-history' of the QCF. Indeed, it is the connection between this recent, formalised process of development and the preceding period of undocumented and unplanned activity that forms the true focus of this publication.

The title of the publication attempts to signify both the importance of the concept of 'credit' in this story, and the long and sometimes arduous road to the creation of a system of credit-based qualifications. Although the QCF explicitly brings together both qualifications and credit in its title, it will be for others to propose an alternative conception of its development that focuses on the 'Q' rather than the 'C' in QCF. The assumption behind this story is that the importation of credit into the process of qualifications reform marks a significant change from previous phases of reform and establishes the opportunity to make a positive break with these previous manifestations of 'reform' in the way that learner achievement is recognised. This is an explicitly 'credit-based' view of credit-based qualifications.

I use the word 'opportunity' here because it is too soon to tell whether these recent reforms have secured a permanent change in the culture of our qualifications system. Despite the potential of the QCF to deliver the usual ambitions of government for radical change, it remains to be seen whether the big idea of 'credit' can survive and prosper in this new place between 'Q' and 'F'.

This is not intended to be an exhaustive chronological account of events leading to the establishing of the QCF. One of the penalties of being a 'participant observer' in this process is that some aspects of this story loom larger than others, simply because they were witnessed at first hand. Somewhere between a comprehensively researched series of secondary texts and the privileged access to first-hand experience of some of these moments sits a balance of objective and subjective perspectives on the story of how the QCF was made. I hope the term 'small steps' conveys an appropriately modest position of the storyteller in this account.

The idea that the QCF has been established through the collective actions of numerous people making small advances over a long period of time is reflected in a description of the development of credit systems in the United States. The author of this description – Sheldon Rothblatt – bemoans the fact that the story of how credit systems in the US came to be developed is lost in the mundane history of the organisations that gradually established them: 'The history of credits is fascinating but essentially obscure... After all, it is administrative history, a tiresome account of tiny details congealing into a system. No heroic personalities combat insurmountable odds... The story is humdrum' (Rothblatt, 1991).

It is my intention that these 'tiny details' should be recorded in some way so that this same 'humdrum story' in the UK acknowledges at least some of the contributions – occasionally by heroic personalities combating insurmountable odds – made to the 'congealing' of this thing we now refer to within the QCF as 'a credit system'.

The piecing together of this story is an explicitly personal process. Although I have attempted to draw on a range of external sources to validate this personal perspective, it will be for the reader to decide how far the personal risks become the idiosyncratic as the text unfolds. In highlighting these fragments of the humdrum, I have followed Jorge Luis Borges' view that in writing about the past we shine a torch backwards through time and select out those things that fall momentarily into the glare of our moving arc of light, that we recognise as familiar from our current viewpoint. We read Gerard Manley Hopkins differently because we are familiar with Dylan Thomas, says Borges (Borges, 1999). In this sense, all history is idiosyncratic, notwithstanding the fact that our torch falls on real moments that can be verified through evidence. If the QCF had not been developed, many of these briefly illuminated moments would have remained in darkness. I claim the privilege of the torch holder in collecting the tiny details together in a way that makes sense to me.

It is probably rare in one's professional life to be able to shine this torch back through time from such an elevated position as a formally constituted framework, secured in legislation. To have been part of both the history and what Stephen Yeo tantalisingly referred to as 'the pre-history' (Yeo, 1998) of credit systems, as well as the making of the QCF, has been a privilege for me, but also an intellectual challenge – albeit a welcome one. This experience, and the opportunity to reflect on the relationship between ideas and practice, as well as between sentiment and the reality of practical progress, forms the background to this volume; a codicil to the internal reading of events in this arcane and particular field of work that has occupied me for some 25 years.

One reason for wanting to record this 'congealing of tiny details' is to mark the importance of individual contributions at various key points in the story. Again, I make no apology for recording these individual contributions in both the text itself and in an occasional footnote. Some of these contributions have indeed been 'heroic' – if not in the drama of the action, then in the dogged perseverance of some committed individuals in the face of often 'insurmountable odds'. The small steps on this journey have not always been in a forward direction, but the big idea of a credit system has passed from one person to another and – despite numerous diversions – has finally been delivered in the form of the QCF.

There is another message in this volume, which is about time and process. Since the announcement by government of its intention to develop the QCF, the process of reform has become more formalised, more subject to plans and projections, more expensive and therefore more closely scrutinised by government itself. It remains to be seen whether some of the elegance and subtlety of the QCF is lost in its implementation through these formal processes. In highlighting the small steps in the development of credit systems prior to this most recent phase, I am trying to shed light on a very different process. The credit system that now underpins the QCF did not spring fully formed from a think tank, a government commission or a research project. It has been developed through experiment, trial, error, theorising and – most of all – through widespread application in practice, subject to collective scrutiny and refinement over a long period. It is a process of development very different from the plans for implementation of the QCF. Indeed, I would argue that it is a process that is very unlikely to be repeated in any public policymaking in the foreseeable future and is all the more precious for that. By implication, this story is also about how to make things that work. Placing the tools of a credit system in the hands of those unfamiliar with its origins and history is no guarantee of its effective application in practice. The big idea of credit may yet prove to be a modest innovation in the hands of those not involved in its development over time.

A further intention behind this publication is to connect the QCF explicitly to its unwritten, as well as its documented, history. In so doing, I hope not only to record the wealth of individual contributions over time (the real meaning of 'small steps') that form the foundations of the QCF, but also to bequeath to those responsible for now taking forward the new framework an understanding of this history which they (whether knowingly or not) now inherit and, at least in the view of this chronicler, have an obligation to acknowledge and to refine further.

Acknowledgements

This book makes repeated references to the people who have influenced my thinking on this subject over many years. I hope that none of them are embarrassed by their inclusion. Similarly, I apologise here to all those others who may have been named, but are covered instead by the 'too numerous to mention' convention to which authors are allowed to have recourse. However, some acknowledgements must be made here.

I begin with thanks to David Browning, who first inspired me about credit, and to Aubrey Black for his quiet wisdom. To my colleagues involved in setting up the South Yorkshire Open College Federation, Robin Fielder, Elaine Smith and (for sentimental reasons) the much-missed Mary Wright. Special thanks for his clear thinking and good humour from those days through to the present go to Brett Kerton. In those early days we received a great deal of support from colleagues in other OCNs, and in particular from Teresa Bergin, Sue Pedder and David Robertson. And special thanks to John Sanders, not just for this early support but for its continuation to the present day.

Caroline Mager connects this early period with the support of NIACE for OCNs, and it is here that my thanks go also to Alan Tuckett, not just for this support, but for his friendship and benign leadership over more than a decade. My thanks go also to Peter Lavender, Carol Taylor, Mick Murray and Alec McAulay for their help and support in actually producing this volume, and to all at NIACE for the opportunity to write it.

The group of people that put together *A Basis for Credit?* deserve special mention, but to Andrew Morris in particular go thanks. A special thank you also to Tony Tait, not just for his perseverance in staying with this agenda when many others had left it, but for his help in filling in some of the missing details from this story that I had forgotten or simply been unaware of. We all owe him a great deal.

To the people who worked with me to set up the Leicestershire OCN and in particular to Alison Hedley, Carol Howett, Lynne Slipper and Marie Thompson, who not only did the real work but also indulged me in my writing for audiences far from Leicester. Thanks to Toni Fazaeli, Annie Merton and Robert Raven for all their support behind the scenes. And to Philip Jones –

still missed – the original inspiration behind today's credit-based Access to HE Diplomas.

Roger Waterhouse, Paul Bridges and Bob Faithorn deserve recognition for supporting the early development of NOCN, as well as credit systems in HE. Sally Kitchener and Lynne Furness were the practical rock on which NOCN was built. To all those others who have come after, including Karan Green and Jill Brunt, thanks are due for transforming a good idea, a desk and a part-time secondment into a multi-million pound organisation. Thanks too to Jonathan Brown, editor of the Journal of Access and Credit Studies, and to Stephen Yeo for his radical thoughts about credit in its pages.

Lest my thanks seem too Anglo-centric, thanks go also to Monica Deasey, Kim Ebrahim, Caroline Egerton, Alison Spencer and especially to Kenn Palmer – not just for his original thinking about credit, but for his comments on my perception of the influence of Wales in this story. Beyond these islands thanks go too to Arjen Deij and to Mike Coles.

It has been a privilege for me to work closely with the group of people responsible for taking forward the work on the QCF in recent years. Thanks to the irreplaceable Ken Boston and the imperturbable Mary Curnock Cook and especially to Sue Georgious, who could have been mentioned in the list of people that helped to build NOCN but will be best remembered as a QCF warrior. Thanks to all the people who carried through the work of the QCF on the ground at QCA – to mix my metaphors horribly it was a great privilege for an old dog to get a second bite of the cherry. Nick Juba, Liz Vidis, Veronica Davids, Richard Garrett and Libby Sharpe are all remembered with fondness. Thanks too to Jon Gamble and Janet Ryland at LSC. Their work behind the scenes has been vital to the success of the QCF.

Lastly, to Beverly Sand, who deserves mention in her own right as a contributor at many stages of this story, as well as a critical friend in reading the text and eliminating the worst of its excesses ('Wilsonisms' as she calls them). But mainly for her enduring support (at times tolerance) for the time and energy I've devoted to this work over the past 20 years and more. This book is first and foremost for her.

1
A new beginning

The intention to develop 'a credit framework for adults' was announced in the July 2003 Skills Strategy White Paper *21st Century Skills: Realising our Potential* (DfES, 2003, p. 74). In the proposal to ministers in June 2008 that recommended that the Qualifications and Credit Framework (QCF) should be implemented, it is *21st Century Skills* that is cited as the starting point for development of the QCF. A great deal of work remained to be done in determining what this 'credit framework' would look like more than five years into the future, but the significance of this policy commitment cannot be overestimated. But where did this reference come from?

The Skills Strategy White Paper of 2003 was seen as a major policy document that would shape the agenda for reform of post-school education and training for years to come. A further White Paper in 2005 consolidated the direction of reform set out in *21st Century Skills* (DfES, 2005) and reiterated the importance of a new credit-based qualifications system in taking forward a broad programme of reforms across post-school education and training.

Two years later, Lord Leitch's report *World Class Skills* (Leitch, 2007) and the government's subsequent response (DfES, 2007) further underlined the importance of the QCF in delivering the 'demand-led' system of skills that, Leitch stated, would be essential if the UK economy and its workforce were to remain internationally competitive in the year 2020. In 2008, in its consultation document on the reform of 14–19 qualifications, the now re-titled Department for Children, Schools and Families (DCSF) proposed that all 14–19 qualifications in England should be developed in the future within 'a credit-based framework' (DCSF, 2008, p. 7). Proposals for bringing 14–19 qualifications into the QCF were presented to the DCSF by the Qualifications and Curriculum Authority (QCA) in January 2009, and a plan and timescale for taking forward this next phase of development of the framework to 2015 is (at the time of writing) being considered within government.

Through these references in key formal documents we can detect a gradual shift in both the importance of the QCF and its conceptual purpose over a five-year period. From the 'adult' credit framework of 2003, through the framework for vocational qualifications of 2005, to the comprehensive framework for all qualifications of 2009, the conceptual scope of the QCF has continued to expand during its process of development. In part this is a testament to the design of the QCF itself, which has always promoted itself as a 'potentially comprehensive' framework (of which more later). Nevertheless, we should note here the unique trajectory of reform that this sequence of reports actually represents.

Having begun its policy life as an adult framework, the QCF then became a framework within which the reform of vocational qualifications, irrespective of age, was to be taken forward; and it is now conceived as a framework within which 14–19 qualifications, including A levels and GCSEs, could also be reformed in the future.[1] This is not the way that things normally happen in education and training policy, and it is certainly not the way in which previous programmes of qualification reform have been undertaken. The idea that a framework based on the needs of adult learners could support the wider reform of vocational qualifications and, having proved its ability to do so, could then be used to support the reform of A levels and GCSEs has no precedent in recent policy formation in education and training. For this reason alone the QCF is worthy of our consideration.

This reverse process of development becomes even more interesting when the history of credit-based frameworks in the UK prior to 2003 is considered. Not only does the QCF originate in a policy context with a focus on the needs of adult learners, but the 'credit' strand of the QCF draws on a long and rich history of recognising the achievements of adult learners in community-based learning, in informal adult learning and in contexts totally outside the 'mainstream' development of qualifications during the same period. Once this 'prehistory' of the QCF is added into the sequence, the process of development from an adult to a comprehensive framework is woven into a parallel process of development from an informal and voluntary towards a formal and regulated framework that makes the trajectory of reform over a 25-year (rather than a five-year) period even more remarkable.

The Skills Strategy, the Leitch Review and the reform of 14–19 qualifications are all based on very different policy imperatives from those that informed the development of credit systems prior to 2003. Can a concept developed in the context of widening access to educational opportunity support a policy of workforce up-skilling in response to international competition? Can a system designed to promote responsiveness to individual needs be deployed to maintain academic standards? Can a system designed to recognise the achievements of marginalised learners in local communities be used to measure the professional development of employees in a large multi-national company? To understand how a credit system can do these things it is necessary to trace its development over a 25-year period. The process of practical application and refinement of the concept of credit in a gradually changing context has produced a powerful set of conceptual tools that can not only be applied to the policy agenda as conceived in the Skills Strategy and the Leitch Review, but also to the emerging strategy of retrenchment and fire-fighting that currently characterises government policy in a period of recession.

One of the reasons for wanting to 'capture' some of this history is its uniqueness. We have not seen anything quite like the development of the QCF before, and I doubt whether we will see anything quite like it again. This is not to suggest that the QCF is a perfect construct or that it is more important than other reforms. It is to acknowledge that the process of policymaking in the twenty-first century in the post-school sector is based on centrally developed strategies honed in think tanks, preceded by detailed consultation and implemented through highly controlled project management processes. Policy no longer originates in grass roots ideas, nurtured locally outside the 'official' framework of development (and sometimes in direct opposition to it) with neither a manifesto commitment nor a government policy document to support it, and without one penny of central government funding to implement it. Yet, prior to 2003, this is exactly how the QCF was developed. It is worth recording how this happened, not only because it reflects how the workings of government have changed over a generation, but also because it is important for those now charged with implementation of the QCF to acknowledge and (it is hoped) to be proud of, this different history. Indeed, as the continuing shrinking of the UK economy sweeps away much of the rationale for reform embodied in policy assumptions prior to 2008, a credit system developed and honed through processes unrelated to formal policymaking may prove even more valuable in ensuring that the QCF can adapt to this changing environment.

In looking back over this long-term history of how this new framework came into being, it is necessary to acknowledge the different strands that contribute to the QCF. Each strand is represented in its name: there is a strand that brings the concept of 'credit' into the framework just as clearly as the strand that brings 'qualifications' into its title. In order to understand how the QCF has been developed (and how it can continue to develop), it is necessary to consider both these strands as equal contributors to the framework. Having acknowledged this parity, this account focuses on the credit strand at the expense of the qualifications strand. I offer no apology for this. There are many other sources of information for those seeking to understand how our post-school qualifications system has developed over recent years. The informal and 'humdrum' development of credit systems over the same period means that they have gone largely (though not totally) unrecorded. In some respects this publication seeks to redress this imbalance.

Nevertheless, this is intended to be an account of how the QCF has been developed. It is not intended simply as a history of credit systems in the UK. In order to understand the particular design constructs and conceptual underpinnings of the QCF, it is necessary to draw on both strands of its history. Despite the wording of *21st Century Skills*, the QCF cannot be understood as a 'credit framework' any more than it can be understood as a 'qualifications framework'. It is the interconnection between these very different strands of development that makes the QCF unique. Indeed, as I argue later in this publication, it is the joining together of these two strands that creates the ability of the QCF to deliver on its potential for radical change in a way that neither the National Qualifications Framework (NQF) nor a credit framework could actually do. There are many people involved in the QCF who are familiar with qualifications. There are some who are familiar with credit systems. Only by creating a synthesis of these often separate cultures can we begin to utilise the unique potential of the QCF as it is implemented in the coming years.

Note

1 At the time of writing, the proposal that A Levels, GCSEs and Diplomas should be brought into the QCF was being considered by ministers.

2

The origins of credit systems in the UK

The story of credit systems in the UK usually begins with an account of the development of modular curriculum structures in certain Higher Education (HE) institutions that drew explicitly on a North American model. The Robbins Report of 1963 (Robbins, 1963) and the Russell Report a decade later (DES, 1973) are identified as creating the policy environment within which the first Higher Education credit schemes were developed. The Open University, established in 1969, is also rightly identified as a major contributor to these early developments in credit systems.

Despite these early precursors, it is the Oakes Committee of 1977 (DES, 1978) and the subsequent publication of the Toyne Report (Toyne, 1979) that mark the formal beginnings of HE credit systems in the UK (though Scotland may lay claim to a longer, if less formal, history). Although the formal outcome of the Toyne Report was the establishing of the Educational Counselling and Credit Transfer information Service (ECCTIS), the report's major contribution to policy was in the formalisation of some of the basic principles and technical constructs of credit systems within UK HE, drawing explicitly on a North American model. We can trace a direct line from the Toyne Report to the establishing of the Council for National Academic Awards (CNAA) Credit Accumulation and Transfer (CAT) Scheme of 1985 (CNAA, 1989), which formed the basis for the credit systems of the polytechnics in England and Wales throughout the 1980s and early 1990s.

It is not the intention of this publication to dwell on the history of credit systems in HE. To do so would insult by implication – at least until 1993 – the comprehensive account of HE credit systems in *Choosing to Change* (the Robertson report) (Robertson, 1994). The influence of HE credit systems is noted, but it is actually the development of credit systems outside HE that is the primary concern of this publication. The influences of the Open University, of the Toyne Report and of the CNAA CAT scheme can all be detected in the early development of credit systems outside HE. Indeed, it is possible to detect (and to record) a continuing influence of HE credit systems on the development of credit-based qualifications that forms the focus of this publication. From the outset, however, these 'other' credit systems claim a different and distinctive history from HE.

A recent exchange of correspondence between the (then) chief executives of the QCA and the Quality Assurance Agency for Higher Education (QAA) illustrates how the development of credit systems inside and outside HE are traced back to very different roots. The chief executive of the QCA proposed a meeting with his QAA counterpart to discuss some of the issues arising in developing links between the QCF and HE credit systems. In his response to this request, the chief executive of the QAA noted that 'Higher Education has some experience in this area', implying of course that such experience did not exist outside HE.[1] Thus the separate beginnings of credit systems inside and outside HE in the UK echo down the years.

In fact, the beginnings of credit systems in the UK outside HE can be traced back to similar origins to those that informed the work of the Oakes Committee and the subsequent Toyne Report. These origins draw consciously on North American curriculum models as well as the work of Oakes and Toyne, which preceded the beginnings of credit systems outside HE by a relatively short period. The critical difference lies not in any major design differences or conceptual models of credit inside and outside HE (though differences there were), but in the simple fact that the Toyne Report was commissioned by a government minister, was published by a department of government and led to the establishing of a publicly-funded national agency (ECCTIS). The origins of credit systems outside HE were altogether less formal, more modest and determinedly local.

No equivalent of the Toyne Report exists outside HE. Indeed, in 1978 it would have seemed rather strange to seek to implement government policy through the introduction of a concept such as 'credit' into the qualifications system. A levels and O levels were well established, and in the policy sphere of vocational qualifications government had recently established the Business and Technology Education Councils (BEC and TEC), the forerunners of BTEC. Developing these new vocational qualifications was conceived very much as a curriculum development process, with practitioners in colleges invited to develop the vocational education curriculum to meet the design requirements set out by BEC and TEC. There was no reference to 'credit' in this process and no conception of either a 'qualifications framework' or a 'credit framework', within which different qualifications might be developed. Indeed, the idea that vocational qualifications should be developed for adult learners, rather than for those 16- to 18-year-olds for whom O levels and A levels were not appropriate, simply did not figure as a consideration in the development of government policy on vocational education and training of this period. From wherever the development of credit systems outside HE might spring, we can be sure that these origins will not be found in a formal policy document or in a high-profile report to a government committee.

To locate the origins of credit systems in other areas of the post-school system, we need to look at the particular phenomenon of Open Colleges, Open

College Federations or Open College Networks (OCNs) that began to develop in different parts of the UK in the late 1970s.[2] The Open College of the North West (OCNW), founded in 1975, is acknowledged as the first of these networks (Percy, 1980). In fact, OCNW made no reference to credit or to credit systems at its inception, drawing more explicitly on the Open University as its inspiration and establishing itself very clearly as a curriculum and course development organisation, rather than an awarding body of any kind. OCNW was followed in 1981 by the Manchester Open College Federation (of which more in the next chapter) and then subsequently by the Open College of South London (OCSL), and by three other London-based networks covering different geographical segments of the capital.

The initial rationale for establishing these London-based OCNs followed closely the model of OCNW – that is, to develop programmes of learning for adults as an alternative to the O level and A level courses that were then the predominant form of provision available outside vocational qualifications. In particular, the London OCNs aimed to develop alternative progression routes to HE for adults outside A levels. The fact that A levels were not the most appropriate route to HE for many adults was formally recognised by the Department of Education and Science in 1978, when it invited Local Education Authorities (LEAs) to set up the first Access to Higher Education Courses to encourage adult learners (and, in particular, adults from ethnic minority communities) to progress to higher education (DES, 1978a). Indeed, it is not too far-fetched to envisage this invitation to develop alternatives to A levels for adult learners as a 'balancing' of the development of BEC and TEC qualifications for younger learners during the same period. No major policy initiative was needed, simply a signal to LEAs that the development of a certain type of provision would be looked upon favourably by government and would therefore be seen as a legitimate object of expenditure by these authorities in the ongoing discharge of their local duties.

In these early days of the London OCNs and alternative access to HE, there were no references to credit systems. The focus was on the development and provision of alternative courses, not on assessment or on the recognition of learner achievement. Nevertheless, the conception of this provision as being an alternative to A levels located it within a policy sphere that would, over time, link it ever more closely to the development of qualifications. In the late 1970s the distinction between 'qualifications' and 'courses' was nowhere near as well-developed as it would become in later decades. In 1978, 'an alternative to A levels' was conceived as a particular curriculum offer. Only gradually would it start to be seen as an alternative form within which learner achievements could be recognised. The origins of credit systems outside HE therefore lie in this emulsion of the concepts of 'provision' and 'achievement'. Indeed, I suggest that it is precisely the joining together of these later-separated ideas that created the primeval stew from which the first concepts of credit emerged in the UK outside HE. We will not find the origins of credit systems in a clearly marked box entitled 'learner achievement'. To locate these beginnings we need to look into murkier and less conceptually well-defined areas in which 'qualifications' and 'curriculum' were - unproblematically at the time - intimately connected. In particular, we need to look at their particular interconnection in the City of Manchester.

Notes

1 Exchange of letters between Ken Boston (QCA) and Peter Williams (QAA) on issues of 'articulation' between the QCF and HE qualifications (2008).

2 For the sake of brevity this publication will use the term 'Open College Network' (OCN) when referring generally to this phenomenon, though in fact very few of these networks actually referred to themselves as 'OCNs' for at least a decade after their inception. Where a specific reference is made to an individual OCN, the actual name of the organisation (at that time) is used.

3

The Manchester model

In 1980 the City of Manchester Education Committee decided to set up a Working Party to investigate the development of an OCN for the city, drawing on the experiences of OCNW and others. The Working Party on Open College Developments (also referred to as 'The Working Party on Alternative Entry to Higher Education' – an illustration of its conceptual origins) produced, over a period of 18 months, the basis for what would become the Manchester Open College Federation (MOCF) (City of Manchester Education Committee, 1981). Notwithstanding this merging of roles in its title, the Working Party received advice from the LEA's inspectorate at its inception that its remit should relate to the needs of *all* adult learners in the city. In other words, the constraints of the DES's earlier invitation to develop alternative courses for entry to HE were explicitly extended by local government officers interested in improving the quality of provision offered to adults in the city. This advice proved critical in moving the MOCF beyond the boundaries of OCNW and the London OCNs and into a consideration of the development of a credit system.

The Working Party was supported by a member of the City Council's Community Education team – Aubrey Black. In his previous role at Didsbury Teacher Training College he had become familiar not only with local Access to HE provision in Manchester, but also with the concept of credit in HE. In 1982, Black was commissioned by the Further Education Unit (FEU) of the DES to write a report on the development of the MOCF through this period and up to the formal constitution of the Federation in March 1982 (Black, 1982).[1] It is during this period that the concept of credit first makes its appearance outside HE in the UK, and Black's report to the FEU is a fascinating account of how the people involved in the development of the MOCF began to use credit in the pursuit of its aim to establish an alternative structure of educational opportunities in Manchester for 'all' adult learners. Despite the earlier development of OCNW and the adoption of a course-based model by the London Open Colleges, it was the Manchester model that came to form the basis for the development of credit systems across England, Wales and Northern Ireland in the coming years. For this reason it is worth looking in some detail at how the concept of credit emerged in Manchester and how it was initially conceived by those responsible for the first credit awards made to learners in the UK.

Although Aubrey Black's report to the FEU is a key source document of the period, it would be wrong to see it simply as a theoretical blueprint from which MOCF developed its credit system. By the time that Black's report was written, the work of MOCF was well under way and some of the propositions that appear in the report were already being tested in practice. The FEU may have been interested in the theory behind the work of MOCF, but Black's report – like many others that followed it from other OCNs in subsequent years – represents a snapshot of a particular moment in the continuous inter-action between theory and practice that informed the development of MOCF, and would inform the development of other OCNs in the future.

The remit of the Open College Working Party to consider the needs of all adult learners in the City of Manchester, rather than those seeking entry to HE, meant that, from the outset, its deliberations encompassed more than just the provision of alternative courses. The first progress report from the Working Party (June 1981) envisioned 'a fully integrated and modular scheme' (City of Manchester Education Committee, 1981a) of provision for adults across the city. The provision of entry to higher education was seen as an important part of this fully integrated scheme, but by no means its only purpose. From the outset, concern about the credibility of such modular courses was consid-ered. An early decision of the Working Party was to establish 'validation arrangements' for MOCF courses, using the validation models developed by Manchester City Polytechnic and the universities of Manchester and Salford. The combination of this concept of modular courses plus validation by HE institutions (HEIs) led the Working Party to put forward in its ideas for further consideration the proposal 'that students would be able to build up a series of "credit awards" into a "matriculation certificate" ' (City of Manchester Educa-tion Committee, 1981).

This first formally recorded reference to credit (outside HE) is notable for several reasons. Firstly, it clearly links the concepts of 'credit' and 'award' – a con-nection that was to become critically important in the later development of credit systems. The idea that a credit is an award made to a learner originates right here at the source of this story and is an integral part of what would come to be defined as a credit system. The implementation of the QCF marks the point at which this concept of credit came to form the basis of the new frame-work. Note, however, that in 1981 there are quotation marks around 'credit awards' – signifying the newness of the concept and the tentative use of it in this initial report. This is an accurate reflection of the way in which the concept of credit emerged into the Manchester model – not as a fully formed and instantly recognisable idea that everyone was able to understand and use, but as a tentative suggestion, not well-defined but worthy of further consideration.

The other interesting part of this initial proposal, in the light of how future credit systems were to develop, is the implicit concept of credit accumulation present in this wording. Indeed, the idea that credits should be 'built up' into a 'matriculation certificate' creates, at the inception of this still hazily formed notion of credit, an echo of the connection between credits and qualifications that forms such a critical feature of the QCF. However, what is even more interesting about this initial proposal from the Working Party is that, by the end of 1981:

> The concept of a 'matriculation certificate' referred to in the June report had now been abandoned and the 'modular scheme' had been replaced by a looser and more open approach. Students would not be required to complete any set pattern of credit awards.
>
> (Black, 1982, p. 10)

How fascinating. At an early stage of development, the connection between 'credits' and 'matriculation certificate' was set aside because the rules that would therefore be set on the accumulation of credits were seen to be too restrictive in relation to the wider ambitions of MOCF. Of course that was demonstrably the case. Tying the award of credit to the concept of matriculation – that is, to meeting the requirements for entry to HE – would restrict the value of credit awards to a small proportion of the adult learners that MOCF set out to serve. In any event:

> To negotiate a 'matriculation certificate' that would be acceptable to the Joint Matriculation Board could be a difficult and protracted matter, and the prospects for a successful outcome were dubious.
>
> (Black, 1982, p. 25)

In essence, if credit awards were developed as an alternative to more traditional qualifications, recognition of these awards by a traditional awarding body was going to be a problem. The solution was simply to detach 'credit awards' from 'matriculation certificate'. In so doing, MOCF opened up the possibility that credit awards could become a means of recognising any and all achievements. However, it also inadvertently undermined the concept of credit accumulation and created a separation of credit from other forms of certification that would characterise the development of credit systems for many years to come. Indeed, one might perceive the reconnection between credits and qualifications as one of the lasting contributions of the QCF. How interesting that this connection was actually present – briefly and only in theory – at the outset of the MOCF's deliberations, before the open definition of credit that was to become a core feature of the Manchester model actually became established. We should not see this as a naïve dismissal of the idea of credit accumulation and transfer. In effect, MOCF deliberately sacrificed this feature of its initial credit system in order to establish the more important principle of an inclusive system that was capable of recognising all learner achievements.

In detaching credit awards from the concept of matriculation, MOCF also consciously abandoned the idea that university validation could underwrite the credibility of these awards. If credits were to be awarded without reference to any particular credit accumulation target (this term was not actually used in the MOCF documents), then the Federation itself would need to underwrite the credibility of these credits. Indeed, despite the dropping of the concept of matriculation, the continuing support of HEIs in Manchester was critical to this credibility. The Working Party began to focus on the systems that would be needed to do this. What is interesting from the perspective of 2009 is that the approach to this credibility issue focused initially not on the assessment of learners' achievements, but on the quality of the courses that they were to be offered:

> The basis of the scheme ... [is] that credit ratings would be conferred upon courses submitted to it [MOCF] and that students who successfully completed the course requirements would be awarded the credits.
>
> (Black, 1982, p. 10)

At this juncture, although the concept of 'credits' is conceptualised in the plural, there is no indication of what 'a credit' is or how credits were to be defined. The implication of the early MOCF documents is that the number of credits would be somehow linked to the size of the courses that learners undertook, but there is no attempt to quantify how many credits might be awarded to an individual learner, or what the relationship between (for example) one credit and two credits might be. Having said this, the MOCF was clear that 'specifications of courses should be based on the outcomes they give rise to, in terms of student competences, rather than syllabus content' (Black, 1982, p. 29).

So the definition of credits as awards made to learners for the achievement of 'competences' preceded any precise specification of what a credit was worth or how its value would be defined. The connection between 'competence' and 'credits' is worthy of note. We are still more than five years from the Review of Vocational Qualifications and the use of the term 'competence' in this context reflects the North American influence in thinking about credit systems. (Prior to writing the FEU Report, Black had been on a study visit to the USA and had been clearly influenced by North American credit systems in his thinking.) Given the later history of 'competence-based qualifications' as an alternative to credit systems, we might have urged Black and his colleagues to establish more explicitly this intimate connection between credit and competence in 1981. However, this issue would be addressed at a later date.

Initially though, the focus of the Working Party was not on the technical features of credits but on the concept of 'level'.

Once again the MOCF faced a conceptual and linguistic problem in trying to establish a structure within which different levels of learner achievement (or should that be 'learner activity?') could be represented. The Working Party was most anxious to establish some means of characterising courses without reference to equivalencies to current courses, such as 'O' or 'A' Levels (Black, 1982, p. 29).

In fact, it found it most difficult to do this. Indeed, the characterisation of O and A levels as courses rather than qualifications surely added to this conceptual difficulty. An initial attempt was made to define three levels of credits which it was proposed would be referred to as 'initial credits', 'minor credits' and 'major credits'. Then the Working Party attempted to create relationships between these concepts, positing, for example, that '3 minors = 1 major' and other similar algorithms. As Black notes in his report:

> at this stage the Working Party had not yet produced a precise vocabulary for discourse... It was using the terms 'courses' and 'credits' interchangeably without perceiving that they were quite separate entities. This may be viewed as a reflection of the inexperience of the education system concerning credit systems.
>
> (Black, 1982, p. 32)

Indeed, although actually it was the confusion between the 'level' of achievement and the 'size' of that achievement that is really striking here. One is reminded of theories of dimensions expanding from a single point in space and time. In the absence not only of a definition of a credit, but also of a definition of level other than 'equivalent to an O or A level', it is perhaps unsurprising that these initial attempts to consider how learner achievement might be valued resulted in a (temporary) merging of what we now consider to be the two essential dimensions of the concept of a credit framework – credits and levels.

It is clear from the deliberations of the Working Party that this original conception of level was not adequate. Not only did it lack any meaningful external reference point, but it also did not take account of learners with basic skill needs – a critical target group not just for MOCF but for the Education Committee. This absence of any clear definition of level was not deemed acceptable to the Education Committee and so the Working Party was asked to reconsider the whole issue of level. It returned with two proposals that would have an important impact on the work of OCNs and on the establishment of the Manchester model. The first proposal was that there should be four levels of achievement within the MOCF. The second proposal was that these levels should be called 'Levels 1, 2, 3 and 4'. The four levels would cover 'basic skills to matriculation equivalent' (City of Manchester Education Committee, 1981) and would be applied to all the courses submitted to the MOCF for 'valida-tion'. In order to elaborate on these proposals, the Working Party also pro-duced a brief description of the kind of courses that would be validated at each level. The descriptors were brief, dependent on examples and related not to learner achievement but to *courses*. Nevertheless, in December 1981 in Manchester, here were the first level descriptors that anticipated those in use today in the QCF. They were to go through a number of refinements and updating over the following years, but in 1981 they bequeathed a sufficiently robust horizontal axis to the MOCF credit system to be adopted for use by the Federation in 1982. They are reproduced verbatim in Table 1:

Table 1 *Credit level descriptors*

Level	Descriptor
Level 1	Courses designed to enable students to establish basic occupational competence in literacy and numeracy skills. Assessment by tutor evaluation of work done during the course.
Level 2	Courses designed to enable students to further develop skills and to stimulate and extend interest in further study. Assessment as for Level 1.
Level 3	Courses designed to enable students to develop: a. Understanding of basic concepts and principles of enquiry in chosen subject areas b. Functional competence in skills areas such as languages, mathematics, creative and interpretative arts In both cases assessment will be by tutor evaluation of an extended piece of work, or of a number of smaller pieces in which the student demonstrates the understanding or skills appropriate to the field of study.
Level 4	Courses designed to enable students to develop: a. The capacity to undertake a study of a problem or theme by application of appropriate principles of enquiry, and to communicate their enquiry and conclusions effectively b. Functional competence in skill areas such as languages, mathematics, creative and interpretative arts, at an advanced level In both cases assessment will be by tutor evaluation of an extended piece of work or a number of pieces of work in which the student demonstrates the appropriate competence.

Source: Working Party on Open College Developments, City of Manchester Education Committee (1981)

From the perspective of 2009, these appear to be unworkable as level descriptors. They refer to the learning process rather than learning outcomes; they use comparative terms ('basic', 'further', 'advanced'), as well as modifiers ('suitably', 'appropriate') that are open to wide interpretation; they make explicit reference to selected subject areas and to both the format and weight of assessment to be deployed. Nevertheless, here in Manchester in 1981, more than seven years before the National Council for Vocational Qualifications (NCVQ) identified its level descriptors and 17 years before the NQF did the same, we have the very first attempt to establish a set of level descriptors with the purpose of locating learner achievement within a comprehensive set of characteristics, clustered together around a simple set of sequential names. The influence of Bloom's Taxonomy on these first level descriptors is apparent (Bloom, 1956). However refined and precise the QCF level descriptors appear in 2009, they can trace their roots back through a series of different descriptors updated on a number of occasions over a 27-year period, each one referring explicitly to its predecessor, to these very first level descriptors produced in Manchester.

In concluding its work of preparing a working structure as the basis for the operations of the MOCF, the Working Party therefore succeeded in establishing a working model of levels that was capable of implementation through the course validation procedures: 'It did, however, fail to complete its task in that it was unable to offer agreed views on ways of computing Credit Values within course levels' (Black, 1982, p. 37).

Consideration had been given to introducing a time element to the definition of credit. A proposal that 60 hours should be taken as the basis for defining a single credit was proposed and debated, but no agreement could be reached on this and the Working Party made no recommendation on the definition of credit to the MOCF prior to its formal launch in March 1982. How ironic that the organisation that is rightfully recognised as the originator of the credit system that has developed into use in the QCF should have begun its formal life without an agreed definition of credit. The issue was soon resolved in practice (again it is necessary to remember that Black wrote his report as the work of MOCF was already under way). At an early meeting of the newly formed organisation, the MOCF:

> decided to follow the principles used by those systems that could provide models, namely the Open University and the American adult education system. In both of these, credit values are determined by course length, measured by study hours, and this method was adopted.
>
> (Black, 1982, p. 38)

'Notional time' it seemed was the only practical option that could be agreed on as the basis for determining credit values. It was also an option that appeared to work well both within US credit systems and within the OU – both significant influences on MOCF. The MOCF then went on to reject the previously discussed proposal that 60 hours should be used as the benchmark to determine the value of a single credit, and decided instead 'that 50 hours should form the unit for a full credit' (Black, 1982, p. 39).

Black offers no rationale for why 50 hours had been chosen. John Sanders, one of MOCF's first development officers, suggests an explanation:

> My memory is that the 50 hours came about as a result of a rough calcu-lation about a typical adult education class at Level 3 requiring 2 hours a week class time for about 12 weeks, plus a roughly equal amount of private study, though this may have been a post-hoc justification.
>
> (Sanders, 2009)

Sanders' indistinct memory and reference to a post-hoc justification confirm that the determination of the basis of credit value is an arbitrary decision. Although the concept of credit value was still tied explicitly to course length, MOCF also reaffirmed 'that credits would be awarded only for satisfactory evi-dence of course completion' (Black, 1982, p. 39).

Almost a decade later, OCN credit systems would be criticised as being 'time-serving' systems, unrelated to learner achievement. This was as untrue at the outset as it was in 1991. Despite the linking of credit values with course length, there was never any suggestion within MOCF that credits would be awarded to learners without quality-assured assessment of their achieve-ments on that course. It is only with the benefit of hindsight that we can extract clearly a concept of learner achievement that is unconnected to the delivery of the curriculum. In 1982 such a separation was beginning to be formulated within MOCF, but the concept of credit still depended on an explicit connection between a learner's achievement and the course that they undertook.

Perhaps surprisingly, MOCF also agreed that the minimum fractional credit that would be available for a course would be one-half (for a notional 25 hours of learning) 'as it was considered that a course of lesser duration could not be expected to give rise to sufficient assessable work' (Black, 1982, p. 39).

Here we have an implied rationale for the adoption of a 'minimum' credit value. The surprising thing is that the MOCF, from the outset, set a value of 'one credit' as the competences that could be achieved in 50 hours of learn-ing, and then immediately decided that it would award 'fractional credits' for courses of half that duration. John Sanders, recollection is again interesting on this point:

The half credit...came about to signify roughly 'a term's worth' of basic skills work (ie [the above formula] without the private study.

(Sanders, 2009)

So the influence of basic skills learners was the key to developing MOCF 'half credits'. As we shall see, the extension of the Manchester model beyond the boundaries of Manchester would call this (apparently hurried) decision into question. Nevertheless, the structure of the MOCF credit system was sufficiently well established to begin accepting courses for recognition (the term 'validation' had been dropped once the connection with matriculation had been broken) for the 1982-3 academic year; 122 courses were recognised by July 1982 and in February 1983 the first credits were issued to learners on an Adult Numeracy course in Newton Heath, and placed in their MOCF Study Passports.[2]

In February 2008, exactly 25 years later, the very first credits were awarded, in Manchester, to the first learners to achieve their credits within the QCF. From these (unfortunately now forgotten) learners in 1983 to Natalie Battle in 2008 seems a lifetime apart, but two members of the team of people that helped to set up the MOCF (Michael Stern and Gordon Conquest) were present to award these first credits to Natalie and three others. In his recollection of the 1983 award ceremony, Gordon Conquest, the first Chair of MOCF, recalled that the process of getting the Federation off the ground in Manchester, and finding resources for it, had been a struggle. He was surprised that it managed to survive at all, let alone be recalled with affection some 25 years later. The reason that MOCF prospered, he surmised, was because 'it was a good idea and people really liked it' (Conquest, 2008). In establishing the Manchester model, Aubrey Black[3] and his colleagues not only bequeathed a set of technical specifications and a commitment to the needs of excluded and under-represented learners to other OCNs, they also bequeathed the notion that awarding credits to learners was 'a good idea'. In the future development of the model, this was to prove as important as the specifications of credits and levels that we trace from these beginnings in Manchester. MOCF's good idea eventually became the QCF's big idea. It was a commitment that would bring OCNs into conflict with many other organisations, not least government itself, over the years. As Michael Sterne reminded his audience in Manchester in 2008:

Opposition used to come from those with lots of qualifications'

(Sterne 2008)

As the account of these beginnings illustrates, the Manchester model was something that emerged from a particular set of circumstances. It was not adopted from any particular external source, though it recognised its debt to others in the adoption of the term 'credit awards'. It was a rough and ready system – good enough for its immediate purpose, but open to further refinement as its scope expanded. It is a testament to the culture of open discussion and mutual agreement that engendered the Manchester model that it was able to adapt and change as the model itself was exported beyond the boundaries of Manchester to become, over time, a national system of credit awards. In its particular form of 1982, the exact model was never adopted outside Manchester. In its basic structure of credits and levels, and its 'study passport', it survives today within the QCF.

Note, however, that in order to develop into a system capable of integration within the technical specifications of a regulated qualifications framework in 2008, it was necessary at the outset to detach credit from its links with formal qualifications (in the form of the matriculation arrangements of O and A levels) and to forge a particular concept of credit that would be taken forward by an independent organisation. In order to ensure that credits served their intended purpose, it was necessary to create a new organisation to award them to learners and to establish this organisation separately from existing awarding bodies. For a brief moment in 1981 it seemed as though credits and qualifications might be developed together. How different the concept of a credit system might have been in these circumstances to the one that was eventually embedded within the regulations of the QCF, and thus rejoined with qualifications, in 2008.

Notes

1 Indeed, Aubrey Black's report constitutes the major source for the account contained in this chapter.

2 I was reminded of this recently when invited to an event in 2009 to mark ten years of Adult Numeracy qualifications. The preceding 16 years have obviously failed to make an impact on the official version of history in this area.

3 In May 1992, Aubrey Black was awarded an honorary degree from the Open University for his work in setting up the first OCN.

4

After Manchester:
The next Open College Networks

From the outset, those involved in the development of MOCF sought – within their limited and locally-targeted resources – both to promote their model outside Manchester and to make links with other emerging Open College organisations in other parts of the UK. As I have tried to show above, the Open College movement (for so it was perceived by those involved in its development in the 1980s) was based around a common set of principles related to the needs and interests of adult learners, rather than around a common framework based on credit systems. Indeed, during the first few years of its existence, MOCF represented a minority perspective within this Open College movement, with the other organisations that came together in this loose alliance of local initiatives ignoring the credit perspective of MOCF. For the time being both OCNW and the London OCNs continued with their separate, course-based approach to achieving these shared objectives.

This community of interests outside the perspective of a credit framework forms an important aspect of the history of OCNs. From the outset, OCNs were never conceived of simply as awarding bodies. What brought them together was always as much to do with a shared commitment to the broader interests of adult learners, and to the development of an 'open' curriculum that would create opportunities for new and different learners to access learning opportunities, as it was about the development of credit systems. The early development of MOCF illustrates clearly the interconnections between this commitment to developing learning opportunities for more and different adults and the credit system that we now see as the significant feature of OCNs.

This integration is best illustrated in 'A Manifesto for Open College Federations', produced in the early days of the MOCF (probably 1983, but the exact date is not recorded) (MOCF, 1983?). Alongside explicit references to credits and levels, it also incorporates references to the accessibility of courses, to the comprehensive range of achievements that should be recognised, to the independence of the federations and their partnership model and to the quality principles that federations should follow. The 12-point manifesto still stands as a testament to the pioneering intentions of MOCF in the early 1980s.[1] It also illustrates clearly how the origins of what was to become the OCN model are based as much on a set of commitments to learners as on a set of technical specifications.

Notwithstanding the relative isolation of the Manchester model within this early grouping of OCNs, once MOCF was established it inevitably attracted interest from other organisations, which became interested in the credit-based approach to recognising achievement pioneered by MOCF. In particular, the MOCF model was exported eastwards and westwards in the early 1980s, and by 1986 both the Merseyside and South Yorkshire OCNs had been established – building on the Manchester model (though it would be another year before their first credits were awarded). This grouping of three neighbouring, northern OCNs marks an important step forward in the development of what was to become the OCN model of credit systems and to the eventual establishing of this model as a national framework that stands as an explicit precursor to the QCF. We should not underestimate the role of MOCF itself – and in particular of David Browning, its first director – in securing this initial development of the Manchester model in its neighbouring localities.

This exporting of the Manchester model to other neighbouring OCNs was important, not only in securing the future development of the OCN model as an explicitly credit-based approach to recognising learner achievement, but also in developing and securing the model itself. It seems strange to be reminded of the fact more than 20 years later, but it really was the case that these first three credit-based OCNs actually adopted three different models of credit system. Not only did each one have a different definition of credit, but there were also two different sets of levels. Far from simply adopting the MOCF model, both the South Yorkshire Open College Federation (SYOCF) and Merseyside Open College Federation (MerOCF) took the basic principles behind the model and adapted them to their own particular circumstances. 'Circumstances' might also include the particular perspectives of individuals within these networks and the external influences that were brought to bear on each different OCN as it was established.

It is important to note here that these adaptations of the initial Manchester model were taken forward with the support and involvement of people from MOCF itself. Rather than the evangelical proselytising of the MOCF model as the one true credit system, the Manchester missionaries actively collaborated with converts who sought to amend the MOCF scriptures in order to promote the idea of a credit system to their local congregations. Again, we are reminded that the OCN credit system itself could not be detached in its development from the wider commitments to widening access and recognising new and different kinds of achievements of adult learners. The connections between these three northern OCNs (and indeed with the very different OCNs in London) were based as much on this wider commitment as on any adherence to a particular model of credit. The Manchester model was never simply adopted, it was always adapted.

This early process of developing the design features of the OCN credit system illustrates how organic the development of this system actually was and how responsive it was to evaluation in practice. The very fact that each OCN was locally based and completely autonomous (as the MOCF manifesto had proposed) enabled this organic process of development to continue throughout the 1980s, with each new OCN refining the design features of the credit system so that it was able to deliver more and more effectively on the wider commitments of the OCN movement. No nationally based initiative could ever have done this. As Aubrey Black has noted, some aspects of the initial MOCF model were established without recourse to testing or trialling. Although the first course-recognition process was able to function on the basis of this initial model, those responsible for establishing it accepted that it would be capable of refinement. There was never any suggestion that other OCNs following Manchester's example would be duty bound to adopt all aspects of this initial model. The local independence of the OCNs that followed the establishment of MOCF was critical to the continuing refinement of the Manchester model over a period of a decade and more. Indeed, these refinements influenced the development of MOCF itself.

So, for example, the initial Manchester model defined a credit in relation to 50 hours of learning. As Black has shown, both 60 hours and 50 hours were considered, but 50 hours was chosen as a fairly arbitrary yardstick and necessitated, as shown above, the award of half-credits.

In developing their own independent organisation, those responsible for establishing SYOCF decided, understandably, that they did not want to offer half-credits to learners (learners in Manchester never liked them), and so an SYOCF credit was defined on the basis of 25 hours of learning rather than 50. Not the most auspicious of beginnings for a credit system that aspired to become widely adopted, but the mathematical connection between 50 and 25 was important. It was a simple multiplier that made the relative values of credits in Manchester and South Yorkshire easily convertible: one MOCF credit was worth two SYOCF credits. And both MOCF and SYOCF agreed that their credits would be offered at four levels of achievement (of which more later), though even at this early stage SYOCF established a revised set of level descriptors from those (already revised) in use in Manchester in 1985.

In 1986 the Merseyside OCF became the third OCN to utilise a credit system. Not only did it redefine a credit as being worth 30 hours (rather than 25 or 50 hours), it also decided that it would offer these credits at three, rather than four, levels of achievement (and proposed a further version of the level descriptors). Notwithstanding its commitment to a credit-based model, MerOCF not only broke the simple mathematical conversion established between MOCF and SYOCF credits, it also disturbed the concept of equivalence between levels of achievement that the first two OCNs had established. These re-definitions by MerOCF of what we perceive as two of the key design features of the QCF – the definitions of credit value and level – illustrate how external, as well as internal, influences have shaped the OCN credit system over the years. The 30-hour unit of credit was adopted because the funding models in use in Merseyside (and in many other LEAs) at the time assumed that a full-time learner in further education studied for approximately 30 hours a week. The logic of tying a definition of credit to some external benchmark outside the world of OCNs was seen as more important to the development of MerOCF at the time than consistency with the credit systems of other OCNs. This benchmarking of credit values against an external measure exposed both the arbitrary nature of the initial choice of 50 hours to calculate MOCF credit values and the purely mathematical logic (that is, the avoidance of half-credits) of SYOCF's 25-hour basis for credit values.

Similarly, the three levels of achievement identified in the initial MerOCF credit system were tied explicitly to Levels 1 to 3 of the recently proposed National Vocational Qualifications (NVQ) framework that arose from the Review of Vocational Qualifications in 1986 (MSC and DES, 1986). Again, tying the development of MerOCF explicitly to the proposed NVQ framework was seen as more important than adopting the four levels of achievement used by both the MOCF and SYOCF. Indeed, the rationale for MerOCF's decision was based clearly on anticipation that, in the future, credits would be transferred between OCN-accredited provision and NVQs. In fact, as a later chapter of this publication makes clear, this future never came close to being realised. Nevertheless, as an independent local organisation, MerOCF was free to make such decisions while remaining part of the Open College movement. In fact, its proposal to recognise only three levels of achievement lasted a very short time and by 1987 MerOCF had adopted a four-level framework consistent with those of other OCNs. The 30-hour unit of credit, however, became the standard that all OCNs adopted in due course (though the rationale for doing so has been lost) and was Merseyside's particular contribution to the OCN model that was to survive well into the twenty-first century.

This then was the landscape of OCNs by 1986. MOCF continued to grow as the neighbouring networks in Merseyside and South Yorkshire established systems based on, but technically different from, the original Manchester model. In London and the North West other Open College organisations continued to operate without reference to a credit system. Embryonic networks were proposed, but not yet established, in other parts of England and Wales. None of the organisations involved in this loose association referred to themselves as an awarding body. What bound them together was a commitment to 'open access' education and to widening opportunities for adult learners, not to the development of a credit system. It was in this context that the first meeting took place in 1986, at Northern College near Barnsley, of the organisation that would become the National Open College Network (NOCN).

Note

1 It was reproduced, for example, by the Northern Ireland OCN to mark the 20th anniversary celebrations of NOCN in 2006.

5

From the local to the national: The creation of NOCN

Although it was the case that the OCNs in Manchester, Merseyside and South Yorkshire had each adopted different technical approaches in developing their approach to recognising learner achievement, and that there was an acceptance of these differences between the three networks, there was also a realisation that, if the credit-based model of OCNs was to grow outside this northern group, it would be necessary to establish a more explicit shared structure within which local OCNs could operate. It was also apparent by 1986 that the credit-based model of the northern OCNs was creating interest in other areas of England and Wales, and that there was a need to offer support and guidance to other embryonic networks now beginning to spring up outside this northern enclave. The call for a national network of OCNs became stronger.

During this time there was also a fierce debate proceeding within the four London Open Colleges about the relative merits of the credit-based system now beginning to lose the term 'Manchester model' and becoming referred to simply as the 'OCN credit system'. These debates were taken into the initial meeting of NOCN, where nine established and embryonic OCNs were represented, as well as other 'fellow travellers' from localities where OCN developments were under consideration. There was no concept of representation at this first meeting; no criteria for determining which organisations should or should not attend; no constitution or standing orders; no officers and no decision-making procedures. The first meeting of NOCN was simply a coming together of people and organisations for whom the term 'Open College' had some meaning.

This is not the place to reproduce the history of OCNs and NOCN, already published to commemorate the 20th anniversary of this event and the 25th anniversary of MOCF as the first OCN (Sanders and Whaley, 2007). Nevertheless, the early history of NOCN has some interesting lessons for awarding bodies now operating, or preparing to operate, within the QCF. In particular, it has some important messages to communicate about how credit systems can be established, nurtured and developed among independent organisations with a shared commitment to extend educational opportunities for adult learners. None of the nine organisations present at this first meeting conceived of itself as an awarding body and there was certainly no suggestion that NOCN should become such an organisation. Within the framework of membership of NOCN, however, these bodies learned to trust and respect each other's differences, to find mutually beneficial ways of working together, and to develop a shared confidence in the continuing development of the credit systems that inevitably and inexorably drew them into closer relationships with each other.

The establishing of NOCN in itself produced a significant upsurge in interest in credit systems. Meetings of NOCN were attended by increasing numbers of people representing a burgeoning network of local organisations with an interest in the OCN credit system. It should be emphasised yet again that there was no formal sanction of this development by government, no encouragement through policy messages about the development of OCNs and no funding at national level to support the establishment of credit systems. Throughout the first two years of its existence, NOCN remained a loose voluntary association of like-minded people involved in broadly similar types of local organisation, operating totally outside the formal structures of qualifications and awarding bodies in the UK. No two OCNs were identical in structure, but all were membership organisations of some kind, based on providers of education and training to (mostly) adult learners that shared a commitment to what were still referred to as open-access learning opportunities.

By early 1988 it was clear that the credit-based model of OCNs (rather than the course-based model of OCNW and the first London networks) would be the basis for developing future networks. A 'Provisional Map of Development' drawn up for a meeting of NOCN in that year identifies 18 networks either established or under development across England and Wales, plus the significant presence of an Accreditation Development Unit in London that would in time transform the four original London Open Colleges into a single, credit-based, London OCN (Browning, 1988). Some of these 18 local initiatives simply faded away when temporary funding or political will, or both, failed to provide the necessary platform of stability to become an OCN. Others (there were five separate networks in Yorkshire and Humberside) joined together before becoming fully operational OCNs.

It was at this stage that the first external resources became available to support the continuing development of OCNs. As NOCN itself had no resources and no staff, it was clearly not in a position to provide any meaningful support to local OCNs seeking start-up resources. However, just as local OCNs had become adept at squeezing resources from short-term funding, from projects and secondments (SYOCF had 11 different sources of funding during its first two years of existence), so NOCN was successful in securing external funding in 1988 from two very different sources.

The first of these sources, perhaps surprisingly, was British Petroleum (BP). BP supported a programme of staff development events during 1988 aimed at nurturing new OCNs and supporting quality improvement in more-established networks. The events contributed significantly to the development of a shared ethos among those working in OCNs and to a considered approach to the further development of new networks. At a time when formal government policy was focused firmly on the development of the NVQ framework, this external recognition gave OCNs a welcome boost and was critical in establishing a national presence for the networks. However, it was the second source of funding that really enabled the second phase of development of OCNs to be consolidated.

In 1987, NIACE established, through a fixed-term source of funding from the DES, the Unit for the Development of Adult Continuing Education (UDACE). As part of the preparation for establishing a programme of work for UDACE, NIACE conducted a series of consultative events around England and Wales to identify perceived priorities for development among adult education practitioners. One of the key priorities that emerged through this process was the need to extend the existing network of OCNs. (Actually this outcome seems to have surprised NIACE – it was not one of the priorities identified by the organisation itself in its initial prospectus for UDACE. To its credit, however, NIACE acted upon what practitioners in the field told it.) By late 1988, through discussions with NOCN, a development programme had been established within UDACE that would lead directly to the establishing of four new OCNs within a year, and to more networks in the longer term. It would also lead to significant improvements in the quality assurance systems of OCNs – indeed to the establishing of the first national quality assurance framework for OCNs. David Browning from MOCF led the project, supported by Caroline Mager from SYOCF. A report on the UDACE OCN project records this process in some detail (UDACE, 1990).

It should be emphasised here that, despite the active role played by NOCN in securing funding from BP and in taking forward the UDACE project, both these activities were aimed at promoting the development of local OCNs. NOCN played a coordinating role, ensuring that the outcomes of the BP and UDACE projects were shared across both operational and embryonic OCNs in England and Wales, but no resources were available for the development of NOCN itself. The focus of development activity during this time remained clearly local, rather than national. Indeed, the importance of local control over systems of recognition and the award of credit was seen as a critical success factor in the further development of OCNs and a strong motivator for the funding of OCNs through local networks of providers. Simply increasing the availability of OCN credit systems to learners was the priority for development in the late 1980s. That these systems should be mutually compatible across local boundaries was seen as desirable but secondary to this primary purpose behind the UDACE OCN project.

Notwithstanding this local focus, it was becoming clear within NOCN itself that the process of bringing new OCNs into the national network could not proceed indefinitely on the same basis as the first three northern OCNs, with their three different credit systems. The formation of new OCNs through the UDACE project forced NOCN to confront the issue of standardisation across these different credit systems. Indeed, the fourth OCN to become operational, in the Black Country, adopted a model that drew on the 30-hour unit of credit from Merseyside, together with the four-level approach to recognising achievement established in Manchester and South Yorkshire. For a brief period there were four credit-based OCNs and four different systems of credits and levels. What had been seen as a positive advantage in the early stages of development – the freedom to test and refine operational credit systems at a local level while remaining part of a national network – was perceived by 1989 as an impediment to further progress. Clearly such an approach to the development of new OCNs could not continue indefinitely, especially as the UDACE project was now allowing more embryonic networks to become operational.

Out of the BP workshops, and stimulated by the decision of the new London Open College Federation and other new OCNs to adopt the Black Country model of credit (a 30-hour unit of credit and four levels of achievement), NOCN agreed to establish the 'Commonality Working Party'. The group was established in late 1988 and by the end of 1989 had produced a report, accepted by NOCN, that effectively secured the Black Country model of credit, rather than any of the three models established by the original northern group of OCNs, as the model adopted by NOCN. All members of the NOCN would, in future, have to subscribe to this model. The loose network of like-minded people of 1986 had become by 1990 a much more formal organisation, with a constitution and with clear membership requirements (though still with no budget, no officers and no headquarters). The three northern OCNs each changed the specifications of their original credit systems (not without some internal opposition in some cases) and by the start of 1990 the concept of a single NOCN framework of credits and levels was firmly established.

From a perspective of 20 years, these discussions about what kind of credit system should be adopted seems like a little local difficulty that would inevitably need to be swept aside in the development of a national network of credit-based OCNs. In fact, the debate about definitions of credits and levels needs to be seen in the wider context of OCNs' commitments to widening participation (the term was gaining currency by 1990) and to recognising the achievements of adult learners. There was a strong current of opinion within the OCN movement that networks should be free to develop their own structures and procedures, that NOCN had no role in determining what these should be and that it was the act of awarding credit in itself that marked the distinctiveness of OCNs, even if these credits had different values in different localities.

The Commonality Working Party (which included representation from Manchester, Merseyside and South Yorkshire OCNs) was made up largely of development officers - ie local practitioners - rather than OCN directors or chairs. The pragmatic views of this group were important in overcoming these occasional expressions of local identity, just as OCNs began to become a significant presence in many parts of England and Wales. The adoption of a common definition of credit and an agreed set of levels (based on a further refinement of the level descriptors) is now seen as a significant and necessary precursor to the next period of expansion. But it took time to establish and was based on a significant level of mutual trust between OCNs, as well as a shared vision of the future.

This shared vision of the future encompassed the concept of 'credit transfer' between OCNs, and the potential for transferring credits between different local networks. However, the operation of a system of credit transfer was not part of the formal rationale for establishing the Commonality Working Party. The brief for the group was primarily concerned with the 'credibility, cohesion and distinctiveness' of NOCN as a national organisation. In 1989 there were no concrete examples of credit transfer between OCNs and the internal documents of NOCN at the time were clearly concerned with consistent approaches to the award of credit across different local networks, not the transferability of credits between them (NOCN, 1990). The decision of NOCN to adopt standard specifications for credits and levels in 1990 established an essential prerequisite for the future development of credit transfer between different OCNs, and the next phase of development of the OCN credit system would focus much more explicitly on the potential of credit transfer.

Before considering the issue of credit transfer between OCNs, it is necessary to step outside this chronology of OCN development, which has been recounted so far in something of a vacuum. The process of developing and refining the OCN credit system during this period took place outside the formal system of qualifications, which itself underwent some significant changes during this period. Before considering the next phase in this process, it is necessary to consider how the development of an OCN credit system related to the separate developments within the qualifications system during the 1980s.

6

Separate and not equal:
Credits and qualifications

It is difficult to envisage from a perspective of 25 years, but when the very first credits were awarded to the very first learners in Manchester in February 1983, the whole area of qualifications in relation to adult learners was effectively a 'policy free' zone. The government had established an agency (the Schools' Curriculum Council, later the Schools' Curriculum and Assessment Agency – SCAA) to oversee quality and standards in O levels (later GCSEs) and A levels, but, as their names imply, these agencies had no remit or interest in the development or delivery of qualifications outside schools. By 1983 the Business Education Council (BEC) and the Technology Education Council (TEC) had merged to become BTEC, but the focus of the Council's work on younger learners remained unchanged. Although it was true that vocational qualifications were offered to adult learners, it was not seen as necessary to subject these offers to the formality of government policy. In fact, government policy on the development of vocational qualifications to meet workforce needs was only just beginning to be formulated. The publication of the New Training Initiative (NTI) policy in 1981 marked the first attempt by government to formulate a national policy in relation to the development of workforce skills (MSC, 1981). The rationale behind the NTI makes interesting reading in 2009: 'If the UK is to meet its training needs in a rapidly changing and increasingly competitive economic environment we need a workforce which is both more highly skilled and more flexible' (MSC, 1981, p. 5).

Even more interesting is the fact that, although the NTI did lead to the development of the Technical and Vocational Training Initiative (TVEI) and the Youth Training Scheme (YTS), its initial focus was not on the reform of qualifications. Nor was it concerned with the needs of adult learners: 'We must develop skill training, including apprenticeship, in such a way as to enable young people entering at different ages and with different educational attainments to acquire agreed standards of skill appropriate to the jobs available' (MSC, 1981).

Two messages from the NTI are clear: the focus of reform should be on skills training rather than qualifications; and skills training is for young people. In this context, the early development of OCN credit systems can clearly be seen to fill a need that was almost entirely absent from the concerns of official policy in relation to qualifications – that is, recognising the achievements of adult learners. We should also note that the rationale for developing OCN credit systems at this juncture was quite different from that set out in the NTI. There is no reference in early OCN documents to competitiveness, raising skill levels or developing a more flexible workforce. The rationale behind these early credit systems is entirely learner-centred and based on principles of widening access and participation in learning. Any notion that the development of credit systems might contribute to economic prosperity or improve the UK's position in the international economy is completely absent from the literature of the times and would be for more than a decade.

This absence of policy was even more marked in provision for adult learners outside skills training. The first OCN credits awarded to learners in 1983 were in recognition of their achievements on a programme designed to improve numeracy skills. It would be some 15 years before policymakers decided that adult numeracy and literacy issues should be tackled through the development of new qualifications, by which time hundreds of thousands of learners across England, Wales and Northern Ireland had achieved OCN credits through literacy and numeracy programmes.

It was to be five years after the publication of the NTI before the connection between its original rationale and the reform of qualifications became an explicit part of government policy. Shortly before the first meeting of NOCN took place in 1986, the government published the outcomes of its *Review of Vocational Qualifications* – the de Ville report (MSC and DES, 1986). The rationale for undertaking this review also makes interesting reading from the perspective of 2009:

> We have a complex and untidy array of vocational qualifications. A free market has operated in vocational qualification and several national systems have grown up … in addition there are regional bodies … and of course there are hundreds of professional bodies. There is no agreement between them on the form, size, shape or status of qualifications, or the terms used to describe them.
>
> (Jessup, 1991, p. 9)

This is one of the first formulations of the infamous 'jungle' of vocational qualifications, the rationalisation of which has informed much government policy in this area over the years.

This then is the form of the qualifications landscape in 1986. The need for reform of vocational qualifications sits alongside a continuing focus on the needs of young people and a formal structure within which only those qualifications offered to school pupils are subject to any form of central regulation. In effect, those early OCNs meeting at Northern College surveyed this landscape and, in relation to the needs of adult learners, they continued to see virgin territory. The OCN credit system did not develop initially in opposition to, or as an alternative to, more formal government policy on the recognition of achievements of adult learners. Until 1986 no such policy existed, and it would be another five years until the possibility that credit systems and reformed vocational qualifications might not be mutually supportive developments actually entered into the field of vision of policymakers.

Following from the publication of the de Ville report, the government announced the following year the establishment of the NCVQ and began a programme of development leading to the first NVQs in 1989. Although OCN credit systems and NVQs developed along entirely different tracks during the late 1980s, it would not be true to say that the two initiatives were hermetically sealed from each other. An examination of how the reform of vocational qualifications influenced the development of OCN credit systems during this period is instructive. It would also be interesting to examine how credit systems influenced the development of NVQs. Unfortunately, there is no evidence that they did.

7

NVQs and credit systems

Subsequent events have perhaps led to an overemphasis of the separateness of the histories of NVQs and credit systems. OCN credit systems did not develop without reference to NVQs. Indeed, it seemed at first that the reform of vocational qualifications would reproduce for younger learners many of the benefits that credit systems sought to deliver to adults. Although in theory NVQs were designed to be offered to learners of all ages, their introduction in 1989 was closely tied to the government's strategy to combat youth unemployment, and in particular to the development of the Youth Training Scheme (YTS) and later Youth Training.[1]

Although more recent critiques of NVQs have focused on the bureaucracy of assessment (Torrance, 2005), the costs of development (Wolf, 1996) and their inability to support skills improvement (Grugulis, 2002), it should be remembered that these aspects of the new vocational qualifications were not yet evident in their early stages of development. In 1987 and 1988, those involved in the development of OCN credit systems noted the unit-based format of NVQs, the practical basis of assessment, the commitment to open access in assessment and the stimulation of accreditation of prior learning as innovative features of the new qualifications that would make them appropriate to adult learners. Notwithstanding what OCN practitioners saw as the design faults of the NVQ framework (in particular, the absence of any recognition of achievements below NVQ Level 1 and the 'silo' nature of qualifications), the initial reaction of people working in OCNs to the introduction of NVQs was largely positive.[2]

The NCVQ also appropriated the language of credit accumulation and transfer to describe the process through which learners could receive certification for the completion of individual NVQ units. Indeed, in 1988 NCVQ formally launched what it referred to as 'a national system of credit accumulation and transfer'. Fourteen awarding bodies 'signed up' to this national system based on an agreement:

> to restructure their qualifications in unit form, where necessary, and to offer the units for separate assessment. They further agreed to recognise the units of the other awarding bodies as credits towards their own qualifications where the units were common.
>
> (NCVQ, 1988, p. 2)

Despite the description of this arrangement as 'credit accumulation and transfer', the use of the term 'credit' in the NVQ system simply describes 'the formal recognition of achievement through certification' (Jessup, 1991, p. 68). Elsewhere in the same Information Note, NCVQ confirms that it 'does not prescribe the size of a unit' in NVQs, which of course would be a necessary feature of a real credit system. This conception of 'unit sharing' as 'credit transfer', and the conflation of 'unit certificate' and 'credit', continued to arise during the QCF tests and trials in 2006-8.

NCVQ's appropriation of the language of credit accumulation and transfer did not have a significant impact on the growth of OCN credit systems. Nor indeed did it establish an alternative concept of credit accumulation and transfer. However, NVQs did have an influence on the development of credit systems in another way. We now take for granted that credits are awarded for the achievement of learning outcomes presented in a unit format. This forms a critical feature of the QCF and was indeed inherited directly from the practice of OCNs. However, the award of OCN credits has not always been based on units as we now conceive them. In fact, this connection between credit value, level and learning outcomes is a relatively recent development and can be traced back directly to the influence of NVQs on OCN credit systems in their initial phase of development.

The outcomes of the NOCN Commonality Working Party in 1989 simply delivered for NOCN a common definition of credit and an agreement to use four levels of achievement. However, these agreed specifications of credit and level were unrelated to the concepts of either learning outcomes or units. The documents produced by individual OCNs at the time make numerous references to 'units', to 'modules', to 'chunks of learning', to 'small steps of achievement' and other similar concepts, but there was no NOCN requirement to base these common specifications of credit value and level on a clear definition of learning outcomes grouped together in a unit format. To many of the people involved in the QCF tests and trials in 2006-8, it appeared that the (unfamiliar) concept of 'credit' was being added in to the (familiar) concept of 'unit'. In fact, for those involved in the development of OCN credit systems in the late 1980s and early 1990s, this process was reversed. Credits (and indeed the concept of credit transfer) and levels pre-date the formal adoption of the unit format now so familiar in credit systems by a number of years.

In Chapter 4 the origins of credit systems are noted during a period when the distinction between 'curriculum' and 'qualifications' or between 'courses' and 'achievement' was far more blurred than it is today. Indeed, the definition of credit, bringing together as it does a measurement of the outcomes of learning with a reference to the process of learning, could perhaps only have originated in such a context. Nevertheless, from the outset, OCN credit systems have always clearly associated the award of credit with the recognition of learner achievement. However, conceptually such credits were achieved through completion of the outcomes of a recognised course or programme, and credit values were established for these courses and programmes, thus perpetuating the implied link between achievement and curriculum that is evident in the first iterations of OCN credit systems. There was no explicit link to learner achievement represented through learning outcomes in a unit format.

During the late 1980s and early 1990s, OCN credit systems began to mature as more OCNs became established and greater collective clarity was established about the operation of credit systems. In particular, we can detect in the debates of this period a clearer focus on credits as a representation of learner achievement, rather than as a measure of the volume of learning. Part of this influence can be attributed to an increased focus on quality assurance arrangements underpinning the award of credit, and the need for clarity in what was being recognised through the award of credit across different OCNs. But there is no doubt that an equally important influence on this gradual separation of 'achievement' from 'course' in OCN credit systems can be attributed to the growing influence of NVQs, and in particular to focus of NVQ units on the assessment of learner achievement rather than on the delivery of a particular curriculum.

By the end of 1988 the approach of the NCVQ to the development of NVQs was becoming well established and a meeting between the NCVQ and the NOCN in December that year confirms the differences of approach between the two organisations: 'there were key differences of approach and intent between OCNs and the NCVQ and we should be clear about these when presenting each other's work in our various developments. They are not the same and we should not suggest that' (Browning, 1988a, p. 1).

At the same time NOCN considered a discussion paper prepared by the Merseyside OCF in which it was argued that, although the competence-based approach of NVQs was too restrictive to encompass the range of achievements that OCNs sought to recognise, nevertheless OCNs should be more explicit about the nature of the achievements that were to be recognised through the award of credit:

> This paper repeats the arguments for a time-based unit of credit, within which a system of learning achievement statements can operate. Such a system would reflect the best traditions of models operating in the United States ... and avoid the excessive claims of models inspired by behaviourist, operationalist objectives.
>
> (MerOCF, 1988, p. 2)

Although the reference to learning outcomes is not quite explicit, the concept of 'learning achievement statements' brings us close to this. As the UDACE

OCN project continued through 1989–90, this approach found favour with the new networks beginning to develop as the NVQ model became more familiar. A full-scale debate was now engendered through OCNs about the adoption of a 'learning outcomes'-based approach to the award of credit. That these learning outcomes should be grouped together in units formed an accepted part of this same debate.

This debate within OCNs became focused during 1990 on the development of the first credit accumulation and transfer agreement between OCNs, of which more in Chapter 10 (NOCN, 1990). This was seen as a logical consequence of the adoption of a common set of design features for the OCN credit system, but it soon became clear that the definitions of credits and levels established through the NOCN Commonality Working Party were not in themselves sufficiently robust to support the mutual confidence between networks that was necessary in order to establish an agreement on the transfer of credits between OCNs. It was necessary to be much clearer about the processes leading to the award of credit, and to be assured that there was comparability of credits and levels across OCNs. In order to do this, consensus was needed on what credits were actually awarded *for*.

As part of the work on the UDACE project, those OCNs that were operational set up through NOCN a 'quality circle', with the intention of supporting newer networks in developing their internal quality systems. Each OCN had a responsibility to sample, evaluate and report on the processes of another network that led to the award of credit to learners. What emerged clearly from this initial exercise was that there was a great deal of discrepancy in the process through which credit values and levels were determined, and a wide variety of forms within which what might be termed 'the curriculum and assessment offer' (in some cases it was not easy to distinguish between these two things) was presented to learners. It became clear that, if credit transfer was to operate effectively between OCNs, it would be necessary to establish a more explicit and more detailed set of requirements leading to the award of credit than simply agreeing definitions of credits and levels.

By the time that the first NOCN CAT agreement was signed, the shift within OCNs to a learning outcomes-based approach was well established. There was consensus among OCNs that identifying the anticipated outcomes of the learning process reflected international best practice in adult learning, and provided a more stable and consistent basis for awarding credit to learners than simply 'course completion'. However, what remained open for debate at this juncture was the precise nature of the relationship between learning outcomes and the learning process within OCN systems. The adoption of a learning outcomes-based approach was established within NOCN through the mutual acceptance of this approach by individual OCNs, not by a definitive requirement of NOCN. Within this mutual acceptance, a variety of forms continued to exist within which this learning outcomes approach was represented. Many OCNs continued to embed learning outcome statements within descriptions of learning activities – a natural consequence of an approach based on the recognition of learning programmes rather than the development of qualifications. The NOCN CAT agreement was based on an acceptance of the importance of learning outcomes, but not on a standard unit format.

The clear separation of assessment from programme delivery and of learning outcomes from the learning process is now accepted as a standard design feature of vocational qualifications. But, as the Review of Vocational Qualifications in 1986 highlighted, this separation is a relatively recent innovation and is clearly based on one of the key design features of NVQs. As the NOCN discussion paper illustrates, the separation of assessment from programme delivery also had the potential to bring positive benefits to learners, especially those learners for whom traditional classroom-based provision was not best suited to their needs. So, although the argument for focusing exclusively on assessment had a different rationale in OCN credit systems from that which informed the development of NVQs, by the early 1990s OCNs had a much clearer focus on assessment than the first networks, and the award of credit became much more explicitly tied to the achievement of learning outcomes than the completion of a programme of study.

The link between learning outcomes and credit marks another significant influence of NVQs on OCN credit systems. Again, the OCN rationale for adopting an outcomes-based approach to assessment was different from NVQs, but the resulting influence on the form of assessment within OCN credit systems is clear to see: 'programmes ... should be designed in such a way as to make explicit, and available for public scrutiny, the "hidden" and "intuitive" assumptions being made by teachers about what they expect students to learn/achieve' (MerOCF, 1988, p. 3).

Thus for OCNs the benefits of a learning outcomes approach are rooted in the rights of individual learners. For NVQs they are rooted in the identification of the competences required by employers. Despite these fundamental differences, in the early 1990s both OCN credit systems and NVQs espoused a learning outcomes-based approach that was still at odds with the accepted orthodoxy of the day.

The third aspect of the NVQ framework that influenced the development of OCN credit systems was the unit format. From the outset OCNs had argued that the adoption of a credit system would support greater flexibility in the delivery of the curriculum and would permit small steps of achievement to be recognised. Indeed, as Robertson reminds us in *Choosing to Change*, credit systems in HE were always linked explicitly to modular programme structures (Robertson, 1994, p. 172).

During the 1980s this connection between credit systems and flexibility in curriculum design was clearly manifested through the work of OCNs. However, there were many different interpretations of 'flexibility' and many different ways in which the delivery of a programme of learning might be connected to the award of credits. In retrospect, it seems as if this connection between flexibility and credit systems was more of an article of faith, supported by local anecdote, than a standard feature of OCN credit systems. Linking the award of credit clearly to the assessment of learning outcomes marked a major step forward in the development of OCN credit systems in the early 1990s; one that was clearly and positively influenced by the parallel development of NVQs. Clustering these learning outcomes into a standard unit format (another feature of NVQs) would take a little longer to establish as a standard feature of credit systems.

It would be wrong though to represent this process of shifting towards units of assessment based on learning outcomes as a straightforward line of development in credit systems in the early 1990s. Some OCNs adopted this approach earlier or more willingly than others. Although the concept of the unit based on learning outcomes was borrowed from NVQs, the actual format of the NVQ unit was not adopted by OCNs. Nor was the particular concept of 'competence' that informed the development of NVQ outcomes embraced within OCN credit systems. Indeed, even among those OCNs that moved most quickly towards a unit-based model, there were several different interpretations of what a 'unit' actually was, as well as a wide variety of interpretation of the concept of learning outcomes. Nevertheless, the influence of NVQs on the development of OCN credit systems during this period is significant, especially in securing a fundamental clarity within OCNs that the focus of quality assurance within their credit systems should be the assessment of learning outcomes and not the quality of the course through which these outcomes were delivered. Such a separation was an essential prerequisite for extending credit systems beyond the boundaries of OCNs themselves and ensuring the wider applicability of credit as a currency of achievement within the QCF.

It would be 1994 before a standard unit format was secured across all OCN credit systems, and again the impetus for that development came from outside the OCN movement itself. In order to locate this next phase of development in a meaningful context, it is necessary to examine how, from their original starting point, OCNs sought to export their credit systems beyond the boundaries of their own networks. To get a flavour of how this process of exporting credit was approached, we need to go back to the South Yorkshire OCN in 1989–90.

Notes

1 Although it should be emphasised that YTS preceded NVQs by some time. In fact, prior to the development of NVQs, MOCF offered accreditation to young people on YTS provision in Manchester.
2 Though the opposite was not the case. Some enthusiasts for the new qualifications predicted that NVQs would lead to the rapid demise of OCN credit systems.

8

Exporting credit: Integrating OCN credit systems with NVQs

It should be recalled that, although the development of NVQs was a direct consequence of the outcomes of the Review of Vocational Qualifications, the de Ville Report itself made no explicit recommendations about the precise form in which NVQs were to be designed and offered. The original conception of the NCVQ was that it would become an accreditation agency for vocational qualifications, playing a similar role to the SCAA in relation to what were still known as 'academic' qualifications. In the event the strategy adopted by NCVQ was not to set accreditation criteria for existing vocational qualifications, but to develop detailed design requirements for a new type of vocational qualification – the NVQ. It took some time for the implications of this strategy to be understood in the post-school sector. Indeed, it was not immediately clear that the gradual elimination of all other vocational qualifications had been the intention of government in establishing NCVQ. During this initial period it was assumed that some accommodation could be found between existing vocational qualifications and these new 'competence-based' qualifications that NCVQ proposed should now be developed.

From the beginnings of the development of the NVQ framework, attempts were made to integrate the wider development of credit systems with the emerging features of the new framework of vocational qualifications. The importance of doing this was accepted from the outset. Despite the rationale for review of vocational qualifications being based almost entirely on the needs of younger learners, it was clear from the outset that NVQs would have an impact on the qualifications offered to all learners. The intention that NVQs should become the sole available vocational qualifications (hence their title) rather than a particular type of qualification – their position in the NQF – was not yet explicit in 1987. Nevertheless, there was no disputing the potential impact that these new qualifications would have in the future. In this context, it was essential for OCNs to consider how their credit systems might relate to this new NVQ framework.

This issue – the relationship between the emerging NVQ framework and OCN credit systems – continued to occupy NOCN during the late 1980s. The tenor of the OCN position had effectively been set by the initial meeting between NCVQ and NOCN in 1988. Although both organisations accepted the differences in approach between their different systems of recognising learner achievement, NOCN still sought ways of establishing connections between them that would benefit adult learners through creating progression opportunities from credits towards an NVQ. No such reciprocal concerns are evident in the development of NVQs, which were established as exclusive qualifications whose intention was to replace existing forms of recognising vocational achievement, not accommodate them. It took a little while for the implications of this approach to become apparent.

The SYOCF response to the initial consultation paper on the NVQ framework makes interesting reading in this context. The response assumes a different approach to the development of NVQs than that subsequently adopted by NCVQ and sets out the explicit hope that 'through NCVQ, relationships can be established between [SYOCF] and national validating bodies that will enable a gradual integration of these developing local and national systems of credit accumulation and transfer' (SYOCF, 1987, p. 2).

This was the conceptual framework within which OCNs envisaged that their credit systems would interact with NVQs – that is, that they would in some way become recognised in their localities as the organisation that would award credits to learners that could then be accumulated towards an NVQ offered by an awarding body. This expectation was made explicit in a report by the author to Sheffield City Council at the end of 1987:

> We may envisage a future system operating in South Yorkshire with the following characteristics:
> (i) Recognition by the major validating bodies of SYOCF credits in vocational areas enabling transfer of these credits towards national awards at each level of NVQ.
>
> (Wilson, 1987, p. 3)

The expectation, of course, never came close to being realised. Nevertheless, work continued within SYOCF and other OCNs to establish links with NVQs as the new qualifications were developed. In 1989 the Manpower Services Commission was prepared to fund a development project in Rotherham LEA 'to enhance opportunities for students to transfer between and progress through OCF and NVQ systems of awards' (SYOCF, 1989, p. 1). The objectives of the project envisaged that SYOCF would:

> Negotiate agreements in principle on recognition, equivalence, credit transfer and exemption between OCFs and National Awarding Bodies ... [and produce] concrete examples of collaboration and articulation between OCF and NVQ systems of awards.
>
> (SYOCF, 1989, p. 1)

It seems that, in some parts of the country at least, hope sprang eternal that the emerging NVQ framework and the existing credit systems of OCNs could somehow be brought together in a single national system of credit accumulation and transfer; not that OCNs were unaware of the difficulties that such an 'integrated' system might present:

> Unfortunately NCVQ has compounded confusion by referring to the design framework of NVQs as 'a system of credit accumulation and transfer'. In fact the NVQ framework is not credit-based ... in itself [it] is not a sufficient vehicle through which a comprehensive institutional system of credit accumulation and transfer can be established.
>
> (Wilson, 1988, p. 2)

The response of national awarding bodies to the proposition that OCN credits might be accumulated towards a vocational qualification accredited by NCVQ was one of bemusement. In particular, the proposition that local credits might count towards an NVQ was conceptually too problematic to address within the criteria and procedures of the NVQ framework. The conceptual distance between a large, national qualifications-awarding body and a comparatively small, local network awarding credits was simply too wide to bridge. The interests of qualifications-awarding bodies were focused on the younger learners that still comprised the great majority of registrations in the late 1980s. OCNs' commitment to adult learners effectively confirmed their position as marginal actors in relation to this qualifications system.

Needless to say, nothing concrete emerged from the SYOCF project and no agreements were ever negotiated through the OCN that permitted learners to accumulate credits towards an NVQ. However, it was not just at local level that this proposition was tested. The potential connection between OCN credits and NVQs was an issue that exercised NOCN too during this period.

Following the initial meeting between representatives of NOCN and NCVQ in December 1988 to discuss the objectives of the UDACE OCN project, there was little formal contact between the two organisations. As the UDACE project began to deliver on its objectives to extend the network of OCNs, so the first NVQs began to be offered to learners. It was nearly two years later, in 1990, that a formal meeting was held at the headquarters of the NCVQ between representatives of the Council (including the Chief Executive) and representatives of NOCN. The subject of the meeting was discussion of the feasibility of establishing an agreement between NOCN and NCVQ that would enable credits awarded by local OCNs to be transferred towards an NVQ, under certain circumstances. From the perception of NOCN, the discussion was about how a new system on which the first learners were now registered (NVQs) might relate to an established system (OCN credits) that had already registered tens

of thousands of adult learners across the eight or nine OCNs now fully operational. From the perception of NCVQ a group of local networks without formal support from government or any significant national resources was
proposing an agreement between equals to the organisation responsible for
the biggest programme of qualifications reform yet undertaken in the UK. The
meeting may have been of people but it was not of minds. NOCN's proposition was greeted with polite but incredulous surprise.

Whatever the perception of OCNs about the potential to extend their
credit systems to NVQs, it was very clearly the perception of NCVQ that the
process of developing the NVQ framework should proceed without reference
to any existing credit system. The following year, NCVQ presented evidence to
the House of Commons Employment Committee on the progress of introducing NVQs (House of Commons, 1991). As part of this evidence, the Deputy
Chief Executive of NCVQ, John Hillier, set out clearly NCVQ's proposals for
further development of vocational qualifications, excluding all reference to
credit systems (House of Commons, 1991, pp. 116-17). Any suggestion that
OCN credit systems and NVQs might both have a role to play in the future
of post-school education was now dismissed. The idea that some form of
credit transfer agreement might now be struck between NCVQ and NOCN
was officially dead and buried.

By the summer of 1991 it was clear that any further development of OCN
credit systems would need to take place without reference to NVQs. As the
intention that NVQs would eventually supersede all other vocational qualifications was still (just) a formal policy position of government, the future for
OCN credit systems seemed far from secure. Despite this uncertainty, however,
OCNs continued to grow and other avenues were beginning to open up
through which the proposition could be sustained that these credit systems
could be extended more widely across the post-school sector. The idea of
exporting credit still flourished, though not all approaches to this objective
proved fruitful. Once again it was in South Yorkshire that an alternative export
strategy to developing formal links with NCVQ and vocational awarding
bodies was tested.

9
Exporting credit:
The first 'credit-rating' experiment

As I noted previously, the independence of local OCNs meant that individual networks were able to experiment with different approaches to the extension of their credit systems. During the late 1980s and early 1990s these experiments in extending the reach of credit systems were taken forward most explicitly through the South Yorkshire OCN. The previous chapter highlights one attempt to 'export credit' through establishing links with NVQs, but there were other attempts that emanated from the same locality. So, for example, Sheffield LEA's project to introduce NVQs across its Further Education (FE) Colleges was managed by the Chair of the OCN, with one of the NVQ project officers also working as an OCN Development Officer. One of the first Accreditation of Prior Learning (APL) projects to be mounted in the UK was run in Sheffield, piloting APL processes within both NVQs and the OCN credit system.[1] Within South Yorkshire at least, the development of an OCN credit system was seen as an integral part of a wider strategy for developing post-school education and training opportunities. The innovative work undertaken during this period was recognised beyond the boundaries of the People's Republic of Sheffield, and representatives from South Yorkshire began to find a national audience for their ideas.

In 1988, I produced a paper for a Further Education Staff College event on 'the modular curriculum'. The paper, entitled 'Modularisation and Credit Accumulation and Transfer', reflects some of the trends in OCN credit systems identified in the preceding chapter on credit systems and NVQs (Wilson, 1988). It sought to separate out the distinctions between curriculum design and delivery (modularisation) and the assessment and certification of learner achievement (credit systems):

> A module is the smallest part of a learning programme that can be validly and reliably assessed... A credit, on the other hand, is a concept of value. It is a means of translating the outcomes of learning into a comprehensive and comprehensible expression of its worth.
>
> (Wilson, 1988a, p. 1)

Although rooted in the experience of working within the OCN credit system in South Yorkshire, the paper sought to encompass a wider perspective:

> The first step in this process [of developing a credit system] is to establish a uniform institutional definition of a credit. In doing so, colleges need to take account of the external equivalence, convertibility and transfer value of such credits, both to other local colleges and beyond.
>
> (Wilson, 1988, p. 5)

As these extracts illustrate, the clear separation of delivery and assessment was still incomplete at this stage of development. The context within which credits were to be awarded was perceived as *learning programmes* rather than qualifications. The key actors in developing a future credit system were seen as *colleges* rather than awarding bodies. Again, we need to remind ourselves that the paper was produced a decade before the introduction of the NQF, and in a context where adult learners hardly registered on the map of existing qualifications. Nevertheless, the paper explicitly argues that the credit system of OCNs could provide the model for a national credit system across the whole post-school sector.

This perspective reflected the views not just of the author, but of a group of colleagues working in the South Yorkshire OCN. The idea that the credit system developed by OCNs could actually be applied more widely and was potentially relevant across all areas of the post-school sector sprang from this experience of working not just in the context of the OCN itself, but in the wider context of developments in the post-school sector. For the first time the idea that the concept of the credit system, though developed by OCNs, could be used beyond the boundaries of OCNs was made explicit. If one considers the relative maturity of the OCN credit system at the time, and the limited number of OCNs actually operational in 1988, such an idea seems, in retrospect, both foolhardy and conceited. Nevertheless, it was a sincerely held belief, and one that informed the continuing development of OCN credit systems for a number of years.

In 1989, SYOCF began another project, again funded by the Manpower Services Commission alongside the NVQ development programme, that aimed to apply the OCN credit system to 'mainstream' qualifications (SYOCF, 1989a). In particular, the project sought to apply the concept of credit to A levels and to BTEC National qualifications. At the time SYOCF accredited a number of Access to HE programmes, and these were in the process of being reviewed to bring them within the scope of the new Council for National Academic Awards/Committee of Vice Chancellors and Principals (CNAA/CVCP) Access Course Recognition Scheme. As part of this review, the SYOCF project proposed to 'credit-rate' BTEC and A level modules and offer them as options within Access to HE programmes, based on an OCN-accredited core. This was the first example of this approach to using credit not as an award made to a learner, but as a way of representing the value of a qualification (or part of a qualification) offered by an awarding body other than an OCN.

The project was not a great success. Although the principle that components of other qualifications might be brought within the scope of a credit-based qualification was to prove technically feasible in the longer term, it became clear through the project that simply credit-rating another qualification, or part of it, actually did nothing either to transform the curriculum offer to learners or to offer them any wider options within their OCN-accredited programme. Simply attaching numbers to other qualifications had no impact on delivery, assessment, registration or certification processes. Decreeing that part of an A level was worth three credits at Level 3 or that a BTEC National module could be valued at six credits was of no practical use if these components of other qualifications could not be offered separately to learners, nor assessed as part of another qualification, nor certificated separately from their parent qualification.

The SYOCF Credit Framework project has long since disappeared into the dustbin of history. In retrospect it can be seen as an attempt to bypass the obduracy of the NCVQ or the lack of interest from other awarding bodies in developing real examples of credit accumulation between OCN systems and vocational qualifications. The process of credit rating required no negotiation and no complex agreements with other organisations. It was a process wholly controlled by SYOCF itself and other organisations need not even be informed of its outcomes (certainly nobody thought to inform BTEC that a module of a BTEC National had received a credit rating of 6 in South Yorkshire).

The practical impact of the Credit Framework project on the lives of learners in South Yorkshire was zero. Its impact on those involved in the project (I wrote the project proposal and Brett Kerton, a member of the project team, went on to become director of the North East Midlands OCN – NEMOCN – and a member of the NOCN executive committee) was more long lasting. For the first time the idea that the credit system had a wider application beyond the boundaries of OCNs was tested in practice. What the project demonstrated was that this wider application could not be based simply on using the mathematical constructs of the OCN credit system (that is, credits and levels), but had to also encompass the structure and processes of assessment and certification that led to the award of credits. Without the active collaboration of the awarding bodies responsible for assessment and certification of the qualifications concerned, the act of credit-rating components of these qualifications was literally pointless.

David Robertson would later characterise this process of credit-rating as 'mass blessing by numbers' (Robertson, 1993). The experience of those who first experimented with this process in South Yorkshire in 1989–90 led to a realisation that, if the OCN credit system was going to be extended beyond the boundaries of OCNs themselves, it had to be based on the award of credits to learners. This would require a radical and thorough-going transformation of the qualifications landscape in the post-school sector, rather than a superficial extension of the numbers in the credit system to existing qualifications. Extracting the numbers from the credit system, and seeking to use them without also seeking to transform the way in which learner achievements were assessed and recognised, was not an effective method of exporting credit beyond the boundaries of OCNs.

In retrospect, two other aspects of the SYOCF credit framework project are worthy of note here. Despite the fact that the project had zero impact on learners, it did engage practitioners in a series of workshops aimed at credit-rating other qualifications. These workshops gave rise to some heated discussions about the perceived equivalence between different qualifications and the difficulties involved in applying a mathematical algorithm (credits and levels) to represent this equivalence. Nevertheless, a series of numbers were generated through this process, and the components of A levels and BTEC Nationals were duly 'blessed' with these numbers.

What this process proved was that applying judgements about relative credit values to qualifications with very different design specifications was actually very difficult. It was simply not possible to take very different design specifications (a BTEC module and an A level component, for example) and calculate from the information presented what an appropriate credit rating might be. Without a common set of design features to compare, people involved in the credit-rating process could have no confidence that the numbers produced through their deliberations were consistent with the decisions of others working from a different set of design features, or that the numbers that emerged from these different processes were comparable with each other or with the real credits actually awarded to learners on Access to HE programmes. This lesson had important implications for the future development of units within OCN credit systems. It was also a lesson that was relearned by the FEU a few years later (of which more in Chapter 15).

Conversely, the discussions about appropriate credit ratings for other qualifications also proved that the numbers themselves were an extremely seductive tool in engaging practitioners in this process. Using the credit system of OCNs as a way of trying to bring a semblance of order to an otherwise chaotic system (the Review of Vocational Qualifications had already characterised vocational qualifications as 'a jungle') (MSC and DES, 1986) was seen by practitioners as an exercise worthy of their time and effort. The problem was, of course, that sprinkling A levels and BTEC Nationals with number dust had zero impact on this jungle. The SYOCF Credit Framework project marked the end of credit-rating experiments within OCNs, but this seduction of numbers would come back time and again during the future development of credit systems outside OCNs.

As the project concluded, the first NVQs were being delivered, and a continuing programme of massive investment in the development of both the new qualifications themselves and the standards that underpinned them was under way. The attempts to export credit systems beyond the boundaries of OCNs through developing credit transfer arrangements with NVQs or through credit-rating mainstream qualifications had failed. The chances that a still modest network of locally-based organisations, unsupported by government policy and without one penny of central government funding to finance their activities, might have a wider impact on the development of the qualifications landscape was, at best, far-fetched. If the OCN credit system was to be extended beyond the boundaries of OCNs themselves, then a long, hard road lay ahead for those that wanted to see such a development. The focus of OCNs now turned towards strengthening their own systems rather than trying to build links with others.

Note

1 And later produced one of the standard texts on the subject *Introducing APEL*, by Maggie Challis Routledge, London, 1993.

10

From commonality to credit transfer

By 1990 an element of 'commonality' had been established across all members of NOCN in relation to credits and levels, and all new networks (which continued to join the national organisation) were required to subscribe to these shared definitions. However, as the debates over the importance of learning outcomes and the experience of credit rating illustrate, there was a rapidly developing understanding across OCNs that, if they were to survive and prosper as independent organisations outside the purview of NCVQ, they needed to establish even more explicit and binding links between their different local credit systems.

NOCN now decided that it should move beyond the simple proposition that all OCNs based their awards to learners on a common set of design features. It was agreed that NOCN should ask all operational OCNs to commit themselves to the mutual recognition of credits by all other member OCNs. This formalisation of the relationship between OCNs would lead to the establishing of the first credit accumulation and transfer agreement between NOCN members in 1990 (NOCN, 1990a). Although this might seem a logical consequence of the development of a common set of design features for OCN credit systems, the mutual confidence that would be required between OCNs to accept the credits offered by all other networks signified a major step forward for NOCN. An organisation built initially on an inclusive model that invited any interested party to become a member, even if that member did not operate a credit system, was now proposing a very different and much more demanding condition of membership (though for a time these differences were accommodated through the concept of Associate Members).

The UDACE project and the additional funding from BP for staff development across OCNs had an important impact on the form of this credit accumulation and transfer agreement. In addition to the common specifications of credits and levels developed through the commonality working group, the agreement also set out, for the first time, proposals on the operational principles for the OCN accreditation process, as well as an agreement on the form within which credits were to be awarded and recorded.

The statements about process within the agreement, which referred simply to 'peer group panels' and 'a system of moderation', mark for the first time a collective understanding between OCNs of the importance of quality assurance systems within individual OCNs to the operation of credit transfer systems between networks. The credit accumulation and transfer agreement marks an explicit step forward from the commonality agreement, and the new OCNs brought into the national network through the UDACE project contributed significantly to this development. The agreement marks an acceptance across NOCN members that mutual recognition of credit depends not just upon common design features, but on mutual confidence in the quality systems leading to the award of credits. The idea of credits as a currency of learner achievement moves a step closer with the signing of the NOCN credit accumulation and transfer agreement.

The agreement also makes explicit reference to a Credit Record 'within which credits are accumulated' and requires credit awards to be issued to learners 'for achievement on recognised learning programmes'. Again, this marks a step forward from the commonality agreement and formalises what was becoming accepted practice within most OCNs. The MOCF Study Passport remained the inspiration for this document, but its name and format moved forward to accommodate this larger network of interests. The credit accumulation and transfer agreement also requires that credits are clearly awarded for achievement and not for the completion of a programme of learning. The distinction between assessment and programme delivery, based on the acceptance of a learning outcomes-based approach, underlies this part of the agreement and finds formal confirmation within it. Indeed, the detachment of the concept of credit from 'a course' and its clear location in the context of quality-assured assessment, leading to the recognition of achievement, was an essential precursor to the signing of the credit transfer agreement.

The idea that the accumulation of credits should be brought together within a Credit Record was one of the key innovations of MOCF. OCN legend has it that the idea of a Study Passport came to Michael Sterne (pace Archimedes) in his bath.[1] From the perspective of 2009 and the numerous (to date unsuccessful) attempts to introduce a comprehensive Record of Achievement or similar document across the post-school sector, it is easy to miss the significance of this development. Nothing like it existed in the UK in 1981 (though once again the North American precedent must be acknowledged) and it clearly anticipates the later development of the QCF Learner Record. Following the MOCF example, individual OCNs developed different formats in which credits were recorded, with different titles and different ways of representing the award of credits to a learner. Although the Commonality Working Group had discussed the idea of a standard format and title for such documents, no proposals from the group were put to NOCN. A paper presented to NOCN in 1988 marks the first proposal that OCNs should award credits in a standard format (Wilson, 1988a). This proposal gathered support as new OCNs

were established through the UDACE project, and from 1990 onwards all credits were awarded in a standard format and recorded in a document called a
Credit Record. Despite the absence of an ICT infrastructure to support this
development, the Credit Record signifies an attempt to create a common format within which credit achievements could be recorded and accumulated
over time. More importantly, it created the basis on which these credits could
actually be transferred between different awarding bodies – that is, between
individual OCNs.

In writing these words, it struck me that 'credit transfer' is actually a paper-
based concept. Within the QCF the operation of what is termed 'credit transfer', supported by a shared Learner Record in which all credits are recorded,
actually requires no real transfer of information at all. In fact, credit transfer
within the QCF operates through the mutual recognition of credits between
awarding bodies, rather than by the physical movement of data between
awarding bodies. Credit transfer within the QCF is a real concept for learners,
as credits really are moved between qualifications and awarding bodies. But for
the awarding bodies themselves, the acceptance of credits awarded by another
awarding body is managed (or will be managed) through the Learner Record
without any movement of data at all. In 1990 such a concept was beyond the
scope of the people involved in developing the NOCN credit accumulation
and transfer agreement, as well as the technology of the time.[2] Any credits
transferred between OCNs would need to be physically moved from one network to another, hence the concern in the NOCN agreement about the format
within which credit achievements were recorded.

In the event, 11 OCNs signed the NOCN credit accumulation and transfer
agreement in Manchester (symbolically)[3] in July 1990 (Sanders and Whaley,
2007, p. 7). Although it marked a step forward from the commonality agreement, the credit accumulation and transfer agreement makes no reference to
units or to qualifications. Despite the clear focus on assessment and achievement within the agreement, the entity that was to be accredited in the OCN
system was not a qualification, but a learning programme. Indeed, in the
absence of an NQF, many awarding bodies operated quality assurance systems
that also drew on a similar model. 'Centre-devised' units within BTEC qualifications were just one manifestation of this feature of qualifications that would
continue until the establishment of the NQF in 1998. In this respect NVQs,
with their highly centralised and explicitly national approach to development,
were very different from the explicitly local approach of OCNs. In between
these two models, other awarding bodies combined national and local
approaches in different ways.

In 1990 it seemed a perfectly feasible and meaningful exercise to develop a
credit accumulation and transfer agreement without reference to qualifications. In particular, the relationship between the needs of adult learners and

the development of qualifications was not at all well established. NOCN might have been a relatively marginal player in relation to the overall numbers of learners registering for and achieving qualifications in 1990 (statistics are not available). But in relation to adult learners, the NOCN was already becoming perceived as a significant force in the post-school sector, and the credit accumulation and transfer agreement did much to stimulate further interest in OCN credit systems.

In retrospect, the NOCN credit accumulation and transfer agreement was far more important for OCNs themselves than it was for learners. Signalling the mutual acceptance of credits between all NOCN members had a significant impact on OCN quality systems and helped to establish credits as a genuine national currency of achievement. The problem was that there was actually very little incentive for a learner to transfer credits between OCNs, as the credits (with the important exception of Access to HE certificates) could not, in 1990, be accumulated towards a qualification. What the agreement exposed, over time, was that the incidence of learners actually transferring credits between OCNs was negligible in some cases and non-existent in others. Learners did indeed move between OCNs and some proudly displayed the different Credit Records issued to them by different networks. But, without qualifications to which credits could be accumulated, credit transfer was actually (though OCNs would argue against this in 1990) pointless. It took the combination of credit systems with qualifications to give a purpose to the process of credit accumulation and transfer, and in 1990 that prospect was a very long way in the future.

My personal opinion is that the postponement of a national system of credit accumulation and transfer until the technology available to support such a system was available was actually a blessed relief for OCNs. The physical transfer of credits issued by one organisation into the Credit Record of another would have been a seriously complicated business, open to many errors. Some years after the NOCN agreement was signed, a young woman approached the then Leicestershire OCN and asked if the credits she had gained previously on her Access to HE course in London could be transferred towards a similar Access to HE course offered by a Leicester college. The college itself was happy to accept that some of the credits could be counted towards her Leicestershire OCN Access to HE Certificate, and this (in Leicestershire) unique incident was duly trumpeted by the OCN.

When the moment came to actually transfer the learner's credits from London to Leicestershire arrived, the problems inherent in the physical transfer of credits became apparent. The actual credits awarded by the London OCN could not physically be transferred to the Leicestershire OCN Credit Record. Not only did the certificate on which the credits were recorded include credits that could, as well as credits that could not, be transferred, but the actual process through which credits were physically attached to the Credit Record in London was quite different from that in Leicestershire. The certificate that recorded the credits simply would not fit into the new Credit Record. In the end, through a one-off process, the relevant credits that counted towards the Leicestershire OCN Access to HE Certificate were re-issued to the learner and marked as duplicates. Credit duplication just does not have the same ring to it as credit transfer, does it?

Notwithstanding these practical difficulties, it should be emphasised that the principle behind the credit transfer agreement – that a learner could take her achievements with one OCN and use them in another OCN – actually worked. And although such examples of credit transfer were rare, the principle that they embodied was extremely important. Despite the fact that the credits that were transferred were not awarded for the achievement of identical learning outcomes, signatories to the NOCN CAT agreement were prepared to accept that these achievements could be deemed to be *of equivalent value* within the programme (again the NOCN CAT agreement was not an agreement between qualifications) to which they were transferred, based on the number of credits awarded at a particular level. The NOCN CAT agreement is based on this important principle: that learning outcomes do not need to be identical in order to be accepted as being of equal value. It is a principle that is embodied in the operational arrangements for the QCF and marks a significant step forward in both flexibility and inclusiveness from the 'unit sharing' concept of credit accumulation and transfer that 14 NVQ awarding bodies had previously signed in 1988 (NCVQ, 1988).

The other important aspect of the NOCN CAT agreement is that it was based on a combination of shared technical specifications (credits and levels), shared quality assurance approaches (learning outcomes, peer group recognition and independent moderation) and mutual trust (embodied in the shared values of OCNs). The process of developing this mutual trust between what were, and still remain, independent organisations accountable to a local/ regional membership has resonance for the same process of developing mutual trust between awarding bodies operating in the QCF. Although the scale may have been smaller in 1990, the issues that had to be overcome before 11 different organisations were prepared to authorise delegates to sign the 1990 NOCN CAT agreement have changed little in the ensuing years.

Notes

1 A legend that Michael himself continued to confirm in his speech to the NIACE 'Recognising Achievement' conference, Manchester, February 2008.
2 Well almost. John Sanders returned from a study visit to the USA in 1990 with a copy of the Michigan Opportunity Card, which included a

microchip – the first we had ever seen – for storing learner data. At about the same time, Pete Ling presented to NOCN a proposal that all OCN Credit Records should incorporate barcodes to record learner achievement. Of course, NOCN had no resources to develop either of these technologies.

3 As one of the signatories was OCNW, which still did not operate a credit system, the symbolism extended beyond the simple signing of the agreement in Manchester to a recognition of the origins of OCNs in the North West.

11

Towards a national credit framework

Following the signing of the NOCN credit accumulation and transfer agreement, work continued both to extend the network of OCNs in England and Wales and to build relationships with other organisations with an interest in credit systems. In 1991 these 'other organisations' were primarily providers rather than awarding bodies. The idea of credit accumulation and transfer was still perceived as an instrument for supporting flexible curriculum offers to learners as much as a method of recognising learner achievement. For OCNs, the drive to extend the offer of recognition to new and different learners formed the main impetus for continued growth. But for providers, and in particular for FE colleges, the credit system offered a structure within which a curriculum could be designed and delivered that was more appropriate to learners than more traditional qualifications.

This is not to say that FE providers were uninterested in recognising learner achievement. Some of the more progressive leaders of FE colleges in the early 1990s saw a close connection between extending the offer of recognition through the award of credit and attracting more and different learners in to their provision. In 1991, NVQs had yet to make a significant impact on the offer to adult learners in colleges, while large areas of the adult curriculum, funded as it was through LEA Schemes of Delegation, were not linked to any requirement to offer a qualification. Outside the established qualifications offered by major awarding bodies such as BTEC and City and Guilds, the OCN credit system continued to expand into areas, particularly at lower levels of achievement, where traditional qualifications were simply not available.

One organisation that developed an interest in credit systems at this period was the Further Education Campaign Group. A relatively short-lived organisation, based on membership of a few dozen large FE colleges, the FE Campaign Group nevertheless established itself as an independent voice, reflecting the views of a group of providers that were formally part of LEA provision. The Campaign Group included within it those FE College Principals seen as the most forward-looking and progressive voices in the sector at the time. As part of its campaigning activities during 1991, the group began to promote the idea that the OCN credit system might be extended more widely to other areas of provision in FE colleges. In this they were naturally supported by members of NOCN. For the first time, some influential voices in the FE sector began to promote the virtues of a credit framework as a comprehensive structure, within which the whole FE curriculum could be offered and learner achievements could be recognised.

At the same time a separate and more fortuitous opportunity arose to promote this same idea. At the beginning of 1991 the government of John Major declared an interest in exploring further the benefits of a 'modular curriculum' in meeting the needs of young people. As part of this 'exploratory activity' (there was no policy decision to pursue modularisation as a feature of the curriculum), the Further Education Unit (FEU) was asked to produce some advice on the potential benefits of a modular curriculum in the FE sector. The FEU, though funded at the time by the DfEE, had established a reputation under the DES during the 1980s as an independent organisation through which innovations in FE could be tested and evaluated prior to implementation. Indeed, one of the key factors that shaped the founding of the FEU in 1976 had been the influence of US Community Colleges and their credit systems on Sir James Hamilton, the civil servant most involved in setting up the FEU.[1] It had close links with the FE Staff College at Coombe Lodge.

Following this invitation from government to consider the implications of a modular curriculum, the FEU invited a group of practitioners drawn from across the sector to meet together over a period of months and to draw up some recommendations for FE colleges on the future development of the modular curriculum. As the author of the 1988 FE Staff College seminar paper on 'Modularisation and Credit Accumulation and Transfer', I was invited to join this group. Indeed, the paper itself was circulated to the group as background reading (along with other documents) prior to its initial meeting.

This FEU group met throughout 1991. The membership of the group included not only myself and the future author of the Robertson Report, but two committee members from the newly established OCNs in London and Surrey and (after its initial meeting) Caroline Mager from the UDACE OCN project. This was not accidental. Tony Tait, the FEU officer responsible for convening the group, had already become interested in credit systems through his experience of working with the South London OCN, and from his study of the credit system at Liverpool Polytechnic (David Robertson again). He ensured that a strong perspective on credit systems informed the work of the group. From the outset the group set about re-interpreting its brief to take it beyond the boundaries of the modular curriculum. To the lasting credit of the FEU Officers involved, including the Director, Geoff Stanton, the FEU supported this process and continued to convene and service the group despite this creative interpretation of its official remit. Instead of a document on the modular curriculum, the group proceeded to develop a blueprint for what for the first time was becoming known as 'a credit framework'. As the group proceeded with its deliberations, the concept of a national credit framework began to be put forward both by NOCN and its members, and also by the FE Campaign Group.

Another organisation that supported this call for a national credit framework in 1991 was the Forum for Access Studies (FAST). The story of how Access to HE programmes came to influence the development of credit-based qualifications is told elsewhere in this publication. However, by 1991 most Access to HE programmes were accredited through OCNs and the officers of FAST were drawn almost exclusively from representatives of OCNs. The Forum became an important medium through which the experiences of OCNs in developing credit-based Access to HE programmes could be shared with a wider group of practitioners.

In November 1991, FAST and the FE Campaign Group organised a joint conference in Coventry entitled 'Towards a national credit framework'. It was the first time that the concept of a national credit framework had been presented in a public arena. Members of both organisations (including myself) made presentations and ran workshops. The event was a sell-out and the response to the call for a national credit framework was enthusiastic and unanimous. However, it should be noted that no representative of government or an agency of government attended the event. The audience was made up largely of representatives of providers (mainly FE colleges). There were hardly any awarding bodies represented, outside OCNs, and neither FAST nor the FE Campaign Group had any structure or resources to take forward the central proposition of the conference – that a national credit framework, based on the OCN credit system, should be established forthwith.

Notwithstanding the fact that there were no practical resources available to support the call for a credit framework, the FAST/FE Campaign Group conference marks a significant step forward in extending the concept of a credit framework beyond the boundaries of OCNs. Although OCN members were actively involved in the event, NOCN itself deliberately avoided active involvement. The proposal that a national credit framework should be established was all the more significant because, formally, it was put forward by two organisations separate from NOCN. The fact that the call for establishing such a framework fell on deaf ears as far as official policy was concerned was entirely expected by both sponsoring organisations. The important thing was engagement with a constituency outside NOCN itself, and in this respect the conference was a resounding success.[2]

The outcomes of the conference might simply have disappeared from view at the end of 1991, but at the beginning of 1992 they were given a major (and entirely expected) boost by the publication of the outcomes of the FEU group's deliberations on the modular curriculum. The title of the FEU's publication was *A Basis for Credit?* (FEU, 1992). Originally entitled *A Basis for*

Credit, the question mark was added in order to prepare the ground for consultation on the proposals within it. The FEU itself was rightly concerned that it should not be seen to be promoting the radical views within the document without wider consultation in the field. The publication of *A Basis for Credit?* marks a key moment in the development of credit systems in the UK and effectively shifted the debate about the merits of a national credit framework to an entirely new level. The influence of those members of OCNs that were part of the group is clearly seen in the publication. This time it seemed as though OCNs had finally succeeded in exporting – with some help from friends – the concept of credit beyond their own credit systems.

Notes

1 Perhaps one of the main reasons why the FEU was keen to fund Aubrey Black's report on MOCF (Black, 1982).
2 Fifteen years later, during the tests and trials of the QCF, an officer of an SSC came up to me and told me that she was at that conference and saw the establishing of the QCF as the realisation of the ambitions set out on that day.

12

A basis for credit?

Despite the introduction of the last-minute question mark, the FEU document is now widely recognised as precisely what it set out to be: the basis for the future development of credit systems outside HE in England, Wales and Northern Ireland. In 1992, *ABC?* flew off the shelves at the FEU. (Of course, the fact that it covered eight sides of A4 and was free helped with its popularity!) It quickly went to a reprint, and then to a further reprint. By the time it was reprinted for the fifth time it was, and remains to this day, the most widely circulated document ever produced by the FEU and by its successor organisations. We may confidently anticipate that, in the era of the Internet download, that position will not change. Tony Tait, who steered the document to its publication, and led FEU's work in promoting it and its successor publications, has every reason to be proud of his achievement.

What made *ABC?* such an instant best-seller? Some years later another document would refer to a credit system as 'an idea whose time has come' (actually, the author was wrong by about a decade).[1] The publication of *ABC?* marks the beginning of this process of becoming. The document circulated widely among FE colleges (far beyond the membership of the FE Campaign Group), throughout OCN networks and among many HEIs. It seems that it also enjoyed a limited readership among awarding bodies. It was well-received by representative bodies in both the school and post-school sectors (for example, by the Secondary Heads Association and by the National Association of Teachers in Further and Higher Education). It reached the libraries of many universities and colleges in North America (triggered no doubt by the explicit reference to 'credit' in the title) and found its way also to Australia and New Zealand. Whether it ever reached the desks of senior civil servants or ministers in Whitehall is not known.

The primary contribution of *ABC?* to the development of credit systems, and to the QCF itself, is that it brings together the definitions of credits and levels previously refined by OCNs and links them explicitly to a proposed specification of a unit that goes beyond any agreed definition then in use within the OCN network. The specification of the unit clearly draws on the experience of developing NVQs, and indeed of other vocational qualifications, and for the first time links the concepts of credit value and level with the other specifications of a unit that are now so familiar to users of the QCF. It is this bringing together of the three key concepts of credits, levels and units that secures *ABC?*'s seminal place in this story.

The *ABC?* specification of a unit has withstood the test of time. The FEU group debated the design features of the unit at some length before agreeing the specification set out in *ABC?* In particular, and for the first time, the agreed focus on learning outcomes as the essential content of the unit was supplemented by the concept of 'assessment criteria'. This term was borrowed explicitly from the 'performance criteria' of NVQs and then extended to ensure that it was able to encompass forms of assessment based on evidence other than performance. It was the first time that learning outcomes and assessment criteria had been linked together explicitly within a document intended for wide circulation, and it was a key development in the extension of the OCN credit system beyond the definitions of credits and levels, and the commitment to recognising the outcomes of learning, that characterised the agreed approach of OCNs in early 1992.

A further proposal in *ABC?* linked closely to the specification of assessment criteria, and about which there was fierce debate within the FEU group, was the decision to remove from the unit specification any reference to assessment methods or assessment instruments. The logic of this position was based again in part on the design principles behind NVQs, and also in part on the intentions of *ABC?* that it should provide *a basis* for the further development of credit systems, rather than a prescriptive blueprint to be followed in all cases. It would be true to say that consensus among the FEU group was reached on the basis that the unit specification put forward in *ABC?* was a minimum specification and that the document had no power of compulsion behind it. Those people or organisations that wanted to add further specifications to those set out in *ABC?* would be perfectly at liberty to do so.

At the time of the publication, the absence of any reference to assessment methodology in the unit specification set out in *ABC?* was seen as the most radical feature of the document. The position taken by the FEU group was based on an idea borrowed from systems theory – that the fewer the design specifications of any system, then the wider would be the usefulness of those specifications to users and the more utilised the system would be. This idea that the design features of a credit framework should set out the minimum specifications required to guarantee consistency and stability in the framework itself, while allowing the widest possible access to it, consciously informs the rationale for the design features of the QCF today. Its origins lie firmly in *ABC?*:

A post-16 CAT framework should use the open system as a model. An open system is one where users adopt, or subscribe to, a set of standards or rules on a voluntary basis because it offers mutual benefits.

(FEU, 1992, p. 3)

Over time, this removal of any reference to assessment methodology, and the link-ing of assessment criteria explicitly to learning outcomes, have proved to be two of the most important innovations introduced by *ABC?* into the development of credit systems. Not only do they open up opportunities for a wide range of assessment methods to be deployed, and therefore enable the achievements of all types of learners in all kinds of contexts to be recognised, but they also intro-duce an important quality assurance mechanism into the unit format. Removing reference to assessment methodology effectively forces issues of consistency and comparability into the assessment criteria of units. Over time this has proved to be a better and more accessible guarantee of consistency and comparability across the assessment of units than focusing on the standardisation of assessment methods. Thus, as the unit specifications set out in *ABC?* were implemented in ensuing years, what was originally seen as a minimum specification for a unit came to be seen as a complete specification.[2] Excluding reference to assessment methodology may have been the basis of an acceptable compromise between dif-ferent views in 1992, but by 1997 it was seen as a forward-looking and critical feature of a credit system that set out to be inclusive in its application.

Of course, in 1992 the proposition that *ABC?* might form the basis of a future national credit framework was put forward without any suggestion that it might be developed as an alternative to a qualifications framework. The pro-posal that a national qualifications framework should be established was still five years away, and it is clear that the audience that *ABC?* addresses is prima-rily an audience of providers, and that the object for reform is not the qualifi-cations system but the organisation and delivery of the curriculum in the post-school sector:

A college could subscribe to the system in two ways; firstly by adopting the framework definitions and system of credit valuation as a way of mapping, comparing and planning its own curriculum offer, and secondly by negotiating agreements with other institutions, HE and employers based on the framework.

(FEU, 1992, p. 3)

For all its prescience in setting out a durable and adaptable specification of the unit that has survived almost unchanged in the unit format of the QCF, reference to qualifications and to awarding bodies constitutes a relatively small part of *ABC?* In 1992 it seemed a perfectly reasonable proposition that a national credit framework could be developed without directly challenging the qualifications system:

The approach proposed here ... is not a new set of qualifications or awards. It is a way of relating existing qualifications (or parts of them) to each other as well as offering enormous potential for creating new units, new qualifications, new awards and new progression routes.

(FEU, 1992, p. 3)

In this extract we see one of the seeds of future controversy about the direction of development for a credit framework in relation to qualifications. However, in 1992 such concerns did not exist. The idea that a credit system could survive and prosper separately from the continuing development of qualifications was not seen as problematic. Indeed, this is exactly how the movement for a national credit framework did develop over the next five years. After *ABC?*, however, credit systems could never again be 'owned' by OCNs.

One area on which it was not possible to reach a consensus, and which is effectively 'fudged' in ABC?, was the issue of levels. That there should be levels in such a framework was not at issue, nor that these levels should represent learner achievements and should be applied to units, rather than to whole qualifications. The problem was how many levels there should be and what they should be called. On these two features of levels, ABC? is equivocal. The 'Framework Levels' in ABC? are 'illustrative' and FEU 'recognises the need for extensive consultation and development of a consensus among users of the framework at a national and local level before ... The definition and number of levels is fixed' (FEU, 1992, p. 5).

The reason for this was the distinction between the OCN system of four levels below HE and the NVQ system of three levels below HE. This left the FEU group in something of a quandary. Although it accepted that four levels of achievement could be identified prior to HE, it also recognised the influence of the NVQ framework in its use of the terms Level 1, Level 2 and Level 3. To propose usage of the OCN terms for levels would immediately create problems in 'selling' the proposals in *ABC?* to the NCVQ. To imply that it was not possible to recognise achievements below NVQ Level 1, when OCNs had been doing just that for nearly a decade, was also not an acceptable position for the FEU group to take. For the time being, the resolution of this discrepancy between NVQ and OCN levels would be postponed.

Notes
1 I refer here to the Fryer Report.
2 A position confirmed in the Regulatory Arrangements for the QCF.

13

Beyond '*A basis for credit?*'

During the time the FEU group was working on the development of *ABC?*, the government announced a change in the structure of the post-school sector that would have a significant impact on the development of the credit framework proposed by the FEU. We forget now that the proposal to remove FE colleges from the control of LEAs and 'set them free' as incorporated institutions did not initially appear as part of an education policy. The incorporation of FE colleges was part of a package of reforms of local government, rather than education. Indeed, evidence suggests it was rather 'tacked on' to the Education and Training White Paper of 1991 as an afterthought to the main agenda of deregulation and competitive tendering of local government services (DfEE/DE/WO 1991).

Notwithstanding its origins, the incorporation of FE colleges in April 1992 had a profound and lasting effect on the terrain of the post-school sector. The publication of *ABC?* in February of that year, and the support of bodies such as the FE Campaign Group for the establishing of a national credit framework, had an important impact on the newly incorporated sector. Although it took a little time for the impact of incorporation to feed into the development of the sector, there is no doubt that a newly independent, rapidly expanding and increasingly confident FE sector in the mid-1990s did much to spread the concept of a national credit framework and to support the rapid expansion of OCNs as the credit-awarding bodies within this framework. In this respect the publication of *ABC?* was perfectly timed.

In April 1992 the OCN movement was not so enthusiastic about these changes to the FE sector. Indeed, the removal of FE colleges from LEA control was seen by many as a severe blow to the continued growth of OCNs. It should be remembered that MOCF itself had been created through an LEA – the City of Manchester – and although subsequent OCNs were usually formed through a more complex set of partnerships, often involving HEIs, LEAs were actively involved in establishing and continuing to support all those OCNs that had signed the first credit accumulation and transfer agreement in 1990. Indeed, as the UDACE project publicised the development of new OCNs, some LEAs began to draw up plans for new networks, funded by and located within the structure of the LEA itself. Prior to the announcement that FE colleges were to be taken out of the control of LEAs, it appeared that the future preferred model of OCN development would be through LEAs themselves.

In 1990, Derbyshire LEA proposed just such a model, but (for reasons that were never clear) having identified a budget to support such a development, it was never implemented. A little later, Leicestershire LEA followed suit, and by March 1991 the first OCN in a decade, brought into being through a minute of an LEA education committee, was founded.[1] At the time this was seen as a significant development – Leicestershire at the time was seen as a beacon of good practice in the provision of adult learning opportunities through its rich network of FE colleges, community colleges and community education centres. The Leicestershire OCN (actually the first OCN to use the word 'Network' in its title – another shift from the more traditional 'Federation' of most OCNs at the time) was seen in 1991 as an important model that would lead to the development of other LEA-based OCNs in the future. That expectation was short-lived. A few months later the intention to remove FE colleges from LEA control was announced and the LEA-based model of OCNs came to an abrupt halt. Only Buckinghamshire (Conservative-controlled throughout the 1990s) followed the Leicestershire model. The big step forward of 1991 was suddenly a sideshow as LEAs prepared for college incorporation. From then on, the development of new OCNs, together with the championing of the idea of a national credit framework, would be led, in the main, by FE colleges.

The year that followed incorporation was in part an unseemly scramble, as the process of incorporation followed its messy path across different LEAs. For every smooth transition from LEA control to 'independence' there was another bitter argument about resources, ownership and legal responsibilities, as colleges (from the perspective of some LEAs) were 'ripped out' of a previously carefully integrated provision covering a range of different types of institution. Meanwhile, the new Further Education Funding Council (FEFC) was created and began to float ideas about how it might exercise its responsibilities in support of its newly independent constituency of FE colleges.

In this volatile context, with significant change now a universal expectation across the post-school sector, the FEU began a follow-up programme of activities in the wake of the runaway success of *ABC?*. These activities followed three tracks. The first was to create a more substantial and detailed set of documents to support the proposal in *ABC?* for the establishing of a national credit framework. The second was to hold a series of events across England and Wales to promote the ideas in *ABC?*. The third was to support the development of organisations that sought to build 'credit frameworks' to take forward the proposals in *ABC?* at local or regional level. Thus, the new FE sector came into being alongside a substantial programme of activity, based around the proposals in *ABC?*.

For the first time in more than a decade, the continuing development of credit systems was now being taken forward by a coalition of interests that went beyond the boundaries of OCNs. Notwithstanding the fact that OCNs themselves had pushed for such an initiative for a number of years and were actively involved in the FEU's programme of activities from the outset, the concept of 'a credit framework' now began to encompass ideas and practice that found expression through publications, events and organisations that were not controlled by OCNs. The two years following the publication of *ABC?* saw both the dramatic expansion of OCNs under the umbrella of calls for the development of a national credit framework, and the beginnings of a distinction in the purposes of such a framework between OCNs and their 'fellow travellers' (Robertson, 1994) in the ongoing development of credit systems. There is no doubt that OCNs benefited from the FEU's programme of activity. There is also no doubt that some of the activities undertaken under the banner of 'a national credit framework' in 1992 and 1993 were based on a very different set of assumptions from those shared by OCNs.

In 1993, I was commissioned by the FEU to produce a series of technical documents to support the continued development of the proposals for a national credit framework contained in *ABC?*. The first of these specifically addressed the question of levels, postponed from *ABC?* itself, and was produced in June 1993. In it are contained both a revised set of level descriptors and proposals for the number and naming of levels within the proposed framework (Wilson, 1993). The names and number of levels represent a working compromise between the OCN and NVQ systems. The principle that the framework should have four levels is put forward, but the OCN naming conventions are abandoned in favour of those of NCVQ. This effectively shifted the existing OCN naming conventions up one level, and left the previous OCN Level 1 nameless. The term 'Entry level' was put forward as an acceptable term for this first level of achievement. Terms such as 'Foundation level', 'Access level', 'Basic level' and 'Level zero' were all considered and rejected as being either too confusing or too pejorative. My recollection from the discussion that preceded the publication is that it was actually Caroline Mager who proposed 'Entry level', but it is in this publication of June 1993 that it is first presented for consideration within the context of developing a national credit framework. It did not go down well with OCNs, who suddenly began to realise that the impetus to the development of credit systems in *ABC?* might be a double-edged sword.

The revised level descriptors were created one afternoon by amalgamating key features of the existing OCN level descriptors and the NCVQ level descriptors with terms extracted from Bloom's *Taxonomy* (Bloom, 1956):

Entry: The achievement of a limited range of basic skills, knowledge and understanding in highly structured and self-referenced contexts which permit the identification of progression from the learner's point of entry to the learning process

One: The achievement of a foundation of competence, knowledge and understanding in a limited range of predictable and structured contexts that permits progression to further levels of achievement

Two: The achievement of a broader range of competences, knowledge and understanding which demonstrates the extension of previous abilities in less predictable and structured contexts and prepares the learner to progress to more complex, autonomous and critical achievements

Three: The achievement of more complex and creative competences, knowledge and understanding in contexts which permit the demonstration of autonomous, analytical and critical abilities that prepare the learner to progress to further independent achievements.

(Wilson, 1993, p. 18)

There is still some way to go in refining the language to create meaningfully separate descriptors, but the evolution of the level descriptors has clearly come a long way from those produced 12 years previously in Manchester (through several revisions by individual OCNs and by NOCN itself), and the future connections with the Northern Ireland CAT Scheme (NICATS) descriptors and those of the QCF itself can clearly be identified.

Before moving on from the descriptors it is worth noting one feature described in this 1993 paper:

we should note the distinctive and subtly different definition of achievement at Entry level ... [where] it is possible for ipsative-referenced achievement (that is, learners' own achievement targets) to be recognised for credit.

(Wilson, 1993, p. 19)

This facility to record what we would now refer to as 'learner-referenced' achievements originates here within the commitment to an 'inclusive' national credit framework and has recently been restored to its original intention within the Entry 1 Level Descriptor for the QCF. Despite the references in 2009 to a 'new' conception of Entry level, this inclusive approach to learner-referenced achievement is actually far from new. Not for the first time in this story, a long-standing feature of credit systems has been 'rediscovered' by those with experience only of qualification systems. This small but symbolic change in the scope of Entry level within the QCF, in comparison with its predecessor, shows once again the importance of bringing together these two separate cultures in a single framework. The story of how Entry level came to be part of the NQF must wait until a later chapter.

The separate paper on levels, incorporated into a fuller document on the technical specifications of a national credit framework, presented to the FEU in October 1993 (Wilson, 1993a), was originally intended as a consultation document, but it was considered too detailed and technical for such a purpose and was used instead as a stimulus paper in some of the specialist seminars on credit systems organised by the FEU in 1993. A shorter version of the paper appeared in a collection of papers published that same year by the FEU, entitled *Discussing Credit* (Wilson, 1993b).

As its title suggests, *Beyond 'A Basis for Credit?'* (Wilson, 1993a) expands on the basic propositions in *ABC?* and sets out some explicit definitions of the key technical features of the proposed credit framework. Two of these features are worthy of note. The definitions of 'credit' and 'credit value' in the document not only secure the specification of credit clearly in relation to learning outcomes, but also remove from the definition those lingering traces of time serving or process that had been part of the subtly evolving definition of credit over a decade or more. By 1993 the definition of credit was almost identical to that used in the QCF – that is, 'an award made to a learner in recognition of achievement' (Wilson, 1993a, p. 11). At the time, it should be noted, the OCN definition of credit embodied in the 1990 CAT agreement referred to 'the definition of the unit of credit as 30 hours of learning activity' (NOCN, 1990, p. 1). Here we see the advances made in the FEU group, and in particular the influence of NVQs on *ABC?*, beginning to create differences between the FEU and OCN models of credit systems.

Although *Beyond 'A Basis for Credit?'* was never formally published by the FEU, it was circulated widely both through the FEU's CAT network and through OCNs. It formed the basis for a series of ongoing discussions – some of them quite heated – within NOCN members about whether or not the specifications in *Beyond ABC?* should be adopted as the revised basis for OCNs' own activities. The re-definition of the level descriptors, the re-naming of the levels and the establishing of what a number of OCNs still saw as a restrictive unit format were all issues of some contention within the OCN network. There was to be no automatic acceptance of the FEU proposals. The pros and cons of changing established OCN practices had to be weighed against the pros and cons of working with other organisations outside the NOCN in the wider development of a national credit framework.

The misgivings of some OCNs about this direction of travel might have been more assuaged if the FEU had chosen to publish the last of the papers it commissioned in 1993. It was written as a companion piece to the technical specifications and was entitled 'Awarding Credit: The Principles of Quality Assurance' (Wilson, 1993c). The paper attempted to show how both awarding bodies and providers might use the technical specifications proposed by the FEU not only to award credits for the successful completion of units, but to combine these units into qualifications. The FEU, understandably, felt that addressing a set of proposals to awarding bodies went beyond the scope of their remit and might bring the organisation into conflict with a powerful group of independent organisations, just as the proposals in *ABC?* were beginning to be taken on by a wide audience of providers. In particular, the newly independent FE colleges were beginning to be enthusiastic in their support for the FEU proposals, and in 1993 the colleges were seen as the key players in taking forward the development of a national credit framework. The quality assurance proposals to support *ABC?* were never published.

The technical papers commissioned by the FEU in 1993 include many of the design features that have found their way into the QCF some 15 years later. Some of these design features (like the level descriptors) were distinctly different from those deployed by OCNs at the time. In some respects the FEU technical specifications presented a challenge to OCNs. Having led the call for establishment of a national credit framework in 1991, they found themselves by 1993 in the midst of a wide-ranging call for the establishment of just such a framework, but based on a set of design features that in some respects differed from their own. The resolution of these differences formed the next challenge for OCNs.

For the FEU, the publication of the (albeit abridged) specifications for a national credit framework in *Discussing Credit* took the proposals in *ABC?* to the next logical stage of development. However, it was also becoming clear that, without the involvement of qualification awarding bodies in taking forward these proposals, OCNs would remain the only organisations capable of recognising learner achievement within the proposed framework. This was a constituency relatively unfamiliar to the FEU, and so the proposals remained couched in terms that addressed the development of the proposed framework through FE colleges and other providers, rather than through awarding bodies. The decision of the FEU not to publish the second technical paper on quality assurance arrangements for the proposed framework arises directly from this targeting of the FEU proposals to its primary audience. Although the call for a national credit framework had plenty of legs left in 1993, its development as a framework separate from qualifications was a logical consequence of the FEU's strategy in promoting the idea of a credit framework through providers.

The proposals in the unpublished *Awarding Credit* focused not just on the necessary processes of assuring quality in developing units to the FEU specifications, but also on the process of accumulating credits to achieve a qualification. In producing these proposals, I drew on my experience of developing a similar model of credit accumulation within the Access to HE programmes validated by many OCNs. Reference has already been made to Access to HE programmes and will be again later in this publication. Now is an appropriate moment to once again step out of the main chronological thread of this publication and to consider in more detail how Access to HE programmes came to influence the development of credit systems.

Note

1 In fact, the County Council approved the establishing of the Leicestershire OCN in the spring of 1990, but it took almost a year to translate the agreement into action.

14

Access to HE programmes and credit systems

In 1978 the government invited FE colleges to set up Access to HE courses explicitly to prepare adults for entry to higher education in areas such as social work, teaching and nursing. The courses were targeted at adults without previous formal qualifications and in particular at members of minority ethnic communities. From this date, Access to HE courses expanded rapidly, the subject areas offered through such courses also expanded, and within a decade most general FE colleges in England and Wales offered Access to HE courses to adult learners. It is difficult to envisage a central government initiative of this kind being established in the twenty-first century without reference to a particular qualification, but this was exactly what was done in 1978 – a further reminder that 'mainstream' qualifications were seen as the preserve of young people at the time. It simply never occurred to the Labour government of the day that such courses, though explicitly encouraged and resourced through the DES, should be linked to a qualification.

Although not linked to the development of a particular qualification, Access to HE courses did offer recognition to learners through certification of some kind. For the first decade of their existence, Access to HE courses offered a range of different certification opportunities to learners. In a number of instances, HEIs themselves – again the polytechnics were the prime actors in this – certificated Access to HE courses. In other instances learners simply received a college certificate attesting to the fact that they had completed their course. Where OCNs were established, they became the awarding bodies for Access to HE courses. In other instances local consortia of FE and HE institutions were formed to certificate the courses, outside the network of OCNs. By 1987 concern was beginning to be expressed about the variety of local and regional arrangements for quality-assuring Access to HE courses. In particular, older universities questioned the quality of these arrangements, as they lacked any national standard against which the outcomes of such courses could be judged.

In fact, as the evidence from both the Royal Society of Arts (RSA) (Ball, 1989) and Her Majesty's Inspectorate (HMI, 1990) reports was later to show, concerns about the quality of such courses were ill-founded. Nevertheless, in response to a DES White Paper on HE in 1987 (DES, 1987), the Committee of

Vice-Chancellors and Principals (CVCP) and the CNAA were asked to jointly establish on behalf of, respectively, universities and polytechnics the Access Courses Recognition Scheme. The scheme was established in 1989 and operated through a network of Authorised Validating Agencies (AVAs) across England and Wales. Each AVA was a consortium of Access providers (mainly FE colleges) and HEIs in a particular locality and about 30 such local consortia were initially established within the scheme. From the outset, OCNs became recognised as AVAs.

It should be noted that the primary responsibility of AVAs was to assure the quality of Access to HE *courses*. As part of their responsibilities, AVAs offered Access to HE certificates to learners successfully completing these courses, but certification was seen as an integral part of their responsibilities for these courses. In this respect, AVAs mirrored the quality assurance responsibilities of universities, rather than those of awarding bodies. This should not surprise us – again the focus of the qualifications system on younger learners needs to be remembered (even in 1987), and overall responsibility for the scheme rested with bodies representative of universities and polytechnics. This focus on the curriculum and learning, rather than on assessment and achievement, mirrors some of the characteristics of OCNs already noted above in this same period. Even where an OCN became an AVA, it still perceived its primary responsibilities as the quality of learning on the Access to HE course, rather than the quality of assessment leading to an Access to HE Certificate.

Notwithstanding this clear difference between the culture of quality that informed the development of AVAs and those of awarding bodies offering vocational qualifications, the influence of AVAs on the development of credit systems can be detected in three different areas of activity. The first of these is the continuing influence of HE credit systems on OCNs. Most polytechnics were involved in their local AVA, and the people involved most actively were often those with a responsibility for the development of credit systems within their institution. AVAs therefore provided a formal and productive structure within which the different but related credit systems developed by polytechnics and OCNs came together. The influence of one on the other is noticeable. Robertson (Robertson, 1994) offers a number of examples of this influence. Indeed, in much of the early 'modelling' of a national credit framework a single framework was envisaged that brought together CNAA and OCN credit systems. Perhaps the institutional barriers to realising this objective were not appreciated in 1989, but in a number of polytechnics the local OCN, operating as an AVA, was seen as part of the institution's overall set of credit accumulation and transfer arrangements.

Secondly, AVAs themselves proved to be a fertile source for a new generation of OCNs that developed during the 1990s. Having established the organisational infrastructure necessary to validate and certificate Access to HE courses, member FE colleges soon began to demand that the AVA use its machinery to validate and certificate other courses. As the FE sector began to grow rapidly following the 1992 incorporation of colleges, so a string of AVAs moved to become OCNs. This movement was particularly strong in the midlands, where AVAs in Birmingham, in Coventry and Warwickshire, and in the North East Midlands, all transformed themselves into OCNs. Indeed, the FEU supported this process explicitly through a project entitled 'From AVA to OCN' (Stott, 1993) as part of its general programme of support for a credit framework following *ABC?*. As more AVAs transformed themselves into OCNs, so Access to HE programmes became, in the main, credit-based provision.

However, the main contribution of Access to HE programmes in influencing the credit system that would eventually be developed to underpin the QCF was in the development of the Access to HE Certificate. As the refining of the OCN concept of credit proceeded, and the influence of NVQs began to separate out more clearly the distinctions between programme delivery and the assessment of achievement, so OCNs began to confront these distinctions within their role as AVAs. The publication of *ABC?* and the subsequent technical specifications of a national credit framework in *Beyond ABC?* added further weight to these distinctions. As these ideas began to influence the practice of OCNs in 1992 and 1993, the continuing integration of learning and assessment, delivery and certification, within the culture of Access to HE programmes, began to appear anomalous to some of those involved in the activities of AVAs.

We should note again here that OCNs did not offer qualifications, and that the OCN credit system made no reference to qualifications. Learning programmes were developed by providers, submitted to OCNs for accreditation, and credits were awarded to learners completing the units that were offered through these programmes. Thus the credits themselves were the awards made to learners. All credits were recorded in a Credit Record, but there was no concept of 'credit accumulation' within traditional OCN systems (despite the rhetoric of the NOCN CAT agreement) because there was no target or external entity towards which credits could be accumulated. In the context within which OCN credit systems developed throughout the 1980s and early 1990s, this approach was perfectly understandable. As the FEU proposals illustrate, a credit framework was perceived primarily as a provider-based structure targeted at adult learners, unrelated to the different qualifications that had been developed primarily for younger learners. When OCNs became AVAs, they were confronted for the first time with a responsibility for awarding something to learners – an Access to HE Certificate – that was not a credit.

Some OCNs responded to this by maintaining separate certification arrangements for their OCN provision – leading to the award of credit – and their AVA provision – leading to the award of an Access to HE Certificate. London

OCF, for example, institutionalised an Access Validation Panel with separate responsibilities from its Quality Assurance Committee. In other OCNs the relationship between credits and Access to HE Certificates was simply fudged. In South Yorkshire, for example, credits were awarded for the achievement of the learning outcomes of individual units, but the Access to HE Certificate was awarded for completion of the Access to HE course – that is, it was unrelated to the award of credits. Although these may seem like strangely convoluted approaches, both were consistent with the distinctions between OCN and AVA concepts of quality, and both were acceptable to the CNAA/CVCP Access Course Recognition Group.

The first OCN to present to CNAA/CVCP an integrated approach to the award of credit and the award of an Access to HE Certificate was the Leicestershire OCN. Its proposal to award an Access to HE Certificate on completion of a set of credit achievement requirements, rather than on completion of an Access to HE course, was not initially well received, and the OCN was asked to re-submit its application to assure CNAA/CVCP that its particular approach to quality assurance on Access to HE programmes would enable the quality of provision, as well as the quality of learning outcomes, to be addressed. At the second attempt, LOCN received its licence to operate as an AVA in 1992. I was responsible for putting together the application and for arguing the case for a quality assurance approach that integrated the award of credit not with the Access to HE course, but with the Access to HE Certificate.

The process of drawing up the submission for approval as an AVA went forward in parallel to the final stages of producing *ABC?* and the beginning of drawing up the full specifications of a national credit framework. Leicestershire OCN was founded in 1991 and became a full member of NOCN in 1992. In its structure and ethos it was heavily influenced by these external processes, and, unencumbered by previous OCN approaches, tied its approaches to quality assurance and certification very clearly to units and learning outcomes from the outset. It sought to reproduce these approaches in relation to Access to HE Certificates when it became an AVA. Such an approach was, at the time, different from the course validation models operated by all other AVAs.

In the Leicestershire OCN, unlike any other AVA at the time, the Access to HE Certificate was awarded *not* for the successful completion of an Access to HE course, but for the successful accumulation of credits required for award of the Certificate. These requirements were set out in a separate document and were called 'rules of combination'. The term was borrowed from HE credit systems but had not been used before by an OCN. The rules of combination effectively tied the award of the Access to HE Certificate into the process of credit accumulation. In other words, it gave the process of credit accumulation meaning as, for the very first time in the OCN credit system, there was a distinct purpose to the process of combining credits in particular ways. CNAA/CVCP were not initially happy with this conception (hence the re-submission of the application), but were eventually persuaded to endorse the Leicestershire OCN model. In so doing they effectively formalised the first structure within which the award of credits and the award of a qualification were integrated through the process of credit accumulation governed by rules of combination.

As part of this structure, the Leicestershire OCN also formalised the concept of 'exemption' by identifying qualifications of equivalent value to clusters of OCN credits within rules of combination. In particular, GCSEs in English and Maths were identified for exemption – a facility that was used from the outset by several Access to HE providers in Leicestershire, who offered GCSEs as an alternative qualification to OCN-accredited units in English and Maths as part of their Access to HE provision. The periodic review conducted by the HE Quality Council (the successor to CNAA/CVCP) of Leicestershire OCN's AVA activity in 1995 notes that the particular model operated by the OCN can 'over time ... stimulate innovation, greater flexibility and wider choice for learners' (HEQC, 1995, p. 8).

The Leicestershire model was gradually taken on by other OCNs in their work as AVAs, particularly by those that joined the national network after the publication of *ABC?*. By the end of the twentieth century, some 95 per cent of Access to HE Certificates were based on the OCN credit system. In 2005, following a review of Access to HE recognition arrangements by QAA (the successor to HEQC), all AVAs were required to be relicensed under new criteria (QAA, 2005). Among these criteria is a requirement that the award of new Access to HE Diplomas should be based on the accumulation of credits through rules of combination. The design specifications of the new Diplomas mirror quite explicitly the main design features of the QCF, creating the possibility that, in due course, Access to HE Diplomas may be offered within the QCF. For the time being, however, Access to HE Diplomas remain a 'cousin' of the QCF, with common ancestry in a previous generation, but with separate quality assurance and regulatory arrangements in the present day.[1]

Although Access to HE programmes have been important in a number of respects in developing OCN credit systems, it is the relationship between the Access to HE Certificate and the credit systems of OCNs that is the key contributor to the design features of the QCF. In Leicestershire in 1992, in a relatively small organisation totally outside the context of mainstream qualifications, we find the first example of a formal system of credit accumulation, based on rules of combination, as the basis for awarding a qualification outside HE. The concept of 'rules of combination' has become more familiar in the context of vocational qualifications in recent years. In 1992 it was an unknown concept in this context. The term becomes known outside HE first through the interaction of OCNs with HEI credit systems, then through the relationship between the credit-awarding and qualification-awarding responsibilities of those OCNs that also operated as AVAs. Once established, the concept was applied more generally to the relationship between credit systems and qualifications, which is exactly its place in the QCF today.

The Access to HE recognition scheme and its successors have played a significant role in helping to form some of the important features of the QCF. In particular, by imposing upon OCNs an external requirement that a certificate be awarded to learners other than a credit, the Access to HE scheme forced OCNs to confront the relationship between credits and qualifications and to find a logical process through which these two separate requirements could be brought together. 'Rules of combination' sounds like a straightforward descriptive term that sits naturally within the QCF. In fact, it has quite specific origins, and a history that can be traced very precisely from this first example in 1992 of its use outside the context of HE credit systems.

Two instances from the introduction of rules of combination within the Leicestershire OCN illustrate both the potential of the concept and the newness of the idea at the time. One of the most innovative Access to HE Certificates developed at the time was an Access to HE Certificate in Performing Arts. Offered by a consortium of providers through the Leicestershire Community Arts programme, the achievement of the Certificate required the completion of a core set of study skills through a local college, plus the completion of three performing arts projects in three different roles (for example, as stage manager, producer, performer, set designer) offered at one of a number of community arts projects across the county. The programme was entirely individualised and simply did not exist as an Access to HE course. Creating rules of combination based on credit accumulation offered a structure within which a completely new set of skills and knowledge could be recognised for a group of learners previously excluded from recognition of their achievements. It remains a great example of how innovative structures for recognising achievement can stimulate creativity in the design and delivery of learning opportunities, and eclipses in its inventiveness anything yet available within the QCF.

A more prosaic reminder of how different this approach to recognising achievement actually was in 1992 came from the recommendations for award of Access to HE Certificates sent to the Leicestershire OCN from a large FE College and countersigned by the (experienced) moderator for the Access to HE programme. It was the administrative officer for the OCN who, in checking the recommendations as part of the certification process, revealed that in fact a number of learners had failed to complete all the requirements of the rules of combination set out in the recognition document for the programme. Despite the experience of both the course leader and the moderator, the process of accumulating credits through rules of combination presented a challenge to more traditional concepts of certification on the Access to HE course.

On further investigation it transpired that the learners *had* completed the requirements of the rules of combination, but they had been wrongly reported by the programme leader and wrongly countersigned by the moderator. As the OCN administrator proved, credit accumulation through rules of combination is actually a very transparent and straightforward concept – providing you know what you are doing. It remains to be seen how awarding bodies utilise the innovative potential of rules of combination in their QCF qualifications and how challenging this approach will be to more traditional methods of awarding qualifications.

This side trip through Access to HE Certificates has once again taken us way ahead of the main route of our journey, which we pick up again in 1993, when the idea of a 'credit movement' began to take shape.

Note

1 Though DIUS subsequently announced that Access to HE Diplomas should be brought into the QCF in the future. How this is to be done is currently a matter for discussion between Ofqual and QAA.

15

OCNs and credit frameworks

By 1993 the FEU was actively promoting the benefits of a national credit framework across the FE sector and was finding a positive reception to this message. Not only were its publications well received, and its events and conferences on the theme of credit well attended, but in different parts of the country new credit projects and credit initiatives were launched, often stimulated directly by the FEU's message. In some cases these new projects were closely aligned with the work of an existing local OCN. In other instances they stimulated the development of a new OCN. In a few cases these credit projects were set up without reference to OCNs, seeking to use the concept of credit for purposes other than recognising the achievements of adult learners – for example to establish 'credit ratings' for other qualifications.

By 1993 the new funding arrangements of the FE Funding Council were established and the FEFC's approach to funding was set out in one of its key documents, *Funding Learning* (FEFC, 1993). The document established funding arrangements that were to transform the FE sector over the following five years. The FEFC's methodology offered considerable incentives for growth, and FE colleges lost little time in planning an expansion of their provision to take account of FEFC's clear intentions to support this growth. The criteria through which FE provision demonstrated that it met the eligibility criteria for funding was set out in a Schedule to the 1992 Act that incorporated colleges and established the FEFC. Schedule 2 became, during the mid-1990s, a platform for the dramatic expansion of the sector.

Schedule 2 also provided a platform for the dramatic expansion of OCNs. Several aspects of the schedule required programmes to be accredited in order to trigger eligibility for funding, and OCN recognition was accepted as an appropriate form of accreditation for a number of areas of provision. This was not an accidental occurrence. By 1993, OCNs were influential enough to ensure that their accreditation system was promoted by FE college principals and other key members of FEFC committees, and that FEFC officers discussed the arrangements for implementing different aspects of Schedule 2 with officers of NOCN.[1] The publication of *Funding Learning* confirmed the important position of OCNs in the expansion of the newly independent sector, and the promotion of the idea of a national credit framework by the FEU lent further weight to the development of OCNs during this period. It is also worth noting the important position that FE principals and senior managers now took up on OCN management committees and boards. The fact that OCNs were controlled by their members, and that FE colleges were the most important of these members, led in some instances to the OCN being used as an explicit instrument for college expansion. The downside of this process would take time to work through the system. In 1993, OCNs were at the beginning of a period of unprecedented expansion.

Of course it was not just OCNs that expanded after college incorporation. Some of the more popular vocational qualifications offered by awarding bodies also experienced rapid expansion during this period, particularly in the relatively new area of Information Technology. In effect, the introduction of the FEFC and its expansionist funding methodology represents the final nail in the coffin of NCVQ's expectation that all vocational qualifications would be brought within the NVQ framework. By 1993 (that is, by the date when it had originally been expected that all vocational qualifications would have been transformed into NVQs), it was clear that this ambition had failed. Just how dramatically it had failed became more and more apparent during the 1990s as awarding bodies introduced many new vocational qualifications, in response to demand mediated through the growth of numbers in the FE sector, outside the NVQ framework. From 1993 onwards the number of new qualifications outside the NVQ framework outstripped the growth of NVQs in each year of the FEFC's existence. And the growth in learner numbers – particularly the numbers of adult learners – on these new vocational qualifications grew even more rapidly. OCNs were one of the major beneficiaries of this growth, but they were by no means alone.

It is during these years of FEFC funding, based on Schedule 2, that it gradually became more and more commonplace to develop qualifications or accredited programmes for adult learners. What some have criticised as 'credentialism' became more and more commonplace as providers sought formal recognition of the achievements of adult learners in order to meet eligibility requirements for funding. Although all parties (funding bodies, awarding bodies, providers and others) supported the principle that adult learners had a right to have their achievements in learning formally recognised (as younger learners had done for many years), there is no doubt that during this period of expansion some adults were forced into assessment and certification arrangements that they did not really want. Tying eligibility for funding so explicitly to the formal recognition of achievement, especially in a context where the expansion of the FE sector was deliberately encouraged, was bound to produce a downside to this principle, and OCNs benefited from this downside just as much as other more traditional awarding bodies. It is a connection that has been broken in the QCF, and which will undoubtedly prove to be a long-term benefit to the new framework.

As both OCN-accredited provision and other vocational qualifications continued to expand from 1993 onwards, NVQs gradually became a smaller proportion of recognised achievements in relation to FEFC funding. Five years after the incorporation of FE colleges, registrations on OCN-accredited provision outnumbered the registrations of all adult learners on A levels, GCSEs, GNVQs and NVQs combined, and around 10 per cent of learners on FEFC programmes in England were registered for an NVQ (FEFC, 1998). But this story is jumping too far ahead. In 1993, OCNs were looking forward to a period of rapid expansion, supported in no small part by the growing demand for a national credit framework based on the FEU proposals. But the internal credit systems of OCNs, based on the NOCN CAT agreement of 1990, were still different from the technical features of a national credit framework proposed in *Beyond ABC?*.

Since 1992 several OCNs had produced guidance notes for organisations using their local accreditation services that were based on the FEU credit framework, but other OCNs continued to operate solely on the basis of the 1990 agreement. During 1993–4 a series of internal debates took place within NOCN about the advantages and disadvantages of changing the OCN credit system to fit precisely the specifications proposed by the FEU. Some of these debates were difficult. For every argument that there were strategic advantages to OCNs in adopting the FEU model, a counter-argument could be put that OCNs were giving up control over something that, until that juncture, had been theirs and theirs alone to determine. There were also concerns about what was perceived by some as abandoning a primary concern with learning in order to focus on assessment and certification. There was no consensus in 1993 about the merits of an outcome-based approach, and indeed there were concerns that the clear distinctions between OCN credits and NVQs would be lost if the FEU credit framework was adopted.

This debate within NOCN was joined during 1993–4 by representatives of several new OCNs that had recently entered the national network. Some of these new OCNs had been influenced strongly by the impetus to credit systems given by *ABC?*. Indeed, one or two OCNs may not have come into existence at all at this time without the climate of support for credit systems provided by the FEU initiative. All OCNs recognised the importance of *ABC?* in contributing to the climate in which OCNs were now beginning to prosper.

By early 1994 the debate within the NOCN was won by the pro-credit framework OCNs, and the specifications of the national credit framework proposed by the FEU were formally adopted as the basis for all OCN credit systems from this date (NOCN, 1994). Despite the FEU's reluctance to refer formally to its proposals as 'The National Credit Framework', this was the title used by NOCN from 1994 onwards. Paradoxically, in so doing, NOCN deliberately sought to signal that the framework within which OCNs operated was no longer conceived as 'The NOCN Framework', but as a wider and more accessible entity which might be used by a number of different organisations for a number of different purposes. In this respect, NOCN was consciously enacting the intentions of the FEU in proposing a national credit framework in a way that the FEU itself never did.[2] So the National Credit Framework formally came into being, some four years before the NQF.[3]

Once again it is important to note at this juncture that the specifications of the National Credit Framework related to units, to learning outcomes, to credits and to levels, but not to qualifications. In adopting the National Credit Framework, NOCN still had no conception of itself as an awarding body, nor did individual OCNs consider that they might offer qualifications. For NOCN the focus for future development of the National Credit Framework was still on the activities of providers, on the accreditation of learning programmes and on the continuing development of OCNs as the credit awarding bodies within this framework in their localities or regions. In effect, the National Credit Framework was conceived as a structure within which the continuing development of OCN credit systems could take place and within which other awarding bodies, if they so chose, could also operate credit systems. This was not, however, a view that the NOCN shared with the FEU.

In the years following the publication of *ABC?* and the continued development of the idea of a credit framework, both the NOCN and FEU (and later its successor organisation, the Further Education Development Agency – FEDA) promoted and used the idea of a credit framework for their own purposes. On many occasions these purposes coincided, and on other occasions they did not. From the perspective of NOCN this was always the risk that would have to be taken in promoting the idea of a National Credit Framework as a shared concept with a range of different applications. The benefits of working alongside an organisation such as the FEU in promoting the benefits of such a framework, especially in the context of a rapidly expanding FE sector in which OCN-accredited provision was growing faster than ever before, outweighed the costs of occasional conflict with the FEU/FEDA in taking forward its different agenda as a development agency rather than as a credit-awarding body.

Within the collective experience of OCNs in 1994 lay both a scepticism about the value of 'credit-rating' qualifications as a method of extending the reach of credit systems, together with the experience of rejection by NCVQ as a partner in the reform of vocational qualifications, and the lack of interest of other awarding bodies in developing links between OCN credits and qualifications. These perspectives, coupled with a self-confidence based on continuing expansion of the OCN network, led NOCN to view the development of a National Credit Framework as a long-term proposition, based explicitly on the expansion of OCN accreditation as the sole mechanism through which provision could be brought within such a framework and learners could be awarded credit for their achievements.

The critical distinction in perspectives between the FEU and NOCN in taking forward the range of possible benefits of a national credit framework was that NOCN viewed the award of credit to learners as the essential focus for delivering these benefits, whereas the FEU saw the award of credit as one in a list of benefits, and that different users might choose to use some of these benefits in their work, and not others – including the awarding of credit to learners. So, for example, both the NOCN and FEU were in agreement that the National Credit Framework could offer:

- greater opportunities to plan learning programmes appropriate to learner needs
- increased choice and opportunities for more varied curriculum combinations
- opportunities for changes in direction without loss of credit
- a basis for high-quality progression routes into education and training
- a common framework for examination and validating bodies supporting the development of both credit accumulation and credit transfer (FEU, 1992, p. 6).

The NOCN's view was that all these benefits were dependent on the development of credit as a system for recognising learner achievement. For the FEU, the mathematical constructs of the credit framework (in particular, the specifications of credit and level) could be detached from this award of credit to learners and could still be used to bring about these wider benefits of a credit framework. This was a perfectly understandable position for a development agency that was not an awarding body to take.

The development of credit initiatives and credit projects based on *ABC?* provided an opportunity for these different perspectives on a credit framework to be put into action in different parts of England and Wales. In England, with one or two exceptions, the development of local or regional credit frameworks took place in collaboration with or through OCNs. One of the exceptions, however, is worthy of note. In 1993 the FEU commissioned the University of London Examinations and Assessment Council (ULEAC) to carry out research on the application of the *ABC?* specifications to a cluster of five A levels. ULEAC was at the time one of the larger A level Boards and later became part of the Edexcel group.

The report of the project confirmed the problems associated with the application of the *ABC?* specifications to existing qualifications (ULEAC, 1993). The report hints that, in fact, people working within ULEAC saw potential benefits in re-designing A levels within the *ABC?* specifications, but that the exercise was 'constrained by an ambivalent attitude towards Advanced Level modularisation by the Schools Examination and Assessment Council', a regulatory forerunner of the QCA.

The ULEAC report provides clear evidence that the proposition that 'a system of credits and levels could overlay existing qualifications' (FEU, 1992a, p. 32) was an approach with acute problems. The report confirms that 'if the exercise were starting from scratch', then it might have been possible to make progress: 'However, working with existing syllabuses provides only limited success' (FEU, 1992a, p. 1).

In fact the ULEAC project produced some interesting examples of how an existing A level syllabus might be represented to learners through the *ABC?* specifications. It confirmed that it would be theoretically possible to present an academic qualification to learners within the unit format proposed in *ABC?*. The problem was, of course, that the development of such units was simply a theoretical exercise on ULEAC's behalf. It required in some subjects (English Literature and French were referred to in particular) a significant re-engineering of the existing syllabus to develop meaningful units. Without an explicit mandate to conduct such a process of reform to A levels, the *ABC?* specifications simply could not be applied.

In a separate strand of activity in the FEU project, ULEAC also conducted a survey of existing A level syllabuses in relation to the *ABC?* specification of credit value. Schools and colleges offering ULEAC A levels, as well as subject experts commissioned by ULEAC, were asked to propose credit values for A levels based on the existing syllabuses in these same five subjects. The ULEAC report concludes: 'The credit value of each unit was sometimes difficult to determine... The findings show a massive variation in time allocation' (FEU, 1992a, p. 2).

Not only were there major differences in the estimations of credit value between schools and colleges, and between providers and subject experts, but even when these estimations were averaged out within each subject they produced overall credit values that were different for each of the five subjects, and in which the largest estimate was more than twice the size of the smallest (FEU, 1992a, p. 2).

These discrepancies should not surprise us. They confirmed the outcomes of the SYOCF project some three years previously (see Chapter 9) and anticipated the outcomes of the Dearing 16-19 Review some three years later (Dearing, 1996). They confirmed one of the basic tenets of successful credit systems, and one which has been carried forward (though not without difficulty) into the QCF; that simply ascribing a credit value to an existing qualification or unit without respecifying the unit to meet the requirements of the credit system is not only a vacuous exercise, but cannot produce the necessary stability and consistency in unit credit values that is an essential prerequisite for the effective functioning of a credit system. This realisation was one of the main impetuses behind NOCN's adoption of the National Credit Framework, and its unit specification, in the year following the ULEAC report.

Notwithstanding the evidence from this research from 1992-3, which confirmed the earlier research in Sheffield in 1989-90, the seductive power of numbers represented through this credit-rating approach would continue to divert energies and generate divisions within the emerging credit movement well into the twenty-first century. The ULEAC report simply confirmed within OCNs that their initial suspicions of the credit-rating approach were well founded. As OCNs began to expand through the 1990s, so the principle that the benefits of a credit system were essentially based on the award of credit to learners, rather than the ascribing of numbers to existing qualifications, remained an unshakeable principle across all OCNs.

By 1994, OCNs in England were too well established, and too well supported by senior managers in FE colleges, to envisage the development of a credit framework outside the OCN structure. Nor did the FEU or any other organisation have the resources to establish an alternative structure to that already put in place through the NOCN. In Wales, however, these conditions did not necessarily apply, and events here began to take a different tack from those in England.

The story of how credit developed differently in Wales is told later in Chapter 25. In England there was a close connection between the development of credit initiatives stimulated by the FEU's activity and the continuing development of OCNs. Three of these initiatives, A Credit Framework for London, the Derbyshire Regional Network and the Leicestershire Progression Accord, are worthy of further consideration here.

Notes

1 Teresa Bergin was particularly influential on this issue.
2 A parallel debate about credit also took place within the FEU. There was by no means a consensus of support for *ABC?* within the organisation. It would have been both difficult and potentially divisive for FEU to have formally proposed the establishing of a National Credit Framework at this time.
3 It was actually Brett Kerton who proposed this 'just do it' approach to adopting the term 'National Credit Framework' by NOCN. Others (including myself) were nervous that such a move might alienate support for OCNs from FEU. It didn't.

16

Credit developments in England

In England the promotion of 'credit' as a conceptual tool by the FEU and FEDA proceeded in parallel with the continuing development of credit systems through OCNs. For the most part the platonic and the concrete interpretations of *ABC?* were mutually supportive. For the first time a significant national organisation was leading a promotional campaign to spread the potential benefits of credit at exactly the moment when the benefits of the OCN credit system were being realised, as FE colleges began to expand their provision within the new FEFC funding arrangements. There is little doubt that the continuing development of new OCNs, as well as the dramatic increases in learner registrations within existing OCNs, would not have happened so quickly during the mid-1990s if the FEU/FEDA promotion of credit had not created such a fertile environment for this growth. Similarly, the FEU/FEDA's own work in England not only drew on the expertise present within OCNs, but used the evidence of learner achievements within OCNs as one of its key arguments in favour of establishing a national credit framework.

This distinction of positions between a development agency and a group of awarding bodies is entirely understandable. In essence, the FEU/FEDA promoted the view that there were a number of potential benefits in establishing a credit framework, of which recognising learner achievement through the award of credit was only one. The other potential benefits of a credit framework – for example, as a curriculum management tool or as a funding mechanism – could be realised separately from the award of credit to learners. Although OCNs also recognised these other potential benefits of a credit framework – indeed, had been the original promoters of some of these ideas – the award of credit remained central to the purpose of establishing a credit framework. In essence, for OCNs these potential wider benefits were critically dependent on the operation of a credit system based on the recognition of learner achievement. For the FEU/FEDA, the award of credit to learners was one of a range of potential benefits, not the critical focus of a credit system.

For a number of years throughout the 1990s these different conceptual starting points were obscured behind a general and rapid spread of the idea of a national credit framework. What joined OCNs and the FEU/FEDA together was, for the most part, more important than what divided them on these different concepts of credit. In this respect developments in England did not produce an alternative model of credit in the same way that they did in Wales. In part this can be attributed to the relative strength of OCNs in England in comparison with the more recently established Welsh OCNs. In part it was also due to the fact that, in relative terms, far more resources were devoted in Wales than in England to developing the concept of a credit framework that was not based on the award of credit to learners. This is not to suggest that there were not important developments in England during this time that extended both the scope of the credit framework idea and brought new partners into the development of credit systems. In England, however, these significant developments took place with the active support and involvement of OCNs, rather than separately from them. Although one or two local 'credit frameworks' were developed without the involvement of OCNs, in England these were short-lived and their influence on the overall development of credit systems was negligible (FEU, 1993).

Three particular credit framework initiatives are noted here. Each one of them was different, all three of them were taken forward with the active involvement of an OCN, and all three were supported and promoted by the FEU/FEDA as positive examples of the potential of credit to deliver benefits far beyond the traditional scope of OCN credit systems. These three initiatives were established in Derbyshire, in London and in Leicestershire.

The Derbyshire Regional Network (DRN) was, both at the time and in retrospect, seen as the most advanced and the most influential of all the regional credit frameworks that were established following the publication of *ABC?*. The network was based on a formal agreement between the newly established NEMOCN and the newly established University of Derby that created the first credit system that genuinely operated across the boundaries between further, community and higher education (Derbyshire Regional Network, 1993). The university adopted a credit system based on an almost identical set of design features to those operated by OCNs. Critically, the definition of credit was common across the whole DRN, and the accreditation arrangements of NEMOCN and the validation systems of the university were offered through the DRN as an integrated structure. Learners were still awarded credit either by the OCN or by the university, depending on what level of achievement they were aiming for, but the recognition of their achievements through the award of credit was made as a standard offer to all learners through the DRN. It is no accident that the main architect of the DRN, Beverly Sand, had previously been Director of the Black Country OCN.

This integrated approach to the development of credit systems through an OCN and an HEI led to the rapid growth of credit-based progression routes into the university from the surrounding network of FE colleges in Derbyshire (and, indeed, in parts of Staffordshire and Nottinghamshire).[1] It also led to the development of programmes that were designed across the traditional boundary between FE and HE, giving learners the opportunity to combine achievements from NEMOCN and the university within a single learning opportunity. The DRN also supported a collaborative approach to unit development across all members of the network. Units developed through FE practitioners were offered within university programmes. Conversely, learners were offered the opportunity to achieve university credits through their FE college programmes. Units were shared between FE providers, and the DRN unit databank became an important local resource for curriculum design and development. (In this respect the DRN did reflect similar developments in Wales.) DRN units began to be used beyond the boundaries of the network itself, though in this pre-internet context unit sharing was a more cumbersome activity. The influence of this particular aspect of the DRN is still current – what is now the East Midlands Region OCN (EMROCN) unit databank contains many thousands of units, freely available through the OCN website, all designed to the same specifications as the QCF. Indeed, in early 2009, the OCNEMR unit databank contained as many units as the QCF itself (www. ocnemr.org.uk/units).

It should be emphasised that all this activity was generated and supported by the institutional members of the DRN itself. There was active support for the development of the DRN from the senior management at the university,[2] while NEMOCN itself had been created in direct response to the demands of FE colleges in Derbyshire and Nottinghamshire. The principals of these colleges were represented on the board of the OCN and gave their active support to the creation and development of the DRN. The network therefore became a proving ground for many of the potential benefits of a credit system set out in *ABC?*. None of the other credit frameworks established during this period actually had the institutional support and the clarity of vision that existed within the DRN. Although institutional changes within the university led to the demise of the network at the turn of the century, the DRN stands today as the most innovative model of collaboration in the delivery of credit systems across the boundary between FE and HE that has yet been established in England.

Another important but very different credit framework was established in London. Known simply as the Credit Framework for London, it was launched in 1995 following a year of development activity that was led by the still relatively new London Open College Federation (LOCF). Support and resources for the Credit Framework for London came from an organisation called London Together, which, in an era before either a London mayor or even a London Development Agency were established, brought together both public sector and private employers, together with various London-based agencies and organisations, to promote the interests of Londoners beyond the boundaries of individual boroughs and individual employers. Funding from London Together permitted LOCF to employ a consultant to put together and promote the idea of a London-wide credit framework, within which both the providers of education and training and the employers of people learning through these providers would collaborate to offer credit-based learning opportunities, and to recognise the achievements of Londoners through the award of credit.

The Credit Framework for London initiative brought together a significant range of both providers and users of education and training in the post-school sector across London. The framework itself was based on a document that was part manifesto, part technical specification for the framework. The document was painstakingly crafted and consulted on by all those with an interest in the framework and was accepted nem. con. at the framework launch event by 90 organisations across London (FEDA, 1995a).

In effect, the Credit Framework for London, which grew explicitly out of the wider interest in credit systems generated by the publication of *ABC?* and the follow-up activities of the FEU, cemented the position of the London OCN as the credit-awarding body for London, and significantly increased the scope and volume of activity of the network, securing its position as the largest OCN and indeed one of the largest awarding bodies in the UK. To this day the OCN London Region remains a larger awarding body than all but a dozen of the awarding bodies in the NQF (in terms of learner registrations and certificated achievements), even though it has never operated within the NQF itself. The Credit Framework for London initiative shows how important the wider influence of the FEU/FEDA was in promoting the benefits of a credit framework, and in so doing securing the position of OCNs as the key awarding bodies for credit in England. In contrast to the experience of Wales, the Credit Framework for London was based on the outset on the active involvement of the local OCN, and on the conception of the framework itself as a structure within which learners could be awarded credit in recognition of their achievements. As a result of the London Together initiative, employers began to make use of OCN accreditation for the first time in significant numbers, a trend that continued to spread through the national network of OCNs throughout the 1990s.

The third initiative in England to break new ground for credit systems was developed in Leicestershire and marked the first significant extension of credit systems to younger learners. The Leicestershire Progression Accord was established in 1994 and remains in place to this day. It has become the model for similar credit-based progression accords and progression agreements throughout England, though none of them has had such a significant impact on its locality as the Leicestershire Accord.

The Leicestershire Progression Accord grew out of a collaboration between the local OCN and the Leicester City Cluster – an organisation first established through the Technical and Vocational Education Initiative in the 1980s, and which acted as a coordinating body for staff and curriculum development activity across schools and colleges in Leicestershire – as it still does (albeit under a different name) in 2009. The aim of the Accord was to establish a series of formal agreements between universities, further education colleges and schools in Leicestershire that would recognise a range of learner achievements outside the scope of the national curriculum, A levels and GCSEs through the award of credit, and then secure agreements from universities and colleges about enhanced offers of progression based on a combination of both 'mainstream' qualifications and credits awarded by the Leicestershire OCN.

The Progression Accord was painstakingly negotiated with both 'receiving' and 'providing' institutions across Leicestershire. Key to its success was the active involvement of De Montfort, Leicester and Loughborough Universities in making offers of university places to local schools and colleges through the Accord. In particular, the Accord was taken up enthusiastically by the three Sixth Form Colleges in the City of Leicester (Leicester abolished school sixth forms in the 1970s). The scope of the Progression Accord was widened each year to include more offers to learners, particularly from the three universities, until, some three years into its operational life, over 300 degree programmes across the universities that were signatories to the Accord made offers to learners based on mainstream qualifications, plus the award of credits for additional achievements.

These additional achievements included community-based projects run through schools and colleges, work experience programmes designed to prepare learners for progression to vocational qualifications, extra curricula activities in schools, as well as outdoor projects and field study programmes that had previously led to no formal recognition. Providers welcomed the Accord because it motivated learners to undertake additional learning and activities that had previously not been well supported. Learners were enthusiastic about the Accord because they soon became aware that achieving credits through these activities enhanced their chances of progressing to the university course or vocational qualification of their choice. Universities liked the Accord because it created an incentive for learners to progress into degree programmes with a richer combination of achievements than just A levels. The nature of the offers made to learners either substituted credit achievements for an A level grade or grades, or enhanced offers of progression by recognising credits as achievements of value, in addition to A level grades.

In an era before the development of Key Skills qualifications, before the Curriculum 2000 reforms and long before 14–19 Diplomas, the Leicestershire Progression Accord marked a significant step forward, both in the recognition of learner achievements outside mainstream qualifications and in extending the experience of credit systems to both practitioners and learners in the 14–19 age range. Although these subsequent initiatives, together with the establishing of performance targets for schools based on examination success rates, have undermined the continued development of the Accord, by the late 1990s several thousand learners a year were earning credits through the Accord and progressing from schools and colleges to universities in the county through the agreements established within the framework of the Accord. Through the Leicestershire Progression Accord, the relevance of credit systems to younger learners was demonstrated unequivocally. The ability of credit systems to secure progression opportunities for younger learners in schools and colleges, by enhancing the range of achievements that were recognised beyond the boundaries of formal qualifications, proved beyond doubt one of the main points put forward in *ABC?* – that a credit framework was relevant to all learners of all ages in all areas of the curriculum. The assumption that credit systems were 'just for adults' was well and truly buried through the Accord, though news of its success seems not to have reached the ears of those who drafted *21st Century Skills* in 2003.

It should be noted that in all the above credit framework initiatives in England, the driving forces behind each local framework were not awarding bodies but universities, FE colleges, schools, employers and other local agencies. Each of the OCNs involved in the three initiatives showed itself adept at responding to the demands of the different organisations involved in developing these credit frameworks. All of them were developed outside the framework of mainstream qualifications and each of them demonstrated the potential scope of credit systems to meet very different needs in their localities. All of them were based on credits as awards made to learners and each one can claim to have added a significant body of evidence to the growing movement across both England and Wales that collectively argued for the establishing of a national credit framework. From the perspective of those people involved in these developments on a day-to-day basis in the mid-1990s, it seemed that this inexorable expansion of the scope of credit systems would inevitably result in the formal establishment of this national framework in the not-too-distant future.

If a national credit framework seemed just around the corner in 1994, one issue that divided credit enthusiasts at the time was the potential scope of such a framework. In particular, the issue of whether such a framework should encompass all post-school achievements, including those in HE, remained contentious. All OCNs included HE institutions in their membership, and the influence of HE credit systems remained strong, even after the demise of the CNAA CAT scheme in 1992. Conversely, the gradual development of OCN credit systems based on the assessment and recognition of learner achievement, rather than on the structuring of the curriculum, created significant divisions between HE and OCN concepts of credit. Perhaps a single credit framework that encompassed HE as well as lower levels of achievement was simply not an attainable goal? To some practitioners in credit systems in the mid-1990s, such a suggestion was unthinkable.

Notes

1 The influence of Brett Kerton, another ex-SYOCF Development Officer and NOCN Board member, must be acknowledged here.
2 Roger Waterhouse, Vice-Chancellor of the University of Derby, had been an active proponent of credit systems during his time at Middlesex Polytechnic, and took this commitment to credit into the university's validation systems.

Choosing not to change:
Credit developments in HE

As the three examples in the previous chapter illustrate, the development of local and regional initiatives based on credit involved in most instances a partnership between universities, colleges, local authorities and other providers. Indeed, as the growth of credit systems outside HE grew and the concept of a national credit framework took hold through the 1990s, there was an assumption among many practitioners that such a framework would include all levels of achievement and encompass all types of provision. Indeed, we can recognise manifestations of this ambition in both the Scottish Credit and Qualifications Framework (SCQF) and the Credit and Qualifications Framework for Wales (CQFW) today. To some people involved in the development of credit systems following the publication of *ABC?*, it would have been unthinkable to envisage a future in which Higher and (for want of a better term) Further Education existed within separate credit frameworks.

This influence of HE on the continuing development of credit systems at lower levels of achievement is actually not so surprising given the origins of OCN credit systems. It should be remembered that the first Open Colleges established in London were each centred around the development of programmes leading into HE and all were physically located within a Polytechnic. The Manchester and South Yorkshire OCNs also began life within a Polytechnic building. The constitution and development plan for Merseyside OCN was drawn up in Liverpool Polytechnic, while the Black Country OCN was based in Wolverhampton Polytechnic. All these early networks drew on the practical support of these HEIs, as well as on HE credit systems for their inspiration. Many OCN officers were employed by polytechnics, others were seconded from their roles in HE to support what was seen as an important and parallel development of credit systems that would benefit the emerging CNAA CAT Scheme (CNAA, 1989).

It should be recalled that it was not just FE colleges that were 'freed from LEA control' in 1992. At the same time, polytechnics were also re-constituted as independent organisations, outside LEA control and given permission to use the word 'university' in their title. Before 1992 the close relationship between polytechnics, FE colleges and community education services was a simple fact of life for three different types of provider all accountable to a single LEA. The influence of HE credit systems on the early development of OCNs was seen as a perfectly logical consequence of this relationship. At the time, credit systems were almost invisible in what became known post-1992 as the 'old' universities (with the singular exception of the Open University), but in the polytechnics a national framework for the development of credit systems had been established through CNAA in the 1980s and this had a strong influence on the wider development of credit systems.

The importance of Access to HE programmes in cementing these relationships between credit systems across the boundary between FE colleges and polytechnics (again Access to HE programmes were initially focused almost exclusively outside the old universities) is noted in Chapter 14. The involvement of polytechnic staff in the development of such programmes, as members of OCN Access to HE recognition panels, and as moderators on accredited programmes, all helped to create and maintain a continuing strong influence of HE credit systems within OCNs.

In retrospect, although the incorporation of FE Colleges in 1992 had a positive impact on the growth of OCNs, the parallel independence of polytechnics and their incorporation into an expanded university sector can be seen to have weakened this previously intimate connection between HE and OCN credit systems. This was not immediately apparent, though a glance down the postal addresses of OCNs in 1995 reveals that – in contrast to the early networks – only around half of them were based in universities. Within the new universities there was still plenty of commitment to the development of credit systems. But there was also a new independence, not just from LEAs, but also from the now disbanded CNAA. It should be recalled that polytechnics made awards not in their own names, but in the name of the CNAA. The CNAA CAT scheme was therefore a scheme devised and controlled by the organisation in whose name polytechnics made their awards. The effect of independence for the new universities severed this connection. In future, the adoption of credit systems, and the development of credit accumulation and transfer arrangements between universities, would be matters for mutual agreement between independent organisations, rather than a collectively owned scheme integrated into the arrangements for making awards. The enthusiasm of many people working in the new universities for credit systems, the continuing influence of the CNAA CAT scheme within these universities and the involvement of HE staff in the development of OCNs, all served to obscure the significance of independence for the new universities on HE CAT schemes for some time.

The significance of the dissolution of CNAA for the future development of HE credit systems was not lost within the Council itself. Prior to its demise, it agreed with the then Departments for Education and Employment to institute a major investigation into the development of HE credit systems. The investigation began in November 1992 and was completed under the auspices of the successor organisation to CNAA: the Higher Education Quality Council (HEQC). Published by HEQC in 1994, *Choosing to Change* remains to this day the key reference point for the development of credit systems in HE, from *The Toyne Report* (Toyne, 1979) to the demise of the CNAA CAT Scheme. Indeed, Peter Toyne himself, then vice chancellor of the newly established Liverpool John Moores University, oversaw the work of one of his staff – David Robertson – in taking forward the project in his capacity as Chair of the HEQC Credit and Access Advisory Group. Robertson himself is a good example of this inter-relationship between HE and OCN credit systems, having written the constitution and development plan for the Merseyside OCN, as well as some of the early NOCN papers.

The Robertson report is crammed with recommendations – primarily to HEQC, but also to a range of other organisations. It is possible to view *Choosing to Change* as a last ditch effort to secure the establishment of a national credit framework, encompassing both FE and HE, by recommending the convergence of credit systems around a shared set of design features. Unfortunately, the audience for Robertson's message had changed significantly between 1992 and 1994. The HEQC, as the organisation charged with maintaining quality across the newly expanded and independent university sector, was (unlike its predecessor) simply unable to deliver on the key recommendations in *Choosing to Change*. In fact, Robertson realised this, and his 'blaze of glory' approach to his task makes entertaining reading from a distance of 15 years. Among the hundreds of recommendations that in effect constitute an attempt to secure the establishing of a culture of credit within UK Education, we note the following:

An effective credit framework must be *comprehensive* and inclusive ... it should be simple in operation and credible in its application (467).

It should be applicable to both higher and further education, to academic and vocational programmes ... and to any form of learning achievement (470).

We recommend that the National Credit Framework should be made up of eight levels of achievement and progression (498).

We recommend that all qualifications, vocational and academic, should be aligned with the levels of the agreed framework with the requirements for credit accumulation towards the qualifications carefully defined (515).

We recommend the establishment of a national credit transcript (529).

We recommend that the achievement of a common credit currency within a comprehensive post-secondary and higher education should be a major objective of policy (500).

Choosing to Change therefore represents not just a seminal challenge to HE credit systems, but it proposes very explicitly the establishing of a single credit system across 'post-secondary and higher' education. Not only that, but it proposes to HEQC that

arrangements for a comprehensive credit system, with a common credit currency, converge in due course around the proposals of the FEU (537).

Given the remit of the organisation publishing the report, and the audience to which it formally addresses itself – that is, to HE – this is a quite stunning proposal. It illustrates, in a way almost impossible to conceive in 2009, the close relationship between HE credit systems and those developed by OCNs (and put forward by the FEU in *ABC?*). Robertson's role in the early development of OCNs was clearly influential here, but we should also recall that he was a member of the group that advised the FEU on *ABC?*.

The publication of *Choosing to Change* caused quite a furore. At the single event organised by HEQC to introduce the document, it was clear that the Council itself was deeply unenthusiastic about Robertson's proposals. Indeed, the register of HEQC's response to its report finds familiar echoes today. Universities, declared the Chief Executive of HEQC in introducing the report at its publication, are independent institutions and HEQC has no remit either to represent their views or to tell them what to do. *Choosing to Change* contained many interesting recommendations, some of which may be taken up with enthusiasm by some universities. But the status of Robertson's recommendations was made clear. They remained 'interesting ideas' to which individual HEIs were invited to respond. There was to be no HEQC strategy to implement the recommendations in *Choosing to Change*.

Some of Robertson's recommendations – as the above extracts illustrate – have very precise parallels in the development of the QCF. Although *Choosing to Change* does not anticipate the NQF, and still envisages qualifications 'aligning with' a national credit framework rather than being an integral part of it, the intellectual weight behind the report and the scope of its recommendations secures its importance in any account of the history of credit systems in the UK. In effect, faced with Robertson's radical proposals, HE chose not to change. Credit systems inside and outside HE began to diverge (with some notable exceptions) and the influence of credit systems within HEIs slowly declined. Robertson's recommendations have actually had more influence outside HE than within it (a fact that he might enjoy). The gradual rediscovery of HE credit systems in the twenty-first century (by which I mean its official rediscovery by national organisations such as QAA and Universities UK, not the continuous fanning of the credit flame by the dedicated enthusiasts of the UK Credit Forum and other HE credit consortia) has been an arduous process, and connections between the QCF and HE credit systems (as a later chapter will attempt to show) are far from simple or secure. Robertson's vision was that determined leadership exercised through HE could lead other sectors into his vision of a single, unified credit framework. It remains to be seen whether an opposite process of leadership can draw a very different twenty-first-century HE system into an updated version of Robertson's vision. From the perspective of 2009, however, such an eventuality seems a very long way off.

In the story of credit systems outside HE, *Choosing to Change* remains an important text. It marks the point at which the idea that credit was owned by HE and adopted by others began to change. Robertson's proposal that HE and FE credit systems should converge 'around the FEU specifications' secured both the intellectual weight of the National Credit Framework proposals set out in *Beyond ABC?* and the importance of an alternative history of credit outside HE. From the moment that HEQC politely parked *Choosing to Change* in its library, the impetus towards further development of credit systems (in England at least) shifted gradually away from HE. Robertson's work confirmed the authority of the FEU model and of OCNs as the key inheritors of the credit tradition of both HE and others. It is no accident that Robertson's recommendations find a clearer resonance in the QCF than in current developments in HE credit systems. The credit movement of the 1990s viewed *Choosing to Change* as a key part of its own history. The QCF cements its place in this story just as surely as HEQC squandered its place in the history of HE credit systems.

18

From local initiatives to a national presence

When *ABC?* was published in 1992 there was a reasonable assumption that the forthcoming general election of that year would produce a change of government. As we now know, this did not happen. Nevertheless, 1992 marks a more subtle watershed in the progress of what we now see as the credit movement of the 1990s. In particular the events of 16 September 1992 – 'Black Wednesday' as it quickly became known – marked the beginning of the end of John Major's government. Although it would be May 1997 before this change actually came about, from 1994 onwards it became increasingly clear that a Labour government would be coming into office, and the calls for the establishing of a national credit framework became increasingly directed towards this anticipated change of government, rather than towards the existing Conservative government.

What also emerges during this period is the use of the term 'credit' as a more general proxy for the introduction of a more flexible, more learner-centred and more modern curriculum in the post-school sector. Beneath the banner of 'credit' were assembled an array of initiatives, projects and campaigns, all directed at the reform of the curriculum (only some of them directed at the reform of qualifications), some of which had only a passing relevance to any concept of a credit framework, but all of which sought enhancement through association with what was now recognised as the key repository of innovation and reform across the post-school sector. In 1993 the FEU established a Credit Accumulation and Transfer Network, supported by an occasional bulletin, the CATalyst. Although the CAT Network did encompass many interesting examples of embryonic credit systems (including those referred to in Chapter 16), it also included some less obviously credit-related initiatives. For example, the July 1993 version of the CATalyst (FEU, 1993) includes accounts of:

- an electronic 'Learning Framework' based at Wirral Metropolitan College which was in effect an embryonic intranet linking three college sites
- the introduction of an Electronic Bulletin Board System within the Surrey TVEE scheme, entitled 'Networking the Network'
- a Performing Arts project developing a 'progression module' for possible use by GCSE, A level and BTEC students

- a project funded by BP Oil to develop a module in Maths leading to Engineering Degrees (FEU, 1993).

These examples illustrate that, in the years following the publication of *ABC?*, the idea of a credit movement not only took hold among practitioners, but also took along with it a whole range of progressive initiatives in the post-school sector with a tenuous (and occasionally with no) connection to the real development of credit systems. This had both positive and negative consequences. The language of credit became much more widely known and used in the post-school sector, far beyond the boundaries of OCNs. However, at the same time the meaning of 'credit' became diluted, stretching out to encompass a range of ideas about a flexible, learner-centred curriculum that sought common cause within the credit movement without engaging directly in the development of credit systems based on the award of credit to learners. From this credit movement emanated numerous calls for a range of reforms to the post-school curriculum targeted increasingly at an anticipated Labour government, rather than its lame-duck predecessor.

These calls were still being voiced primarily by the providers of post-school education and training. In particular, the Association for Colleges (AfC) – the forerunner of today's Association of Colleges (AoC) – was active in garnering support for the establishing of a national credit framework. In 1994 the AfC, together with five other worthy organisations, produced a public call for the establishing of a national credit framework (AfC et al., 1994). It is worth noting the names of the AfC's partners in this call:

- the Girls' School Association
- the Headmasters' Conference
- the Secondary Heads Association
- the Sixth Form Colleges' Association
- the Society for Headmasters and Headmistresses in Independent Schools.

Hardly a roll call of revolutionary threats to the established order. This call for establishment of a national credit framework was a reflection of the overwhelming support for such an idea among providers at the time. In particular, it demonstrates the significant impact that both the FEU/FEDA campaigns, and the growth of OCNs, had had on FE colleges and other providers. The AfC document calls for the 'unitisation' of all qualifications based on the standard unit specification in *ABC?*. In other words, it rejects by implication the idea that credit-rating of existing qualifications would support the other changes called for to reform the post-compulsory curriculum, and calls instead for the adoption of a basic structure within which a genuine credit system could operate.

There was never any real expectation from the signatories of this document that the Conservative government would accede to the demands for a national credit framework. In fact, the document was directed as much at an anticipated Labour government as the government of the day. It confirms the appearance of a genuine credit movement in England and is a testament to the power of both the FEU/FEDA in promoting the concept of a credit framework and the OCNs in demonstrating the potential scope of credit systems to move beyond the boundaries of their origins in community-based and informal adult learning to become a potentially comprehensive framework for recognising learner achievements, even (potentially) those of pupils in independent girls' schools.

By 1995 the spread of OCNs across England, Wales and Northern Ireland was almost complete. There were 26 operational OCNs and six more under development. Learner registrations exceeded 250,000 in that year and would double by 1997. In 1996 over a million credits were awarded across the OCN network. An embryonic OCN was established in Scotland. It seemed that this phenomenal growth, plus the wide support from the AfC and its partners, would simply impel an incoming Labour government to establish a national credit framework as a formal structure for the continuing development of credit systems across the UK. This growth took place within the context of the development of an increasingly important policy initiative, led by the FEFC, that cemented the concept of 'widening participation' into the policy landscape of the post-school sector.

The FEFC's Widening Participation Committee was established in late 1994 and began work in 1995. It was chaired by Helena Kennedy QC and continued its work over a period of two years, taking evidence from all parts of the FE sector and stimulating initiatives at both local and national level aimed at widening participation in FE. And by Further Education in 1995, Kennedy meant 'everything that does not happen in schools or universities' (Kennedy, 1997). The Widening Participation Committee took a very broad view of the sector, and also took a very broad view of the actions that needed to be taken in order to deliver on its objectives.

It should be remembered that the Widening Participation Committee was set up under the auspices of a Conservative government (with representatives of the then Department for Education and Employment acting as assessors to the Committee). It should also be remembered that the Committee's work was undertaken during the long, slow demise of this government and the increasing certainty that a change of government would be brought about in 1997. In the event the timing of the Committee was perfect. The Kennedy Report – *Learning Works* – was published in June 1997, one month after the return of a Labour government. The Kennedy Report was enthusiastically welcomed by David Blunkett, the new Secretary of State for Education and Employment, and it seemed the report would effectively set the agenda for change in FE for the new government.

Many of the recommendations in *Learning Works* (actually, Kennedy refers to them explicitly as her 'Agenda for Change') relate to funding, to changes in what would now be termed 'the machinery of government', and to the responsibilities of other agencies (for example, broadcasters) to promote widening participation. However, two of Kennedy's recommendations relate directly to structural changes within the FE sector. These are (Kennedy, 1997):

- launch a credit accumulation system, to be operative within five years.
- create new 'Pathways to Learning' – a unitised system for recognising achievement.

In the body of the report, Kennedy expands on these aspects of her agenda for change. Her proposals on the first part of this agenda are very explicit:

> There should be a national framework of credit for further education, similar to that already developed in Wales and by open college networks... It will require funding to be available which recognises achievement at unit level. There are already examples of local credit frameworks and FEDA has provided us with one route map to develop the approach on a national basis.
>
> (Kennedy, 1997, pp. 86–7)

Kennedy's recommendation is unequivocal, and yet – as previous chapters of this publication have tried to illustrate – it accommodates both conceptions of what is meant by a credit framework. It recognises the systems developed by OCNs, but explicitly identifies Wales as being different. It recognises the importance of the work done in 'local credit frameworks' (Kennedy took a close interest in the work of the Derbyshire Regional Network and was given an honorary degree by the University of Derby for her work on Widening Participation in FE), but also acknowledges the 'route map' proposed by FEDA, which combines a credit-rating approach adopted in Wales with the award of credit approach of OCNs. In her second recommendation about the development of 'Learning Pathways', Kennedy draws explicitly on some of the practice that the Widening Participation Committee had identified within OCNs:

> at the heart of the pathway will be a planned programme of learning support, accredited so that its learning outcomes are recognised.
>
> (Kennedy, 1997, p. 86)

Kennedy also recognises the importance of Access to HE certificates as a model for the future development of qualifications. In a section of her report entitled 'We know how to do it', she writes:

> Programmes which offer adults access to higher education provide a good example... Learners are able to collect credit for each unit studied and to build up a record of achievement which counts towards their overall qualification.
>
> (Kennedy, 1997, pp. 79–80)

Kennedy's report therefore reflects the continuation of this twin-track approach to the development of credit systems that had been unfolding throughout the life of the Widening Participation Committee. Nevertheless, the appearance of these recommendations in such a high-profile and well-received report at such a juncture lent great weight to the arguments already advanced in support of a national credit framework, and led to an expectation that it would be simply a matter of time before the incoming Labour government acted on Kennedy's recommendations.

This expectation was further raised by the announcement by David Blunkett, days after the publication of *Learning Works,* that he was establishing a National Advisory Group for Continuing Education and Lifelong Learning (NAGCELL) with Professor Bob Fryer (then Principal of Northern College) as its chair. It should be remembered that *Learning Works* had been commissioned by the FEFC, not by government. Blunkett decided he needed a more wide-ranging report directly to government before setting out a programme of action. However, NAGCELL was established as a short-life group, with an implicit expectation that it would build on the work undertaken in the production of the Kennedy Report. The Fryer Report, *Learning for the Twenty-First Century*, was published in November 1997 (Fryer, 1997).

As expected, Fryer explicitly endorsed the Kennedy proposals and took them a stage further. A whole chapter of *Learning for the Twenty-First Century* (Chapter 14: Measuring Achievement) is devoted to a detailed argument in favour of 'developing a unit-based, credit framework'. However, unlike the Kennedy Report, and for the first time in such a report in England, Fryer explicitly links the development of a unit-based credit framework to the reform of qualifications. His Chapter 14 extols the benefits of 'developing unit-based qualifications within a credit framework', including:

• Provide the means to reduce duplication and overlap in the qualifications framework by requiring components of qualifications to be justified on a unit-by-unit basis.

- Encourage adults and those not currently participating in education to work towards achieving nationally recognised qualifications by the recognition of achievement of units towards a qualification.
- Ensure that qualifications formed from agreed combinations of mandatory and optional units will meet the divers [sic] needs of employers and individual learners.
- Encourage parity of esteem between academic and vocational qualifications.

(Fryer, 1997, p. 82)

Fryer also proposed the establishing of 'A Learning Record', within which the achievements of all learners would be recognised.

Critically, Fryer also says that taking forward the development of unit-based qualifications within a credit framework 'is clearly a task which should fall principally to the Qualifications and Curriculum Authority (QCA) to give leadership' (Fryer, 1997, p. 83).

This leadership would be of 'the national partnership' proposed by Kennedy to develop a credit framework in *Learning Works*. Thus, while building explicitly on Kennedy's recommendations, Fryer locates the development of a credit framework very clearly within the context of qualifications reform, the first time this connection is made so explicitly in a major policy document. Reference is often made to 'Kennedy and Fryer' as two reports with very similar perspectives. However, in relation to the development of credit systems, one marks a significant step forward from the other. At the same time we can detect a diminishing of scope in the Fryer report in comparison with Kennedy. This reflects the different remits of the FEFC Widening Participation Committee (and Kennedy's view that FE included 'everything outside schools and universities') and NAGCELL, with its focus on the relatively new concept of Lifelong Learning that, despite its literal meaning (and Fryer's personal emphasis on this meaning), was already being perceived by government as a concept to replace the increasingly unfashionable 'adult education'. To understand how this concept of lifelong learning fitted into the new government's overall conception of how unit-based qualifications within a credit framework might be developed, it is necessary to look outside the scope of both the Kennedy and Fryer reports, and focus on the separate issue of qualifications reform in England in this same period.

Before leaving *Learning for the Twenty-First Century*, it is worth noting a few interesting personal connections. Bob Fryer was, for a time, a member of the Executive Committee of the South Yorkshire OCN. When the very first credits were awarded to learners by SYOCF in Barnsley in 1987, they were presented by the then leader of Sheffield City Council, one David Blunkett. The first meeting of the National Open College was held at Northern College.

David Browning, who chaired that first meeting of NOCN, had been a lecturer at Northern College before leaving to become Director of the Manchester OCN. One of the key advisers to NAGCELL was Alan Tuckett from NIACE. In 1996, I began working for NIACE as a development officer and produced advice on credit systems for Alan to feed into NAGCELL. Given this network of connections it is hardly surprising that, unlike *Learning Works,* Fryer's chapter on developing credit systems draws very explicitly on the experience of OCNs and locates the award of credit to learners very clearly at the heart of his recommendations. Although *Learning in the Twenty-First Century* makes a passing reference to work in Wales, it makes no reference to FEDA's road map for development. Indeed, the recommendation that QCA should lead further development of credit-based qualifications effectively signals the end of the idea of a credit framework as a provider-led development, rather than one to be taken forward through awarding bodies and the newly established qualifications regulators.

One more connection needs to be noted. The person who organised the presentation of the first awards to learners by David Blunkett in Barnsley was Caroline Mager, from the South Yorkshire OCN. Caroline then went on to work with David Browning on the UDACE OCN project in the late 1980s and was also a member of the group that produced *A Basis for Credit?.* In 1995 she began another, temporary, role as part of the secretariat to the Dearing Review of 16–19 qualifications. Before taking up the post-Fryer story of credit systems, we need to take a step back to the Dearing Review and the separate story of qualifications reform in the 1990s.

19

The reform of qualifications

In the twenty-first century we have become used to reform agendas being set by major reports, or being brought on by significant crises in the system. So, for example, the Skills Strategy White Paper and the Leitch Review of Skills are clear drivers for the reform of vocational qualifications. The A level debacle of 2002 and the subsequent Tomlinson Report form the basis for the current programme for reform of 14–19 qualifications. However, no such crisis or major report seems to have brought about the review of 16–19 qualifications conducted by Lord Dearing in 1995–6 (Dearing, 1996). Dearing had previously been responsible for advising government on the development of the National Curriculum and would go on to produce a report on the reform of HE. In retrospect one might wonder if the DfEE had not simply asked Dearing to 'call in' on 16–19 qualifications on his journey from schools to universities – an impression not dismissed by the frequent references to his third report on HE as 'The Second Dearing Report' (Dearing, 1997).

Dearing's remit was to 'strengthen, consolidate and improve' the framework of 16–19 qualifications. In doing so he was instructed explicitly to 'maintain the rigour of A levels' and 'to continue to build on the current development of GNVQs' (Dearing, 1996, p. 42). In other words, any radical changes in the current offer of qualifications to 16- to 19-year-olds were excluded. Dearing was expected to make recommendations about 'preparing young people for work and higher education ... minimising waste ... [and] securing maximum value for money' (Dearing, 1996, p. 42).

In fact, the outcomes of the review – both intended and accidental – were more far reaching than this rather modest remit would suggest.

The conduct of the Dearing Review during the 12 months leading to the publication of his report in March 1996 took place during a time of unprecedented interest in the development of credit systems, as I have tried to show in the previous chapter. David Robertson had produced *Choosing to Change* some six months before the start of Dearing's work. FEDA continued to argue the case for a credit framework, and were represented on the 'support group' for the review. The AfC and partners' statement was widely circulated, the work on credit in Wales had a high profile and OCNs continued to grow. It seemed that the review offered the opportunity to build a credit system into the future development of qualifications for 16- to 19-year-olds. The question was, would Dearing make such a recommendation in his report to government?

The review was conducted both through the receipt of written submissions and through a series of consultation events across England and Wales (the formal scope of Dearing's remit). The weight of opinion in favour of introducing a credit system into 16–19 qualifications was impressive. Not only were there numerous written submissions that argued this case, but at every consultation event in England and Wales the case for a credit framework was put, and put by many different organisations with a range of different interests. In Wales in particular, one might have been forgiven for assuming that the purpose of the Dearing Review was to introduce a credit system into 16–19 qualifications. At the London consultation conference, Dearing had to plead with delegates to raise issues 'other than credit' in their contributions.

Despite this weight of opinion, Dearing's hands were effectively tied by his remit. The introduction of a credit system into 16–19 qualifications would have brought about significant structural change to both A levels and to GNVQs, which Dearing had been instructed to avoid. At the launch of his final report in March 1996, Dearing acknowledged the 'very high level of interest' in credit systems that had been revealed through the consultation, but regretted that he was unable to include any recommendations on the development of credit within 16–19 qualifications in his report to government.[1] At the time, this seemed like an opportunity lost, but in reality the arguments for a credit framework, despite their widespread support across the post-school sector, had had little impact on national government by 1996. The purpose of the review was as much to cement the triple track approach to qualifications (A levels, GNVQs and NVQs) as it was to bring about any significant reforms.

Notwithstanding this limited remit, Dearing's first and most lasting recommendation was that government should establish a national framework of qualifications to bring about 'greater coherence' in the offer of qualifications to 16- to 19-year-olds:

> A first step towards coherence is to bring the present academic, applied and vocational pathways into a common framework covering all achievements. A common framework would help people understand where qualifications stand in relation to each other ... [and] should also be capable of recognising other major qualifications currently available which meet nationally accepted criteria, but fall outside the three main qualifications pathways.
>
> (Dearing, 1996, p. 6)

As we know, the government of the day accepted this primary recommendation of Dearing's report and less than a year later the legislation was introduced to establish this first iteration of Dearing's recommended national framework of qualifications - the NQF. In a related and equally important recommendation, Dearing also proposed that the NCVQ and the SCAA should be brought together into 'one single statutory body'. Although his proposed title for this body was a 'national qualifications authority', the same legislation that established the NQF also established the QCA as this agency in England - together with its Welsh and Northern Irish counterparts. Interestingly, the creation of the QCA and the NQF was literally the last act of the Major government - nodded through Parliament on the last day before the 1997 general election was announced, with the agreement of the Labour whips, and given royal assent as Labour assumed power. In effect, the NQF was a Conservative bequest to the incoming government, willingly accepted by Labour ministers-in-waiting in April 1997. This conscious acceptance of the NQF was to have repercussions in 1998 when Labour came to set out its proposals for taking forward the recommendations of the Kennedy and Fryer reports.

Dearing's recommendations on establishing a national framework of qualifications are worthy of closer examination. They had a direct impact on the drafting of the legislation that brought about the establishing of the NQF, and they clearly reveal the conceptual underpinnings of the framework. Firstly, it is worth noting that Dearing's recommendations arose explicitly from a remit related to 16- to 19-year-olds, yet related explicitly to NVQs and 'other major qualifications' irrespective of the age of the people undertaking them. Not for the first time a reform aimed at younger learners was deemed to be good enough for adults.

Secondly, the purpose of bringing qualifications into an NQF was expressed in terms of 'coherence', 'clearer understanding' and 'comparability' (Dearing, 1996). Placing qualifications in the framework was effectively an end in itself. In other words, the NQF was a self-referencing structure: the purpose of bringing qualifications into the framework was so that they could be in the framework. There is no suggestion in Dearing's recommendations that the NQF might play any role in reforming or restructuring qualifications - remember this was excluded from his remit - and so the recommendations, faithfully carried through into the Education Act of 1997 that established the NQF (DfES, 1997), are entirely passive in their construct, in marked contrast to the rationale for developing the QCF. From the outset the NQF was, in Michael Young's terms, a 'weak' framework (Young, 2003).

Finally, it is worth noting the distinction Dearing draws between 'the three main pathways' of A levels and GCSEs, GNVQs and NVQs, and 'other major qualifications'. Dearing proposed explicitly that these 'present' qualifications should be brought into the framework, and that other qualifications should then be recognised if they met 'nationally accepted criteria'. This is, in fact, exactly how the NQF was set up. On the first day of its existence, all A levels,

GCSEs, GNVQs and NVQs became part of the framework, and other qualifications (primarily vocational qualifications) then had to be submitted and accredited against criteria produced by the regulators. Again, the contrast with the process of building the QCF, with its single set of regulations applied to all qualifications, is marked and instructive.

Despite this restricted view of the purpose of a national framework of qualifications and the absence of any reference to credit in Dearing's final report, the outcomes of the Dearing Review did take on board one of the design features of the NOCN credit framework, and this was also accepted as a design feature of the NQF. This design feature was the adoption of Entry level as an accepted level of learner achievement within the NQF. As neither the NCVQ nor SCAA had a current remit for the recognition of achievement at this level, we must see this as an innovation in Dearing's proposals. The establishing of Entry level within the first iteration of the national framework of qualifications not only vindicated the long-held view of OCNs that learners had the right for their achievements at this level to be recognised, it also borrowed the term 'Entry level' directly from the OCN experience. Other terms (for example, 'Access Level' and 'Foundation Level') were considered, but the same logic that had led OCNs to accept 'Entry level' in 1994 also persuaded Dearing. Although the case for Entry level was made during the Review, it was tied explicitly to the wider arguments in favour of a credit framework. Extracting it from this context and highlighting the value of Entry level within the NQF was one creative bit of drafting in the final Dearing report, for which we should thank Caroline Mager.

Dearing made other recommendations in his report which were not taken up at the time. In particular, his proposals for 'National Certificates' and 'National Diplomas', that would be achieved through combining qualifications from one of the 'main pathways' with new key skills qualifications, would be taken up a decade later by 14-19 Diplomas. However, one of Dearing's recommendations that was acted upon was his proposal to establish an 'AS Level' qualification with a value of 'half an A level'. Little could this 'simple postman' (Dearing's familiar description of himself)[2] have realised that, in its attempts to define exactly how an A level could be halved, the organisation created by his report, together with a Secretary of State for Education, would be consumed by the crisis of A level grades in 2002 that would lead, eventually, to the dismantling of this first iteration of a national framework of qualifications and its replacement by the QCF. But that part of the story lies some way in the future.

Looking back over this period from 1995 to 1997, the continuing conception of the outgoing Conservative government was that qualifications were for young people (hence Dearing), while the needs of adult learners should be addressed through a range of initiatives other than qualifications reform (hence Kennedy). Dearing's apology for being unable to make recommendations about credit systems in his report on qualifications systems illustrates perfectly the official demarcation line set by government between qualifications (young people) and credit systems (adults). In inheriting the NQF at the demise of the Major government, David Blunkett and co. also accepted this demarcation line. The Fryer Report, for the first time, sought to bring together these previously separate strands of policymaking, by locating the further development of credit systems very clearly within the context of qualifications reform. In 1997 it remained to be seen whether the new Labour government would accept this crossing of the policy line between credit and qualifications that Fryer proposed.

Notes

1 Although an appendix to the report included a rehearsal of some of the issues related to credit.
2 He had previously been a long-serving chairman of the Post Office.

20

The learning age and the onward march of credit

In June 1997 the incoming Labour government had the Kennedy Report in front of them, had set up NAGCELL to advise on the publication of the Fryer Report, and had inherited from the outgoing administration a commitment to establish a new national framework of qualifications. It had other educational commitments derived from its manifesto (in particular, the establishing of a new 'University for Industry'), but, with the publication of *Learning for the Twenty-First Century* in late 1997 (the Fryer Report), the stage seemed to be set for the establishment of a clear policy to take forward the development of a national framework of credit-based qualifications. Despite Dearing's misgivings, here was the ideal opportunity for a new government to instruct its new agency – the QCA – to bring together Dearing's proposals for a national framework of qualifications, with the recommendations of Fryer-out-of-Kennedy that this new framework should be based on a credit system.

In February 1998 the DfEE published a White Paper setting out its plans for the 'Lifelong Learning Sector' (the term was now embraced by government), entitled *The Learning Age* (DfEE, 1998b). The foreword to the White Paper was written by David Blunkett (that is, not by a civil servant) and stands as one of the most positive and forward-looking introductions to a government White Paper on education in the post-war period. The ambitious sub-title of *The Learning Age: A Renaissance for a New Britain* captured the optimistic and ambitious mood of the time. It promised a very different approach to policy in post-school education, with the learner and learning at the centre of this new direction. If the reader was in any doubt about the progeny of *The Learning Age*, then the insertion of a quote from the Fryer Report above the heading of Chapter One reminded them of where the White Paper came from: 'This country needs to develop a new learning culture, a culture of lifelong learning for all' (Fryer, 1997, p. 3).

An initial reading of *The Learning Age* gave cause for optimism about the development of a credit-based framework of qualifications. The chapter on recognising achievement is littered with clues about the government's intentions. For example:

We propose to examine how qualifications targeted at adults can ... be taken in small sections (6.12).

We propose that the qualification system should be developed to recognise that learning can take place in many different forms (6.13).

Many adults returning to learning want to take small steps. A full national qualification may not be the right goal for them to start with (6.15).

Many (including the Fryer and Kennedy committees) have called for a system in which people ... can build up recognition for bits of learning at a time (6.15).

Having set out the rationale for a more flexible and responsive system for recognising learner achievements, *The Learning Age* then goes on to refer explicitly to the development of a credit system. Not only that but, taking a lead from the Kennedy Report, it suggests that a system of credit-based qualifications might be developed along the lines of Access to HE certificates: 'It may be possible to develop, within further education, a system of commonly understood credits as currently happens with arrangements for access to higher education for adults' (6.16).

Having set out this possibility, *The Learning Age* then starts to expand on this idea: 'This would be aimed at those undertaking courses which prepare for full qualifications... This would not prevent people from studying a particular unit even if they were not seeking a full qualification' (6.16).

There then follows a consultation question that asks people if they think 'a system of credit accumulation and transfer is a sensible goal'. The response to this consultation question was overwhelmingly positive, with some 90 per cent of respondents favouring this approach. It seemed that *The Learning Age* was setting the groundwork for the development of the system of credit-based qualifications, regulated by the QCA, that Fryer had envisaged.

In retrospect it is possible to read *The Learning Age* outside the cloud of optimism that still pervaded the post-school sector in February 1998. In addition to the references to the development of a credit system, the same chapter on recognising achievement contains other interesting commitments and proposals from government. It is divided into sub-headings, including 'Qualifications for Young people' (p. 64) and 'Qualifications for adults' (p. 66) – thereby instituting a policy separation of qualifications by age that has been reinforced over the years. Prior to *The Learning Age*, no such divisions in policy are in evidence as qualifications were assumed to be developed for young people, even if they might be taken by adults. The rhetoric of lifelong learning in *The Learning Age* is significantly compromised by this distinction.

The Learning Age sets out the government's policy framework for the QCA and the NQF without any reference to credit systems. It confirms that A levels, GCSEs and GNVQs will continue to be offered to young people, without reference to any reform of these qualifications (pace Dearing). It commits the government 'to develop and promote NVQs' for adults and to encourage more adults to take A levels, GCSEs and GNVQs, again without any reference to credit. Comparing the statements about a credit system with these clear commitments related to qualifications, we can see the equivocation in *The Learning Age* very clearly. So, for example, the ability to take qualifications in small sections could be offered through the unitised format of NVQs, without reference to a credit system. The reference to small steps of achievement that do not lead to a full qualification could mean that such achievements would fall outside the national framework of qualifications. In this context the reference to credits being made available to 'those undertaking courses which prepare for full qualifications' (6.16) can be read to confirm that such credits would be separate from the qualifications system. And where the references to qualifications use the terms 'we will' and 'we want', references to credits are far more equivocal: 'it may be possible', 'many have called for', or 'we may need to go further' (6.15 & 6.16).

In retrospect, the optimism about *The Learning Age* seems sadly misplaced. Indeed, one might suspect it had been written with the clear intention of making an appropriate series of references to the development of credit systems without any commitment whatsoever. It might also be read as an attempt to re-assert the importance of mainstream qualifications against the arguments for development of a credit system. It may even be suspected that, in writing the chapter on recognising achievement, civil servants asked the advice of people working in the newly established QCA (which effectively consisted of the people previously working for the SCAA and NCVQ) about how the recommendations of Kennedy and Fryer might be incorporated into a White Paper that also considered the outcomes of the Dearing Review. We may assume that formal advice from this source was not enthusiastic about a credit system. Reading the White Paper over a decade later, one is left with the overwhelming impression that the intentions of this part of *The Learning Age* were actually to stifle and marginalise any further development of credit systems, to incorporate further development into a continuing debate based on uncertainty and conjecture, and to get on with the Dearing agenda of building a national framework of qualifications that excluded any reference to credit systems.

It took some time before the reality of policy development outside the process of consultation on *The Learning Age* began to be appreciated by those who had promoted the development of credit-based qualifications. Indeed, the optimism of the White Paper continued to feed the growth of

OCN registrations and awards throughout 1997 and 1998. We can now see though that *The Learning Age* marks a turning point in the development of credit systems through the 1990s. It seemed for a time that the rapid growth of both OCNs and local credit frameworks after 1992, the support for the development of a national credit framework from AfC and its partners, the recommendations of Kennedy and Fryer, the creation of the NQF and the accession of a Labour government would all lead, inexorably, to the establishing of the NQF as a qualifications framework based on credit.

The extent of this consensus is revealed in a Joint Statement issued by a group of organisations at the end of 1998. The statement called for:

> ...a high quality, unitised credit-based qualifications framework encompassing all achievement post-14.
>
> (AoC et al., 1998, p. 1)

The list of organisations supporting this call is impressive[1] and is worth recording in its entirety:

- Association of Colleges
- Further Education Development Agency
- Fforwm (the association of FE colleges in Wales)
- Joint Council for Vocational Qualifications (City & Guilds, Edexcel and RSA)
- National Association of Teachers in Further and Higher Education
- National Education Advisory Board
- National Institute for Adult Continuing Education
- Northern Ireland Credit Accumulation and Transfer System
- National Open College Network
- National Union of Teachers
- University Central Admissions Service.

Notwithstanding the overwhelming pressure on the still relatively new Labour government to establish the NQF as a credit-based qualifications framework, by the end of 1998 it became clear that that ambition had been thwarted and that any further development of credit systems would take place outside the development of the NQF. It seemed at the time that a huge opportunity had been lost (Gosling, 2001). In fact, it had merely been delayed – albeit by a decade.

Had the QCF been established in 1998 rather than 2008, it would have been perceived as the natural outcome of an inexorable process of change that delivered its logical outcome at exactly the moment when there was maximum support for, and maximum understanding of, credit systems across the post-school sector. How much easier would have been the process of developing the QCF and how much more quickly it could have been implemented had it arrived at this historically ideal moment. In retrospect, the expectations about delivery of such a framework in 1998 were misplaced and naïve in relation to the main drivers of reform (SCAA and NCVQ) that led to the establishing of the NQF as an alternative to, rather than an accommodation of, the movement for a national credit framework. The onward march of credit had, for the time being anyway, been halted.

Talking later to colleagues in the QCA about these early beginnings of the NQF, I was struck by how completely insulated the development of the new qualifications framework was from the debates about credit and the apparently inexorable growth of credit systems that were taking place at exactly the moment when the NQF was being established. From a reading of policy documents of the time, from understanding how the policies of the new Labour government were being formulated, and from seeing the scope of the consensus in favour of a credit-based qualifications framework – one might be led to conclude that the decision to proceed with development of the NQF without reference to credit systems was a close-run thing based on knife-edge decisions by new ministers and civil servants in Whitehall. If so, then the officers of the QCA charged with developing the NQF (who were all drawn in the first instance either from the NCVQ or SCAA) were blissfully unaware of these debates.[2] The idea that the NQF might actually have begun life in 1998 as a framework of credit-based qualifications is greeted with a quizzical raising of eyebrows. Very few people involved in actually setting up the NQF within QCA knew a thing about credit systems or were aware of the apparent consensus that had been established by 1998 about the desirability of a credit-based qualifications system. Some people may have thought we were close to bringing together credits and qualifications in 1998, but those people did not work for the QCA.

Notes

1 Once again the role of Tony Tait in bringing together these organisations needs to be acknowledged.
2 My thanks to Alan Greig for these insights.

21

Coming to terms with a divided system

Of course we need to recall that *The Learning Age* was not the first White Paper produced by the new Labour government. In December 1997, *Qualifying for Success* had set out a programme of reform based not only on the proposals in the Dearing Report, but also on the previous recommendations for reform of NVQs (Beaumont, 1995) and GNVQs (Capey, 1996). It included proposals (following Dearing) for the reform of A levels and the development of AS levels through the 'Curriculum 2000' programme. We may characterise *Qualifying for Success* as an opportunity lost to bring about radical reform of the qualifications system that a new government could have instituted. Instead, the Labour government continued with the damaging cycle of constant piecemeal and poorly planned reform that had characterised previous attempts to reform the qualifications system. Introducing *Qualifying for Success* to a conference in December 1997, Baroness Blackstone said: 'We need to move away from the damaging cycle of constant piecemeal and poorly planned reform that has characterised the past.'

Despite David Blunkett's announcement in the introduction to *Qualifying for Success* that the government intended to create 'a qualifications framework for the new millennium', the influence of the Dearing Review, with its explicit requirements to preserve A levels, build on the 'success' of GNVQs and ignore NVQs (having already been considered in the 1995 Beaumont Review), hardly created the context for a radical review. The response of FEDA to *Qualifying for Success* was scathing (FEDA, 1998), along with many other responses that accused the government of missing an opportunity for more wholesale reform and, in particular, missing the opportunity to establish a credit system within the national framework of qualifications. Notwithstanding David Blunkett's introduction (surely this one *was* written by a civil servant), *Qualifying for Success* had a marginal impact on the twenty-first century.

Following the publication of *Qualifying for Success* and the equivocal references to a credit framework in *The Learning Age*, it was becoming clearer that there was to be no coming together of the processes of qualifications reform and continuing development of credit systems. These separate processes were confirmed in a letter from Baroness Blackstone to the QCA in April 1998, in which she asked the new Authority to begin the reform of A levels through the Curriculum 2000 initiative, to continue to develop GNVQs and at the same time 'to investigate further the potential benefits of credit-based qualifications for adult and vocational learning' (DfEE, 1998a).

Here was confirmation that the future development of credit systems was to be put on hold. Responsibility for further development was taken away from a development agency (FEDA) and placed in the hands of the qualifications regulator. Of course in 1998 the QCA had priorities other than 'the potential benefits of credit' to worry about – such as the establishing of the NQF – and the 'investigation' of these benefits was placed on a back burner in the long grass outside the tent. The previous practitioner-based energy that had driven the development of credit systems and fuelled the demands for a national credit framework was siphoned off through *The Learning Age* and effectively nullified by the Blackstone letter. The future development of credit systems would take place outside the development of the NQF and would be placed in the safe hands of the QCA itself to ensure that this separation of regulation from investigation could be properly maintained.

From the Blackstone letter to the 2003 Skills Strategy marks a period of five years and two months. During this period no practical progress on the development of credit systems was taken forward by the QCA. From the 2003 Skills Strategy to the publication of the *Regulatory Arrangements for the Qualifications and Credit Framework* in August 2008 marks a period of five years and two months. What a difference a formal announcement, a proper remit, strong leadership and a clear focus on the objectives of the reform process can make. But again that story comes later.

The immediate effect of the Blackstone letter on the development of credit systems was negligible. Registrations through OCNs continued to grow rapidly. In 1996–7 more adult learners registered for credits with an OCN than registered for A levels, GCSEs and GNVQs combined. In 1997–8, OCNs recorded the biggest single year-on-year increase in both learners registered and credits awarded. For the first time credits were awarded to learners in every part of England, Wales and Northern Ireland. However, the significance of this separate development of credit systems, signalled in *Qualifying for Success* and *The Learning Age* and confirmed by the Blackstone letter of April 1998, was not lost on the OCN movement. In June 1998, I wrote in an article for NOCN:

> I therefore suggest to all those colleagues that have been involved in arguing for the development of a national credit framework in the past that we now need to leave this concept behind and re-focus our energies on the development of credit-based qualifications.
>
> (Wilson, 1998)

The crux of the argument put forward in this paper was that, in the longer term, it would not be possible to deliver on the potential benefits of a credit framework advanced in *ABC?* in a context where a national framework of qualifications was established that purported to be comprehensive in its reach, as the NQF promised to be. In 1992, with the remit of regulation of qualifications limited to A levels and GCSEs (through SCAA) and NVQs (via the NCVQ) and the focus of qualifications almost exclusively on the needs of young people, it was possible to envisage the development of a national credit framework that would simply grow to fill the considerable spaces in the post-school sector outside the remit of these bodies. By 1998, with the advent of the QCA and its programme for development of the NQF, these open spaces were in serious danger of disappearing. Indeed, along with the creation of the NQF, *Qualifying for Success* had also signalled (another of Dearing's recommendations) that future funding of provision in the post-school sector would be linked explicitly to the accreditation of qualifications in the NQF.

It was in this context of a dramatic expansion of the scope of regulation of qualifications, of the linking of regulation and funding systems, and of the apparent demise of the hopes for establishing a national credit framework, that members of NOCN met during 1997 and 1998 to consider how the best interests of OCNs might be protected and extended in this environment. On the surface there was no evidence of crisis. The expansion of OCNs that had begun with *ABC?* and the incorporation of colleges in 1992 continued right the way through the remainder of the decade. As *Qualifying for Success* signalled the intentions of government to pursue the development of a qualifications framework without reference to credit, the NOCN was experiencing its most successful year ever and preparing for a further year of rapid growth (NOCN, 1998).

Just as the debates leading up to the adoption of the specifications of the National Credit Framework set out in *ABC?* had divided OCNs in 1993, so the debate about moving on from this same framework caused similar divisions five years later. Nevertheless, at its AGM in 1998, NOCN took a decision to become an awarding body and to seek recognition for accreditation of its qualifications within the NQF. What Michael Freeston refers to as 'the accidental awarding body' (Freeston, 1996) actually came about as the result of a lengthy period of discussion about the appropriate strategy for continuing to develop credit systems in the context of a statutory national framework of qualifications backed by a system of public funding. Despite the failure of the Labour government to establish the NQF as a framework of credit-based qualifications, NOCN took the decision to engage with the new framework and to develop its own credit-based qualifications within that framework. It was to prove more difficult to do this than anticipated.

22

The relationship between credits and qualifications

It was clearly essential for NOCN to take this step in 1998, though final recognition as an awarding body in the NQF would not be completed until early 2000. However, there were a couple of moments in the previous history of NOCN where an alternative organisational relationship between credit systems and qualifications might have been established. Neither of these initiatives proved significant, but they are worthy of note here in the context of credit accumulation and transfer within the QCF. As I have shown in Chapter 8, the earlier attempts to link OCN credits with NVQs came to nothing as the restrictive nature of the NVQ framework gradually emerged.

Nevertheless, OCNs saw the possibility of using the BTEC qualification framework as a way of establishing a concept of 'equivalence' with NVQs. A proposition was made to BTEC by NOCN and a meeting was held at BTEC's London offices to discuss the proposition. In effect, NOCN suggested to BTEC that OCN credits might be accepted towards the achievement of a BTEC qualification. A pilot project was proposed through which OCNs would develop units explicitly designed to meet the requirements of optional units within BTEC qualifications. Learners achieving credits on these units (which would be jointly validated by BTEC and NOCN) would be able to count these credits towards a BTEC qualification. From the perspective of NOCN the proposal made perfect sense. OCNs awarded credits, not qualifications. BTEC awarded qualifications, not credits. NOCN had no intention (then) of becoming an awarding body. It seemed that OCNs might offer BTEC access to new groups of learners, while BTEC might offer OCN learners a chance to transfer credits to a national qualification. However, the idea that credits from a local awarding body might be transferred towards a qualification offered by a national awarding body was perhaps too ambitious a concept in 1990. Although the meeting with BTEC ended cordially, nothing came of the proposal.

The same idea was discussed subsequently with RSA, and here it seemed that RSA was more receptive to the idea that, outside the NVQ framework, some arrangements for joint recognition of OCN credits might be agreed that would allow these credits to be transferred towards an RSA qualification. Initially, it proved too complicated to find a working relationship between OCNs and the RSA that would permit this credit transfer function to operate, but after a series of meetings an agreement was struck and three OCNs in the Midlands took part in a pilot programme, in which RSA effectively agreed a devolved set of quality assurance arrangements, and through which the OCNs concerned recognised learner achievements through the award of credits. The learners achieving these credits could claim an RSA qualification on completion of their programme of study.

The tortuous negotiations and lengthy agreement between OCNs and RSA eventually supported a handful of learners to achieve OCN credits and use these to claim an RSA qualification. The additional RSA qualification had to be paid for and, although a number of learners actually achieved the credits necessary to claim the RSA award, only a small number actually paid for their RSA certificate. Nevertheless, somewhere out there from the period 1992-3 there are learners who can genuinely claim to be the first people to achieve a national qualification awarded by the RSA (now Oxford, Cambridge and RSA Examinations – OCR) on the basis of credit accumulation. As with BTEC, relationships with OCR remained cordial, but there was no enthusiasm (especially once the RSA had become part of OCR) to extend the initial pilot.

Had either the relationship with BTEC or the RSA or (much more interestingly) with both awarding bodies taken off in the early 1990s, then NOCN might never have become an awarding body. The principle that credits awarded through a local OCN could be accumulated towards a qualification offered by a national awarding body could, in theory, have developed across all OCNs and all awarding bodies. Rather than become an awarding body in its own right, NOCN might have become a broker, underwriting the quality systems of OCNs in order to provide national awarding bodies with the assurances they need in order to be able to accept the transferability of credits towards a qualification. The agreement between the RSA and NOCN to pilot this relationship with three OCNs in the early 1990s proves that, though practically complex, it was technically feasible in a context where such decisions rested with the awarding body itself, outside the framework of regulation. Had such a set of relationships been well established by 1998 then it might have been possible to take these relationships into the NQF. In the event this simply was not an option and, in order to protect the interests of both individual OCNs and their learners, in 1998 NOCN declared its intention to become a recognised awarding body in its own right.

This protection of the interests of individual OCNs and learners was essential, given the expressed aim of QCA that, by 2003, all achievements would be recognised within the NQF, and there would be no public funding of any achievements outside it. (Echoes of the NCVQ's intentions a decade earlier are clearly audible.) NOCN was sceptical at the time of the QCA's intentions: 'By some time in the early twenty-first century, according to the published ambitions of the QCA ... The achievements of all learners will be able to be represented within the NQF. Well, that remains to be seen' (Wilson, 1998, p. 3).

NOCN's scepticism was well founded. In the five years from 1998 to 2003 more than three million learners were awarded over seven million credits on accredited programmes that continued to be offered outside the NQF (NOCN, 2003). Indeed, part of the rationale for reforming the NQF set out in the Skills Strategy document of that same year (2003) was that it had manifestly failed in its ambition to be a comprehensive framework. But once again that story waits ahead. In becoming an awarding body within the NQF, NOCN set out to prove that it was possible to develop credit-based qualifications in a regulated framework, even if such qualifications would be the preserve of a single awarding body, rather than a characteristic of the NQF itself. On the way to becoming an awarding body itself, NOCN had built an agreement with an existing national awarding body – RSA – that demonstrated in practice both the possibility that a credit system and a qualifications system could be brought together and that credits awarded by one organisation could be counted towards a qualification offered by another. For the development of the QCF, both precedents, though based on very small numbers of learners, would prove to be hugely significant.

Once again, though, NOCN was choosing (or rather was forced to choose) a long, hard road to achieving its aims. Demonstrating that credit-based qualifications could be established within the NQF was one thing (though even this proved much more difficult to achieve than had been anticipated). But unless credits were capable of transfer between qualifications offered by other awarding bodies, then the idea that a credit system might operate within the NQF would be an empty claim. By the time NOCN eventually became recognised as an awarding body within the NQF, it was clear that, despite the enthusiasms for credit systems in the 1990s, the twenty-first century had arrived with the prospect of a national framework of credit-based qualifications as far away as it had ever been.

I have focused at some length in this story on the alternative approaches to the development of a credit system espoused by OCNs on one hand and by the FEU/FEDA et al. on the other. The establishment of the QCF clearly marks the ascendancy of one concept of credit system over another. In 2001 no such distinction could be drawn. It seemed that both approaches were actually leading to the same dead end. Perhaps, after all, the alternative strategies for developing credit systems advanced by the FEU and FEDA in the mid-1990s would have been more fruitful than NOCN's continuing insistence that the development of a genuine credit system had to be based on the award of credits to learners.

23

'Credit' without credits: The myth of unitisation

The term 'credit' has many meanings. The temptation to find a way of adding 'crunch' into the title of this volume was resisted, but everyone is familiar with the word in one way or another. Even within the world of education and training, the terms 'giving credit' and 'getting credit' are familiar. So, for example, instructions to the markers of A level scripts in the NQF Code of Practice for General Qualifications requires assessors to 'give credit' for particular kinds of answers to questions. The idea that learners 'get credit' for their educational attainments is a generally understood term within assessment regimes totally unrelated to any system of credit accumulation and transfer. Sometimes it is necessary to be clear about the specific use of the term 'credit' to describe an award made to a learner and its more general use to mean simply acknowledging achievement in some way.

One of the ways of de-coding which use of the term 'credit' is being deployed is what I call 'the plural test'. Basically, if you see the word 'credit' in a document and you add an 's' to make it 'credits', and the sentence remains meaningful, then you are talking 'real credits'. If by pluralising 'credit' you render the sentence meaningless (as in the case of the A level Code of Practice), then you have a more general use of the term 'credit' that should alert you to the possibility that maybe a different concept of credit is being deployed. The plural test is a good Occam's razor in reading what people write about credit systems.

As I have tried to show in previous chapters, building a credit system through the gradual extension of the award of credit to learners in a context where formal government policy ignores such a system, and invests significant resources in alternative approaches to recognising learner achievement, is a difficult and hard road to travel. This road is made even more difficult if the context within which credit systems are developed is local, voluntary and demand driven, while formal government policy extols national approaches through the extension of statutory regulation in support of centrally determined targets. In such a context there are pressures on those arguing for the development of credit systems to seek alternative ways of moving the credit agenda (plural test?) forward in ways that might be more acceptable to central government and therefore more likely to bring about the introduction of such a credit system. From 1994 onwards the credit movement accommodated these alternative perspectives on how best to take forward the development of credit systems. For the most part they co-existed, sometimes uneasily, and differences of opinion over strategy were obscured by success as OCNs expanded and the FEU/FEDA conferences, projects and publications on credit reached an ever-wider audience. But the plural test reveals two distinct strategies for taking forward 'credit' in the mid-to-late 1990s.

The process of building relationships between credit and qualifications through the negotiation of agreements between local OCNs and national awarding bodies was a difficult and time-consuming (and ultimately futile) exercise. Although both credits and qualifications represented structures within which learner achievements could be recognised and represented, it was clear from the attempts to forge links between these two different structures that a massive gulf in conceptual understanding of credit systems existed within awarding bodies. The same could not be said in reverse – from the outset OCNs had understood very clearly the characteristics of qualifications and had devised credit systems to overcome some of these characteristics. As the rationale for establishing MOCF, and the early proposals to link OCN developments with NVQs illustrate, there was no lack of awareness about the development of qualifications among those involved in credit systems. Indeed, throughout the 1990s, OCNs were constantly being asked to justify their existence and to account for the distinctions between credit systems and qualifications, as they attempted to expand the scope and scale of their offer to learners (Kerton, 1993).

It must also be said that, despite the civility with which the discussions between OCNs and BTEC or the RSA were conducted, the links between credit systems and qualifications were never perceived by awarding bodies as a relationship between equals. This can be explained in the most part by an understandable prejudice by national organisations against local ones. There are many areas of human endeavour where such prejudices do not exist or where a reverse prejudice exists – that is, one that favours the local over the national – but the recognition of learner achievement is not one of them. I use the term prejudice here because, taking the 1986 Review of Vocational Qualifications (MSC and DES, 1986) as the document that sets the tone for this enshrinement of the national, there is actually not one of its major recommendations that directly attacks local approaches to the recognition of achievement. However, the establishing of the NCVQ, and the gradual elevation of national approaches to the development of standards and qualifications, firmly secured this prejudice against the local during the 1990s.

The formula:

qualifications = national = good

versus:

credits = local = bad

was to have a profound influence on the ability of OCNs, even working within the framework of NOCN, to build relationships with qualifications-awarding bodies. This was true even before the advent of the NQF. After this the local approaches of OCNs were even further marginalised, bringing about the establishment of NOCN as a national awarding body. Perhaps OCNs may have been able to overcome some of these prejudices if they had not been so proud of their localness. A glance at the promotional literature of OCNs in this period is informative. The whole rationale for OCN credit systems is wrapped up in a series of characteristics that deliberately contrast their approach to those of national qualifications-awarding bodies. OCNs, say their own leaflets and bulletins, offer 'flexible' approaches to accreditation that are 'responsive' to local needs and 'easily accessible' to local organisations. They are able to 'tailor' programmes to suit particular needs and to 'customise' assessment arrangements in response to 'individual needs'. In fact, the striking thing about what OCNs were saying about their credit systems in the 1990s is how closely they anticipate the rationale for qualifications reform of the twenty-first century. However, all these different attributes of OCN credit systems were explicitly and confidently linked to localness as an incontestable virtue of these systems. Such was the growing confidence of OCNs through the 1990s that the deliberate representation of credit systems as being different from national qualifications became an integral part of their promotional strategy.

As we have noted, this opposition to the 'rigid', 'inflexible', 'distant' system of national qualifications had to change in response to the advent of the NQF. However, even before this, the approach of OCNs to building links with qualifications had begun to expose differences with the FEU (later FEDA) in its attempts to promote the benefits of credit systems. It was clear from these early attempts to build relationships with both BTEC and the RSA that this was not going to be a useful method for delivering an integrated system of credit and qualifications in the foreseeable future. In its promotion of credit systems as a potentially useful tool in reforming qualifications, the FEU were presented with a problem of how to play down the localness of OCN credit systems in their work with awarding bodies and other national organisations. As an organisation with a national remit (in England and Wales), the 'credits = local = bad' equation presented a distinct problem for the FEU in its advocacy of the benefits of a credit system.

The national dimension of the FEU's approach to promoting the benefits of a credit system focused on the potential role of credit in relation to qualifications. Indeed, the term 'national qualifications' appears throughout FEU and later FEDA publications during this period, further accentuating the distinctions with local systems of recognising achievement through credit. Notwithstanding this identification of 'the national' with qualifications, the FEU had no remit to reform qualifications, no constituency among awarding bodies and very little influence over NCVQ, SCAA or (later) QCA. National qualifications in this context were a given phenomenon that had to be addressed in taking forward credit, not an alternative system of recognising achievement that could be ignored while building local alternatives. From this anxiety about the role of credit in relation to qualifications emerged a subtly different argument for the development of a credit framework that began to be advanced by the FEU from 1994 onwards. These proposals are set out most clearly in an FEU document simply entitled *A Framework for Credit* (FEU, 1995).

In this alternative approach to those of OCNs, the FEU first acknowledged some of the technical difficulties or complexities that could arise through the introduction of credit systems. The creation of consistent and stable credit values could take some time. There were still many people who did not understand the implications of a credit system and others who were opposed to the introduction of such a system. Credits were controversial. Government was suspicious of the potential of credit systems to undermine national standards (shades of the NCVQ position). In summary, although some of the features of a national credit framework that were advanced in *ABC?* and subsequent documents were accepted as being useful contributors to the debate about reforming qualifications, others were not seen as so useful. In particular, the credits bits of a credit framework were controversial. If these more controversial aspects of the FEU proposals could be modified and brought closer to mainstream debates about qualifications reform, then perhaps there might be more chance of the FEU's proposals being listened to in the debates about the merits of a credit system.

In pursuit of this strategy, the FEU began to produce proposals to soften some of the perceived hard edges of credit systems as operated by OCNs in order to make them more acceptable to a wider audience. So, for example, the FEU suggested in *A Framework for Credit*: 'It is useful to distinguish between the ascribing of *size* to a unit (in terms of notional learning hours), and the ascribing of a *credit value.*'

The rationale for this separation was: 'It is possible for a group of institutions to agree about the size of a unit (for example, for timetabling purposes) without all of them agreeing to recognise its credit value.'

In other words, 'size' was a useful characteristic of units, but 'size expressed as a credit value' was unnecessarily controversial. The FEU then went on to propose that if the size of a unit *was* to be expressed in terms of its credit value, then 'the *context* and *purpose* for which the value is recognised should be stated'.

So, for example, one of these purposes (but not the only one) was that the credit value of a unit could be used as the basis for awarding credit to learners. There may be other purposes (for example, the comparison of the relative sizes of national qualifications) for which credit values might be established.

The FEU proposals in a *Framework for Credit* mark a distinct moment in the development of the credit movement during the 1990s. Two features of the FEU proposals are highlighted above. The effect of these was, firstly, to disconnect the concept of unit from the definition of credit value, and the second was to disconnect the establishing of credit values from the award of credit. From the first of these proposals arose the development of the concept of unitisation. From the second developed the concept of credit-rating, of which more in the next chapter. Thus, in seeking an accommodation between the proposals for a national credit framework and the persistent ignoring of these calls by government in the development of qualifications, the FEU proposed two 'modifications' to its initial proposals that, from the perspective of OCNs, struck two mortal blows to the core purpose of a credit framework – the award of credit to learners.

It is interesting that the origins of the term 'unitisation' have been lost. The term is seen as an integral and accepted part of the current landscape of qualifications, particularly vocational qualifications. In the development of the QCF, a distinction has been made between a unitised qualifications system and a unit-based qualifications system. (In some quarters the distinction has yet to be established – the QCF is still characterised as an exercise in unitisation.) In fact, although the term 'unit' had long been familiar, the concept of unitisation begins to be used around this time in a modified argument for qualifications reform that draws on the idea of a credit system, but tries to bypass the controversial (and local) term 'credit' in so doing. We might think in 2009 that 'unitisation' has been with us as long as units, but it has not. 'Unitisation' very explicitly seeks to present to a national audience the proposition that flexibility can be introduced into the qualifications system without necessarily importing credit into that system. The term was coined by the FEU in the mid-1990s, precisely to distinguish its proposals from those of the NOCN. The fact that the concept was first formally advanced in a document called *A Framework for Credit* may be seen in retrospect as unfortunate, ironic or disingenuous.

To be fair to the FEU, it was not the intention behind the proposals in *A Framework for Credit* to attack the core of the OCN model of a credit system. What was intended was to present a more subtle form of tactics for the development of a national credit framework, rather than to undermine the concept of the framework itself. This tactic, and it can be detected clearly in the proposed redefinitions quoted above (the FEU refers to them as a 'tidying up of terminology'), was to dismantle the integrated set of definitions set out in *ABC?* and present instead a *sequential* approach to the development of a credit framework that took account of the political realities of the mid-1990s, and in particular the misgivings about local credit systems as a feature of a proposal for national reform. So the first step in this process was to disconnect the specification of a unit from the definition of credit and substitute instead the concept of 'size' as a feature of the unit, this size to be expressed in terms of 'notional learning time'.

Once the awkward concept of credit value was removed from the unit specification, the benefits of unitisation could then be presented to a wider and more accepting audience. To the benefits of unitisation could be added – if people wished – credit values and, again if people wished, these credit values may, or may not, lead to the award of credit to learners ('by those pesky local OCNs', one can almost detect as a footnote). This then was the FEU's sequential strategy. First sell the benefits of units with a size expressed in notional learning time. Then, once all qualifications are unitised in this way, sell the benefits of converting the notional learning times into credit values. Now you have a simple metric through which to compare achievements on individual qualifications. Then, if necessary (that is, if the unit is not already certificated as part of a national qualification), credit could be awarded for the successful completion of the unit. All units would have credit values, but only those outside national qualifications would lead to the award of credit, a distinction that cements the separation of local credit systems from national qualifications. A pragmatic strategy, claimed the FEU, but one that would deliver results in relation to national qualifications far more quickly than the continuing extension of OCN accreditation.

In this 1995 publication (which I suggest fails the plural test in its use of the term 'credit') the concept of both size and credit value appear in the unit specification. However, it did not take long for the credit value specification to begin to disappear. By 1996 it seemed that unitisation had managed to detach itself from its origins quite successfully. In his essay on unitisation (Stanton, 1997), Geoff Stanton (who had recently left the FEU in its transition to FEDA) defines 'unitization' as 'the analysis of existing qualifications into units of achievement' and proposes a set of characteristics for these units, including 'a unique title, learning outcome statements, assessment criteria, level and size'. Notice anything missing? Along with the omission of 'credit value' though, the concept of units as 'the building blocks' of qualifications, a concept central to the QCF, is also missing. Instead of building up units into qualifications, qualifications are now 'analysed into' units – in other words, the qualification, rather than the unit, is restored to the centre of the known universe. Note also the kind of qualifications that would be analysed into units – existing qualifications. So, no need for any changes at all, just take your existing qualification and analyse them into units. No wonder unitisation became such an acceptable idea.

Confirmation that the process of unitisation need have no impact at all on qualifications design was confirmed in *A Framework for Credit*: 'in the interests of the learners as well as government policy, existing units embodying standards recognised nationally by the NCVQ and SCAA should be used as they stand'.

In other words, even the watered down, credit-less unit specification advanced in *A Framework for Credit* need not be used where units already existed. It was sufficient that a qualification be analysed into units to meet the requirements of unitisation. Despite the initial attempts by the FEU (reflected in Geoff Stanton's paper) to define 'unitisation' in relation to a particular unit format, once the concept of a unit became separated from the specification of credit value that tied it into the proposal for a credit framework, it became impossible to defend the particular specifications of a unit first set out in *ABC?* and (fatally, as it transpired) modified in *A Framework for Credit*. Once it was posited that where a qualification was already unitised then the unit specification (even without credit value) need not be applied, unitisation became a process devoid of real meaning and slipped easily into the linguistic discourse of the existing qualifications system without having the slightest impact on the format of qualifications.

Thus the sequential strategy advanced by the FEU for the introduction of a credit framework actually fell at the very first hurdle. The concept of unitisation not only removed 'credit' from the unit specification proposed in *ABC?*, it also quite quickly lost all its other defining characteristics as well. As 'existing units embodying standards nationally recognised by the NCVQ and SCAA' included units without any size indicator, without a level, without in some instances learning outcomes and in many instances without assessment criteria, the idea that consistency and stability in the award of credit was critically dependent on a standard unit format (a proposition in 1995 being powerfully proven to be true by the rapidly improving consistency and comparability of OCN credits based on the *ABC?* specification) was effectively dismissed by this tidying-up of the new language of unitisation.

In retrospect, *A Framework for Credit* represents the outcome of a continuing struggle within FEU to take forward and preserve the integrity of the proposals in *ABC?*. The change of organisation from FEU to FEDA, and the change of leadership of the organisation, led to a review of its work on credit and a distancing from some of its previous positions. The influence of FEU's officers in Wales is also in evidence in the paper. Despite the attempts by Tony Tait and others to maintain the clarity and simplicity of the proposals first advanced in *ABC?* and in *Beyond ABC?*, the publication of *A Framework for Credit* represents a compromise within FEU between these different ideas of how credits should relate to qualifications. Its influence on practice (in England at any rate) was minimal. Its influence on policy was less.

The final word on unitisation rests with the QCA and the definition of 'unit' that was established in the initial iteration of the NQF. A more prosaic definition than that put forward by the FEU or FEDA, it nevertheless re-locates the qualification at centre stage and in so doing consigns the notion of unitisation as a process of positive change to the outer darkness. The definition of a unit used in the NQF remains to this day: 'the smallest part of a qualification that is capable of certification in its own right' (QCA et al., 2004, p. 50).

Note that this definition allows for the parts of qualifications to be specified in any way that an awarding body chooses. In the event, apart from NOCN, no NQF awarding body chose to adopt the *ABC?* unit specifications (with or without credit value) and, indeed, some awarding bodies chose to use a number of different specifications for different kinds of qualification. The resulting 'jungle of units' contributed as much as any other design feature to the problems of the NQF, and the adoption of the original FEU unit specification within the QCF marks a restoration of the unit format to its original home in a credit system and (incidentally) marks the end of unitisation as a phenomenon.

The QCF may drive a stake through the heart of unitisation, but its real death is captured in the NQF definition of a unit. Indeed, although it marks the victory of the status quo, my hat is doffed to the QCA officer who, by accident or design, defined a unit in this way and in so doing firmly slammed the lid on the idea of unitisation as a process of change. To appreciate the simple beauty of the definition, one needs to subject it to an Aristotelian syllogism:

- if a unit is the smallest part of a qualification that is capable of certification and
- if all qualifications lead to a certificate
- then all qualifications have a smallest certificatable part
- therefore all qualifications are unitised.

The implication of the definition is perhaps best illustrated by the characterisation of GCSEs by the QCA as 'single unit qualifications'. The process that the FEU suggested would be a long and difficult one, completed at the stroke of a bureaucrat's pen. Unitisation, RIP.

24

'Credit' without credits:
The seduction of credit-rating

A Framework for Credit was one of the last FEU publications. Soon after it appeared, in April 1995, the FEU became the Further Education Development Agency (FEDA) and the subsequent *Framework Guidelines* (FEU, 1995a; FEDA, 1995) appeared under both the FEU and FEDA banners. The transition from the FEU to FEDA signals the end of the 'high point' of support for the development of a credit framework.[1] By the end of 1995, FEDA's new work plan was published and, although support for credit-related developments continued to form part of FEDA's work, the active promotion of local credit consortia and the high-profile advocacy of credit systems that the FEU had originated were gradually reduced to the publication of occasional leaflets and reports. In England, *A Framework for Credit* and its follow-up guidelines attested to the continuing wider support for development of a credit system but had a minimal influence on practice.

In its influence on OCN credit systems, the contrast between *ABC?* and the subsequent technical documents published by the FEU in 1993, with *A Framework for Credit*, and its subsequent documents in 1995–6 is worthy of note. As I have tried to show in Chapter 15, the FEU's 1993 *Technical Specifications for a national credit framework* (Wilson, 1993b) sparked off a major debate within OCNs and effectively triggered the changes within OCN credit systems that led to the NOCN's adoption of the National Credit Framework specifications in 1994. The 1995 and 1996 FEU/FEDA publications led to no such debate and brought about no changes to the credit system adopted by NOCN. It may be slightly arch to claim that in fact from 1994 onwards the NOCN credit system was the true reflection of the power behind the proposals in *ABC?*, while *A Framework for Credit* represents a gradual squandering of the clarity of purpose in the initial vision by the FEU and its successor organisation. Certainly, the maintenance of the initial credit framework specifications based on *ABC?*, and the ignoring of the 'modifications' put forward in *A Framework for Credit*, led to the huge expansion of OCN credit systems in the latter half of the 1990s. From 1994 onwards no FEU or FEDA publication had a significant impact on practice within credit systems in England, though this is not to deny the continuing importance of FEDA in putting forward arguments to policymakers in favour of a credit system.

There is no doubt, however, that the support of the FEU for credit systems had given a significant boost to OCNs and to NOCN's own national credit framework. It had helped to complete the coverage of OCNs across England, Wales and Northern Ireland, and had significantly enhanced both awareness of and the status of OCN credit systems. By the time that the transition from the FEU to FEDA was complete, these gains had been firmly secured and consolidated. From 1996 onwards the leadership of the credit movement in England lay clearly with NOCN, and the rapid expansion of OCN credit systems over the remainder of the twentieth century was the clearest manifestation of the continued growth of this credit movement.

A Framework for Credit and its subsequent *Framework Guidelines* also bequeathed to the credit movement an alternative concept of credit. In the previous chapter, I identified the source of this alternative definition, and traced the rise of the concept of unitisation that arose during this period. *A Framework for Credit* also exposed one of the issues that had continued to divide the FEU and OCN views of credit systems – an issue that had actually been present from the publication of *ABC?* onwards, but which really came to a head within *A Framework for Credit*. This was the issue of credit-rating. In *A Framework for Credit*, the FEU proposed that the ascribing of credit value to a unit need not necessarily lead to the award of credit. In other words, credit value could be ascribed to a unit for other reasons. *A Framework for Credit* refers, for example, to the use of credit values to 'equate qualifications intended to be similar'.

These alternative uses of the terms 'credit' and 'credit value' caused much anxiety within OCNs. Once the concept of credit value became detached from the process leading to the award of credit to a learner, the currency value of credits themselves was threatened. For OCNs the determination of unit credit values was a means to an end – the award of credit. *A Framework for Credit* implied that the ascribing of credit value to units could be an end in itself. This dilution of the concept of credit, coupled with the acceptance that units could be defined in many different ways (the inevitable consequence of unitisation), led to the proposition that credit could be used to establish a numerical value for existing qualifications and that the establishing of credit values through a standard unit format, and the award of credits to learners, were not essential features of a credit system. This alternative view of a credit system became known over time as 'credit-rating'.

Like unitisation, credit-rating was attractive to people and organisations that saw credit essentially as a descriptive tool rather than as a way of transforming the way in which learner achievements were recognised. We should not be surprised that a development agency like the FEU/FEDA adopted a view of a credit system within which it had a role to play, while awarding bodies such as OCNs opposed so vociferously a conceptualisation of credit that was not an award made to a learner. It should also be remembered that it was an OCN (South Yorkshire) that actually undertook the first credit-rating project in the UK in 1989–90. The lessons of this project (that is, that credit-rating was a literally pointless exercise) were not lost on OCNs. The FEU/ULEAC project in 1992 confirmed these lessons. Nevertheless, by 1996, this alternative view of credit had become clearly established within FEDA, to the extent that FEDA's first independent publication on credit actually makes only passing reference to the award of credit to learners, focusing instead on the use of credit as 'a way of comparing achievement across qualifications'. *FEDA's 2020 Vision* (FEDA, 1996) marks clearly the shift away from the OCN model of credit towards this alternative system of credit rating.

Within *FEDA's 2020 Vision* a rather strange world is envisaged. It is a world in which familiar qualifications exist side-by-side with credits. To quote one example:

> Jo has achieved one A level worth 18 credits at Level 3, one GCSE (5 credits at Level 2) and a unit in secretarial skills (5 credits at Level 1). Anyone interested in Jo's achievements can understand and compare them with the achievements of others.
>
> (FEDA, 1996, p. 5)

Note how credit is no longer used to recognise Jo's achievements (her qualifications and units do that), but to 'understand and compare them' with other achievements. Whether the attachment of numbers to existing qualifications actually *does* help to compare Jo's achievements with others is a moot point. Even if true, this is hardly a visionary view of the purpose of credit systems in comparison with the radical messages in *ABC?*.

The credit framework proposed in *FEDA's 2020 Vision* deploys this approach to credit-rating alongside 'unitising existing qualifications'. It goes on to note that 'many qualifications, for example, NVQs and GNVQs are already expressed in units' [original punctuation] (FEDA, 1996, p. 6).

So not only has the concept of credit value become detached from the award of credit, it has also become detached from the unit. Credit values can be attached to either units or qualifications and unitisation need not be directly connected to credit-rating. The benefits of such an approach are described as follows: 'This vision need not alter the value or characteristics of existing qualifications' (FEDA, 1996, p. 4).

Indeed, this is the crux of the argument for credit-rating. It is a process that borrows key terminology from real credit systems and in so doing breaks the critical connection with credit as an award made to a learner. Once defused in this way, the process can then be presented as a useful way of understanding and comparing existing qualifications by attaching a so-called credit value to these qualifications. The concept of attaching credit value belies the superficial nature of the process. 'Credit as an afterthought' is hardly an approach that is going to challenge existing systems, and of course this is its purpose. *FEDA's 2020 Vision* effectively envisages a world in 2020 where GNVQs still exist (not great vision there I think), but where every qualification has a number attached through a process of credit-rating. All completely painless and, as FEDA points out, an approach that 'need not alter' anything (FEDA, 1996, p. 4). Again, not quite the vision promised in *ABC?*.

It is possible that FEDA's credit-rating proposals would simply have faded away in time. No strategy was proposed to implement them and no agency was charged with taking them forward. Awarding bodies saw no reason to adopt FEDA's proposals and the shift of focus away from awarding credits to learners and towards comparing the values of existing qualifications effectively marginalised FEDA's core audience – FE colleges – from the credit-rating process (FEDA assumed that this was a process that would be undertaken by awarding bodies, perhaps with the advice of a development agency), at precisely the time that FE colleges were rapidly expanding their involvement in OCN credit systems. It would be wrong to characterise *FEDA's 2020 Vision* as abandoning all support for a more radical view of the transformative power of credit systems, and certainly the concept of a credit movement that included both FEDA and OCNs held together throughout the 1990s. The diversion of credit-rating might simply have been swept away in the tide of expansion of OCNs during the late 1990s had it not been taken up so enthusiastically in Wales. It is at this juncture that this story turns to the development of credit in this part of the UK, inviting readers to apply the plural test to the use of this term at appropriate intervals.

Note

1 One of the speculations at the time was that the publication of *ABC?* was one of the main reasons why the FEU became FEDA, and why Geoff Stanton did not become FEDA's first director. No evidence exists to suggest this was true, but Colin Flint, late of the FE Campaign Group, pondered the possibility publicly at the time.

25

The development of credit in Wales

As we have seen, the official attitude towards credit systems in the early 1990s veered between hostility and indifference. The popular support for a credit framework that developed through the early 1990s acted as a counterbalance to this 'official' view, but it failed to have an impact on government policy. In England in particular, and outside the very different policy climate of HE, the idea that credit systems might undermine the development of competence-based qualifications appears to underpin policymaking (or the lack of it) in relation to credit systems for the Conservative governments of the early and mid-1990s.

This view did not necessarily extend to other parts of the UK. Indeed, during this same period, Scotland, Wales and Northern Ireland all put in place various initiatives relating to credit systems either with the support of, or at least without opposition from, the responsible departments of government. Both NICATS (Department of Education Northern Ireland, 1999) and the SCQF (SCQF, 2002) are referred to later in this publication.

By 1992 there were three credit-awarding bodies operating in Wales. Although initially none of these organisations used the term 'OCN', they evolved into the three Welsh OCNs in due course. The first network had been established in South West Wales in 1990 with support from the UDACE OCN project. The North Wales OCN was set up in 1991, followed by the South East Wales OCN, the largest of the three, in 1992. Like their English counterparts, the Welsh OCNs expanded considerably following the incorporation of Welsh FE colleges and the establishing of funding arrangements through the new Welsh FE Funding Council (ELWa), which recognised OCN accreditation as a fundable learning achievement. Once established, it seemed likely that the Welsh OCNs would simply develop along the same lines as their English counterparts and that there would be no separate history of credit developments in Wales worth recording in this story. In fact, things turned out rather differently, and once again it is necessary to begin an account of this other history by taking a few steps backwards in time.

In the early 1990s a major project was undertaken in Gwent to modularise the curriculum offered through the recently established Gwent College. Formed from the merger of five previous colleges, Gwent Tertiary College was the largest in Wales, enrolling around 20 per cent of learners in the Principality. The Gwent Modularisation Project was funded by Gwent TEC, and consisted mainly of a series of curriculum development groups in different vocational areas, each one charged with modularising the curriculum in that area. After an initial evaluation of the work of the project, it was decided that, despite its title, the project was in fact involved in a process of unit development. In other words it was seeking to restructure the assessments offered to learners, rather than the organisation of programme delivery in the college. The Modularisation Project, building on the proposals that emerged from the FEU during the lifetime of the project, consciously adopted the FEU's proposed unit specification as the basis for its later development activity (FEU, 1993). It should be remembered that, prior to the establishing of the NQF, the development of assessment was seen as much the business of a college as it was of an awarding body – especially for vocational learners, who were very much the focus of Gwent TEC's funding priorities. Although the newly established local OCN was involved in the project and was represented on its Steering Group, the process of unit development took place outside the scope of OCN accreditation. Large numbers of units were produced based on (some of them rather loosely) the FEU specification, but the purpose of developing units was centred clearly on the internal offer of assessment within Gwent College rather than on the award of credit from the local OCN. Although the Gwent Modularisation Project had very little impact on the structure and assessment of qualifications in Gwent, it did produce a significant bank of units, some of them with credit values. It also led to demands from the people involved in the process of unit writing that – not unreasonably – their work should be reflected in the qualifications offered to learners in Gwent. The recognition of learner achievement, it seemed, was the missing ingredient in the project.

The experiences of the Gwent project, taken together with the FEU's emerging interest in unitisation and credit-rating, led to the next phase of development in Wales: the Welsh Credit and Modularisation project, which began life in 1993. Even prior to devolution, the Education Department of the Welsh Office was prepared to put resources into a project based on credit, even though its UK counterpart was unwilling to support any similar developments in England. The Welsh Credit and Modularisation project had the resources to employ staff, engage practitioners in its activities and promote the idea of a credit framework for Wales. There was no parallel initiative in England, and consequently no resources to support any similar activity. The idea of a credit framework in England, though promoted through the FEU/FEDA publications and advocated by many other individuals and organisations, was carried forward primarily by the expansion of OCNs and the spread of credit-based provision through the expanding FE system.

In Wales, the Credit and Modularisation project not only had a project director and a support team, it also drew on the resources of the FEU/FEDA's Welsh office. In effect the project became a test bed for the FEU concept of a credit framework set out in *A Framework for Credit*. Indeed, the influence of the Welsh Credit and Modularisation project is clear within *FEDA's 2020 Vision*, which draws heavily on the experience of work in Wales and makes several explicit references to the 'national credit scheme' already operating in Wales. It is during this period, prior to the establishing of the NQF, when the idea of a Welsh Credit Framework first emerges as a potential model that could be extended to England. The idea that, in relation to developments in Wales, England was lagging behind in the development of credit becomes rooted during the first three years of the Welsh Credit and Modularisation project. From 1997 onwards we can detect a conscious representation of credit (plural test) developments in Wales as a model simply awaiting extension to more backward parts of the UK, once the advances of Welsh pioneers are recognised by recalcitrant bureaucrats in Whitehall. Some vestiges of this perceived advanced state of credit developments in Wales in comparison with England can still be detected in 2009, and have certainly been voiced at various stages in the earlier development of the QCF.

In fact, the Welsh Credit and Modularisation project was based primarily on the twin diversions of unitisation and credit-rating. Resources were channelled not into the development of credit as a currency of learner achievement, but into the establishing of a 'unit library' (drawing from the Gwent experience) and into the development of an infrastructure for establishing 'numerical values' (FEDA, 1996) for units and qualifications, in order that they can be compared with each other. By 2001 the unit library had become known as the CREDIS databank and soon the project itself became transformed into the CREDIS project. This combination of unitisation and credit-rating of qualifications soon became the distinctive hallmarks of CREDIS.

The infrastructure of the CREDIS project and its close connections with FEDA Wales were established separately from the three OCNs in Wales. There was no direct funding through the project for the development of the OCNs' infrastructure, nor was there a clear drive from CREDIS to promote the award of credit to learners (rather than the credit-rating of units and qualifications) as the purpose of the credit framework in Wales. Nevertheless, there is no doubt that the Welsh OCNs benefited from the CREDIS project. Not only did CREDIS stimulate the development of units for the databank, it also promoted the general idea of credit as a positive benefit to learners in Wales. Although CREDIS continued to ascribe what it called 'credit values' to units and qualifications through its credit-rating activities, no credits were ever awarded for these qualifications and no qualification-awarding body ever adopted the FEU credit system proposed in *ABC?*. If the activities of CREDIS were to be translated into the award of credit to learners in Wales, there was only one form of recognition available – the award of credit by a Welsh OCN.

In effect, the CREDIS project nurtured both these visions of a credit framework during this period. While formally promoting the FEDA model of unitisation plus credit-rating of existing qualifications, it also stimulated a great deal of practitioner-based interest in credit and channelled significant energies into the process of unit development. Where units were developed for the CREDIS databank that conformed to the FEU specifications, with a credit value determined through the unit development process, these units could form part of an OCN-accredited programme, and many of them did so. Indeed, the development of the CREDIS databank and the experiences of OCNs in Wales in taking units from the databank and locating them within accredited programmes marked a subtle but significant shift in OCN practice, that spread slowly from Wales across the whole of the NOCN network during the late 1990s.

It should be recalled that, although some OCNs had used a standard unit format in the early 1990s, it was not until 1994 that all OCNs agreed to adopt the FEU unit format proposed in *ABC?*, and it was not until 1997 that OCNs were established in every part of England, Wales and Northern Ireland (a period that matches closely the initial three years of the CREDIS project). As OCNs were dependent on their own local resources for development, the process of unit development within OCNs took place as an integral part of the overall process of recognition. It should also be recalled that the accreditation model of OCNs focused on locally developed programmes, rather than on nationally developed qualifications. Even where initiatives such as the Derbyshire Regional Network or the Leicestershire Progression Accord stimulated the development of new units, these were developed from the outset through the programme accreditation arrangements of OCNs. The adoption of the unit format by OCNs had secured an important step forward in detaching the process of assessment based on units leading to the award of credit from the delivery of a modular curriculum. However, during this period, units were still developed for OCN accreditation within the context of a programme rather than a qualification.

If one looks at the process through which OCNs established credit values for units during this period, the connections to programme delivery are clearly apparent. How much was known about how a programme was delivered and how learners were taught were explicit questions asked of unit developers through OCN development and recognition processes throughout this period. The process of slowly detaching the concept of credit from its roots in the curriculum and locating it firmly in the arena of learner achievement was still proceeding as OCNs expanded. The idea of a national qualifications framework was still in the future and the expansion of OCNs from 1994 to 1997 was intimately tied up with the expansion of the FE system (in both England and

Wales) – and in particular the expansion of learning opportunities in adult and community education – that still constituted the primary reference point for OCNs in the development of their credit systems.

The CREDIS project began to change the relationship between units and OCN credit systems. For the first time units began to be developed that met the specifications of the NOCN National Credit Framework, but had not been developed through a process established and controlled by the OCN itself. For the very first time, units were presented to OCNs for accreditation outside the known structure of a learning programme, and stripped of information from a particular provider about how they were delivered in an institution. The Welsh OCNs needed to respond to this growing demand, stimulated by the CREDIS project. In doing so, as members of NOCN, they engaged other OCNs in addressing this issue and so the first unit recognition panels were established – led by Welsh OCNs, but involving other OCNs from the outset.

Thus, by establishing an infrastructure for the development of a credit framework – perhaps more properly referred to as 'a framework of units' – different from that operated by OCNs, the CREDIS project set in train a process that gradually led to a change in the accreditation practices of OCNs. The influence of CREDIS through the Welsh OCNs stimulated NOCN to establish effective procedures that underwrote unit credit values and enabled these credit values to be established with confidence outside the structure of an accredited programme. Stripped of information about programme delivery, OCNs were forced to focus attention on the information contained in the unit itself to establish its level and credit value. In so doing, OCN credit systems were further refined and the establishment of credit as a currency of achievement moved a step closer. In this respect we can identify a positive impact of the CREDIS project on the future development of the QCF, but it was an influence that was mediated through OCNs, not a direct outcome of the project itself.

Although initially the concept of unit recognition caused anxieties among OCN practitioners, it soon led to a noticeable improvement in unit quality as OCN development officers and recognition panels demanded clearer learning outcomes, more measurable assessment criteria and more meaningful unit titles. Gradually the initial concern among OCNs, that detaching the process of unit development from the learning programmes through which units were to be delivered would lead to eccentric or unstable credit values, became dissipated through the improvement of unit quality and the focusing of OCN quality systems on guidance and support for unit writers. It is from this period that the first unit writing guides begin to appear among OCNs, and the sharing of good practice through NOCN soon led to unit development models that are clearly reflected in the QCF today. Not for the first time, the unanticipated consequences of the development of an alternative view of credit in Wales brought benefits to the continued refinement of the OCN credit systems that led into the development of the QCF.

Another outcome of the CREDIS project that had a longer-term impact on the development of OCNs was the establishing of the CREDIS unit databank itself. It should be remembered that the databank was established prior to the availability of web-based methods of sharing data. In effect, the CREDIS databank was an occasionally updated CD of units, circulated (at considerable cost – the first edition of the unit databank was priced at £300 per CD) among FE colleges and other key providers in Wales. The target audience for the databank was still, prior to the creation of the NQF, not awarding bodies but providers. The CREDIS unit databank also included a mixture of different types of unit. Following the logic of FEDA's position that 'some qualifications like NVQs and GNVQs are already unitised' (FEDA, 2006), units from these qualifications appeared in the CREDIS databank, even though they did not conform to the unit specifications still being promoted in *FEDA's 2020 Vision* and in the literature of the CREDIS project itself. Some units had credit ratings attached (for example, CREDIS agreed a standard credit-rating of three – in old money – for all Advanced GNVQ units), while some NVQ units were credit-rated through CREDIS panels and entered into the databank. Where units were developed to the agreed unit specifications, some of them led to the award of credit and others, in keeping with the view of credit value in *A Framework for Credit*, did not.

Though widely circulated, the CREDIS unit databank had no impact on the qualifications system (learners in Wales were not awarded credit through their NVQs or GNVQs). However, it did have an impact on the thinking of OCNs – again led by Welsh OCNs. In a system where individual units could be recognised separately from learning programmes, these units could be shared across different learning programmes, thereby extending the availability of these units to learners and creating efficiencies in the process of unit development. Perhaps unsurprisingly it was from the North Wales OCN – that is, the network that operated across one of the most geographically dispersed populations in England and Wales – that the idea of a national unit library, held by NOCN and available to all OCNs, was first mooted. The three Welsh OCNs, together with the OCNs in Greater Manchester and North and West Yorkshire, came together to establish this first unit library and – unlike its CREDIS predecessor – it was made freely available to anyone that wished to use it.

Although it took some years for the technology to catch up with the idea, NOCN's web-based unit databank, and indeed the dispersed unit databanks of all OCNs, took their inspiration (if not their technology or their purpose) from this first OCN electronic unit library. The unit databank that supports the QCF has its origins in this period of development. Indeed, at the time of writing, the unit databank available through the website of OCN Wales[1] is still far more accessible, far easier to search and more extensive in scope than the (so-called) QCF unit databank.

It is worth noting another shift that took place in the shift from a CD-based CREDIS databank to a web-based OCN unit library. As the CREDIS project did not award credits, it sought to protect its databank asset through control of access to its CDs. The disks were not able to be copied and so providers, primarily FE colleges, had to pay a hefty price for access to the information on the CREDIS CD. In contrast, the OCN unit library was made freely accessible to users and the control exercised by OCNs was not over access to the information in the library, but over the processes of assessment and certification leading to the award of credit. Control of quality rather than control of access to information led to the development of a very different and a very much more widely used OCN unit library than was ever the case with the CREDIS databank. There was no suggestion that credit-rated NVQ and GNVQ units in the CREDIS databank would be offered outside these qualifications and, as these units did not conform to national credit framework specifications, they were of no interest to OCNs.

The OCN unit library also supported the development of unit-sharing processes across OCNs. Although unit sharing had been seen for some time within NOCN as an important mechanism for sharing good practice and improving unit quality, the development of a web-based unit library supported this process much more easily than previous paper-based systems. The development of an openly accessible unit library also illustrated to OCNs the importance of freely sharing units without recourse to protection through intellectual property rights (IPR). Long before the Institute of Public Policy Research recognised the impossibility of protecting IPR in digital format (Withers, 2006), OCN unit developers gave up any claims to IPR over units in the interests of establishing cost-effective and rational systems for developing units across a national credit system. The CREDIS experience of the Welsh OCNs again led to an unexpected benefit to all OCNs as their expansion continued through the late 1990s.

Soon NOCN itself was leading the development of mutual recognition of selected national programmes across all OCNs, based on shared units. This enabled NOCN to begin to promote its services to national organisations, and the development of national programmes with organisations such as the Trades Union Congress, The Workers Educational Association and BBC Education began to establish a national presence for NOCN that laid the ground for its later development as an awarding body. The detachment of the process of unit recognition from the accreditation of local learning programmes and the sharing of units across OCNs were the necessary technical developments within OCNs that permitted this forward shift in credit systems. Though separate from the development of the idea of a Welsh Credit Framework now advanced through the CREDIS project and the OCN unit library, the influence of developments in Wales on the practice of OCN credit systems can be seen in retrospect as accidentally positive. Notwithstanding these long-term spin-offs, the formal development of a Welsh Credit Framework as something separate from the NOCN framework, within which the Welsh OCNs (and later OCN Wales) operated, continued to be based on credit-rating and unitisation well into the twenty-first century.

The CREDIS project was extended beyond its initial three-year life and witnessed both the proposal to establish a national qualifications framework and, a little later, the creation of the Welsh Assembly Government. This combination of the creation of the NQF plus devolution led to a shift in perspective in Wales and to the creation of the CQFW Project. This project built explicitly on the CREDIS model, but sought to accommodate the CREDIS approach within the realities of the NQF. The CQFW Project also built quite explicitly on the importance of keeping Welsh developments ahead of those in England. There was still a view at the turn of the century, perhaps held more forcefully in the newly created devolved administration, that Wales was showing the way for England in the development of a credit framework, and this was undoubtedly a spur to the continuing separate development of credit through the new project. The continuing influence of the CQFW on the QCF is taken up later in this story.

Before leaving events in Wales, it is important to emphasise that the development of the Wales Credit and Modularisation Project, through CREDIS and the CQFW Project to the CQFW itself, constitute only part of the story of credit in Wales. There is another and often overlooked part of the story, and that is about the development of the Welsh OCNs and the influence of these three OCNs on the overall development of OCN credit systems. Thus the concept of credit in Wales is not simply about the CQFW and its predecessor initiatives. Indeed, when the occasion has arisen (for example, when producing reports to ministers or publishing statistics about the growth of credit in Wales), it has suited these initiatives to include within their reports figures relating to the numbers of learners being awarded credit in Wales. Notwithstanding the focus of the CQFW and its predecessors on unitisation and credit-rating based on the FEDA model, the only credits awarded in Wales (outside HE) until well into the twenty-first century were those awarded by Welsh OCNs. It is true that the significant resources pumped into the Welsh post-16 sector through the CREDIS project had a beneficial effect on the growth of the three Welsh OCNs from 1994 to 1997. However, it is also true that, for example, the three neighbouring OCNs in Central England, Leicestershire and the North East Midlands actually grew at a faster rate than their Welsh counterparts during this same period, without one penny of public funding to stimulate their development.

Nevertheless, as we have tried to show, the indirect impact of events in Wales, mediated through the involvement of Welsh OCNs on the development and refinement of NOCN's credit system during this period, helped NOCN itself to prepare the ground to become an awarding body. Just as the advent of the NQF brought a shift in perspective in Wales, so it also produced a shift within the wider development of OCN credit systems. It is in this context of the continuing development of OCN credit systems in response to the advent of the NQF that we return to events outside Wales.

Note

1 In 2009 OCN Wales became a separate organisation from NOCN and re-named itself Agored Cymru. www.agored.org.uk.

26

Good in theory: The NICATS initiative

As we note above, the ambivalence of ministers and civil servants in England towards the demand for a national credit framework did not extend to other areas of the UK. In 1996, following the lead taken previously by its Welsh counterpart, the Department of Education Northern Ireland (DENI) launched a three-year project designed to establish the Northern Ireland Credit Accumulation and Transfer System (NICATS). The project itself led on to the NICATS Implementation Programme, which lasted for a further three years until 2002 before formal responsibility for NICATS passed to the Council for Curriculum, Examinations and Assessment (CCEA) as the qualifications regulator for Northern Ireland.

Like both the CQFW and the SCQF, NICATS was conceived from the outset as a system that would operate across all educational sectors in Northern Ireland, including schools, FE and HE. Like CQFW and SCQF, it was also established as an 'enabling' system, designed to facilitate cross-institutional collaboration in developing credit systems, rather than as a regulated or statutory initiative. It should be emphasised that NICATS had a very clear commitment from all three universities, from all 17 FE colleges and from the CCEA itself to its objectives. In the context of Northern Ireland in the mid-1990s (NICATS was established prior to the NQF it should be noted), such an approach was both logical and uncontested. Progress on developing NICATS would be made through collaborative activity between partners and a 'bottom-up' approach to development (Department of Education Northern Ireland, 1999, p. 37), rather than through an imposed requirement of government.

What is interesting about NICATS and sets it apart in some way from both SCQF and (even more so) from CQFW was its explicit reference to itself as a CAT system rather than a framework. This was important in two respects. Firstly, it imbued the NICATS project (at least in its initial phase) with a more dynamic set of objectives than those developed in Wales. NICATS was seen very clearly as an instrument through which benefits could be delivered to learners in Northern Ireland. There was no suggestion that being part of NICATS was sufficient in itself – a more difficult case to establish for a system than a framework I suggest. The CAT system aimed 'to maximise opportunities for participation and achievement in education and training in Northern

Ireland' (NICATS, 1999, p. 4) and the rationale for the project is clearly rooted in concerns to improve Northern Ireland's historically poor performance in these areas in comparison with other UK jurisdictions, as well as to target the 'educationally disadvantaged' in the province.

This focus on a credit system rather than a credit framework also led NICATS to adopt without equivocation the OCN definition of credit as an award made to a learner, and this too set it apart from developments in Wales. Having said this, other aspects of the NICATS project did draw more closely on the Welsh experience, as well as on the work of the FEU and FEDA already considered in this publication. The objective of establishing a single CAT system across all educational sectors, including HE, also necessitated the adoption of design features that allowed for the different operations of credit systems in FE and HE. So, for example, NICATS makes a distinction between 'general' and 'specific' credit within its design features. These terms are drawn directly from HE experience and have little relevance to the use of credit in FE (the terms have never been used by OCNs, for example). Nevertheless, they were adopted as design features for a single CAT system in Northern Ireland.

Notwithstanding its name, the NICATS project drew inspiration explicitly from other credit framework initiatives, and in its final report this language of credit frameworks is woven into the outcomes of the project, even where examples of the application of credit seem to be potentially inconsistent with the definition of credit adopted by NICATS. So, for example, NICATS is seen as a potential 'tool for clarifying the relationship between qualifications' (Department of Education Northern Ireland, 1999, p. 26) and quotes directly from FEDA's *2020 Vision* publication in support of this application of NICATS, even though it is clear that there is no suggestion that 'a system of credit accumulation and transfer' should operate across these compared qualifications.

In fact, NICATS represents a halfway house in its proposals for Northern Ireland, actively promoting the award of credit and the development of CAT systems as tools to bring benefits to learners in the province, while at the same time drawing on some of the FEDA proposals that informed the development of credit-rating arrangements in Wales, and the use of 'credit' as a metric for comparing qualifications rather than as a tool for recognising learner achievement. Its commitment to include HE within its CAT system also placed constraints on NICATS' ability to implement some of its more radical proposals, as it made no recommendations as to how its proposals might be implemented. In the event, the NICATS Implementation Project continued both the work begun by the NICATS Project itself and the approach to collaborative development based on practitioner actions that had produced some of the more concrete outcomes of the NICATS Project.

One of these outcomes, which had lasting consequences both within and outside Northern Ireland, was the development of the NICATS Level Descriptors.

This was a major strand of work within the project, straddling as it did both the OCN and FEDA concepts of credit and engaging both FE and HE (and, indeed, representatives of the school system) in this particular development. The NICATS Level Descriptors were produced through a thorough and painstaking process of drafting, consultation, re-drafting, further consultation and testing that finally resulted in a comprehensive set of level descriptors that have survived well beyond the demise of NICATS itself, and have provided the level descriptors currently used in the CQFW, the descriptors recommended for use within HE Credit Frameworks in England, Wales and Northern Ireland, and – most importantly – have been a primary influence on the level descriptors for the QCF itself. Although level descriptors existed prior to NICATS, there is little doubt that the primary influence on current level descriptors both within the QCF itself and outside it derives from this painstaking work undertaken by colleagues in Northern Ireland through the NICATS Project.

Although the NICATS Implementation Project became involved in the work undertaken by CQFW and FEDA on credit-rating qualifications through the UK Credit Equivalence Project (of which more later), NICATS maintained its separate identity, based around its clear commitment to the principle of CAT, into the early part of the twenty-first century. The influence of the Northern Ireland OCN on the development of NICATS was always more important than the influence of Welsh OCNs on the CQFW (the Director of the NICATS Implementation Project was a member of the board of the Northern Ireland OCN – NIOCN) and the continuing focus on credit as an award to a learner remains in place throughout NICATS' history. By late 2002 it was clear that, not least because of the continuing influence of HE on efforts to implement NICATS as a comprehensive system, the CAT system itself simply could not be implemented in the manner originally conceived in the NICATS Project. Responsibility for NICATS passed formally to the CCEA, but little was done to take it forward, until of course the announcement in the 2003 Skills Strategy White Paper opened up a new chapter of credit-based developments in Northern Ireland. The CCEA was given responsibility for leading these developments in Northern Ireland, with a ready-made, in-house expert to hand in Caroline Egerton, who had been involved in NICATS from the outset and now emerged as a key person within the CCEA to take forward the development of the QCF in Northern Ireland. The close collaboration between the QCA and CCEA in all stages of development of the QCF, including the joint commitment to the initial proposals for the Framework for Achievement (FfA; again covered in a later chapter), is based on this integration of the NICATS experience within the CCEA and contrasts notably with experiences in Wales, where the continuing separation of responsibilities for taking forward the CQFW and for the development of the QCF through the Welsh Qualifications Regulator has led to a much less smooth and much more difficult process of development. It now seems that the initial ambitions of NICATS will be realised (at least outside HE) through the QCF in a way that they could never have been realised through NICATS itself. Again, the contrast with the CQFW, which remains as a separately constituted entity in Wales, outside the development of the QCF, is interesting.

27

Units, qualifications and rationalisation

Although it is actually quite difficult to identify an explicit policy of rationalisation of qualifications in 2009 (as employers continue to be subsidised by the Department for Business, Innovation and Skills to seek recognition as awarding bodies in the QCF), there is no doubt that such rationalisation has informed qualifications reform for at least a decade. The characterisation of qualifications as a jungle originates in the 1986 de Ville Report, and the remit to rationalise explicitly informs the establishing of the NQF itself in 1998. In between these two dates there was a dramatic expansion of the number of vocational qualifications, and the number of awarding bodies offering vocational qualifications in England, Wales and Northern Ireland. Indeed, during the initial years of expansion of the FE sector following college incorporation, the idea of qualifications rationalisation seems to go missing for a time, to reappear in the lead-up to establishment of the NQF.

This process of rationalisation (and its apparent absence during the early years of FEFC-funded expansion) presented particular issues for OCN credit systems. Whatever other interpretations of 'qualifications rationalisation' there might have been during the 1990s, an emphasis on 'the national' was certainly a consistent attribute of this concept. From the perspective of government there was no suggestion that growth in the FE sector should be supported through the development of local qualifications. Having said this, the recurrent blind spot of governments in relation to adult learners in this period is still evident. Although qualifications had to be national, other forms of recognising achievement outside the qualifications system (including the award of credit) that were targeted at adult learners could continue to be local providing they were not classified as qualifications. Such distinctions presented interesting problems for OCNs and for NOCN, especially in the accreditation of learning programmes that were apparently vocational in intent. The resolution of these tensions makes an interesting, on occasions almost farcical, story, as the demand for OCN accreditation grew and the concerns of the DfEE about rationalisation began to be re-asserted once the implications of FEFC funding to support expansion of the sector in England became apparent in the mid-1990s. Indeed, maintaining eligibility for funding of adult vocational learning became one of the most important features of the rationale behind NOCN's decision in 1998 to become an awarding body in the NQF.

Actually, although the decision to seek the status of a recognised awarding body in the new NQF marked a significant shift in both the objectives of NOCN and in the structure, funding and constitution of the organisation, technically NOCN had been acting as a named awarding body for some five years before this date. It took on this role from 1993 onwards when Schedule 2 of the 1992 Education Act came into force and the DfEE became the guardian of the vocational qualifications approved under Schedule 2(a) of the Act that were listed by the Department as being eligible for FEFC funding. In the absence of any regulatory structure or any processes for recognition or approval of individual qualifications, the DfEE was actually dependent on awarding bodies to inform them of the qualifications that should be included on this list and would therefore be eligible for public funding.

As we have seen, the years from 1992 onwards marked the beginning of a rapid increase in OCN credit systems, which coincided with the growth of the newly independent FE sector. In no small part this growth was the result of the ability of OCNs to meet the requirements for approval (and therefore of funding) of one section or another of Schedule 2. Indeed, apart from Schedule 2(b) – A levels and GCSEs – OCN accreditation was acceptable for FEFC funding under all sections of the Schedule from 2(a) to 2(j). For all other sections of the Schedule it was the individual local OCN that was recognised by the FEFC. Under Schedule 2(a) only national awarding bodies were recognised, and so NOCN agreed that it would be the named awarding body through which local OCNs would propose their vocational qualifications for approval.

In fact, these OCN entries on the list of approved vocational qualifications were not really qualifications at all in the currently accepted definition of the term, but were actually locally developed programmes accredited by an individual OCN. In some cases these 'qualifications' might be offered by a number of different providers, but in most instances they were unique to a provider, perhaps being offered to only ten or 12 learners a year. When an OCN accredited a new programme in a vocational area (and by no means all OCN programmes were vocational in nature), it forwarded the title of this programme to NOCN, where it was collected together with other such titles and periodically forwarded to the DfEE, where it was duly added to the list of approved vocational qualifications. At this juncture, it should be noted that, despite the rationale for developing NVQs to replace all other qualifications, the incorporation of FE colleges and the development of the FEFC's funding methodology were intended to fuel an expansion of the new sector. In this climate there was no explicit policy on the rationalisation of qualifications. Indeed, the increase in the number of qualifications available to learners in the sector was in itself seen as a symptom of this growth and therefore as a positive indicator that the reform of the sector was having its intended effect.

NOCN therefore continued to add 'qualifications' to the DfEE's Schedule 2(a) list throughout 1994 and 1995 as individual OCNs expanded into new vocational areas. The expansion of the list did not increase directly in proportion to the development of newly accredited programmes, however, as OCNs, developing such programmes in an area where a Schedule 2(a) title already existed, simply used the existing title for their new programme, thereby ensuring that it could be funded through the approved list. As the DfEE was only interested in the titles of each qualification, there was no requirement for programmes accredited by OCNs to be the same as each other in different localities. As long as the approved title was used and recorded in returns to the FEFC, any OCN-accredited programme based on that title could be funded. Indeed, NOCN itself encouraged OCNs to use existing approved titles wherever possible, in order to reduce the number of new titles it forwarded to the DfEE at regular intervals. There was also a Welsh Addendum to the Schedule 2(a) list, which meant that Welsh OCNs reported new titles directly to the Welsh Office (still in the name of the NOCN) rather than the DfEE. The Welsh Addendum added many more titles to the approved list, including a number that were identical, or almost identical, to those being added by the NOCN in England via the DfEE, as well as some that were very different.[1]

Even within the expansionist culture of the FE sector in the mid-1990s, such a rapid increase in the number of approved vocational qualifications (more accurately in qualification titles) could not proceed indefinitely. Of course, NOCN was not the only awarding body adding new titles to the list during this period, but it was the only one adding these titles on behalf of the 25 or more functioning OCNs that were actually developing them. It was also the only one classifying locally-accredited programmes as 'national' qualifications. By 1995–6 NOCN was, it appeared, on its way to becoming one of the largest vocational awarding bodies in England and Wales, based on the number of so-called qualifications on the Schedule 2(a) list. Of course, in terms of the number of learners registered on these qualifications, NOCN was still a very small vocational awarding body. In fact, this was the point. Representatives of NOCN were summoned to a meeting in Sheffield (to where responsibility for the Schedule 2(a) list had recently been transferred from London) to explain the growth (the term 'proliferation' was not yet in popular use) of NOCN's approved vocational qualifications and to agree with officers of the Department a strategy for reducing the numbers of listed qualifications to 'a reasonable number' over time.

At first this exercise was based exclusively on qualification titles. DfEE officers would identify titles that were not very vocational in form – that is, that did not include the name of a sector, an industry, an employment role or a job title – and ask for these to be removed from the list. Then they identified titles that were similar to each other and asked that these be consolidated. NOCN complied with the DfEE's wishes. The number of titles was reduced, but the impact on what was actually offered by OCNs was negligible. Individual OCNs simply changed titles to comply with the revised list and continued to offer the accredited programmes under these titles as they had done previously, enabling providers to continue to claim funding under Schedule 2(a).

The DfEE's next strategy was to set a target for the reduction of titles on the list and ask awarding bodies to remove from the list those titles that they wished, in order to reach their required target. Again, NOCN negotiated with its member OCNs a consolidation of titles in related areas to meet these targets, and again the NOCN Schedule 2(a) list remained largely intact, with minimal impact on the actual provision of accredited programmes offered by OCNs under each title. NOCN also insisted that any newly accredited programmes in these vocational areas offered by OCNs should use an existing title from the list. Over the period 1995 to 1997 this process of consolidation gradually produced a situation where, behind one approved title on the DfEE's list, there existed perhaps 20 or more different programmes offered by perhaps ten or 12 OCNs. Each programme was different, each of them built around units developed by the provider offering the programme. Behind each title on the DfEE list there could in theory have been hundreds of different units that were offered to learners. The distinction between a qualification and an accredited programme was still perhaps not entirely understood by DfEE officers. However, the next stage in this process of rationalisation (now the term was becoming used more often) would expose this distinction and force NOCN to confront this issue directly with OCNs.

Within the structure of NOCN, OCNs have always willingly shared both examples of practice and the outcomes of this practice. Once OCNs agreed to adopt a standard unit specification in 1994, local networks began to share units. This process of unit sharing became more common as new OCNs were established, with the support of an existing OCN as a 'mentor'. As I have tried to show in Chapter 25 above, the influence of the CREDIS project in Wales was also an important stimulus to the unit-sharing process. NOCN itself also coordinated the 'joint accreditation' of programmes across OCNs to meet the growing demand for OCN accreditation from national organisations, leading to the sharing of more units. Nevertheless, in 1997 the great majority of units offered through programmes accredited by OCNs were particular to a single provider. It was in this context that the DfEE moved to the next stage of rationalisation in the process of approval under Schedule 2(a) and asked for each qualification on the approved list to be submitted for scrutiny to the DfEE itself. In so doing, DfEE officers already had one eye on the future process of accreditation of qualifications that would be set up by the QCA and were determined to 'clean up' the Schedule 2(a) list in anticipation of this shift in responsibility.

For the first time in this process, NOCN was now required to present to the DfEE for approval one single specification for each approved qualification title on the Schedule 2(a) list. It should be noted that, in terms of the overall scope of OCN accreditation, the Schedule 2(a) list constituted a small minority of learner registrations and awards across the network in 1998. However, with the prospect of a new, regulated NQF on the horizon, and having taken a decision to become an awarding body in the new framework, transforming previously accredited programmes into qualifications as defined by the QCA, would be a critically important task in developing credit-based qualifications in the NQF. Preparing qualification specifications for the DfEE through NOCN was seen as an essential dry run to prepare OCNs for transition to their continuing development within the context of a regulated national framework of qualifications.

By 1998 the national network of OCNs was well established and 30 networks were fully operational. Each network was an independent organisation, with its own governing body and staff. NOCN itself was perceived as a structure within which the collective interests of OCNs could be represented, rather than an organisation in its own right. Although NOCN had established a head office in 1996, with three part-time staff and a small budget drawn from subscriptions from OCNs, the budget and staffing of the smallest OCN in the network was greater than NOCN's. Indeed, it was not until 1998 that NOCN, in preparation for recognition within the NQF, established itself as an independent legal entity rather than an informal association of local OCNs. It was in this context that the process of preparing qualification specifications for approval by the DfEE was undertaken.

As it had no resources of its own to do this, NOCN formed a series of clusters drawn from OCNs themselves in each sector/subject area where it was agreed a qualification specification needed to be developed. Each cluster of OCNs was asked to draw up a qualification specification by reviewing all the locally accredited programmes related to that qualification and producing a single, detailed specification for each qualification, drawing on the best elements of these locally accredited programmes. The exercise was sometimes difficult, subject to many discussions about the relative merits of one OCN programme in comparison with another, and presented a notable coordination challenge to NOCN. Nevertheless, out of this process came three important lessons about the process of structuring credit-based qualifications that would be relevant to the development of the QCF.

The first lesson from this exercise was that it was possible for a number of independent awarding bodies (that is, individual OCNs) to work together to produce a shared qualification specification, even though a number of them had strong vested interests in the existing qualifications on the Schedule 2(a) list. The adoption of a standard unit format proved to be an essential prerequisite of this process, as it allowed direct comparisons to be made between individual units and allowed a focus on unit content, rather than unit structure through the process of qualification development. The process required compromise from some OCNs and agreements on re-writing units to accommodate different perspectives within a single specification, but at the end of the process it proved possible to create over a hundred rationalised qualification specifications that could be shared across OCNs and within which individual networks could, with some compromises, meet the needs of individual learners within their locality. Of course, the process was also dependent both on good will and on a shared vision of the purpose of such an activity. Given these prerequisites, individual OCNs managed to overcome the technical problems presented by this significant shift from locally accredited programmes to national qualification specifications. The sharing of units between OCNs lay at the heart of this change.

The second important outcome of this process relates to the quality of the units that formed the basis of each specification. Although the standard unit format proposed in *ABC?* had been adopted by all NOCN members in 1994, the national network was still incomplete at that juncture. It would be 1996-7 before a fully operational national network of OCNs was established, and during this period each local network accredited thousands of new programmes based on tens of thousands of new units (as well as a small number of shared units). NOCN did have a quality review process in place during this period, and each OCN had a responsibility to monitor and report on the activities of another OCN, based on review criteria established through NOCN. However, given the relative strengths of individual OCNs in relation to NOCN in this period and the dependence on local OCN staff to conduct this review, there was very little detailed scrutiny of the process of unit development during this period of rapid growth.

Preparing qualification specifications for Schedule 2(a) approval changed that significantly. For the first time, groups of OCNs were asked to come together to examine existing units from a variety of accredited programmes and to produce a single qualification specification based on an identified set of units. The process led to the elimination of a number of units deemed to be of poor quality and the re-writing of many others. In effect, the enforced rationalisation of the DfEE engendered a thorough quality review of OCN units, based on the mutual actions of individual OCNs, that had an undoubtedly positive effect on unit quality. Notwithstanding the fact that only a minor proportion of OCN provision was touched by this exercise, the process of review and re-writing of units had a longer-term positive impact on unit quality across all OCN-accredited provision, and led to the development of much more thorough and well-tested guidance on the process of developing good quality units throughout all NOCN members. Despite the problems caused by the process, the outcomes of enforced collaboration in developing qualification specifications had a positive impact on unit quality.

The third lesson that was learned by OCNs during this process of preparing qualification specifications was that, in order to accommodate the range of individual learner needs that had been met through locally accredited programmes, it was necessary to develop flexible qualification structures that offered a wide range of unit choices. To develop these flexible structures, OCNs turned to their own experiences of developing rules of combination for Access to HE Certificates, and applied this experience to the development of rules of combination for these approved vocational qualifications. For the first time a set of vocational qualifications was developed that was based explicitly on the principle that credits could be combined in particular ways through rules of combination linked to each qualification specification. In comparison to the rules of combination for Access to HE Certificates, these first Schedule 2(a) rules were more limited. In essence, they were based around a basic core and options model, with a number of different ways of grouping optional units to permit the maximum range of choices, including (a radical feature at the time) the opportunity to achieve credits at a level lower than the qualification itself. However, in comparison with the rules of combination for the QCF, this initial set of rules did not include the opportunity to count 'credits from other units' (the DfEE insisted that all units had to be named in the specification); did not include the facility to identify 'credit from equivalent units' (as there were no other credit-based qualifications capable of being equivalent); nor did they encompass the concept of exemption (although this was a feature of Access to HE Certificates, it was another concept that the DfEE would not accept). Despite these limitations, OCNs learned a great deal about how to develop rules of combination through this process of qualification development for DfEE approval, and some of the key features of qualification design in the QCF can be detected in these first nationally developed, credit-based qualifications that appeared on the DfEE's approved Schedule 2(a) list in 1998-9.

It should be emphasised that, despite the DfEE's explicit anticipation of the introduction of the NQF and the detailed scrutiny of qualifications submitted for Schedule 2(a) approval by NOCN during this period immediately prior to implementation of the NQF, these first credit-based qualifications produced by NOCN were still developed in an unregulated context, with both the criteria for and the process of approval developed pragmatically by a small group of DfEE officers in response to the pressures to rationalise qualifications that grew significantly from the publication of the Dearing Report on 16-19 qualifications, and continues (albeit in a modified form) to this day. This 'phoney war' – with DfEE officers playing the role of 'proto-accreditors' in a Schedule

2(a) list prior to the establishment of the actual QCA accreditation criteria in 2000 (QCA et al., 2000) – appeared to demonstrate to NOCN that it would be technically feasible to establish credit-based qualifications within the NQF and that therefore the continuing development of credit systems could continue in tandem with the establishment of a regulated framework of qualifications. In the real context of the NQF, this proved much more difficult to achieve than had been anticipated in the dry run with the DfEE in establishing approved qualifications through the Schedule 2(a) list. In 1999, however, with overall registrations and certifications through OCNs still expanding significantly, optimism about the ability of OCNs to continue to operate both inside and outside a regulated NQF remained high. Meanwhile, the NQF itself was becoming more clearly formed as the QCA began the process of establishing the new framework.

Once again, this episode in the development of OCN credit systems shows how a creative response to an external requirement produced changes to practice that, in the longer term, helped to prepare for the development of the QCF. The continuing efforts of the DfEE to rationalise the list of 'NOCN Vocational Qualifications' during this period, and the continuing efforts of NOCN officers (led, it must be said, by myself) to obscure the rapid expansion of locally accredited OCN programmes behind acceptable forms of NOCN titles, seems almost comic in retrospect. Nevertheless, the experience gradually brought home to OCNs the importance of being able to share units easily, to have mutual confidence in unit quality across networks and to develop qualification structures capable of protecting local diversity and responsiveness within a genuinely national structure. All these features are present in the QCF. History repeating itself, the first time as farce.

Note

1 Including the infamous 'Love Spoon Carving' qualification.

28
The establishing of the NQF

In 2008 the European Commission produced a map that aimed to show how National Qualifications Frameworks (NQFs) were developing both within the European Union and in applicant and aspiring EU Member States (Coles, 2008). The map showed four Member States with established NQFs (the UK, Ireland, France and Malta), 24 States with a commitment to develop an NQF of some kind in the future, and only three States (Greece, Norway and Sweden) without an explicit commitment to develop an NQF. The Commission also acknowledged the influence of other international examples of NQFs (for example, in Australia, New Zealand and South Africa) on European developments. An OECD study (OECD, 2007) confirms this growing influence of NQFs on the education systems of many countries. Both the European Commission and the OECD draw explicit connections between the development of NQFs and the implementation of policies of lifelong learning in countries that have adopted, or plan to adopt, such frameworks. Conceptually, therefore, NQFs are seen as tools that have the potential to support structural changes in the development of national systems of qualifications, to the benefit of people throughout their learning lives. Although France is usually acknowledged as the first of these NQFs, it is the UK that is often seen as a model for other frameworks. Of course, the UK includes the development of a separate national framework of qualifications in Scotland, but in relation to this publication it is the NQF first established in England, Wales and Northern Ireland in 1998 that commands our attention.

When looking back at the rationale for establishing the NQF in England, Wales and Northern Ireland, we detect none of these conceptual influences that inform the current European and international debates about the potential benefits of NQFs. There is no suggestion in 1998 that the NQF would be a strategic tool in the context of lifelong learning. Indeed, this first iteration of a national framework of qualifications in England, Wales and Northern Ireland (the QCF being the second) is based primarily on expediency rather than any strategic goals and is as limited in its scope as its modest origins might lead us to anticipate. To understand why the NQF was developed, we need to go back once again to the Dearing Review of 16-19 qualifications and the policy context in which the review was conducted.

As I have tried to show in Chapter 19 above, the Dearing Review was tightly constrained in its remit. The scope of this remit was effectively set by the 1991 White Paper *Education and Training for the 21st Century* (DES/DE/WO, 1991), which established the policy context for qualifications reform for the remainder of the period of Conservative government and beyond. The primary focus of the White Paper was on the needs of young people (adult learners were still noticeable by their absence from any policy debate about qualifications) and, in particular, on the form of the qualifications system that should be offered to them prior to entry to the workforce. In 1991 government strategy in relation to qualifications reform was still primarily limited to preparing young people for a career and, although it was accepted that adults would continue to gain qualifications after entry to the workforce, this was of little strategic interest to government. Wider twenty-first-century concerns about raising workforce skill levels were still focused on the skills of entrants to the labour market in 1991. Raising the skill levels of young people was strategically important to government; continuing to raise skill levels among adults already in the workforce was less easy to identify as important.

The late 1980s had seen significant increases in the numbers of young people studying and achieving A levels, and in particular modular A levels. As numbers increased, familiar concerns about maintaining standards were voiced – a continued expansion of A level numbers might be perceived as a dilution of the 'gold standard' against which other qualifications were measured. At the same time it had become obvious that NVQs were not an appropriate qualification for many 16- to 19-year-olds in full-time education wishing to study a vocational qualification. The 1991 White Paper proposed the introduction of GNVQs as a third track option for 16- to 19-year-olds that would sit between the academic A level route and the occupational NVQ route. The White Paper also proposed restrictions on A level and GCSE coursework in an attempt to limit the further development of modular A levels, that – it was suggested – might be easier to achieve than qualifications based on an end-point examination. It's also interesting to note that the White Paper also suggested that 'overarching' diplomas might be developed that would enable young people to count achievements from different tracks towards the award of a diploma. This suggestion was not pursued further.

The establishing of GNVQs and the restrictions on flexibility placed on GCSEs and A levels effectively established the triple-track system of qualifications for young people that continues (in a slightly different form) to this day. Future expansion, it was assumed, could be managed by offering young people the opportunity to combine more general and vocational studies in this new middle track. At the same time the standards of the academic track could be maintained within this context of expansion. The shortcomings of this triple-track approach have informed much of the criticism of our 14-19 qualifications system over the past two decades (Hodgson et al., 1997). Indeed, *Education and Training for the 21st Century* can be seen as a conscious attempt to re-assert these separate qualification tracks against the growing criticism of this approach that coalesced around the 1990 argument in favour of 'A British Baccalaureate' (Finegold, 1990). In marked contrast to the 1991 White Paper, the Baccalaureate group argued against separate qualification tracks and in favour of a 'unified' qualification system based on a single set of 16-19 qualifications.[1] It was an argument that did not find favour with the Major government. Indeed, opposition to the Baccalaureate idea probably ensured that the 1991 White Paper's proposals for overarching diplomas were not pursued.

This is the context that informed the remit of the Dearing Review. Dearing's remit can therefore be seen as a conscious attempt to head off any attempts to use the review of 16-19 qualifications as a way of undoing this triple-track approach. As Michael Young has argued, given the restrictions on his remit, Dearing probably made as much progress as he could in shifting 16-19 qualifications towards a more unified system (Young, 1997). Indeed, at the time the shift towards a single national framework of qualifications, with a single regulatory body that merged the previously separate responsibilities of the SCAA and NCVQ, was perceived as one of Dearing's more positive recommendations.

Nevertheless, the establishing of the NQF followed the limitations of the Dearing Review and the logic of the triple-track system of academic, applied and occupational qualifications established by the Major government. Notwithstanding the victory of Labour in the 1997 general election, the incoming government, in accepting the passage of the 1997 Education Act, effectively secured this conceptualisation of qualification tracks into the NQF. The legislation that created both the NQF and QCA was based on the logic of Dearing's recommendations, framed as they were by Conservative opposition to a unified approach to 16-19 qualifications. As we have shown above, concern for the needs of adult learners was simply absent from the core of this debate.

Not only did the first iteration of this national framework of qualifications institutionalise this divided structure of 16-19 qualifications, it also, taking its lead again from the remit of the Dearing Review, accepted A levels, GCSEs, GNVQs and NVQs into the NQF without any changes to their structures. This ensured that the NQF would, from the outset, be a 'weak' framework – that is, a framework without any remit to require changes to any of these existing qualifications in order to become part of it (Young, 1997). Indeed, the rationale for establishing the NQF is almost entirely organisational in concept. There is no suggestion that the NQF might be a policy instrument for facilitating or enforcing desirable changes in the structure or delivery of qualifications, nor that the NQF might have a positive role to play in developing a learning culture capable of supporting a shift towards lifelong learning. Instead, the rationale for the NQF is best exemplified in the introduction to its first set of regulatory arrangements (QCA et al., 2000, p. 4): 'In accordance with national policy, the regulatory authorities will establish a clear, coherent and inclusive national qualifications framework ... in which accredited qualifications are grouped according to purpose and level of demand.'

This first iteration of a national framework of qualifications was essentially a hybrid structure. Although it established a single regulatory body (actually separate regulatory bodies for England, Wales and Northern Ireland) to oversee the new NQF, it also deliberately institutionalised the separation of qualification tracks within the new framework and, less deliberately, created an effective hierarchy of qualifications in the NQF by accepting the most significant qualifications offered to 16- to 19-year-olds into the framework without change, and then developed a set of bureaucratic and (despite its objective) exclusive procedures designed to limit the accessibility of the NQF to other qualifications outside these 16–19 tracks. Tying the accreditation of qualifications in the NQF explicitly to public funding in England and Wales was one mechanism that assured the approach to admitting new qualifications into the framework was never going to be 'inclusive'. At the same time the advent of the NQF signified an end to the idea that, outside the qualifications offered to people in full-time education or training, voluntarism and choice would continue to be the primary features that informed qualifications design and delivery. In effect, the requirement that all qualifications, irrespective of which age group was their primary target for registrations, would need to comply with the regulatory requirements of the NQF if they were to be considered eligible for public funding marks the beginning of the end of the system of qualifications that had been offered to adult learners since the early 1980s, and which, for want of a better term, we might characterise as being 'demand led'.

It should also be recalled that, as in the 1991 White Paper, Dearing had also called for the development of a series of overarching 'National Awards' at each level of the NQF. Indeed, Dearing's conceptualisation of the NQF in his report identifies these National Awards as the significant qualifications in the framework (Dearing, 1996). In the event, of course, these 'Dearing Diplomas' were never developed, but the concept of the NQF in Dearing's report without these new qualifications is considerably diminished. It should be remembered that the NQF was actually conceived as 'a national framework of qualifications' (Dearing, 1996). In other words, it was the qualifications, rather than the framework itself, that gave the NQF its particular form. The contrast with the QCF is worthy of note. In this second iteration of an NQF in England, Wales and Northern Ireland, it is the framework itself, rather than the qualifications within it, in which the concept of 'the national' resides. In this context, implementing the NQF without the new National Awards significantly undermined the rationale for Dearing's initial recommendations in favour of a single framework. It would take some time before this omission could be addressed.

This then was the NQF that began to function in 1999. Derived from a report with a very restricted remit; focused on the needs of 16- to 19-year-olds; institutionalising the existing divisions between different types of qualification; almost entirely bureaucratic in concept; based essentially on the characteristics of qualifications rather than on the characteristics of the framework itself; deriving its internal culture from two previous organisations collectively responsible for a minority of qualifications offered to individuals (and a small minority offered to learners in the FE sector); and (as I have shown in Chapter 19) eschewing the opportunity to build into the framework any reference to credit – the NQF was from the outset a very particular construct, hidebound by the limitations of both policy and culture in its scope, remit and ethos. This was the instrument of government policy that now faced those still intent on taking forward the development of credit systems in the twenty-first century.

It should be noted in passing that the legislation that supported the establishing of the NQF and gave statutory powers to the regulators is actually quite open and permissive in form (arguably, as good legislation should be). With one or two relatively minor amendments contained in the 2008 Education and Skills Act (DIUS, 2008), the legislation that supported the creation of the NQF in 1998 is the same that supports the QCF in 2009 (though in England some further changes will result from the legislation to create an independent qualifications regulator in the Office for Regulation of Qualifications and Examinations – Ofqual) (BIS, 2009). The first iteration of the NQF was constrained primarily by the policy context of the Dearing Review and partly by the paucity of vision of those commissioned to actually develop the framework, with their backgrounds in either the NCVQ or SCAA. Ten years later a different policy context, a different leadership in the QCA and a conscious decision to draw on the experiences of credit systems outside the NQF enabled a very different type of framework to be established on the basis of almost identical legislation.

The lessons of this experience of developing a second iteration of the NQF just a few years after the initial version are not lost on colleagues in Europe and beyond, who now look to the QCF as a way of avoiding some of the pitfalls in creating an NQF based on limited and pragmatic objectives, rather than a dynamic vision of a changed future system of recognising achievement. In relation to the EU or OECD concept of a national qualifications framework as a strategic policy instrument, linked explicitly to the development of lifelong learning, the QCF is actually a much more recognisable framework to international observers than its predecessor (OECD, 2007). The story of the QCF in an international context is picked up in a later chapter.

Note
1 Including the young David Miliband, an experience that would become important a decade later when he became a junior minister in the DfES.

29

Credit systems inside and outside the NQF

As I note in Chapter 21, the Blackstone letter of April 1998 confirmed to the QCA that the Labour government wished to implement the Dearing proposals for maintaining a triple-track approach to qualifications development, while introducing AS levels into the 'general' (the term 'academic' was now falling out of use) track. The letter also asked the QCA to take forward further investigative work on 'unitisation and credit' for 'adult and vocational learning'. In 1999 a White Paper, entitled *Learning to Succeed*, elaborated government policy further in this area (DfEE, 1999). It confirmed the implication behind the process of establishing the NQF – that is, that qualifications for 16- to 19-year-olds were to be structurally different from qualifications for adults within the NQF because 'the needs of adult learners are different' (DfEE, 1999).

This was a new development in qualifications policy. Although previous policy documents had based recommendations on the needs of 16- to 19-year-olds, there was also an explicit assumption (rightly or wrongly) that any reforms would also apply to adult learners. Of course, in previous contexts adults had been free to choose qualifications and other forms of accreditation outside the previous scope of regulated qualifications. Now that the NQF was established, the working assumption was that the achievements of adult learners would also be recognised within the same framework. However, it was also recognised (fuelled in part by the growth in both OCN accreditation and in other vocational qualifications during the 1990s) that A levels, GCSEs and GNVQs were failing to meet the needs of adult learners, and were accounting for an increasingly smaller proportion of adult learner registrations across the FE sector. In this context, *Learning to Succeed* represents a logical step forward in relation to the NQF. For the first time it institutionalised within the national system of qualifications a distinction between qualifications aimed at different age groups. Although one might anticipate this as an inevitable outcome of a recommendation to establish a national framework of qualifications that arose explicitly from a review of 16–19 qualifications, it should be noted that Dearing himself rejected this division and, indeed, viewed the establishing of the NQF as a mechanism for ensuring equal esteem for all qualifications, irrespective of the age group at which they were targeted. *Learning to Succeed* effectively undermined this aspiration.

Notwithstanding this shift in policy, *Learning to Succeed* seemed to create the possibility that unitised, credit-based qualifications might be established within the NQF, targeted explicitly at adult learners. The assumption that the needs of adult learners could be met through the introduction of AS levels and the reform of GNVQs was now formally abandoned. Although *Learning to Succeed* therefore added an additional layer of constraint and complexity into the development of the NQF, it also created a new conceptual space entitled 'qualifications for adults', within which new credit-based qualifications might be developed. In this context the first position paper on unitisation and credit, produced by the QCA as part of its continuing investigatory role, was received in the summer of 1999 with some interest.

The QCA position paper *Unitisation and Credit in the National Qualifications Framework* (QCA, 1999) begins to illustrate the problems of asking a regulatory body to take forward further investigation outside its regulatory remit. I reviewed the QCA paper in an article in *Adults Learning*, entitled 'It's credit Jim, but not as we know it' (Wilson, 1999). In effect, the QCA's concept of credit was based not on the OCN definition of an award made to a learner, but on FEDA's proposition that credit was a way of measuring and comparing the achievements of learners. How ironic that, in assuming responsibility for the further development of credit systems from FEDA in 1998, the QCA failed to conceptualise credit as an award. Indeed, the QCA had gone further – again building on ideas emerging from both FEDA and from Wales – suggesting that credit and unitisation were actually separate concepts, and that it would be possible to establish some of the benefits proposed in *ABC?* and in subsequent FEU/FEDA publications by simply unitising qualifications – that is, by 'analysing them' into smaller components – rather than by establishing a credit system to recognise learner achievements on these units. It should be noted that the QCA paper was actually published prior to the 2000 *Statutory Regulations* for the NQF, and so the magnificent *coup de grace* dealt to the concept of unitisation in the definition of a unit in that document had yet to materialise.

The QCA paper, which formed the basis of advice to ministers the following year, effectively excluded any reference to credit in the development of qualifications in the NQF. Although units were now deemed to be 'a good thing' (even in the context of 16–19 qualifications), credits were seen as either too complicated or unnecessary in the ongoing development of the NQF. 'Unitisation good, credits bad' appeared to be the watchword of the day within the QCA. *Unitisation and Credit within the NQF* draws very clearly on the FEDA/CREDIS model of credit and served to confirm that the QCA's thinking about credit continued to separate credit from the regulation of qualifications. Indeed, the ability to introduce unitisation separately from a credit system and 'without changing any existing qualifications' was advanced as a positive argument in favour of the QCA's position. Whatever the reason for this failure to build on the practical delivery of credit systems through OCNs, which were at the zenith of their scope and influence in 1999–2000, the failure of the QCA to support the development of credit-based qualifications within the NQF from 2000 onwards marks the end of that particular hope for the further development of credit systems.

We may identify this period following the QCA's advice to ministers on unitisation and credit in 1999, and the fact that 2000–1 marked the first year ever in which OCNs did not experience an increase in registrations or credits awarded, as the beginning of the decline in what had become known as the credit movement. The QCA's position confirmed that the unitisation and credit-rating approach to developing a credit system advocated by FEDA and CREDIS was not going to deliver a credit system that bore any resemblance to that developed by OCNs (hence the title of my article in *Adults Learning*). Notwithstanding this manifest failure of the sequential strategy of developing a credit system through unitisation and credit-rating, there was no evidence that the NOCN approach would deliver such a system either. The position of the QCA on credit also manifested itself in the practical problems experienced by the NOCN in putting forward credit-based qualifications for submission to the NQF. The advent of the twenty-first century effectively marked a low point in the struggle to establish a national system of credit-based qualifications.

30

Driving a wedge between credit and qualifications

Once the NQF was formally launched, and A levels, GCSEs, GNVQs and NVQs had all been admitted to the framework, the QCA and its regulatory partners began work on admitting other qualifications to the NQF. Vocational qualifications outside the NVQ/GNVQ structure constituted the great majority of these qualifications. The process was not without its difficulties from the start. A test case brought by one awarding body established the principle that the QCA had no remit to recognise awarding bodies themselves, but only the qualifications they offered within the NQF (as many awarding bodies continued to offer qualifications outside the NQF, this was an important principle). A compromise position was established through which the QCA agreed that it would divide the process of qualification recognition into two parts: that which was common to all the qualifications offered by an awarding body in the NQF (Part A); and that which was particular to a single qualification (Part B).

This compromise established a de facto process for recognising an awarding body's overall approach to qualifications design and delivery. It also put down a marker to the new regulators that awarding bodies had concerns over the potential power of the QCA and its partners to limit their business opportunities, and had not necessarily bought in to the idea of a comprehensive regulated framework.[1]

This early legal challenge to the QCA's powers also served to highlight another issue, which was to prove problematic for NOCN in its aims to bring credit-based qualifications into the NQF. Not only did the QCA not have any powers to recognise awarding bodies, it also had no powers to recognise anything other than a qualification.[2] For all other awarding bodies bringing their products into the NQF, this was not a problem as these products were all qualifications. For NOCN, however, qualifications were defined through the accumulation of credits and a credit was – as an absolutely non-negotiable principle for OCNs – an award made to a learner. NOCN and QCA were now faced with a conundrum. If NOCN's quality systems leading to the award of a qualification were based on the accumulation of credits and the QCA had no remit to recognise the credits that made up this qualification, how could NOCN demonstrate to the QCA that its quality systems leading to the award of a qualification met required standards?

During the period between the formal establishing of the QCA in 1998 and the launch of the NQF in 1999, numerous meetings were held between NOCN and QCA officers to tease out this conundrum. At the same time, of course, QCA's work on unitisation and credit was proceeding and, as QCA's 1999 position paper revealed (QCA, 1999), the assumed definition of credit that the Authority was using in this work was based on the view of credit adopted by FEDA and used in the CREDIS framework in Wales, not the definition used by NOCN. These meetings between QCA and NOCN during 1998-9 also revealed a more practical problem. The QCA officers responsible for dealing with NOCN's Part A submission were drawn almost exclusively from staff previously employed by NCVQ. It soon became clear that none of them had any experience or knowledge of credit systems. Indeed, some of them had no experience of any vocational qualifications outside the NVQ framework. It also became clear that they had no contact with the QCA officer responsible for taking forward the 'further work' on unitisation and credit. The regulation of qualifications and the investigation of credits continued to be entirely separate activities within QCA.

NOCN's initial draft submission to QCA was based on the experience developed in the previous two years of preparing qualifications for submission to the DfEE for inclusion on the Schedule 2(a) list of vocational qualifications, approved for Learning and Skills Council (LSC) funding (see Chapter 27). It soon became clear that QCA's approach to the accreditation of qualifications in the NQF would be quite different and more problematic. It should not be assumed that NOCN was the only awarding body that had problems with this new process. Indeed, QCA's reputation as an overly bureaucratic regulator of the NQF became well established, as awarding body after awarding body found that the process of accreditation was more difficult and much lengthier than they had anticipated. This is not the place to deal with these wider problems, though they did have an impact on the policy decisions leading up to the decision to reform the NQF in 2003. The impact on NOCN, and on the development of credit-based qualifications within the NQF, was significant.

Whether this was the inevitable result of the emerging policy on credit evident in the Dearing Report, in *The Learning Age* and in *Learning to Succeed;* whether it was the particular result of the approach adopted by QCA to its separate remits from government on the implementation of the NQF and the further investigation of unitisation and credit; or whether it was simply the result of the people involved in these processes is open to debate. Certainly, the 'policy steer' was clear: from Dearing's concept of credit systems as 'complementary local provision rather than a replication of national awards' (Dearing, 1996, p. 28); through *The Learning Age's* reference to credit as appropriate for 'courses that prepare people for full qualifications'; to the clear separation of qualification development and further investigation of credit in the Blackstone letter; and the absence of any reference to credit systems in *Learning to Succeed* – the concept of credit gradually shifted from its significant role in the Kennedy and Fryer reports to its marginal impact on the NQF as a framework based clearly on the primacy of qualifications for 16- to 19-year-olds. The change from 1997 to 1999 is marked. The determination of QCA to ensure that its responsibilities for further work on unitisation and credit were hermetically sealed from its responsibilities to establish the NQF simply gave practical manifestation to these policy intentions. The end result – the exclusion of credit-based qualifications from the NQF – was, in retrospect, a perfectly logical outcome of these processes.

It took NOCN some time to work through the implications of this logic. The original Part A submission to the QCA, based on the development of qualifications by NOCN through rules of combination linked to the accumulation of credits awarded by individual OCNs, was debated, amended, rejected and subsequently withdrawn. Eventually an agreement was reached in 2000 through which NOCN, consistent with its decision in 1997, became accepted as an awarding body within the NQF. To accomplish this NOCN had to strip out of its submission to the QCA any reference to credit or to the accumulation of credit through the completion of individual units. In effect, the price of becoming an awarding body in the NQF for NOCN was to lose any formal recognition of the processes through which credit was actually awarded to learners throughout the OCN network,

NOCN became recognised as an awarding body within the NQF just like any other awarding body – that is, without any reference to credits or to the accumulation and transfer of credits within qualifications. Although OCNs continued to award credits through the processes that had been agreed within the National Credit Framework, the separation of NOCN qualifications from OCN credits was now formalised. NOCN became an awarding body within the NQF, but it was not an awarding body for credit-based qualifications. The arrangements for awarding credit for achievements on locally accredited OCN programmes were formally separated from the arrangements leading to the award of NOCN qualifications within the NQF. The experiences of OCNs in developing credit-based qualifications for the DfEE Schedule 2(a) list were lost, and the separation of NOCN's qualification-awarding responsibilities from those of OCNs in recognising learner achievement through the award of credit were formalised. Although initially it seemed that it would be possible to take forward the development of credit-based qualifications within the NQF by creating examples of these qualifications and then (as in the past) negotiating agreements on credit transfer with other awarding bodies, this opportunity was now lost. In retrospect, it matters little whether this blocking of credit-based qualifications in the NQF was a conscious outcome of government policy or a combination of policy steer and interpretation in practice by QCA officers. The end result was that the strategy of NOCN to seek recognition by QCA, in order to develop credit-based qualifications within the NQF, came to nothing.

This separation of national qualifications from local credits created a serious internal headache for NOCN and led to pronounced tensions between NOCN and its constituent members. It also created serious practical difficulties for NOCN in developing qualifications to meet NQF requirements that were effectively cut off from the experience and the creative energies of the OCN network. Although both NOCN and local OCNs continued to survive and to offer valued local services to adult learners, NOCN's inward focus as it dealt with these problems effectively exacerbated the decline of the credit movement by removing its active leadership from a national presence. It seemed that, by the end of 2000, the onward march of credit had been truly halted.

Notes

1   It also showed that the civil servants who drafted the 1997 Education Act had not done a very good job, a mistake that was put right in the tidying up legislation in the 2008 Education and Skills Act, Section 159, that prepared the ground for the introduction of the QCF. Although the legislation that created the NQF was almost fit-for-purpose for the QCF, this was one change that was indeed necessary.

2   The 2008 Education and Skills Act also addresses this problem, creating a legal requirement for awarding bodies to offer both qualifications and credits.

31

What we talk about when we talk about credit[1]

By 2001 it was clear that the credit movement, which had sustained both the development of OCNs and the establishing of numerous local and regional credit initiatives during the 1990s, was running out of steam – at least in England. Registrations and certifications of learners through OCNs began to level off and would soon begin a steady decline. The numerous local credit frameworks or similar initiatives that had sprung up after *ABC?* also began to disappear from the map. The further investigation of the benefits of a credit system continued within the QCA at a seemingly ever-slower pace, still totally disconnected from the implementation of the NQF. Some of the leading figures who had promoted credit systems during the previous decade also began to slip off the map, as retirement, promotion, fatigue or re-organisation took their toll on many of those who had established NOCN or contributed to *ABC?*. In 2002 the creation of the Learning and Skills Development Agency (LSDA), to support the newly created Learning and Skills Sector, also marked a further shift away from practical support for the concrete development of credit systems in the activities of the new agency in comparison to its predecessors, FEDA and FEU.

Only in Wales, it seemed, were developments linked to credit proceeding with any support from government. The (still relatively new) Welsh Assembly Government sponsored the development of the CQFW Project, also supported by the LSDA (DYSG) in Wales. The CQFW Project was funded (with support from the European Social Fund) by ELWa – the Welsh funding agency for post-school education and training. The project aimed to build explicitly on the previous work on credit-rating of qualifications, initially developed by the FEU/FEDA and then taken forward within the CREDIS initiative. As with these previous manifestations of credit in Wales, the CQFW Project was taken forward separately from the development of OCN credit systems in Wales and led to the establishment in 2002 of the CQFW itself.

The CQFW was established through a policy decision of the Welsh Assembly and was formally launched by Jane Davidson, then Minister for Education, Lifelong Learning and Skills in the Welsh Assembly government. Despite this relatively high profile of the CQFW, it had negligible impact on the development of the NQF in Wales, which proceeded to be established without reference to credit-based qualifications through joint regulatory activity with the qualifications authorities in England and Northern Ireland. OCNs in Wales (later to combine into a single OCN Wales[2]) were excluded from the NQF through exactly the same set of regulatory requirements as their counterparts in England and Northern Ireland. In this critical respect the CQFW, though it raised the profile of credit in Wales, reflected exactly the same view of credit systems that applied in England and Northern Ireland – that is, as an initiative separate from the formal development of the NQF across these three UK jurisdictions.

In Scotland the concept of credit developed along slightly different lines. Here a group of national agencies came together, with the support of the Scottish Executive, to establish the SCQF. The development of the SCQF began with a consultation in March 1999 (SQA, 1999) and resulted in the formal launch of the framework in 2002. In effect, the SCQF brought together the previous experience of HEIs in developing the Scottish Credit Accumulation and Transfer (SCOTCAT) framework, and that of the Scottish Qualifications Authority (SQA), the regulator and awarding body for lower levels of qualification in Scotland. The SCQF aims to bring together all 'mainstream' Scottish qualifications in a single framework of levels and credits, and also 'to help employers, learners and the public in general to understand how various qualifications can contribute to improving the knowledge and skills of the workforce' (Hart, 2002, p. 24).

The SCQF identifies 12 levels of achievement. Although this makes it distinctive from other UK frameworks, it is actually the different definition of 'credit' that is more important to this particular story:

> SCQF points are used to quantify learning and give it a value or currency. These general credit points are allocated to assessed outcomes of learning... In common with other credit systems, the SCQF works on the basis that a full year's learning should be worth 120 points.
>
> (Hart, 2002, p. 26)

The difference from the credit systems developed by OCNs in other parts of the UK is marked. In effect, the SCQF takes the credit system developed in HE and applies it to qualifications at all levels of the framework. Note that 'general credit points' are *allocated* to qualifications. There is no concept of credit as an award. A credit point 'represents 10 notional hours of learner effort' (Hart, 2002, p. 28) and the process of allocation of these points is unrelated to any concept of awarding credit to learners.

This use of credit points in the SCQF is entirely consistent with the framework's aims of 'making the Scottish system of qualifications easier to understand and use ... and providing a national language for describing all learning opportunities' (Hart, 2002, p. 24).

It is clear that the system that operates within the SCQF is a 'system of qualifications' and not a credit system. The SCQF is not, and was never intended to be, a regulated framework. It is established explicitly as an enabling or descriptive framework (Gallagher, 2005) and as such is not able to support the development of credit as a comprehensive currency of learner achievement. Nevertheless, the SCQF offers a model of how a particular concept of credit, derived principally from the experience of HEIs, can be applied to a national framework. Those involved in the local development of credit systems in other parts of the UK during this period, and noting the continuing lack of any national policy commitment to the development of credit systems in England, pointed to the SCQF as proof that it would be possible to establish a national framework based on credit in England without undermining the integrity of the qualifications system.

Ironically, during this period of separate development of credit systems and the NQF in England, Wales and Northern Ireland, examples of credit-based qualification frameworks were beginning to be established in both New Zealand and in parts of Australia. Although the models of qualification frameworks established in the Southern Hemisphere were conceptually different from those established in the UK, both the New Zealand framework (www.nzqa.govt.nz/nqf) and the Victoria state qualifications framework (www.vrqa.vic.gov.au/creditmatrix) acknowledged the influence of UK credit systems in their development. For a time in the early twenty-first century, it seemed as though the development of credit systems through the 1990s might have more influence on qualifications systems overseas than in the UK itself – or at least in its English jurisdiction.

The high point of the credit movement in England had passed by the time both the SCQF and the CQFW were launched. It was clear by 2001 that the attempt to carry the experience of developing operational credit systems into a newly established, regulated qualifications framework had failed. Although the QCA remained formally responsible for taking forward the further development of credit through its 1998 remit from government, the conception of credit that had now solidified within the QCA's work was based not on the actual experiences of OCNs in operating credit systems, but on the theoretical potential benefits of credit promoted over the previous decade by the FEU/FEDA. In this the QCA was influenced to an extent by the development of both the SCQF and CQFW, with their different definitions and concepts of credit. During these early years of the twenty-first century, it became increasingly important to sustain a theoretical concept of credit as the continuing development of the NQF gradually choked off the further development of operational credit systems across England, Wales and Northern Ireland.

One of the outlets for this continuing exploration of the potential benefits of credit systems was the work commissioned by the Cabinet Office Strategy

Unit in 2001 to investigate the future needs of the British workforce in the face of growing international competition. The Strategy Unit (previously known as the Performance and Innovation Unit – PIU) produced two influential reports entitled *In Demand: Adult Skills in the 21st Century*. The first report (Part 1) appeared in November 2001; Part 2 was published a year later (Performance and Innovation Unit, 2001; Strategy Unit, 2002). The second report was published alongside the LSC's *Workforce Development Strategy* (LSC, 2002). The importance of the Cabinet Office in policy development during this period should not be underestimated. Indeed, one of the lasting criticisms of the Blair government was the pre-eminent influence of the Cabinet Office during this time, often to the detriment of the relevant department of government. *In Demand* certainly lends credence to this perception. The foreword is written by the Prime Minister alone, without reference to the DfES, and the publication of the second report alongside one of the first major reports from the newly created LSC serves to underline the impression that, in this area, the Cabinet Office, rather than the relevant department of government, was leading policy development.

In 2001, Ufi (the organisation that should have become the University for Industry, had not someone pointed out that it was actually the prerogative of the crown, rather than the government of the day, to bestow the title of 'university') organised an invitational seminar to which a number of key agencies were invited – including the LSC, QCA, DfES and the Strategy Unit – to put the case for a framework of credit-based qualifications. The background reading for the seminar was the NIACE publication *Lifelong Qualifications* (Wilson, 1999a). Shortly after this seminar, I was invited to present the document to a small group of people working on *In Demand*. Copies of *Lifelong Qualifications* were circulated within the PIU, together with FEDA's *Qualifications for the Future* (FEDA, 2000). The first *In Demand* report shows both these influences. In the course of preparing the second report, the PIU/Strategy Unit also organised a seminar at the Cabinet Office (one of the worst meeting venues in the whole of London) in April 2002, in order to gather expert opinion from the field to 'consider the case for introducing credits into the qualifications system' (PIU, 2002, p. 15). The net result of this work behind the scenes was to continue to breathe life into the potential benefits of a credit system, and this is illustrated in the two *In Demand* reports. In Part 1 there was a specific reference to the potential role of a credit system:

> In order to support a demand-led system and to respond to rapid changes in the workplace, more flexibility is needed in the qualifications system. The process for developing and approving ... new qualifications needs to become faster and more responsive. A credit-based system in

which individuals can build up to a full qualification over time could help individuals and employers tailor qualifications more to their needs.

> (Performance and Innovation Unit, 2001, para. 25)

There was also a brief reference in Part 2 of *In demand* for the need to establish 'a more flexible and responsive qualifications system' (Strategy Unit, 2002, p. 18). In particular, the Strategy Unit recommended:

> The qualification system needs to be flexible and responsive enough to balance the demands of employers and individuals whilst maintaining quality and status. This will be achieved through enhancing structures by which qualifications are designed and approved and through increasing the opportunities for unit-based achievement.
>
> (Strategy Unit, 2002, paras 52 and 53)

Although the explicit references to credit in Part 1 of the report are absent from Part 2 of *In Demand* (is it possible that QCA was asked for its advice on wording prior to final publication of the report?), the Strategy Unit's recommendations are interesting in three respects.

Firstly, and for the first time, we now have an influential government policy document that makes explicit reference to the flexibility and responsiveness of a credit system and 'unit-based achievement', in the context not of widening participation or increasing learner choice, but in the context of economic modernisation and workforce development. The arguments advanced by OCNs over a number of years (reflected in *Lasers in the Jungle* (Wilson, 1995) and *Lifelong Qualifications*) that the credit system had relevance to employers, and in particular to the recognition of skills and knowledge in a rapidly changing economic environment, were now advanced within a formal policy document.

Secondly, *In Demand* plots a series of related policy initiatives that it expects to follow the publication of its second report. These include both the follow-up to the FE Strategy document *Success for All* and the follow up to the '14–19 proposals' (of which more in the next section), and, critically, the publication of the Skills Strategy targeted for June 2003 (Strategy Unit, 2002, para. 95). The influence of the Strategy Unit reports on these key departmentally-led publications in 2002 and 2003 is clear.

Thirdly, *In Demand* signals clearly the need for further reform of the qualifications system. The reference to enhancing the structures through which qualifications are designed and approved gives a clue not only to the Strategy Unit's thinking in relation to the role of the QCA and its partner regulatory authorities, but to the scope of the changes that *In Demand* envisages. In order to increase opportunities for unit-based achievement it will be necessary, says the Strategy Unit, to target reform at the 'qualification system' and the structures through which 'qualifications are designed and approved' (Strategy Unit, 2002, paras 52 and 53), rather than by introducing a new set of qualifications into the system. This proposition anticipates the Skills Strategy recommendation on credit the following year and once again seeks to relocate the development of 'unit-based achievement' within the reform of the qualifications system, rather than as an adjunct to it.

By the time the second *In Demand* report was published, it was clear that the influence of the Cabinet Office on other government departments was starting to produce a more systematic approach to the further development of a credit system. The election of David Miliband to Parliament that year and his almost immediate appointment as Minister of State for School Standards, cemented the connection between the policy works of the Cabinet Office and the DfES. Notwithstanding his formal focus on school standards, Miliband immediately began to take an interest in the wider development of the post-14 education system, and in particular on how the recommendations in *In Demand* about credit systems might be taken forward by the qualifications regulator. In the year prior to publication of the 2003 Skills Strategy White Paper, it seemed that there may yet be some movement towards the development of a credit system. However, there was still no clear view about how this should be taken forward, or indeed what the relationship between credits and qualifications might actually be. In particular, the QCA remained lukewarm about the development of credit-based qualifications. However, from August 2002, it was not just QCA that was invited to be involved in developing policy on credit.

Notes
1 With apologies to Raymond Carver.
2 Now Agored Cymru.

32

Unitisation or credit?
The phoney war of 2002

In June 2002, Estelle Morris launched a consultation on the DfES' strategy for reforming FE and training. *Success for All – Reforming Further Education and Training* (DfES, 2002). As part of this strategy the DfES undertook to work with both QCA and LSC: 'to review the barriers affecting the take up of qualifications, exploring the opportunities for opening up of unit achievement, the feasibility of a credit-based approach and the funding implications' (DfES, 2002, p. 24).

In August of that year David Miliband wrote to both QCA and LSC, asking them to take forward this commitment. Miliband's letter to both organisations refers explicitly to the potential benefits of a credit-based system:

> A credit-based system must serve to increase participation, support progression into further learning, including access into higher education, and promote recognition of cumulative achievement by allowing individuals to build up to a qualification over time.
>
> (Miliband, 2002)

Not only does Miliband ask QCA to 'consider the case for a credit-based approach to qualifications' (Miliband, 2002), but he makes very clear reference to a system of credit accumulation and transfer 'building up' to the achievement of a qualification. It seemed that the appointment of Miliband to the DfES had brought about a clearer and more radical view of the potential benefits of a credit system into play. However, alongside this characterisation of credit systems, Miliband's letter also invites QCA to take forward a separate strand of work: 'In relation to unitisation, I would like you to build on the work you have already done to prepare ... a plan for the promotion and phased implementation of a unitised system of qualifications in England.'

The division between unitisation and credit that emerged from the FEDA model of credit in the late 1990s, and was manifested in QCA's initial progress report to the DfES in 1999 (QCA, 1999), is still maintained in Miliband's letter of 2002. It anticipates: 'One of the benefits of having a unitised system will be the flexibility that this offers to the individual learner to accumulate the most appropriate units for their, or their employers, needs,' which, it might be argued, is clearly a benefit of a credit system, rather than of unitisation. It is clear that, in fact, the distinction between unitisation and credit is not based on any technical separation of these ideas, but on the limitations of policy: 'The Authority's work on credits should proceed independently of its remit to review the national qualifications framework' (Miliband, 2002).

In other words, the unitisation plan should be developed within the structure of the existing NQF, while the 'as yet ill-defined credit-based approach' is something that requires 'clear demonstration of added value and demand'. Thus unitisation should proceed, while the option to add credits to qualifications once unitised signals that the sequential approach to developing a credit system is still the model in the minds of the DfES. Nevertheless, we should see Miliband's letter as an explicit attempt to shift the work of the QCA forward at a faster rate than the previous four years and to ensure that, although 'unitisation' is the approved policy label, continuing consideration of the benefits of a credit system did not disappear from the agenda.

This updated remit for the QCA was supplemented by a parallel letter to LSC (Miliband, 2002a), asking the Council to take forward additional work on credit systems. In particular, the LSC was asked to ... 'explore and evaluate locally devised approaches to credits ... not leading necessarily to formal qualifications', as well as advising the DfES on how credits could be used in funding and 'as a measure of value added'. Thus, in addition to a clear separation of unitisation and credit in the remit to the QCA, the DfES also now makes a distinction between local and national uses of credit – that is, between credit inside and credit outside a qualification system. Although the remit to the LSC seems marginalised in relation to the QCA, Miliband's letter actually gives the Council scope for creativity in taking forward its brief (albeit 'locally'): 'I would like the Council to consider how it might support innovation locally ... for example through employer-led development projects, developing partnerships between colleges and universities ... and by promoting access to qualifications and units.'

In effect, the DfES was bringing the LSC into its strategy for development in order to ginger up the QCA's cautious approach since 1998, and to provide the opportunity for an alternative, provider-based constituency to influence the future direction of policy on credit systems. Both the QCA and LSC were asked to report back to the DfES on their different remits in October 2002, in order that their recommendations could influence the publication of *Success for All* in its final form (DfES, 2002a).

The two organisations produced their reports to the Minister in October 2002 as requested. QCA, which had appointed an officer and consultants to lead on its credit work, and who had produced its 1999 report, used this same internal team to produce its report to Miliband. The LSC, without such in-house resources and given the need to move quickly, commissioned the LSDA to undertake work on its behalf. The Council also asked LSDA to seek particular advice and contributions from NOCN, as its remit referred in several instances to the 'local credit systems' of OCNs. The LSDA report was produced for the LSC by Tony Tait, still a key advocate for credit systems over a decade after his work in producing *ABC?* (Tait, 2002).

The QCA report, though subtly different in tone, still focuses primarily on unitisation and remains sceptical about credit systems (QCA, 2002). As requested, QCA includes in the report a plan for unitisation that betrays the superficial nature of the application of the concept in practice. Re-reading the QCA report and comparing it to the process of developing the QCF, one is struck by the modesty of the Authority's 'unitisation plan'. The report confirms that 'the current criteria require each [qualification] to have a unitised structure where appropriate and approximately three quarters of qualifications are unitised'.

The report then goes on to account for the remaining 25 per cent of qualifications under three headings. GCSEs, the report recommends, are an exceptional case and should be treated separately. In a second group of small qualifications, 'unitisation would fragment the qualification' (QCA, 2002, p. 4), which, given the concept of unitisation as 'analysing the qualification into its constituent parts', is an interesting problem to have discovered. In a third group, 'the awarding body has not yet adapted its systems to cope with unitisation' (QCA, 2002, p. 4), even though, as the QCA states, 'a unitised structure' is a regulatory requirement. The QCA then goes on to propose a four-year programme of unitisation to bring the exceptions in this third category into the NQF by 'the end of summer 2007' (QCA, 2002, p. 10). Not exactly a rip-roaring pace of change, especially as GCSEs and 'small qualifications' account for a goodly proportion of the missing 25 per cent, and the remainder fall within the scope of an existing regulatory requirement.

The other noticeable feature of the QCA report is how its plans to develop 'size indicators' for units tortuously avoid the 'c' word. Keeping the polluting concept of credit outside the squeaky clean world of unitisation is sometimes only achieved with superhuman grammatical effort. The QCA draws on both published (QCA, 1999) and unpublished (Houston, 2002) reports to record its scepticism about the possibility of applying a size indicator to units based on 'notional learning time'. As the QCA's 1999 report on *Flexibility for Adult Learners* notes: 'The tool [sic] of notional learning time as a means of measuring size was moderately supported but a greater number of respondents opposed it' (QCA, 1999, p. 4).

Indeed, this opposition included all OCNs and many other credit consortia. The idea that 'notional time' rather than credit value should be used as a size indicator for units originates again in the FEDA model of credit, and was opposed in 1999 by all those organisations familiar with OCN credit systems. Three years later this scepticism remains:

> Work carried out in 2002 indicates deep-rooted views that a time-related measurement is unworkable in some contexts ... [and] many NTOs consulted thought that linking National Occupational Standards to any time-based measurement is completely inappropriate.
>
> (QCA, 2002, p. 7)

The fact that OCNs would support these views is not the point at issue here. Although the term 'credit' is never mentioned in this section of the QCA report, this remains a thinly veiled attack on credit systems by proxy. The opportunity to attack 'time-based measurement' without reference to credit is offered by the separation of 'unit size' from credit value by the FEU in 1995. Of course, the fact that one of the authors of the 2002 report to the QCA also worked for NCVQ in 1991 may or may not have influenced this view. Despite its lack of enthusiasm for developing these size indicators, QCA proposes to government (as requested) a plan to phase in such indicators on a voluntary basis from 2003–7 and then introduce them as a regulatory requirement for all qualifications by 2011.

If the QCA is not very enthusiastic about size indicators based on notional learning time, it is even less enthusiastic about credit. The report clearly regards credit as an adjunct to unitisation and therefore dwells at some length on whether it would be worthwhile undertaking additional work (referred to several times as 'complex' or 'difficult') to add this feature into the NQF. Taking its lead from Miliband's letter and the separate brief given to the LSC, the QCA report emphasises the local qualities of credit systems: 'credit can be used effectively on a small scale... There are examples of effective use by local consortia rather than whole regions' (QCA, 2002, p. 16); 'The impact of credit agreements appears to work best in these well-supported local environments' (QCA, 2002, p. 17).

The sceptical tone of the QCA's 1999 report gives way to the patronising tone of 2002. Noting that credit systems are 'strongly supported' by FE colleges and would bring 'increased flexibility for employers', the report then goes on to note that 'the use of credit points [sic] could have a negative impact on the value of qualifications in the national qualifications framework' (QCA, 2002, p. 18). This leads to a conclusion in the report that 'QCA has continuing doubts about the manageability of a potential national credit transfer system. The benefits of a national system ... need to be weighed against possible major implementation problems' (QCA, 2002, p. 19).

In the end the QCA recommends to the DfES work to develop 'draft principles' to guide the development of credit-based qualifications in England, with appropriate linkages to Wales, Northern Ireland and Scotland, followed by consultation on those principles. If the QCA's proposals on unitisation are modest, those on credit are positively self-deprecating. The outcomes of the report stand in stark contrast to each other. Four-and-a-half years after accepting its remit from Baroness Blackstone, the QCA's two recommendations are to develop some 'credit principles' and consult on them, while work on unitisation continues until 2011. It was in anticipation of precisely this kind of outcome that the DfES also asked the LSC to produce a less constrained report.

The LSC report is basically a summary of the report produced for the Council by LSDA, in consultation with NOCN. This dual influence is signalled in an early section of the LSC report that notes:

> There are currently two distinct uses of credit frameworks operating in the UK, namely:
>
> - The application of credit as a measure of achievement to any qualification or accreditation process
> - The award of credit(s).
>
> (LSC, 2002a, para. 17)

This characterisation, taken verbatim from the LSDA report, is the first time that such a distinction is made in such a public document, and is an indication of the collaborative approach of both NOCN and LSDA in their work for the LSC. It signifies both a distinction between LSDA's approach and those of its predecessor, FEDA, and a growing realisation between LSDA and NOCN that, now the high point of the credit movement had clearly passed and NOCN's strategy of creating exemplar credit-based qualifications in the NQF had not been realised, both organisations needed to be seen to be working together to convince the DfES to move forward on developing a credit system.

Where the QCA's report is sceptical and problem-oriented, the LSC's is optimistic and positive in its consideration of the various applications of credit systems outside the NQF. The LSC report also, by implication, criticises both QCA and government itself for not taking a clearer and more proactive stand on the development of credit systems when presented with the opportunity to do so. The LSC report notes a telling repudiation of QCA's anticipated recommendation on credit: 'Our research shows that there is a strong case for adopting or adapting what has already been established rather than starting from first principles' (LSC, 2002a, para. 9).

The report is no less critical of government itself:

> There is strong evidence that local innovation and responsiveness would develop further and faster if a number of support mechanisms were put in place... The uncertainty about credit is constraining further local

development and, in the Council's view there is a need for the endorse-
ment of ... credits at national policy level.

(LSC, 2002a, para. 34)

The report goes on to make a number of recommendations aimed at moving
the development of credit systems forward and taking stakeholders (including
QCA) with the LSC in this process. The report concludes:

> The Council considers that sufficient initial evidence has been found to
> support the view that the application of credits within a properly struc-
> tured credit framework can progress the development of education and
> training policy in a number of important areas... There is now a need to
> promote the development of a national system of credit in order to sus-
> tain progress.
>
> (LSC, 2002a, paras 43 & 44)

So, in October 2002, two separate reports on credit sat on David Miliband's
desk: one sceptical about credit systems, advising on a period of consultation
on draft principles for credit while proposing a lengthy process of continued
'unitisation' over a period of eight years; the other proposing a more urgent
and concrete set of actions (thanks to the influence of Tony Tait) to take forward the development of credit systems through a 'National Working Group'
on credit, to be established immediately and led by the LSC. Faced with these
distinctly different sets of recommendations from the two organisations he
had asked to take forward this work, Miliband did what any self-respecting
minister should have done and accepted the recommendations of both
reports. The QCA was invited to continue with its work on unitisation and to
develop some credit principles, while the LSC was asked to convene a
National Credit Advisory Group to take forward credit developments on a
wider front. In the event, *Success for All* was published in November 2002
with a passing reference to the need for 'greater flexibility in the qualifications
system' and confirmation that 'the LSC and QCA are working together to
increase availability of, and funding for, units... The QCA is currently considering how a unitised qualifications system might ... respond more flexibly to
employer needs' (DfES, 2002a, p. 24).

However, despite all the activity of the preceding months, and Miliband's
response to the QCA and LSC reports, *Success for All* contained no mention
of credit. It seemed that, despite the attempt to raise the profile of credit systems during 2002, the key policy document of that year failed to acknowledge its existence. That, plus the shift from positive advocacy of credit
systems in *In Demand* Part 1 to support for unit-based qualifications in *In
Demand* Part 2, which was released at the same time as *Success for All*, led

experienced 'creditologists' to doubt once more whether the creation of a National Credit Advisory Group was anything more than one more diversion from action on the implementation of a national system of credit-based qualifications. Of course, the introduction to *Success for All* was written by Charles Clarke rather than Estelle Morris, as had been anticipated. The story of how this change came about turned out to be far more important in the longer-term process of qualifications reform than any reference to credit, or the lack of it, in *Success for All*. Indeed, the whole sequence of events from Miliband's letters to the QCA and the LSC onwards in 2002 barely warranted a second glance from those following the continuing saga of qualifications reform in the post-Dearing era. In the process leading to the establishment of the QCF, 2002 turned out to be an extremely important year, but this importance had nothing to do with the events described in this chapter.

33

From reform to disaster:
The debacle of 2002

As I noted above in Chapter 21, the reforms that followed the publication of the Dearing Report on 16-19 qualifications failed to bring about the establishing of the NQF as a framework of credit-based qualifications. Indeed, this was one of the clear and intended consequences of the Dearing Review. However, like many such reports, there were also unintended consequences that arose from Dearing's recommendations, and one of these unintended consequences was to be critical in creating the political circumstances that led to the establishing of the QCF. We will never know what a credit-based NQF might have looked like in 1998. It's entirely possible that the events of 2002 might have unfolded in exactly the same way and that the clamour for reform might have undermined the case for credit-based qualifications in exactly the same way that the NQF, perhaps unfairly, was undermined by the A level controversy of 2002. In the event, however, one of the recommendations that Dearing *did* make – that a new AS level qualification should be established with a value of half an A level – would prove to be as instrumental in bringing about the development of credit-based qualifications in the longer term as the one he failed to make in 1996.

Before considering further the impact and the implications of the events of 2002, we need to turn first to a report published that same year as part of the standard procedures of government in creating publicly-funded agencies with statutory responsibilities. Five years after the 1997 Education Act led to the establishment of the QCA, the Cabinet Office – as it was required to do after five years – conducted a review of the work of the Authority. The review of QCA was announced in October 2001 and reported the following June. Although the focus of the review was primarily on the performance of the large exam boards for GCSEs and A levels, the review also encompassed vocational qualifications. In particular, the review evaluated the process through which vocational qualifications had been brought into the NQF during its initial phase of development.

The outcomes of the review were not positive. The *Guardian's* summary of the Cabinet Office report highlights the main problems:

> Pupils and teachers get a sloppy and unsatisfactory service from exam boards according to a Cabinet Office report that has condemned the

public examination system as fraught with delays and errors... Guidance
is inadequate, while the paperwork related to the system is unnecessarily complicated and duplicative.

(Smithers, 2002)

Although the language of the *Guardian* report focuses on the exam boards,
the responses of vocational awarding bodies to the Cabinet Office consultation
for the review were equally damning. The process through which 'other' vocational qualifications (that is, other than NVQs or GNVQs) had been accredited
(or in some cases had failed to be accredited) within the NQF was con-
demned as time-consuming, bureaucratic and inconsistent. Numerous examples of failure to meet promised deadlines for responses or decisions were
cited. The inconsistencies of decisions by QCA officers in different sectors or
subject areas were highlighted by many awarding bodies. Some awarding bodies complained that their qualifications were being excluded from the NQF
simply because a competitor's qualification had been accredited at an earlier
date, thereby discrediting the second submission as 'unnecessary duplication'.
Taken together with the rumblings of discontent about the introduction of the
Curriculum 2000 reforms from general awarding bodies that were beginning
to emerge during the review, the report made uncomfortable reading for QCA
(Cabinet Office, 2002).

Of course, as the *Guardian* article admits in its last line, the report also
includes some positive elements among this overall negative evaluation of the
QCA's performance. In the light of the later events of 2002, the Quinquennial
Review has perhaps diminished in its significance on the future development
of the QCA and the NQF. Nevertheless, there are some important messages in
the Cabinet Office report that are worthy of note. The most important thing to
note, of course, is that the report was written by the same arm of government
that had already published *In Demand* Part 1 and was in the process of producing Part 2. In this context, the accusations of bureaucracy, inconsistency
and lack of responsiveness to the needs of individual learners take on a more
serious complexion. The quinquennial review seemed to confirm to the
Cabinet Office that the QCA itself might be an impediment to the reform programme it envisaged in the *In Demand* reports. Taken together with the other
problems for QCA that arose during 2002, we can be fairly certain that those
people from the Cabinet Office that led the work on the Skills Strategy in
2003 would have been well disposed towards the view that qualifications
reform would need to be a major plank of any strategy based on the ideas in
the *In Demand* reports.

The publication of the Quinquennial Review report in June 2002 was
quickly forgotten as the events of the summer of 2002 started to unfold. The
seeds of the problem had been sown through the Curriculum 2000 reforms

and the development of AS levels as part of a new 'two-stage' A level. The technical details of these reforms lie beyond the scope of this paper, but, as the House of Commons Select Committee later decided in its review of the affair, the primary cause of the problem was the government's decision to ignore both the pleas of awarding bodies and the advice of QCA in pressing ahead with the implementation of the new AS levels, without an initial pilot programme to test the new arrangements for marking and determining grades for both the AS levels themselves and the new A levels of which they formed a part. The decision to rush into these new A2 exams (the second part of the two-part A level) without piloting them first was the main cause of the problems of that summer's exam period in the view of Mike Tomlinson, in his inquiry into the debacle (*The Independent*, 2003).

The crisis began with complaints from schools that exam boards had been unfairly lowering grades in both AS and A level units in order to 'protect standards'. In reality, the protection of standards was manifested through a fear of exam boards that their new qualifications might be seen as too easy, so grade boundaries were adjusted to take account of these fears. The lack of any clear guidance from QCA on this issue (it seems that the implications of the new AS/A2 structure had simply not been anticipated in advance) led to one awarding body, OCR, interpreting this issue of standards differently from the other two A level boards. As the welter of criticism from schools and the threat of legal action by the parents of students whose grades had been adjusted downwards grew over the summer, the first casualty of the crisis was Ron McClone, the Chief Executive of OCR, who resigned in August 2002.

Mike Tomlinson was appointed to head an independent inquiry into the crisis in late August and immediately the scale of the problem became apparent. Tomlinson's initial assessment of the issues to be addressed suggested that up to 450,000 A and AS level papers may have to be checked and the grades of some 100,000 students may need to be reviewed. In his resignation letter, Ron McClone made it clear that he felt OCR had been pushed into suppressing 'grade inflation' in A levels by QCA officers. It was not long before the pressure on Sir William Stubbs, Chairman of the QCA, became too much for even his hardy constitution to bear and, with great and very public reluctance, he tendered his resignation to Estelle Morris, the Secretary of State for Education (*The Independent*, 2002).

The sorry saga was completed in early October when Estelle Morris also resigned. Although she cited a range of reasons for her resignation and could not herself be held accountable for pushing through the Curriculum 2000 reforms against the advice of both the QCA and DfES officials (that responsibility was David Blunkett's), nevertheless the connection between the events of the summer of 2002 and her leaving were too clear to warrant dispute. So, the A level fiasco claimed three high-profile victims in the space of six weeks during the summer of 2002. In the middle of all this, one might have been for-given for not noticing that a new chief executive had taken up post at QCA. Although Ken Boston's first weeks in the job were consumed almost entirely with the A levels crisis and the Tomlinson Inquiry, it was not long before the new Chief Executive began to signal to both government and to those involved in the design and delivery of qualifications that QCA might become a different kind of organisation once the dust had settled. Tomlinson's report was delivered in April 2003 (*The Independent*, 2003), by which time talk of further qualification reform was clearly back on the political agenda.

In retrospect, we can see that Ken Boston's tenure as Chief Executive of the QCA was bounded by two crises. Having taken up his post just before the A level crisis of 2002 exploded, he left it at the end of 2008 as a victim of the 'SATs' fiasco of that year. Despite these crisis-induced 'book-ends' to his term in office, the ethos of his period at the QCA is one of calm and persistent pursuit of a progressive agenda for reform, with a clear focus on the interests of learn-ers. This steady support for the development of the QCF, which passed from policy announcement one year into his tenure to implementation one month before its end, should not be underestimated.

Although the events of summer 2002 were focused on one new (or partly new) qualification, and in particular on the actions of one awarding body, the criticism of the qualifications system went much wider. Indeed, the resigna-tions of Bill Stubbs and Estelle Morris only served to confirm the impression that there was a general and serious malaise in the system, rather than a tech-nical problem that could be ironed out by issuing clearer guidance in subse-quent years (which was the immediate solution to the problem and, judging by the lack of a similar crisis in 2003, one that apparently worked). Having delivered his report, Mike Tomlinson was immediately commissioned to pro-duce a further report on the future development of 14–19 qualifications to overcome the problems raised by the experiences of 2002. This time (and unlike Dearing in 1996), Tomlinson was given an open brief to produce pro-posals for the future. There was to be no protection of existing qualifications in the remit – the reputation of A levels as the gold standard of qualifications had been severely shaken by the crisis of 2002 – and the expectation from the outset was that Tomlinson would produce a set of recommendations that pro-posed a radical shake-up of the whole system.

Of course, Tomlinson's remit focused solely on general qualifications. Notwithstanding this technical limitation, the commissioning of the Tomlinson Review of 14–19 qualifications set the tone for a wider shake-up of the qualifi-cations system. It was in this context that the DfES produced, in July 2003, the much anticipated Skills Strategy White Paper, *21st Century Skills: Realising Our Potential* (DfES et al., 2003).

34

Skills, modernisation and credit

We are now almost at the point where this story began. All the various reports and papers submitted to ministers in the process of developing the QCF and preparing for its implementation refer back to *21st Century Skills: Realising Our Potential* as the origin for development of the framework. As we have seen, the two Strategy Unit reports of November 2001 and November 2002 prepared the ground for the release of the Skills Strategy White Paper in July 2003. The White Paper was trailed well in advance, consultation was extensive and sections of the document circulated widely in draft format to ensure that the different interests groups both inside and outside government were able to locate the references that they wished to see inside the strategy. The White Paper was published by four government departments, including – unusually – the Treasury, and was seen across government as an important blueprint for future reform. Like many such cross-departmental documents, Cabinet Office staff were involved in much of the drafting work.

Chapter 5 of *21st Century Skills* is entitled 'Reforming Qualifications and Training Programmes'. Not long before the final publication of the White Paper, a draft of this chapter was circulated for comment to selected contacts outside government. Although there were several references to the need to make qualifications more flexible and more responsive to the demands of employers, there was no explicit reference to credit in the document. Indeed, such was the low-key nature of the QCA's further investigation of credit systems in the five years since Baroness Blackstone had asked the Authority to take on this work that such an omission was hardly unexpected. There were references to the need for unitisation, but by 2003 this term had been fully incorporated into descriptive accounts of the existing NQF and carried no meaningful implication of change. Just as the explicit reference to credit in Part 1 of *In Demand* had been weakened to a reference to units in Part 2, so it seemed that the Skills Strategy White Paper would continue to omit any meaningful reference to credit. The later draft of Chapter 5 seemed to confirm this view. However, between this draft and the published version of *21st Century Skills* that appeared about a month later, the text of Chapter 5 was changed.

Why this late change was made, who drafted it and who was responsible for approving its inclusion in the White Paper are all matters for continuing speculation. My guess is that someone from the Strategy Unit, with close links to the 'reformist tendency' in the DfES and connections in the policy world recently inhabited by David Miliband, added some late text to Chapter 5, and in so doing created an additional reform objective for the skills strategy. No doubt the work of the QCA was considered, and the actual wording of the text suggests that perhaps colleagues in Wales were also influential in this late insertion. Perhaps the LSDA report on Credit Systems of that year also had an influence (Tait, 2003). But the wording also clearly goes beyond these parameters and includes features of the system of credit-based qualifications that had apparently slipped off the political agenda. This was no one-line throw-away reference either – the commitment was clearly spelt out and is worth repeating in full here:

> The consultation on the Skills Strategy has shown widespread support for developing a national credit framework for adults. This is seen as a way of offering the greatest flexibility and responsiveness, with units of qualifications being assigned credit based on a standard system. Supporters argue that adult learners can more easily build up units of credit over time towards qualifications, transferring that achievement between different providers if they wish, and having more choice in the units of qualifications that they combine. Employers can combine together units of qualifications drawn from different sources to form the training programme that best suits their needs.
>
> (DfES et al., 2003, 5.39)

Note that the term 'supporters argue' harks back very explicitly to the language of *The Learning Age* (DfEE, 1998). Note also that, despite the positive language of this paragraph, there is no explicit commitment to action contained within it. Is it possible that, as in *The Learning Age,* credit systems would be praised at second hand and then subject to yet more 'investigation'? The following paragraph confirms that this time there would be action rather than words:

> Building on the preparatory work already undertaken, we believe that the time has come to commit to developing a credit framework for adults.
>
> (DfES et al., 2003, 5.40).

Those of us who had been the 'arguing supporters' of credit systems for some 20 years read these lines in amazement. Notwithstanding the fact that it still referred to a credit framework and was focused on the needs of adults, the commitment was both unequivocal and considered. Unlike previous references to credit, this one clearly linked the process of credit accumulation to the achievement of qualifications, made explicit reference to credit transfer and implied that the writer understood the concept of 'rules of combination'. The echo of the Fryer Report 'an idea whose time has come', is surely deliberate. In the section of the document that follows this extract, the White Paper charges 'QCA and key partners' with taking forward the development of 'a joint programme to develop a shared approach to a credit system which could be expanded over time to a national credit framework' (DfES et al., 2003, 5.40). It seems that the additional work on credit systems commissioned from both the QCA and LSC in late 2002 had actually, if belatedly, born fruit.

The opportunity to take forward the further development of credit systems within – for the very first time – a positive and high-profile policy commitment, linked to a major programme of reform, presented itself almost out of the blue. The question was – had the commitment come too late? By 2003 it was clear that the high water mark of OCN credit systems had passed, and that the coalition of interests that had gathered to support *ABC?* and later the AoC's demands had dissipated. Although the arguments for a credit system were still being made, they were made by fewer people representing a smaller range of interests and with a declining base of (relevant) evidence to support the arguments in favour of such a system. It seems, however, that this time the arguments were being made to the right people and the positive messages about credit systems were not being intercepted en route to the White Paper.

In retrospect, the linking of credit systems with arguments in favour of responsiveness to employer demand and flexibility in a rapidly changing economic environment proved to be more powerful in 2003 than had the arguments about inclusion and widening participation in 1997. Although arguments about individual choice and recognising achievements suffused both contexts, it was clear that the rationale for accepting the case for a national credit framework was based on a very different set of preconceptions than would have been the case if Dearing or Blunkett had accepted the same case at an earlier date. It also brought into play a new set of key partners in taking forward the development of credit systems that had little or no experience of the 'pre-history of credit', including most awarding bodies, all Sector Skills Councils (SSCs) and, of course, the regulatory authorities themselves.

The other obvious fact about the announcement in the White Paper was its explicit connection to the Skills Strategy. Although it was nice to be wanted, it was also clear that credit systems were wanted in a particular context. How might the previous history of credit systems – the 'case' that government now indicated it was prepared to accept – provide models for the future development of credit systems within the Skills Strategy? How might the pioneers of the Manchester model of credit react to the proposition that, instead of using credit systems to recognise the achievements of excluded and disadvantaged learners, the government now proposed to use them to 'help businesses achieve the productivity, innovation and productivity needed to compete' and 'improve...efficiency in the demand and supply of different skills' (DfES, 2003, p. 7)? How might 'QCA and key partners' engage with this previous history of credit systems in taking forward the programme of reform that was signalled by *21st Century Skills*? Once the shock of reading the commitment of government in the White Paper had receded, these were the thoughts that began to circulate among the now less numerous, still partly incredulous and temporarily bemused set of credit enthusiasts who contemplated what would now happen to realise this commitment.

The Skills Strategy White Paper undoubtedly signals the beginning of the process that led to the launch of the QCF five years later. It is also undoubtedly the single most important (in fact, the only explicit) policy commitment (in England) to the development of credit within the national framework of qualifications that has yet been seen (the main reason why it has been seized on and delivered so concretely). Nevertheless, as I have tried to show, the White Paper was by no means either the beginning or the end of the story. The development of the QCF was far from an inevitable consequence of the White Paper commitment. Once the announcement was made, the struggle to interpret its practical manifestation began.

The commitment in the White Paper refers explicitly to 'the preparatory work already undertaken'. What was this 'preparatory work'? Does it refer to the QCA's position paper on unitisation and credit? To the CQFW? To the recommendations in *In demand*? To the work of the FEU/FEDA/LSDA? Or to the 20-year history of OCN developments that had finally driven the concept of a credit system firmly into the perspective of policymakers? All these questions were unanswered in *21st Century Skills* and remained open to be contested as soon as the announcement in the White Paper was made. All worshippers in the broad church of credit received the news of 2003 with great interest. But which vision of the promised land would prevail?

I would argue that the QCF actually over-delivers the Skills Strategy commitment and goes beyond what government was actually imagining it was asking for in 2003. This is not to characterise the QCF as opportunist, but it is to suggest that there were a number of important decisions yet to be made in developing the QCF that were not an inevitable outcome of the commitment in *21st Century Skills*. There was still a great deal of work to be done to transform the commitment to an adult credit framework into the implementation of the QCF. It is to this path from 2003 onwards that this story now turns.

35

England expects

As with many such commitments, it took a little while for the mists that surrounded the Skills Strategy to clear and to reveal exactly how the government wished the commitment to develop an adult credit framework to be taken forward. It also became clear that the Skills Strategy commitment was not perceived as a mandate for change in Wales. In effect, the commitment to an adult credit framework was seen at the outset as an English policy. Although Northern Ireland took its lead from the Skills Strategy commitment and was content to align its own developments with those in England, this was not the case in Wales. In this context, the QCF was in danger of becoming trapped in a constitutional vacuum. Although the NQF had been created prior to devolution through an act of the Westminster parliament, and responsibility for maintenance of the NQF was shared equally across England, Wales and Northern Ireland, responsibility for educational policy in Wales rested with the Welsh Assembly government. In theory, any reform of the NQF would require the consent of all three governments. In practice, the position of the UK government would be critical to the future of the QCF.

The existence of the CQFW in Wales also presented a potential impediment to making progress across all three countries. Why would Wales want to develop an adult credit framework when, it was argued, it already had one? Indeed, there were already suggestions by the end of 2003 that the CQFW model should simply be extended to England and Northern Ireland (MacNamara, 2003). The Federation of Awarding Bodies (FAB) produced a paper welcoming the announcement of 'A Credit Framework in England', and stating explicitly that it had been 'actively involved in the development of the CQFW and would wish to bring to the developments in England the understanding that we have gained' (Federation of Awarding Bodies, 2003, p. 3).

As the paper makes clear, this 'understanding' includes the assertion that 'unitisation is the foundation of a credit framework' and that '"credit" is a means of measuring achieved learning ... [that] would provide an easily, but more detailed means of interpreting relative achievement, and in particular partial achievement', and that this approach could 'bring added value to the qualifications framework' (Federation of Awarding Bodies, 2003, p. 5).

The FAB view is clear and is based very explicitly on the FEDA/CQFW model of unitisation and credit-rating. Interestingly, the FAB paper suggests that 'It is over 10 years since credit was first advanced as a means of recognising small episodes of learning' (Federation of Awarding Bodies, 2003, p. 1), which seems to deny explicitly the previous experience of one of its own members (NOCN), as well as locating the starting point for 'credit' clearly in the FEU/FEDA tradition.

The suggestion that the CQFW model might be adopted in England and Northern Ireland, and that there was no need to address the Skills Strategy commitment in Wales, placed QCA in a difficult position. As in 1998, it once again threatened to drive a wedge between the role of the Authority as a regulator of qualifications, which it carried out in partnership with Wales and Northern Ireland, and its role in taking forward the development of an adult credit framework in England at the behest of the DfES. The potential geographical limitation of the framework was accentuated by QCA's remit to work closely with the LSC in developing this new framework, a remit that served to accentuate the English nature of the proposed reform.

In the first instance – that is, in the latter part of 2003 and the early months of 2004 – it seemed as though the policy commitment in the Skills Strategy might not bear fruit. The LSC convened a National Advisory Group on credit that included many of the usual suspects, with an intention that this group should advise the Council on how it might support the development of an adult credit framework that was somehow detached from any responsibility for reform of the NQF. Meanwhile, QCA was asked to continue to take forward its own work on credit in this new context, but there was no indication in 2003 that QCA perceived this remit as in any way requiring a reform of the NQF. The 'investigative work' of QCA since 1998 led directly into the production and refinement of a set of 'Principles for a Credit Framework for England' that were produced by QCA in draft form in late 2003, debated and amended at some length through the LSC Credit Advisory Group and published in final form in February 2004 (QCA and LSC, 2004).

The Credit Principles mark a shift from the earlier FAB proposals. The process of consultation through the National Credit Advisory Group, which included several experienced OCN practitioners (including myself), had restored the central role of credit as an award to learners, rather than a measure of comparability between achievements. Although the *Credit Principles* still allow that 'The credit framework can be used for several purposes and applications, providing a common and consistent way to recognise, measure, value and compare achievement' (QCA and LSC, 2004, p. 2), it is clear in its opening statement that 'The aim of a credit framework for England is to provide a means by which credit can be gained by learners for their achievement' (QCA and LSC, 2004, p. 2).

Notwithstanding this significant difference from the unitisation and credit-rating model, the *Credit Principles* are clearly located in a context in which it is assumed that the credit framework will be established within the regulations and requirements of the NQF: 'The aim is to build on the shared ownership and processes of the NQF... All qualifications accredited to the NQF will be expected to have credit value assigned to their units' (QCA and LSC, 2004, pp. 6-9). The *Credit Principles* document then goes on to set out a glossary of terms which it acknowledges 'are drawn from the Credit Common Accord for Wales'.

Principles for a Credit Framework for England therefore constitutes an interim stage in the development of thinking about the QCF between its initial July 2003 policy reference in *21st Century Skills* and its first technical specification in November 2004. Although building explicitly on aspects of the CQFW model as FAB had suggested, the *Principles* also accommodate the central definition of credit as an award made to a learner and propose that the introduction of the credit framework will actually have an impact of some kind on existing qualifications. The implication of the *Principles* document is that QCA accepted that the development of the credit framework in England would be taken forward as part of its regulatory functions, albeit without radical reform of the NQF. Although the unitisation and credit-rating model had become established in Wales, the residual strength of OCN credit systems in England made it impossible to import that model directly across the border without also acknowledging the alternative history of credit systems based on awards made to learners. The *Credit Principles* document accomplishes this break with the CQFW model without putting forward in its place an explicit alternative. In this sense it is a document that perfectly represents the transitional nature of the shift towards the QCF model that was taking place at this time.

Through the development of these *Credit Principles*, and through several meetings of the LSC National Credit Advisory Group, some of the debates from the 1990s about the nature and purpose of a credit framework and the relationship between such a credit framework and the national qualifications system were revisited. In 2003-4, however, the context for this debate had shifted. Though now at the beginning of a period of (relative) decline, the OCN credit system had proved itself to be robust enough and attractive enough to both learners and providers to be a more powerful model for reform than had been the case at the time of the Dearing Review of 16-19 qualifications. The LSDA's role in promoting the benefits of a credit system was both less prominent and (as its joint work with the NOCN for the LSC had shown) more collaborative than either FEDA's or the FEU's in the 1990s. In this context the principle that a credit framework should be based around the award of credits to learners, rather than the allocation of numerical values to units and qualifications, was accepted more readily in 2004 than it had been in 1996.

There was also a very clear exposition in *21st Century Skills* that the development of an adult credit framework was seen as an integral part of an explicit series of reforms to the qualification system. The influence of the *In Demand* papers is significant here. Not only that, but there was a very clear indication in the White Paper that QCA in particular should now build on its previous work in actually implementing this credit framework. In this context it would be difficult for QCA to continue to treat a credit framework as a continuing strand of development activity, separate from its work as a regulator.

Once QCA had accepted this role, and the principle was established that the credit framework in England would be built on the central aim of awarding credit to learners, it became obvious by the spring of 2004 that the implementation of the Skills Strategy Commitment would need to involve some significant reform of the NQF. The ongoing process of unitisation which was seen as the key to introducing more flexibility into the NQF was (as I have tried to show above) having no noticeable impact on the structure of qualifications in the existing national framework. Despite FAB's concerns, QCA reiterated its commitment to the development of credit-based qualifications in its presentation of the Credit Principles and assumed that work would now begin on the development of awarding body processes, within the NQF, that would result in the award of credit to learners and to the ability of learners to accumulate these credits towards a qualification (Boston, 2004).

During the spring of 2004 QCA began to advance the proposition that the reform of qualifications through unitisation and the development of a credit framework should be brought together in a single process of reform. Indeed, such proposals had been advanced through the National Credit Advisory Group since the autumn of 2003. Of course, the implications of such a move for the English nature of the credit framework and for the assumption that reform should take place within the NQF were potentially profound.

We should not underestimate the importance of the lead taken by QCA itself at this stage of the debate about the precise nature of the credit-based reforms. Ken Boston's appointment as Chief Executive led to a distinct change in both ethos and direction for QCA. Boston was a natural reformer, with a wider vision than his predecessors and some experience of qualifications reform (and, indeed, of credit systems) in his native Australia. By the time *21st Century Skills* was published, internal restructuring within QCA had already swept aside a number of QCA's old hands and brought in some new appointments from outside the organisation. In particular, some of the senior staff that QCA had inherited at its inception from NCVQ and SCAA left the organisation in 2003. Late that year, Mary Curnock Cook was appointed as Director of Vocational Qualifications and charged with taking forward QCA's commitments within the Skills Strategy, including the development of a credit framework. Boston spoke publicly in favour of 'a single framework of qualifications, based on credit', and Curnock Cook backed his vision in her public statements. By early 2004 it was clear that there was an appetite for reform within the QCA itself and that the development of a framework of qualifications based on a credit system was now to be the focus for this reform process.

This shift was formally confirmed in a revised remit from the DfES to the QCA and LSC in April 2004 that brought together the previously separate remits for vocational qualifications reform and development of a credit framework. It was this shift that finally enabled QCA to go beyond its previous work on 'investigating the benefits' of a credit framework and start to embed the concept of credit into the heart of its vocational qualifications reform programme. Unlike its response to the Blackstone letter of 1998, a different regime at QCA took its obligations for reform seriously enough to ensure that, from April 2004 onwards, the development of a credit framework and the reform of qualifications would be seen as a single process of reform. In the summer of 2004 the appointment of Sue Georgious, with her long experience of work both in an OCN and (latterly) as the Acting Chief Executive of NOCN, to the post of Head of Vocational Learning and Qualifications, cemented this single reform process.

Thus, although the 2003 White Paper is rightly seen as the policy launch pad for the QCF, it should be emphasised that the QCF was not the only possible outcome of this policy commitment. Alternative interpretations of the commitment to an adult credit framework might have held sway. The continuing repercussions of the 2002 A level crisis not only created the objective conditions for a radical reform of the qualifications system, they also brought about a change in both the culture of QCA and in the people responsible for taking forward the Skills Strategy commitment within the organisation that would be essential for the creation of the QCF.

Dearing may have passed up the opportunity to recommend a credit-based NQF from the outset when the credit movement was at its strongest, but perhaps the outcomes of the Dearing Review actually created by accident a firmer basis for the QCF to develop than the development of the NQF and A/AS levels that were the intended outcomes of his report. A few years later, and following the A level fiasco of 2002, a combination of a clear policy commitment, different personalities and a changed organisational culture created conditions for success in the reform process that were simply not present in 1997.

36

What kind of framework? And what kind of credit?

Even with a clear remit that brought together the development of a credit framework within the overall programme of qualifications reform, there was still a wide range of options to consider about the kind of credit and qualifications framework that should be developed. Although it was clear that a straight importing of the CQFW model would not meet the expectations of government in *21st Century Skills*, the *Principles for a Credit Framework for England* still held open the possibility that some form of hybrid model of a credit framework might be developed that drew on both the Welsh and Scottish experiences in establishing a different kind of framework in England.

The SCQF was formally launched in 2002 (SCQF, 2002). It brought together within a single framework both HE qualifications and qualifications offered through the SQA. Although the SQA has statutory responsibility for the regulation of some of the qualifications in the SCQF, the framework itself is not a regulated framework. The position of the SQA, which has both a regulatory function and an awarding function in Scotland, is very different from that of either regulators or awarding bodies in the rest of the UK. The inclusion of HE within the scope of the SCQF also made it quite different in concept from the proposed reforms in *21st Century Skills*. There was also an assumption from the outset that, as the QCA was to lead this particular reform, the new framework would be a regulated framework. And there was no remit in Scotland to reform the framework of qualifications regulated by the SQA.

For these reasons, it was accepted at an early stage of the reform process that the new framework would not be based on the SCQF model. Although important lessons might be drawn from the Scottish experience, there was no expectation that the particular characteristics of the SCQF could or should be reproduced in England, Wales and Northern Ireland. The DfES required that any new framework should 'align and articulate' with the SCQF (of which more later), but would not be modelled on its design features. The *Credit Principles* document confirmed this 'separate but aligned' model.

The CQFW presented a more complex issue for qualifications reform. Although similar in many ways to the SCQF - for example, it includes HE in its scope and is an 'enabling', not a regulatory, framework - the CQFW operated in one of the three UK jurisdictions covered by the existing NQF. If - as government expected – the reform of qualifications would bring about changes to the NQF, then this would by definition have an impact on Wales and therefore on the CQFW. The involvement of awarding bodies in the CQFW Credit Common Accord was also a factor to consider in the practical process of taking forward the reform agenda. There was, therefore, an expectation among the people involved in CQFW activity that, as the Credit Principles had implied, some of the characteristics of the Welsh model of credit would be taken into the QCF. As we have seen in a previous chapter, the model of credit adopted by the CQFW was based on quite a different history from that which had evolved through OCNs in England, Wales and Northern Ireland. In order to understand why the Welsh model was rejected as the basis for the reform programme in England, it is necessary to delve in a little more detail into the workings of the CQFW.

The CQFW, announced in 2002, was formally launched at almost exactly the same time as *21st Century Skills* was published (CQFW, 2003). However, as we have seen previously, the CQFW Project, which preceded the implementation of the framework, built explicitly on the work undertaken through the Welsh Modularisation and Credit Project and the subsequent CREDIS Project. The costs of maintaining and updating the CREDIS database in its CD-based format meant that the CQFW Project gradually dropped the focus of the CREDIS Project on unitisation and focused its energies primarily on the credit-rating of qualifications. In conjunction with both FEDA (and later the LSDA) and NICATS, the CQFW Project launched in 2001 the UK Credit Equivalence Project.

The UK Credit Equivalence Project, as its name suggests, aimed to:

Establish agreed credit equivalences for nationally recognised qualifications and their constituent units that will enable learners, deliverers of learning, gatekeepers and employers to compare qualifications and make judgements on how accredited portions of learning relate to one another.

(NICATS, 2002)

The connections with the previous work of CREDIS, based on FEDA's conception of credit as a tool for comparing achievements, are clear. Note that awarding bodies are absent from the list of beneficiaries of credit equivalence and, indeed, awarding bodies are not referred to in the approach to 'ascribing credit equivalence', described in the outline to the project. During 2001 and 2002 the Project established a range of 'credit equivalences' for qualifications through a process of scrutinising the documentation related to the qualification or constituent 'accredited portions', and comparing it with the definition of credit used in the CQFW Project, which had, in order to accommodate the fact that HEIs in Wales were also part of the Project, now shifted from the previously used 30-hour unit of credit to a ten-hour unit of credit. Among the credit equivalences established through the Project were the following:

- an A level, AS Level or AVCE unit = 9 credits at level 3
- a GNVQ Intermediate unit = 10 credits at level 2
- a GCSE (grades A* to C) = 15 credits at level 2
- a GCSE (Grade D and below) = 15 credits at level 1

(NICATS, 2002)

The figures for A levels correspond precisely to 2007 CQFW equivalences, though the figures for GCSEs from CQFW in 2008 adjust credit ratings upwards to 18. The UK Credit Equivalence Project website also notes: 'The CQFW project is currently credit equivalencing [sic] all professional qualifications offered within Wales.'

As the last entry on the UK Credit Equivalence Project website is dated 8 October 2002, it is difficult to ascertain what happened to these equivalences and whether they were ever used. There is no evidence that they appeared on any information produced about the qualifications or units in question. Indeed, it is unclear whether or not the awarding bodies responsible for these qualifications were even aware that such credit equivalences had been established. Conversely, there is also no evidence that these equivalences were used by OCNs in Wales (or Northern Ireland) in their processes leading to the award of credit. This is hardly surprising, as credit-rating (or 'credit equivalencing') cannot lead to the award of credit. Despite the rather impressive title, it seems as though the UK Credit Equivalence Project actually embodies Robertson's 'mass blessing by numbers' at its most pointless.

The aim of establishing credit equivalences for 'all Post-16 education' was one of the principle aims of the CQFW Project and informed the concept of the CQFW itself. Although the CQFW does identify credit as an award made to a learner, the CQFW also 'brings all accredited learning into a single unifying structure' (CQFW, 2003, p. 3). The CQFW map of learning and progression routes is certainly comprehensive and, indeed, it extends far beyond the list of qualifications with credit equivalence. What then is the relationship between credit and qualifications in the CQFW? As the CQFW implementation plan makes clear: 'The existing national qualifications frameworks are not being replaced and will be maintained through all the mainstream qualifications' (CQFW, 2003, p. 3).

Taken together with the definition of credit and the concept of credit equivalence, it becomes clear that, in the CQFW, credits and qualifications are actually two *different* ways of recognising learner achievement, and that the concept of credit equivalence allows one to be compared with the other while remaining separate. The FEDA proposition that a credit framework could be established that 'need not alter the value or characteristics of existing qualifications' (FEDA, 1996, p. 4) manifests itself clearly within the concept of the CQFW. In other words, if learning leads to a qualification in Wales then it is part of the CQFW. If it leads to the award of credit outside these 'existing national qualifications frameworks', then it is also part of the CQFW. Clearly, this conception of credits and qualifications being separate rather than integral entities within the CQFW gives the framework a very different character from the QCF.

Actually, the CQFW does envisage a potential connection between credits and qualifications: 'Recognition of partial achievement will be available, once credit value has been assigned to units for individuals who otherwise might be considered to have failed' (CQFW, 2003, p. 3).

This deficit model (credits are available to learners who fail whole qualifications) informs the perceived connection between credits and qualifications within the CQFW. It is completely absent (and rightly so) from the QCF. The idea that credits represent 'partial achievement' is dependent on a qualifications-based rather than a credit-based concept of a framework. Such a conception derives inevitably from an approach that uses credit to compare the value of qualifications, rather than to recognise learner achievement. Of course, it was necessary to establish such a model in order to draw awarding bodies into involvement in the Credit Common Accord, while at the same time maintaining the separation of credits and qualifications in the CQFW model. Although events in Wales have moved on, this concept of credit as partial achievement illustrates why, in this important respect, the CQFW offered from the outset an inappropriate model to take into the QCF.

In one respect, however, the CQFW does mark an advance on previous credit developments in Wales. This is because, unlike its predecessor projects, the CQFW has involved awarding bodies (as well as other partners of course) in its work. These bodies have become involved in the CQFW through the development of its Credit Common Accord (CQFW, 2006). The Accord is an attempt to fuse together the use of credit as a measure of comparability between qualifications and as an award made to a learner. Awarding bodies are 'recognised' within the terms of the Accord, either to 'assign credit value' to a unit or qualification, or to award credit to learners. However, the Accord is clear: 'Recognised Bodies that choose to assign credit to units [rather than to qualifications] are not required to award that credit' (CQFW, 2003, p. 7).

In this respect, the Accord mirrors precisely FEDA's proposals in *A Framework for Credit* that the 'ascribing' of credit value to a unit is a possible end in itself, rather than a means through which credit is awarded to learners. This was the experience of credit that the ten awarding bodies involved in the development of the Accord during 2003–5 shared through their activity within the CQFW. The experiences of these awarding bodies are captured in a 2005 report entitled *Learning from Experience* (Lillis et al., 2005). What is clear from the full report (though not from the Executive Summary) is that the process followed by most awarding bodies involved credit-rating existing qualifications and units. Credits were assigned to units that did not conform to CQFW's own unit specifications (as well as some that did), but only a handful of credits were actually awarded by one of the awarding bodies involved in the development of the Accord. In effect, the Accord maintained the process of credit-rating previously developed in Wales and extended it to a group of awarding bodies. In so doing, it created an experience of credit for some of the people working in these awarding bodies that was actually very different from that which informed the development of the QCF.

This collective experience of the operation of an alternative model of credit was formalised through the commissioning of FAB to take forward the work in developing and evaluating the Accord (*Learning from Experience* was formally commissioned by FAB, rather than by the CQFW itself). Representatives of the ten awarding bodies involved in the project met together under the auspices of the FAB Credit Group, and it was this group that transmitted the experience of credit in the CQFW into both their own individual awarding bodies and to the wider FAB community. None of the Welsh OCNs were involved in this work.

When the remit for bringing together the reform of qualifications with the development of a credit framework was announced, it was the FAB Credit Group, and its collective experience, that led the responses of many awarding bodies to the QCA's initial proposals. The fact that these proposals were quite different from the CQFW caused some consternation within this group. Why, asked FAB, did the QCA not adopt the CQFW approach? Why was 'the experience of the awarding body community' being ignored in the development of the new framework? For example:

> the CQFW has worked with many awarding bodies on the assignment of credit to existing NQF qualifications ... that should be built on... QCA's proposals advocate a completely different approach rather than building on known and tested practice.
>
> (Joint Council for Qualifications, 2005)

Actually, of course, the QCA *was* building on 'known and tested practice', but it was not the practice of credit-rating 'existing NQF qualifications' that was taking place in the CQFW, it was the practice of awarding credits to learners that had been developed by OCNs over the previous 25 years. Indeed, while ten awarding bodies were establishing this 'known and tested practice' in Wales during 2004-5 that led to the award of credits to four learners, the three Welsh OCNs awarded some 350,000 credits to 110,000 learners in the same period. Although there were undoubtedly positive experiences for these awarding bodies emerging from their involvement in the CQFW Project, in one critical respect - the awarding of credit to learners - they offered almost no evidence of practice. *Learning from Experience* simply confirmed what was already known to the QCA - that the CQFW model was not appropriate for the development of the QCF, and that it would be necessary to look outside the experiences of awarding bodies in the NQF if the ambitions of government for the new framework were to be realised.

Lest this sounds too harsh an account of the CQFW and too dismissive an assessment of FAB's role in the development of the QCF, it should be noted that both the CQFW and FAB have also contributed positively to the development of the new framework. An internal paper for QCA and LSC entitled *Learning from Learning From Experience* (Wilson, 2005), is sub-titled 'How We Propose to Build on the Work of the CQFW', and there is no doubt that the work of the CQFW Project in keeping alive the idea of credit during the difficult years before the publication of *21st Century Skills* has contributed positively to the QCF. Similarly, some of FAB's early pre-conceptions about what a credit framework actually was have been modified as the QCF has developed, and once again there are positive contributions to the overall development of the QCF that FAB has led.

These extracts also focus on the early debates about the relevance of the CQFW to the development of the QCF in the two years or so after *21st Century Skills*. By the time *Learning from Experience* was published, the compromise agreement of Autumn 2005 was in place and responsibility for taking forward the development of what was to become the QCF in Wales was placed firmly in the hands of the Welsh Qualifications Regulator. It was clear from this date that the QCF would be a regulated framework, eventually replacing the NQF, and would not adopt the CQFW 'enabling framework' model across the three countries. Although the 'unitisation plus credit-rating' model was still promoted through FAB as a potential model for the QCF, the CQFW itself took on board the lessons of the Credit Works report (Lillis et al., 2005). The CQFW model itself changed considerably in the subsequent three years. Indeed, one might almost be tempted to say that as the QCF developed it had a positive impact on the CQFW itself.

Ultimately though, the reason why neither the CQFW nor the SCQF were appropriate models to build on in developing the QCF is rooted in the fact that both are 'enabling' rather than regulatory frameworks. The evaluation of the SCQF makes precisely this point about both frameworks (Gallagher, 2005). They are essentially descriptive rather than dynamic frameworks and they are simply too 'weak' - in Michael Young's terms (Young, 2003) - to carry forward the expectations of government that the introduction of a credit system would lead to radical changes in qualifications. The unitisation and credit-rating approach effectively creates a framework model that is an end in itself. The expectation is that placing a qualification in the framework will enable it to be compared with other qualifications – just being in the framework is sufficient. Despite the other genuinely credit-based activities that have informed the development of the CQFW in recent years, this idea of the CQFW as an end in itself is clearly present in the initial manifestation of that framework. The QCF, however, is a means to an end. Placing qualifications in the framework is a step along the way to establishing a system of credit accumulation and transfer that can deliver greater responsiveness, inclusion, accessibility and less bureaucracy into the qualifications system. To achieve that requires a strong framework (again using Young's typology), and this strength is based on regulation. Neither the CQFW nor the SCQF are strong enough to deliver on these objectives of government policy. Indeed, neither were established with this intention. To deliver these objectives required the creation of a unique framework, not the cloning of an existing one.

Consideration of the models of credit that exist in Wales and Scotland again takes us outside the narrative thread of the story of the QCF. In early 2004, although a single remit had been constructed that ensured credit and qualifications reform would proceed in tandem, this was still an English initiative. It was also now being taken forward by an organisation (QCA) whose previous track record on credit did not inspire confidence that it would move quickly in developing a new framework of credit-based qualifications. Despite this track record, the reform process that delivered the QCF for implementation proved to be in good hands.

37

A framework for achievement

From the spring of 2004 it became clear that QCA was beginning to take a more radical view of the reform process than had previously been the case within the organisation. Bolstered by its new remit from the DfES and by the ongoing work of the Tomlinson Committee with its proposals for sweeping changes to 14–19 qualifications, QCA began for the first time to conceptualise its reform remit in terms of a 'new' framework of qualifications that would replace the existing NQF. Ken Boston led this change, openly criticising the NQF in public pronouncements as being unable to support the development of a qualifications system fit for the twenty-first century. Mary Curnock Cook followed his lead, setting out the case for a new framework, based on credit, within which learner achievements could be recognised. In a relatively short space of time the QCA moved from the publication of its *Principles for a Credit Framework for England* to a position where it began to use its authority as a regulator to propose a different basis for the future regulation of qualifications. In this it was supported fully by the LSC – itself becoming more openly critical of the NQF. Thus the two key agencies in England responsible for taking forward the Skills Strategy commitment to an adult credit framework together formed a joint vision for qualifications reform that, for the first time, located the concept of credit explicitly within a process that would lead to significant changes to the NQF.

It was at a seminar for senior civil servants, organised by the DfES in Sheffield, that Curnock Cook first set out the concept of 'a new framework for recognising achievement'. Her presentation was well received and the small group of people working on the new remit for reforming vocational qualifications, based on a credit system, took their lead from this presentation to refer to their work under the title of 'A Framework for Recognising Achievement'. Translating Curnock Cook's label into a formal title cemented the idea of a new framework. In a short space of time the framework for Recognising Achievement became shortened to 'The FRA', and by the summer of 2004 the public presentation of QCA's commitment to an adult credit framework became transformed into the development of the FRA. QCA proposed that the FRA would be developed as a unit-based qualifications framework, underpinned by a system of credit accumulation and transfer, and work began within QCA on developing the technical specifications and operational rules for the new framework. Although QCA's proposals were well received in Northern Ireland, it should be noted once again that the FRA was an English concept. When it was first mooted as the primary objective of the qualifications reform process, QCA and LSC were reminded that a Credit and Qualifications Framework already existed in Wales. The FRA clearly was going to be an English framework.

It was not only in Wales that the QCA's conception of a new framework to replace the NQF caused some consternation. Suddenly, it seemed, the regulator was outstripping the demands from the field for qualifications reform. Despite the sometimes stinging criticisms of the NQF, made by many awarding bodies in their evidence to the Quinquennial Review of QCA, the proposal that the NQF should be replaced by a new framework clearly went beyond the expectations of a number of awarding bodies. It seemed that, although in favour of reform, many of them did not like change.[1] FAB put forward an alternative view of how the commitment to an adult credit framework might be realised (Federation of Awarding Bodies, 2003), as did John V. Williams, the Chief Executive of the qualifications regulator for Wales. As we have shown, these alternative views were based explicitly on the model of credit-rating adopted by CQFW. It was not necessary to undertake a wholesale reform of the NQF, argued FAB and Williams. What was needed was a process through which existing qualifications, both inside and outside the NQF, could be credit-rated.

To their credit, neither the QCA nor the LSC were persuaded by these alternative proposals. Robertson's characterisation of credit-rating as 'mass blessing by numbers' found an echo in the QCA's rejection of the CQFW model as inadequate to support the expectations of government for reform. By late summer 2004, Sue Georgious was in post at QCA and starting to take a lead on the FRA proposals. Senior staff at QCA and LSC had little difficulty in selling to the DfES the idea that, if the reform partners were going to deliver on the expectations of government set out in the Skills Strategy, the NQF would need to be replaced by a new FRA.

Before the FRA saw the light of day, however, it became necessary to change its name. OCR wrote a letter to the QCA, claiming that 'Recognising Achievement' was a tag line owned by OCR and that any use of the name by the QCA in its new framework would be challenged by the awarding body as an infringement of its copyright. The idea that 'Recognising Achievement' was a term capable of being copyrighted came as interesting news to some awarding bodies (the term had been used publicly by OCNs since the 1980s). Nevertheless, on the advice of its solicitors, QCA decided that the term 'FRA' should be dropped, to be replaced by the simpler 'Framework for Achievement (FfA)'. Work began in the autumn of 2004 to prepare for formal consultation on the establishing of the FfA as the planned replacement for the NQF.

The publication of the consultation paper *A Framework for Achievement* (QCA, 2004), in November 2004, marks the point at which QCA, which had two years previously perceived credit as something that required 'further investigation' until 2011, was transformed into the leader of the development of a new framework of credit and qualifications. The proposals for the FfA were launched by a powerful supporting speech from Ken Boston, which left his audience in no doubt about the commitment of QCA to take forward the reform of the qualifications system, and by equally solid support for the development of the FfA from the LSC. The publication of the FfA proposals marks, in England, the point in the Skills Strategy agenda where it was no longer possible to think of qualifications reform as simply a process of 'adding credit' to existing qualifications. Once the proposals in *A Framework for Achievement* had been published for consultation, the basic structure of the future process of qualifications reform was set.

The publication of the FfA proposals also marks the point at which the original concept of credit set out in the MOCF documents of 1981 makes a public reappearance in the story of qualifications reform. By 2004 it was clear that the long period of practical development of credit systems throughout the 1990s was in decline. Nevertheless, the FfA proposals were clearly based on a continuation of this 'credit tradition'. Although the practical implementation of local credit systems had come to a halt by the early twenty-first century, the theoretical basis of such systems had not been destroyed or forgotten. The FfA proposals mirror both *ABC?* and the later National Credit Framework specifications agreed by the NOCN in 1994. Such has been the influence of the FfA proposals on the development of the QCF that it is worth noting in some detail here the key features of the document.

The FfA consultation document contains a very clear definition of credit as *an award made to a learner*. In this it is unequivocal, and represents a clear break from the concept of credit produced just a few months previously in the *Principles for a Credit Framework for England*. During the course of 2004 we can therefore trace a clear focusing of the concept of credit from an enhancement to existing qualifications, to an award within a new framework of credit-based qualifications. The FfA document confirms this shift by proposing that all awarding bodies should be recognised within the new framework to award both credits and qualifications. In so doing, the FfA proposals reach explicitly beyond the existing remit of awarding bodies in the NQF in 2004 and signal the need for a new set of regulatory arrangements to support the new framework.

The FfA proposals also reproduce almost exactly the specification of a unit first set out in *ABC?* and subsequently adopted by all OCNs. The proposal that there should be 'a standard electronic template' for all units, based on the existing specifications of units in the National Credit Framework, was seen by those experienced in the development of credit systems – that is, by those with experience of work in OCNs – as an essential prerequisite for the development of robust and stable credit values. For those organisations without this experience, the proposal was seen as an impediment to flexibility and as part of an insidious attempt to 'nationalise' (the word was used on several occasions during this period) awarding bodies. Although the proposal received clear support from the field in the FfA consultation, the establishing of a single-unit template for the new framework proved to be a matter of continuing, if gradually diminishing, debate in the process of establishing the QCF.

There was also much concern over the proposal within the FfA consultation that all units should be placed in a unit databank and would be made freely available to all users within the framework. There was much opposition to this proposal from awarding bodies – again, the accusation that the FfA was an attack on their commercial freedom was heard – and, indeed, there were threats of legal action against QCA in more than one response to the FfA consultation if this proposal was enacted. In the event, despite a clear majority of respondents that agreed with this proposal, it was decided not to pursue this particular feature of the FfA in taking forward the further development of the new framework. The implications of this decision are considered later in this publication.

The most radical feature of the FfA proposals also secured a significant majority of favourable responses and, perhaps surprisingly, raised few objections from awarding bodies. Perhaps one reason for this was because the April 2004 remit to proceed with development of the FfA referred explicitly to the concept of 'mutual recognition of units' as being one of the design features of the new framework that the DfES expected to be built into the FfA. QCA interpreted this brief in relation to the establishment of a system of credit accumulation and transfer:

> Thus mutual recognition places a collective obligation on all awarding bodies to recognise and accept the credits awarded by other awarding bodies within the framework... Mutual recognition will operate within the rules of combination for a qualification.
>
> (QCA, 2004, pp. 22-3)

Thus the FfA proposals made explicit the commitment to credit accumulation and transfer as the 'underpinning system' for recognising achievement within the new framework. It placed a particular interpretation on QCA's remit to establish 'mutual recognition' of units that actually went beyond the formal brief from the DfES and held that mutual recognition should be extended to the achievements of learners, not just to the design of qualifications. This marked a significant step forward and effectively cemented the concept of credit accumulation and transfer into the new framework. In fact, the proposal went further than this. By locating the concept of mutual recognition within the 'rules of combination for a qualification', the FfA proposals not only tied the future definition of a qualification explicitly into the underpinning credit system for the framework, they also ensured that the powers of the regulators to accredit qualifications could be brought to bear on the future operation of this system of credit accumulation and transfer. This was to prove a critical feature of the FfA and one that has been carried forward into the QCF. Within a single specification, the FfA proposal therefore redefines fundamentally the nature of a qualification and secures the position of the credit as the currency of achievement within the new framework. It remains a pivotal concept in binding together credits and qualifications in an integrated system that effectively gives the QCF its name, and distinguishes it clearly from either the CQFW or the SCQF.[2]

There were other significant proposals in the FfA consultation that prefigure and anticipate the final form in which the QCF was developed. In particular, there are clear hints about a different approach to regulation and to the possibility that organisations other than awarding bodies might be recognised to operate within the new framework. Some of these features are considered later in this publication.

The consultation on the FfA closed in February 2005 and towards the end of March QCA published a report on the outcomes of the consultation (QCA, 2005). It demonstrated strong support for the FfA proposals across the post-school sector. In particular, the proposals on awarding credit, on development of an electronic credit transcript, and on the ability to transfer credits between qualifications and awarding bodies, all received overwhelmingly positive responses. However, the responses to the FfA consultation also revealed that some awarding bodies had serious concerns about the proposals for the new framework. The statistics show that awarding bodies were equally divided on many issues between the pros and cons of the FfA. But behind the statistics the FfA proposals drew sustained criticism, both from individual awarding bodies (particularly larger awarding bodies) and from FAB and the JCQ, to some of the FfA proposals.

As the report on the FfA consultation makes clear: 'The consultation document was not intended to provide the sole basis for moving to the design stage of the new framework' (QCA, 2005, p. 6).

However: 'The consultation process has ... given us the basis for securing some of the technical features of the new framework' (QCA, 2005, p. 3); and it is these technical features, as well as the consultation process itself, that mark the most significant outcomes of the FfA consultation. In effect, the outcomes of the FfA consultation confirm the concept of credit as an award made to a learner and secure for the future development of the QCF a set of technical specifications that restore the previous influence of the OCN experience on the development of the framework, as opposed to the alternative model developed by FEDA and implemented through the CQFW. By March 2005 the key technical features of the QCF had been exposed to consultation and most of them had secured significant support across the post-school sector. The consultation also revealed a high level of concern about the development of the new framework among some awarding bodies and the necessity for further work to be undertaken with these organisations, either to allay fears (some of the responses to the FfA consultation were based on basic misunderstandings of some of its proposals – for example, on the definition of a unit), or to support the case for reform through more evidence and (in some cases) more persuasive argument.

It should be remembered, though, that the report on the FfA consultation was still an English report. Although the FfA proposals were also subject to a formal process of consultation in Northern Ireland (with very similar outcomes), there was no consultation on the FfA in Wales. Instead, an alternative set of proposals was subject to a less formal process of consultation, and this confirmed that, although there was general support for the development of a framework of credits and qualifications in Wales, this should be taken forward through the continued development of the CQFW, and, critically, should not involve the replacement of the NQF by a new framework. Although no general invitation to comment on these alternative proposals in Wales was ever issued in England, the Welsh proposals received positive support from the very same awarding bodies, and from JCQ and FAB, that were most vociferously opposed to the FfA proposals in England and Northern Ireland.

By the spring of 2005 it was clear that, in the space of a little over a year, QCA had been transformed from an organisation that was an impediment to reform to an organisation that now wanted to push the scope of qualifications reform far beyond the comfort zone of a number of awarding bodies. It was also clear that the FfA proposals had drawn clear lines between the direction of qualifications reform in England and Northern Ireland from the preferred path for development in Wales. These were issues that needed to be resolved before the reform process could move forward. Unfortunately, the FfA consultation could not have been more badly timed to address this need. The report on the outcomes of the consultation was delivered to the DfES at the end of March 2005 and the following day the government announced its intention to hold a general election in May. From that date all concrete activity on the qualifications reform programme was suspended until the election of a new government. Indeed, it would be some considerable time before the process of reform leading to the QCF would get back on track.

Notes

1 With due respect to Mark Twain.
2 Although there were a number of technical issues to resolve. See *Devilish Details* (Wilson, 2004).

38

Cold feet and twiddling thumbs

What happened to the process of qualifications reform in the year from April 2005 to March 2006? After all general elections there is an inevitable hiatus, as new ministers and junior ministers get a grip on their new portfolios. In the DfES there was a significant change, with Ivan Lewis – one of the longest-serving junior ministers for Lifelong Learning and Skills – being replaced by Phil Hope. In the summer of 2005 there was also a considerable movement of senior civil servants and a new group of civil servants in the DfES assumed responsibility for taking forward the programme of qualifications reform. The hiatus brought about by these changes was to last quite some time.

The consultation on the FfA, though it had identified wide support for the proposals for a new framework based on a credit system, had also exposed some serious fault lines in taking forward the new framework. The opposition of some larger awarding bodies to some of the design features of the FfA had been made clear during the consultation (several responses to QCA were copied 'for information' to the DfES), and the alternative consultation in Wales also revealed concerns about the future of the CQFW if the FfA were to go ahead. To these voices of concern about the direction of reform were added those from some (by no means all) SSCs. In particular, a small number of SSCs was concerned by the implication in the FfA consultation that NVQs might disappear in the transition to a new framework. There was concern in some quarters that existing qualifications 'valued by employers' would need to be changed in order to bring them into the FfA. The warning bells began to sound when a representative of an SSC at a consultation event on the FfA quoted the preferred position of those opposed to change down the years: 'If it's not broken, don't fix it.' Personally, I reach for my sledgehammer whenever I hear that phrase. I much prefer Tom Peters' update of it in *Liberation Management:* 'If it's not broken, break it'. (Peters, 1992, p. 577).

The pause in the process of development in 2005 allowed those with concerns about the direction of reform to regroup and to press their case for alternatives with the new civil servants and junior ministers at the DfES. At the same time, the results of the FfA consultation allowed senior staff at QCA and LSC to continue to promote the benefits of the FfA as the preferred model for a reformed framework. In June 2005 QCA, LSC and the Skills for Business network wrote to Phil Hope setting out their proposals for further work, and asking for 'a clear mandate to proceed with the development and implementation of the Framework for Achievement' (Boston, 2005a, p. 6).

The June 2005 proposals contained some adjustments to the FfA model to accommodate the concerns of the more vociferous opponents of the proposals. So, for example, the letter to Phil Hope suggested that 'we explore models for an appropriate structure for ownership and management of the unit databank and units within it that accommodate and test awarding body concerns'. (Boston, 2005a, p. 3).

In other words, the contentious proposition that all units in the FfA databank would be shared was to be dropped, and a model would be tested in which both shared and 'owned' units could be placed in the unit databank.

The letter also proposed a revision of the proposed timetable for implementation, with a period of 'initial building' from 2006 to 2008 to be followed by a review of progress and a formal evaluation of the FfA model, before proceeding to full implementation. Although these were important concessions designed to re-engage key awarding bodies in the reform process, the letter was also unequivocal on wishing to proceed with the development of the FfA across England, Wales and Northern Ireland. It was also uncompromising on the basic principle of credit accumulation and transfer:

> We recommend that the principles of credit accumulation and transfer must be established for all achievements within the FfA and that all awarding bodies operating within the FfA will be required to recognise credits awarded by all other awarding bodies.
>
> (Boston, 2005a, p. 4)

Phil Hope's response to these proposals was positive, but did not deliver the 'clear mandate' that had been asked for. The new minister wanted to:

> have full confidence that all the key parties understand and agree on the way forward... You are still in the process of building the consensus which will be necessary to move to the next stage of development. In particular the awarding bodies clearly have a strong interest in your proposals, and I know you are in close and continuing dialogue with them.
>
> (Hope, 2005)

In summary, QCA needed to ensure that awarding bodies were signed up to the FfA proposals before agreeing to proceed with further development. More work needed to be done before a clear mandate for implementation could be agreed. Without at least the tacit support of awarding bodies for the reform proposals, it seemed as though progress towards the QCF would be stalled.

It also became clear that the new government was going to take a strong line on the development of skills and had some different ideas from its predecessors as to how the Skills Strategy should be taken forward. Two years after the White Paper on *21st Century Skills*, a second Skills Strategy White Paper was published in July 2005. *Getting On in Business, Getting On at Work* (DfES et al., 2005) reiterated the government's commitment to the qualifications reform programme and to the development of a framework of credit-based qualifications as the key feature of these reforms. It also hinted at new roles for SSCs in the reform process, to ensure that reform remained a demand-led process that reflected the needs of employers. The Skills Strategy White Paper of 2005 marks a further shift away from the concept of Lifelong Learning, set out in *The Learning Age* seven years previously, towards an increasingly narrow view of post-school education and training policy as the delivery of the skills demanded by employers. In order to take forward the proposals for development in the FfA, it would be necessary to reflect this increasing emphasis on employer-based demand for skills.

At the same time, the focus of public attention on qualifications reform was being drawn towards the future development of qualifications for 14- to 19-year-olds. The publication of the Tomlinson Report in October 2004 (Working Group on 14-19 Reform, 2004) was followed in March 2005 with the formal response of the DfES and the proposal that, rather than the wholesale reform of A levels and GCSEs proposed by Tomlinson, new 14-19 Diplomas would be developed as an additional, rather than a replacement, qualification for A levels and GCSEs. The outcomes of the FfA consultation were effectively drowned by the chorus of dismay and disappointment that greeted the DfES's announcement about the new diplomas. The rejection of the Tomlinson recommendations and the argument about the form of the new diplomas meant that work on the development of a new qualifications framework was relegated for a time down the political agenda. In July 2005 QCA was charged with taking forward the development of the new 14-19 Diplomas. In the DfES' remit to QCA, no reference was made to the FfA or to the reform of vocational qualifications. Not only would A levels and GCSEs continue to be excluded from the programme of qualifications reform, but the stage was now set for the new diplomas also to be developed separately from this process. This separation was not QCA's preferred position. In a speech in May 2005, Ken Boston argued explicitly once more for a single framework of qualifications 'from 14 to 90', based on a credit system (Boston, 2005b). However, throughout the summer of 2005 it was clear that senior civil servants were preoccupied with establishing a programme for developing the new diplomas. Taking forward the development of the FfA was clearly not such a high priority.

Despite the separate work on qualifications reform conducted in Wales while England and Northern Ireland consulted on the FfA proposals, there was one issue in the FfA proposals on which all respondents were agreed; that the new framework should extend to all three UK jurisdictions. Notwithstanding the existence of the CQFW, there was no enthusiasm for establishing the FfA as a purely English (or even as an English/Northern Irish) framework. On this issue, even those awarding bodies that argued in favour of the CQFW approach were clear – whatever model for future development was selected, it should be a model that operated across England, Wales and Northern Ireland. No awarding body wanted to risk a position in which qualifications offered in Wales would be differently specified from those in England. Any suggestion that the FfA would replace the NQF in England and Northern Ireland, but not in Wales, was politically unacceptable, as well as being legally questionable.

In the summer of 2005 the new ministerial team at the DfES found themselves in a constitutional quandary. The FfA proposals clearly signalled a need for wholesale reform of the NQF. The NQF was a framework established in law across England, Wales and Northern Ireland. The devolution of responsibility for educational matters to the Welsh Assembly government meant that the DfES would find it difficult to enforce the reform of the NQF in Wales. It seemed for a time that not only could the Welsh Assembly government refuse to be part of a programme of reform to establish a new framework of credit-based qualifications, it could also block any attempt to take forward such a reform in England because the governments in all three countries needed to agree on the reform of the NQF. It seemed the reform process had reached an impasse, a position that continued unresolved into the autumn of 2005.

Although the DfES was prepared to challenge directly the alternative view of qualifications reform within the Welsh Assembly government, a more subtle approach was required to overcome the objections to the FfA model put forward by some larger awarding bodies. Phil Hope's invitation to QCA and its partners to continue to 'build consensus' with awarding bodies presented the opportunity for FAB and JCQ to present an alternative model for reform. In September 2005, FAB and JCQ put forward these alternative proposals to QCA (McNamara, 2005). They included the following:

> We continue to maintain that it is possible and desirable to include existing qualifications ... in the new framework.

> We ... see little benefit in a wholesale approach to sharing units across awarding bodies.

> Many general and specialised qualifications are not currently unitised and must be permitted to transfer to the framework in their existing form... In doing so we should draw on the recent Welsh experience and the expertise developed by awarding bodies.

> (McNamara, 2005, p. 2)

The JCQ paper was supported by the Chief Executive of ACCAC, offering in his contribution to 'organise, for a future meeting, a proper presentation of the CQFW' (Williams, 2005, p. 1).

The JCQ proposals may have found favour in Wales, but they were not supported by QCA, nor by the LSC, and the debate continued late into 2005. Phil Hope announced to the FAB conference in November 2005 that, if necessary, he would 'bang some heads together' to get the reform process moving again.

There remained clear differences of view between the QCA/LSC and JCQ/FAB positions at this juncture. However, there were positive aspects to this exchange of views as well. There was no challenge to the principle of credit accumulation and transfer in the JCQ/FAB position, and the two organisations declared themselves to be 'entirely comfortable' with the proposals for a period of trialling (though they wanted more discussions about the purpose of these trials). Not only did JCQ and FAB fully support the development of a new framework across England, Wales and Northern Ireland, they also wished to see such a framework encompass all qualifications (that is, not just vocational qualifications) for all learners of all ages. In this respect, JCQ and FAB were helping to push the boundaries of policymaking beyond those within which QCA and LSC were required to operate.

Overcoming this apparent impasse with Wales was helped in the autumn of 2005 by the publication of the Evaluation Report on the CQFW that was produced for FAB by Credit Works (Lillis et al., 2005). QCA produced an analysis of the CQFW report and it was this analysis that informed the future banging together of heads that Phil Hope promised. In effect, the Credit Works report highlighted the differences between the CQFW and the FfA proposals, provided useful ammunition to QCA and LSC in seeking to develop an alternative model for credit and qualifications, and confirmed that in the critical areas of awarding, accumulating and transferring credits towards qualifications there was very little evidence of activity within the CQFW that was relevant to the FfA.

A similar approach was taken to the role of SSCs in the reform programme. It was clear from *Getting On in Business, Getting On at Work* that government expected SSCs to take a more pro-active role in voicing employer demand in the identification of skills needs and in the development of qualifications to meet these needs. It was also clear that the DfES expected QCA to adopt a less hands-on approach to the future accreditation of vocational qualifications, shifting its role to supporting employer demand as represented through SSCs and their qualifications strategy for their sector. The process of shifting this responsibility away from QCA and into the hands of SSCs was also a matter for some negotiation behind the scenes, as the DfES planned for the next phase of the qualifications reform process.

It was November 2005 before the next phase of development of the new framework was formally authorised and the machinery to take forward the reform process was put in place. However, although the new arrangements brought a number of compromises to the proposals put forward in the FfA consultation, the key commitment to the development of a new qualifications framework, based on a system of credit accumulation and transfer, remained intact. Whatever options might be available to government in taking forward the further implementation of the Skills Strategy set out in the 2005 White Paper, it was clear that these could not be achieved without a radical reform of the NQF. Faced with a choice of going forward on the basis of the FfA model or reverting to an attempt to fix the problems of the qualifications system within the existing NQF, the government clearly and explicitly chose the former course of action.

These then were the strategies used by government, pressed by both QCA and LSC, to get the qualifications reform process back on track. Heads were banged together to bring Wales into the reform process. Concessions to the original FfA model (particularly on unit ownership) were made to engage awarding bodies with the emerging model of the QCF. A greater role was engineered for SSCs to bring them more explicitly into the qualifications reform process. And the whole timeframe for reform (except – although few noticed at the time – the date by which the reform process should be completed) was subjected to a two-year breathing space during which time the QCF proposals would be tested and trialled. Only following these tests and trials would a decision to implement the new framework be made. These were the pragmatic steps taken during the autumn of 2005 to get the reform process back on track after the outcomes of the consultation on the FfA had confirmed such positive support for the new framework, prior to the 2005 general election.

Note

1 See Chapter 36 for details of this report.

39

A UK-wide programme of reform

In the end (almost) eight months passed between the submission of the consultation report on the FfA to the DfES and the renewal of a formal remit to proceed with the development of a new framework of qualifications in November 2005. At times it seemed as though the reform proposals might be derailed or that the more radical features of the FfA proposals would need to be withdrawn. Although the second Skills Strategy White Paper reiterated the commitment to reform, and referred explicitly to the development of a unit-based qualifications framework, underpinned by a system of credit accumulation and transfer, the new civil servants at the DfES wanted to secure a continuation of the reform process based on consensus. Meetings with the senior officers of large awarding bodies and with representatives of FAB and JCQ revealed continuing concerns with some of the FfA proposals. Individual SSCs also made representations to the DfES about their concerns over NVQs. Discussions continued with representatives of the Welsh Assembly government. The overall strategy of government during this period is described in the previous chapter.

During the long hot summer of 2005 QCA, which now clearly held, in partnership with the LSC, the mantle of reform, made an explicit attempt to widen the basis of understanding of the FfA proposals through a series of invitational seminars, to which representatives of awarding bodies, SSCs and other key agencies were invited. The original series of eight seminars proved so successful that six of them were repeated. Papers were produced for each seminar; some of them by QCA itself, others by representatives of awarding bodies and SSCs. The second series of seminars presented the opportunity to revise some of these initial papers and present some more refined ideas for discussion. Some of the key issues of contention in the FfA consultation process were unpicked (for example, the rationale behind a standard unit template), as well as some of the issues that had been signalled for future development (for example, grading in credit-based qualifications). The seminar series offered some breathing space for deeper consideration of the FfA proposals, while the future of the reform programme was being hammered out behind the scenes. Although the outcomes of the seminars were impossible to quantify, there is no doubt that some people from some awarding bodies and SSCs became engaged with the FfA proposals during this period in a way that had simply not been possible through the formal consultation process. In the difficult months of summer and early autumn of 2005, with the future direction of the reform programme in the balance, it is just possible that the seminar series had an impact beyond its modest aims. In engaging individuals and organisations in an open, and at times quite formally academic, dialogue about the proposals for a new framework, the seminar series created a climate of considered discussion, rather than entrenched sniping, from fixed positions that helped to maintain the impetus for reform through the summer of 2005.

The seminar series showed that the process of reform was not just about policymaking. During this time, and faced with a period without a clear remit or direction for its work, QCA instituted a more subtle process of extending the reach of the reform programme. The 2005 FfA seminar papers constitute an interesting collection of contributions to the development of the new framework, aimed not at implementing the FfA proposals, but in engaging key organisations and individuals in a series of theoretical debates about different aspects of the new framework. Although by the end of the summer of 2005 there was still no consensus about the direction of reform, there was dialogue between some of the key actors in the reform process. The time would have passed anyway, but not so productively.

In November 2005 the DfES produced its solution to these competing pressures on the future direction of qualifications reform. It sought to bring together all interested parties in a revised programme of reform that would be overseen not by QCA but by the DfES itself, under the chairmanship of a senior civil servant, Peter Lauener. The so-called Lauener Group was constituted at the invitation of Phil Hope and met for the first time in December 2005. The group sought to organise the reform programme under four key strands of work, with a different constituency in the reform consensus taking a lead on each strand. The four strands would be brought together under the heading of the UK Vocational Qualifications Reform Programme (UKVQRP), and the Lauener group quickly formalised its role as the UKVQRP Board.

As the four strands of activity began to emerge and the machinery to manage and operate the overall programme of reform began to be put in place in early 2006, it seemed at first that some of the impetus behind the FfA proposals had been lost and that there was a distinct danger that the direction of reform would be dissipated as each strand of the reform programme pursued its own objectives. In practice, however, the establishing of the UKVQRP proved to be an effective vehicle for taking forward the development of the new framework, as it removed some of the more contentious issues from within the scope of the framework itself, as well as ensuring that all the key agencies, including awarding bodies and SSCs, were engaged in the reform programme. Although it added a layer of bureaucracy to the whole development programme, the DfES' 'big tent' approach actually got the development of the QCF back on track.

As the 2005 White Paper had signalled, the DfES expected SSCs to play a more proactive role in helping to move towards the demand-led model that lay at the heart of the Skills Strategy. This was reflected in the fact that the Sector Skills Development Agency (SSDA) was given responsibility for taking forward the development of Sector Qualifications Strategies (SQSs). This responsibility had fallen previously to QCA, and the FfA proposals had included several references to the interaction between the FfA and SSCs. The removal of this responsibility from QCA actually proved to be of great benefit to the development of the QCF. In effect, the separation of responsibility for framework development (which stayed with QCA), and for determining what kind of vocational qualifications should be developed within the framework (the essence of SQSs), enabled the framework itself to be developed without reference to any particular qualification.

This was to prove a significant moment in allowing the QCF to recapture one of the original ideas behind the proposals for a credit framework – that it should be a comprehensive framework capable of recognising all learner achievements at all levels. In fact, the original proposal for an adult credit framework within a White Paper devoted explicitly to the development of skills meant that, at the outset, the formal remit for development of the QCF had to overcome two distinct limitations on its ambition to be a comprehensive framework. The development of qualifications targeted at 14- to 19-year-olds would soon become a reality during the test and trial programme. But the removal from QCA of responsibility for determining what should be the content of the vocational qualifications that were submitted to the QCF enabled the framework to be developed without explicit reference to vocational qualifications, or indeed to any type of qualification. Within its strand of the reform process, QCA and its partner regulators were now able to develop a framework based solely on design features rather than the content of qualifications, and were therefore able to transcend the limits of vocational qualifications still present in the overall concept of the UKVQRP. In so doing, the ground was prepared for the possibility that general qualifications might be brought into the framework in the future.

In addition to this separation of sector qualifications reform from the development of the new framework, the new arrangements for the UKVQRP also created a strand of work related to the rationalisation of existing qualifications. In their submissions to the DfES, both JCQ and FAB had argued that, in fact, the NQF was not as complicated a structure as it seemed to be, and that it would be possible to simplify the apparent complexity of the NQF by reducing the number of qualifications that were offered through the existing framework. A strand of the UKVQRP was created through which this contention could be tested and evaluated. It seemed at first that this strand of work might become an alternative model of reform to the QCF – that is, a demonstration that it was unnecessary to develop a new framework in order to achieve the objective of rationalisation of the qualifications system. Indeed, there is little doubt that this alternative view was consciously held by key actors in some awarding bodies. JCQ and FAB were given responsibility for taking forward this strand of work, and it provided a focus for their activity within the UKVQRP that effectively kept them preoccupied with the existing NQF, leaving QCA and its partner regulators (of which more below) free to concentrate on the development of the QCF. As a tactic for including awarding bodies in the reform process, while restricting their ability to undermine the development of the new framework, it was an astute move on the part of the DfES.

The last strand of work related to the development of funding models to support the reform of vocational qualifications, and the LSC was asked to lead this strand. In effect, this meant that the LSC was able to focus its attention on supporting the development of the QCF. Thus the establishment of the UKVQRP created four strands of work (a fifth strand on marketing and communications was led by the DfES itself), each led by one of the four key stakeholders (QCA, LSC, SSDA and JCQ/FAB), with two strands (SQSs and funding) linked explicitly to the development of the key strand (the QCF) and a fourth strand tied to the (now clearly time-limited) NQF. It took a while for these relationships between the strands to work out during 2006, but there is little doubt that the UKVQRP structure actually ensured that, over time, the QCF would become the focus for the overall reform programme. In addition, of course, the establishing of the UKVQRP also ensured that the new framework would not be just an English construct, but would encompass England, Wales and Northern Ireland.

Thus, from late 2005, formal responsibility for taking forward the development of the new framework fell not just to QCA, but also to its partner regulators in Wales and Northern Ireland. One immediate consequence of this widening of responsibility was that the term 'Framework for Achievement' was dropped from the reform programme. This was seen in Wales as an English construct (despite its use in Northern Ireland too) and, as part of the wheeling and dealing that eventually brought ACCAC (the regulatory authority for Wales) into the 'Framework Development' strand of the UKVQRP, the term 'FfA' was sacrificed. 'Sacrificed in favour of what?' was a question that remained unanswered for quite some time during the first part of 2006. Those involved in this strand of development were instructed simply to refer to 'the framework'. Even 'The Framework' was banned – lowercase letters only were permitted. This led to some very strange grammatical constructs in the publicity of the time. In the spoken word the FfA became 'the framework previously known as the FfA', but it was generally agreed that the inclusion of the Welsh and Northern

Irish regulators in the big tent of the UKVQRP was worth a bit of tongue-twisting. In the event it was the summer of 2006 before a new term for 'the framework' was eventually agreed.

The other, more subtle, effect of joining together QCA, ACCAC and the CCEA. to take forward the development of the framework. was to gradually marginalise the impact of the CQFW on the further development of the QCF. As the CQFW was not a regulated framework. ACCAC held no responsibility within the framework development strand of the UKVQRP to promote or defend the interests of the CQFW. It was agreed that the CQFW would continue to exist in Wales as a separate construct from the framework and that ACCAC's role in the reform programme lay solely within its remit for the regulation of qualifications in Wales, and not to the wider interest of the Welsh Assembly government in promoting the CQFW. In effect, the new regulated framework would become part of the CQFW. In charging the three regulatory authorities with responsibility for taking forward the development of the framework, the DfES signalled clearly that the QCF would become a regulated framework, replacing the NQF, and not an 'enabling' framework that encompassed the NQF.

From November 2005 then, the further development of the FfA became one of four strands in a broader programme of reform under the banner of UK Vocational Qualifications Reform. Although at first this seemed to relegate the importance of the 'framework development' strand of the reform programme, the advantages of the UKVQRP structure soon became apparent. Arguments about what kind of qualifications might populate the new framework were separated from considerations about its design features, enabling the QCF to be developed as a genuinely comprehensive framework. The issue of rationalisation was separated from the process of developing the new framework and the problem of rationalisation became tied explicitly to the NQF, rather than the new framework. The new framework would be a three-country framework, as England and Northern Ireland had wished, and it would be a regulated framework, replacing the NQF. And in all this the principle of credit accumulation and transfer as the underpinning system for all qualifications in the new framework was reaffirmed in the UKVQRP's remit. By the spring of 2006 it seemed that progress towards the QCF was moving forward once again.

In the development of the QCF, 2005–6 was a difficult year for those involved. At certain points in the year it seemed as though the DfES might be persuaded to drop the FfA model. At other points it seemed possible that the whole reform initiative would run out of steam before permission to proceed to the next phase of development was agreed. In the event. a combination of sound leadership within both QCA and LSC, consensus-building by the development team, a combination of astute political judgement and fortunately positive pragmatism within the DfES, together with some tactical misjudgements among those opposed to the FfA model, saw the process of moving towards a new framework of credit-based qualifications back on track by the spring of 2006. Despite the continuing lack of a name, preparations now began to shift the framework from its design stage into a more concrete stage of development.

40

Testing and trialling the new framework

In the process of moving the development of the new framework forward after the publication of the report on the FfA consultation, a significant compromise was made in the proposed timing of development. Initially, it had been proposed to begin work on developing the new framework from January 2006. The outcome of the protracted negotiations of 2005 was an agreement that the new framework would be tested and trialled from 2006 to 2008. Initially, it was hoped the test-and-trial programme could begin early in 2006, but resources for the programme were not found until the 2006-7 financial year, and so the UKVQRP agreed that the test-and-trial programme should run for two years from April 2006. In the event, the process of identifying and contracting with the various test-and-trial projects took some time to conclude, and in practice the tests and trials of the QCF ran from September 2006 to April 2008. The test-and-trial programme itself was therefore a product of the negotiated settlement brokered by the DfES in the autumn of 2005. It had not been part of the original timetable put forward in the FfA consultation, which had envisaged a period of further development activity in 2005-7, leading to full implementation from September 2007. For those who still harboured doubts about the FfA model, the test-and-trial programme represented a significant brake on the original timetable for development of the new framework, and (for some) a further opportunity to re-evaluate the potential benefits of the new framework before moving to implementation.

Predictably, there was much discussion within the UKVQRP about the scope and objectives of the test-and-trial programme. So, for example, it took some time to agree that the purpose of the test-and-trial programme would be to test a single framework model based on the main design features of the FfA, but modified to take account of the compromise agreements reached during the latter part of 2005. An alternative proposal that the test-and-trial programme should be used to compare the relative merits of the FfA model and an alternative approach, based on the CQFW, was rejected by the UKVQRP on the advice of the regulatory authorities. It also took some time to establish the separation of responsibilities for taking forward the test-and-trial programme with the development of SQSs. Where an SQS ended and the design features of the new framework began would continue to be a contested boundary throughout the test-and-trial programme. Indeed, as the QCF is implemented, this tension between what is a design feature of the QCF and what is the characteristic of a qualification within it is still apparent in some sectors.

In theory the test-and-trial programme extended the developmental phase of the QCF quite considerably. In practice, however, it was agreed that the credits and qualifications actually awarded to learners during this period would be real. So although SSCs, awarding bodies, providers and the regulators themselves would be testing and trialling different aspects of the new framework, from a learner's perspective it would be a real framework during this period. Although the regulatory basis of the QCF would remain unchanged (that is, the old regulatory criteria for the NQF would form the statutory basis on which qualifications would be accredited and awarded), it was agreed by all concerned that learners themselves should not be subject to the concept of testing and trialling. Having agreed this position, the logic of the QCF began to assert itself quite quickly. Once the first awards were made in the QCF, it is actually difficult to conceive of anything other than an external event of some kind that could have prevented the QCF proceeding inexorably towards implementation, despite the formal position of government that a decision on implementation would not be made until the (successful) end of the tests and trials.

Preparation for the test-and-trial programme also took place in the context of the interim report from Lord Leitch's Review of Skills, which had been published in late 2005 (Leitch, 2005). Although the interim report contained many of the positive messages about qualifications reform that had been included in both Skills Strategy White Papers, the main impact of the interim Leitch report was to up the stakes on the need for radical and rapid reforms. In effect, Leitch undermined the case for a conservative approach to qualifications reform and injected an urgency into the reform programme that had been in danger of disappearing during 2005. The positive noises about the Leitch Review emanating from the Treasury also lent weight to the DfES' argument that more resources would be needed if QCA was to support the Leitch agenda through the tests and trials of the new framework. During the early months of 2006, the DfES became more proactive advocates for the tests and trials of the new framework, securing adequate resources to support the programme over the following two financial years. Linking the development of the QCF with the Leitch agenda was also an important feature of the work of the LSC in supporting the new framework. Given the drive to accelerate the reform programme engendered by Leitch, it might seem that the test-and-trial programme for the new framework represented an untimely obstacle to the reform process. However, the benefits of engagement with awarding bodies and SSCs presented by the tests and trials outweighed the disadvantages of slowing down the pace of reform at the very moment when the government was being urged to do the opposite.

The announcement that the DfES had approved the next stage of development of the new framework brought renewed interest in the framework from awarding bodies, sector bodies and providers. Events were held to publicise the opportunity to become part of the test-and-trial programme, and expressions of interest in being part of the tests and trials were received from all parts of the post-school sector. The framework development team at QCA began the process of setting out criteria for involvement in the tests and trials, and for inviting proposals against these criteria from organisations interested in becoming part of the programme. These criteria were developed to take account of the fact that different actors would need to get involved in the tests and trials at a stage appropriate to their needs, and that some providers and awarding bodies had more experience of operating within credit systems than others. A sequential approach was adopted, beginning with the development of units and working through the anticipated systems that would operate in the new framework to award, accumulate and transfer credits. Organisations were invited to identify priorities for involvement in the tests and trials that would take them through this sequence as far as they possibly could. For some organisations, this might mean simply that the process of unit development would be trialled. For others it might mean that units and qualifications could be developed and credits and qualifications awarded to learners.

On the surface, this seemed like a sensible approach to the test-and-trial programme. In fact, the lack of real connections with credit systems for most awarding bodies and SSCs meant that the primary focus of the test-and-trial programme would be the development of units with a credit value and level to meet the framework specifications. In effect, the test-and-trial programme focused on proving to a new set of organisations and individuals that which had already been proven over a decade previously after the specifications of the National Credit Framework had been adopted by NOCN. The real tests for the QCF – the development of rules of combination, the operation of credit accumulation and transfer, and the use of the learner record to support the credit system – all lay well beyond the scope of the test-and-trial programme to address in any practical way. But these realisations lay in the future as the test-and-trial programme moved slowly forward.

Once the test-and-trial programme was formally announced, it became essential to resolve the issue of naming the new framework. This was decided shortly before the tests and trials began (though technically the name was agreed as a 'working title' to be reviewed at the end of the test-and-trial programme). The adoption of a name brought an end to the strange period during early 2006 when the term 'the framework' was required to be used in all public utterances about, well, about 'the framework'. The term 'Qualifications and Credit Framework' was actually put forward by the Chief Executive of ACCAC (reversing the positions of credit and qualifications in the CQFW) in order to distance the new framework from the previously 'English' FfA. Within QCA the adoption of the term QCF became known as the 'briar patch' solution, with Ken Boston playing the role of the apparently innocent rabbit succumbing to the wiles of his foxy counterpart in Wales.

The adoption of the term 'QCF' marks the formal securing of the connection between credits and qualifications that lies at the core of the framework. It also marks the end of the concept of a credit framework separate from a qualifications framework. Most importantly, it enshrines the concept of credit alongside qualifications in a single, comprehensive framework. The 15-year legacy of credit as a local initiative, outside the national system of qualifications, was finally laid to rest. Although the extension of the FfA model to Wales took some negotiating during 2005, the adoption of the term QCF in 2006 (something the FfA development team itself had not dared to suggest) marks a significant contribution to the establishment of a three-country framework of credit-based qualifications. From 2006 onwards, the QCF could develop exactly as its name promised.

In preparation for the test-and-trial programme, the QCF development team (now including colleagues from Wales and Northern Ireland, as well as those based at QCA) developed a Support Pack for individual projects. Within the Support Pack was a document entitled 'Working Specification for the Qualifications and Credit Framework Tests and Trials' (QCA et al., 2006). This represented an amended version of the framework model put forward in the FfA consultation of 2004. In the introduction to the working specification the sources for the model are acknowledged. Although the FfA consultation document is the primary source for the working specification, other contributions are formally acknowledged, including:

- contributions to the series of technical seminars ... run by QCA from May to July 2005
- QCA/FAB/JCQ synthesis paper
- advice from ministers at the DfES
- evaluation reports on other frameworks in the UK and internationally
- Credit and Qualifications Framework for Wales Credit Common Accord
- Northern Ireland Credit Accumulation and Transfer System.

(QCA et al., 2006, pp. 4–5)

The working specification for the tests and trials therefore represents not only a refinement of the framework model put forward in the FfA consultation, it also explicitly acknowledges the process of negotiation and consensus-building that took place during the year between the FfA consultation report and the formal beginning of the tests and trials of the QCF. The working specification is a genuine refinement of the FfA model. The framework development team spent a great deal of time and energy during 2005–6 in developing the framework model, both to accommodate the concerns of some stakeholders and to ensure that the model was still capable of delivering the objectives of the reform programme. Notwithstanding the characterisation of this refined framework model as an object for testing and trialling, the working specification clearly informs the *Regulatory Arrangements* that form the basis for implementation of the QCF.

As the process of identifying organisations that would lead projects in the test-and-trial programme proceeded, a further impediment to the development of the QCF arose. This was an entirely self-imposed problem and arose from the procurement practices of QCA. Having submitted an initial proposal that identified the objectives of a project within the tests and trials, QCA then invited each prospective project to develop a full Project Initiation Document, followed by a Project Plan, on the basis of which each prospective project was issued with a contract based on QCA's standard procurement procedures. The amounts of money available to each individual project were relatively small, and the costs of administration for some organisations proved prohibitive. In addition, a number of awarding bodies refused to sign the standard contract issued to them by QCA, on the grounds that QCA would – it seemed – own the copyright of any materials produced through a project in receipt of funds, including, of course, any units. Given the sensitivity of this issue, it was not surprising that, several months into the formal period of testing and trialling, only one or two of the projected 25–30 projects had actually signed a contract. To quote from an informal discussion with one project leader:

> We bid for £10,000. We've spent close to £5,000 on legal advice and another £5,000 on staff time trying to agree a contract and a project plan, and we haven't actually produced a damn thing yet. It would have been a lot easier, and a lot cheaper, to agree to do it for nothing.

Whether or not the figures quoted were accurate is impossible to verify, but the strength of feeling about the contracting process is not in dispute and was reproduced across many projects. In effect, the bureaucratic processes of QCA threatened to strangle the enthusiasm of many organisations that wanted to be part of the test-and-trial programme. A slightly ironic position for QCA to find itself in, given the objectives of the QCF development programme.

A further problem awaited some projects further down the line. Despite the formal support of the LSC for the test-and-trial programme, the delay in starting the tests and trials and the difficulty in getting many projects off the ground meant that, by the time providers wished to register learners on programmes leading to an award within the QCF, there was no guarantee of funding from local LSC budgets, as the process of allocating funding to providers in the

2006–7 financial year had already been concluded. There were simply no additional LSC funds available to support the test-and-trial programme, despite the best efforts of those responsible for supporting the qualifications reform programme at the LSC National Office. So, in spite of the fact that QCA and LSC had been consistent advocates for moving forward with the development of the new framework as quickly as possible after the formal consultation on the FfA, when the green light was given by ministers to proceed with the test-and-trial programme, a combination of delays and bureaucracy meant that by the end of 2006 there was actually very little testing and trialling taking place.

A second phase of development in the test-and-trial programme was instituted in February 2007. This time QCA did not require a lengthy period of negotiation over project plans, and a much-simplified process of contracting was introduced (a victory for the QCF team over the procurement team within QCA). Indeed, some of the organisations that joined the test-and-trial programme in this second phase actually began work at about the same time as the most delayed of projects in the first phase. By the end of the 2006–7 financial year, 50 separate test and trial projects were running across England, Wales and Northern Ireland. It seemed as though the settlement of the autumn of 2005, which deliberately traded a slower pace of reform for a more inclusive involvement in it, was bearing fruit.

Although it took some time to build up momentum, by the spring of 2007 the test-and-trial programme seemed to be moving the development of the QCF forward again towards implementation. What was actually happening in the tests and trials? What kind of projects were being undertaken? Who was involved? How was the QCF model actually being tested and trialled? How did the actual practice of the programme contribute to (or deflect from) progress towards the implementation of the QCF? These are questions addressed in a following chapter in this story. Before addressing these questions though, another strand of activity took place in the overall development of the QCF that ran in parallel to the first phase of the test-and-trial programme. This strand sought to locate the QCF in the international context of developing credit and qualification frameworks. The outcomes of this work are worthy of note and were important in securing the technical basis of the QCF that was subject to testing and trialling.

41

Best of breed:
The QCF in an international context

Although the particular history of credit systems inherited by the QCF is unique to the UK, the concept of credit has a distinctly international dimension. Indeed, the early pioneers of credit systems in the UK, both in HE and through OCNs, explicitly acknowledged the credit systems of the USA and Canada as inspirational sources for their proposals. More recently, though, more widely, international interest has grown in the development of national qualification frameworks as explicit instruments of policy. The recent establishment of the European Qualifications Framework (EQF) and its growing influence on national policies is the most important current manifestation of this interest (European Commission, 2005), but the growth of national qualification frameworks is far from simply a European phenomenon. The Organisation for Economic Co-operation and Development (OECD) has recently published the outcomes of a comparative study of qualifications systems in 23 different countries (OECD, 2007) that attests to the continuing growth of national qualifications frameworks across the world.

As part of the process of developing the QCF, PricewaterhouseCoopers (PwC) and the University of Oxford jointly undertook an independent review of more than 60 academic studies of credit and qualifications frameworks, covering six countries (PricewaterhouseCoopers, 2007). This academic review, which sought to draw lessons from and comparisons with elements of these six other systems, formed an integral part of PwC's independent review of the first year of development of the QCF and is the most thorough review of credit and qualifications systems undertaken to date in an international context.

The Oxford University review concluded that, although there were certain similarities between the proposed technical features and operational processes of the QCF and other international frameworks, there was no other framework that existed anywhere in the world that was sufficiently close in design and intention to the QCF to provide a comparable model. So, for example, although the New Zealand Framework (Philips, 2003) was a 'strong' framework in Michael Young's typology (Young, 2003), it was too closely tied to the development of vocational qualifications to provide a useful model for the QCF's comprehensive ambitions. The South African Framework (Ensor, 2003) aimed to encompass HE, but South African universities opposed the imposition of the framework and resisted all attempts to universalise its design features, weakening the intentions of the framework considerably. The Australian Framework (Keating, 2003) shares some design similarities with the QCF, but is a weaker framework that has been unable to overcome the different approaches to qualifications design and credit systems operated by individual state governments.

Both the Oxford University study and the OECD report reveal that, although national qualifications frameworks exist or are being developed in a number of European countries, there is little evidence that these frameworks are being developed in conjunction with credit systems. Although there exist both a European Credit System (ECTS) for HE and a European Credit System for Vocational Education and Training (ECVET), there is little evidence from Europe that these credit systems are influencing the development of national qualifications frameworks in any way.[1] Indeed, it is possible to detect a distinct antipathy within the education and training systems of some significant European countries (for example, France, Germany and Italy) between the 'competence-based' culture, within which the growth of NQFs has proceeded, and the process-based culture of higher education, within which most credit systems outside the UK (although 'system' is perhaps too generous a term) have developed.

In this context the QCF provides an interesting and challenging model for other national qualifications frameworks in Europe and beyond. Although a small number of other European countries have actually implemented an NQF (France, Ireland and Malta) and most European countries have decided to implement or are considering the implementation of an NQF (Greece, Norway and Sweden are the only exceptions to this second category) (Coles, 2008), the UK is unique among European countries in having established one NQF and in now seeking to replace it with a second iteration – the QCF. This sends interesting messages to those European countries that are just embarking on the development of an initial model of an NQF. As the OECD study makes clear, simply having an NQF is, in itself, no guarantee that policy intentions can be effectively realised. The importance lies in developing an NQF that is appropriate to the particular needs and structures of national education and training systems. In effect, the development of the QCF signals the decision of the UK government that (at least for three-quarters of its jurisdiction) the original model of an NQF adopted was not fit for purpose for the policy aims of the wider national system in the twenty-first century. This message is being communicated across Europe as the momentum behind the development of the EQF begins to grow, and more and more European countries become interested in the joining together of credit and qualifications in a 'second generation NQF' in England, Wales and Northern Ireland.

What fascinates many European observers about the QCF is the fact that it very explicitly seeks to combine the learning outcomes-led approach to the framework to which all signatories to the EQF are publicly committed, with a credit-based approach to qualifications design and development. This fusion of what are still seen in many European countries as opposing traditions of curriculum design and assessment is what interests many European observers of the development of the QCF. On the surface it seems that, in an attempt to reform its 'First Generation NQF', the UK government has encouraged the insertion into an explicitly outcomes-based and progressive model of qualifications the development of an old-fashioned process-based concept of credit. Is this not (say some European commentators) a step backwards rather than a far-reaching reform?

Of course, there are echoes here of the NCVQ criticism of credit systems in the early 1990s. Indeed, it is a reminder to those involved in the development of the QCF about just how far the concept of credit has come since its first importation from North America some 30 years ago. A European observer of credit systems as they operate in the USA or Canada may indeed be forgiven for missing the connection between credits and learning outcomes that exists within the UK. The origins of the concept of credit in the US education system, based as it is on 'the Carnegie hour', precedes the development of a learning outcomes-based approach to curriculum design and assessment by so many years as to be perceived as the product of a bygone era. To re-quote Rothblatt at greater length:

> The history of units (credits) is ... essentially obscure... Over half a century the various elements of the American educational system grew together to form the everyday curricular structure so familiar today [but] a connected account does not exist. After all, it is administrative history, a tiresome account of tiny details congealing into a system... The story is humdrum.
>
> (Robertson, 1994, p. 117)

It is this obscure story that informs much thinking in Europe about credit systems, rather than the practical example of the QCF itself. Although recent reforms to the ECVET system move it some way towards the resolution of this conflict between outcomes-led and process-based views of credit systems at a European level, within individual EU member states this conflict remains alive and well. In the early discussions about the development of the EQF, there were suggestions from the UK (supported by one or two other European countries) that the EQF should be developed into a European Credit and Qualifications Framework. Such a development is still many years away – if it ever secures a foothold in Europe at all.[2] Having said this, there is an increasing interest in the QCF as a potential model for the development of other European frameworks. It remains to be seen whether the QCF model can be reproduced in other European countries or, indeed, in other countries worldwide.

One reason why the QCF model may not be easily exportable is because it is designed (as the OECD recommends) to take account of the particular structures that exist in the lifelong learning sector in England, Wales and Northern Ireland. One of the key features of the sector is the existence of a large number of independent, commercial or charitable organisations that are formally charged with carrying out assessment and certification of learner achievement, within a structure overseen by an industry regulator (actually by three regulators, one for each jurisdiction). Whether the existence of what these organisations themselves now refer to as 'the awarding community' has a positive or negative influence on the qualification system is not at issue here. What is important is that the QCF has been designed explicitly to deliver a set of reform objectives which the awarding community is invited to share and help to deliver, and that such a community exists in very few other countries in the world.

Interestingly, the PwC/Oxford University study makes very little reference to this distinctive characteristic of the qualifications system in England, Wales and Northern Ireland (Scotland is, once again, a different model). However, as the OECD study makes clear, where 'strong' qualifications frameworks have been, or are planned to be, established in many parts of the world, the functioning of the quality assurance and/or awarding functions in such frameworks are almost invariably the responsibility of a public body, either at national or regional level. In this context the role of such frameworks in delivering policy is much clearer and more direct than is the case with the QCF. So, for example, the development of a qualifications system in Spain (OECD, 2007) is taking place through a series of legislative interventions from both the General State Administration and the various Autonomous Regions. Although the balance of responsibilities varies in different contexts, it is very clearly a reform carried out by public bodies, based on explicit legislation, in which the 'thread of policy' clearly connects the intentions of the 'Organic Acts' that have created the system with the actions of accountable public servants in its delivery. The relevance of the QCF to the Spanish qualifications system, and indeed to many other similar systems, is perhaps more tenuous than we would like to think.

The OECD study also includes examples of 'weaker' frameworks. Rather than basing such frameworks on legislation and statutory requirements, these 'descriptive' or 'enabling' frameworks are conceived of as partnerships in which national and/or regional governments take a lead in the development of voluntary associations based on institutional collaboration. The examples of Germany and Austria might be quoted here, though the SCQF is also noted in the Oxford University study as such a framework. In these weaker frameworks responsibility for assessment and certification remain clearly at institutional level. (Where universities are brought into these frameworks, as the South

African experience illustrates, these weaker models predominate.) Such models make the process of utilising NQFs to deliver on policy objectives more complex and more long term, though the process of engaging stakeholders in the development of the framework may be easier.

What makes the QCF unique is that it seeks to combine the statutory powers of a strong, regulated framework with the operation of a 'qualifications market', within which independent organisations are expected to operate in response to incentives presented by that market. To this unique combination is added the requirement for awarding bodies to recognise for transfer the credits awarded by all other independent operators in this market. In so doing, the regulations of the QCF explicitly create a market interdependence between all members of the awarding community that is designed to deliver benefits to the end-consumers in this market – that is, to learners. The uniqueness of the QCF internationally in bringing together these characteristics may continue for some time to come. Having said that, the move towards public/private partnerships in taking forward national qualifications frameworks in other countries (for example, in Japan) (OECD, 2007) may yet make the QCF an attractive future model for other countries to adopt or adapt.

Of course, the views of some members of the UK awarding community have been highly critical of the QCF during its process of development. What makes the QCF both radical and unique as an international model is also one of the things that constitutes the most serious challenges to current practice among awarding bodies in the UK. The regulatory requirement that all credits must be recognised for the purposes of credit transfer within all qualifications in the QCF has not been universally welcomed by all members of the awarding community. No wonder some of them prefer the enabling models of the CQFW or the SCQF, where no such requirement exists. Just how awarding bodies respond to the challenge of credit accumulation and transfer will determine whether they survive and prosper in the QCF.

It is possible to envisage a model of development in which an awarding organisation adapts to the QCF, extends the scope of its business and contributes to the expansion of the qualifications market that is one of government's policy intentions in implementing the new framework. It is also possible to imagine the opposite. What is not possible is to create a clear 'policy thread' between the regulatory requirements of the QCF and the behaviour of the independent organisations that will operate within the framework. That luxury may be available in other countries seeking to develop qualifications systems, but the QCF has a harder road to travel. The unique combination in the QCF of regulated market and credit system remains, as PwC characterises it in its evaluation report, 'best of breed', in relation to all other international models of such frameworks (PricewaterhouseCoopers, 2007).

Before leaving behind this international dimension of the QCF, one cannot help but remark on the fact that the Oxford University/PwC study makes no reference to the numerous sources of information and ideas about credit systems available to it in England. Of course, it is an explicitly 'international' study, but it does include references to relevant documents in Wales and Scotland, as well as to comparative studies of qualifications (rather than credit) frameworks written and/or published in England. However, the vast range of sources and documents that reside in every OCN about credit systems remain untapped as a theoretical resource to support the QCF. It is the official version of previous history that holds sway in the PwC report, rather than the relevant version. Or maybe it is just that the 'pre-history' of credit systems in England is buried too deep in Google. In any event, the Oxford University/PwC evidence provides powerful academic support for the QCF, based on international comparisons. I cannot help thinking that some domestic evidence would have made the case even more powerful.

Notes

1 This position may well change in the future in Europe, where plans are in place to develop closer links between a new ECVET system and the EQF.
2 Though see footnote 1.

42

Half-way there:
The first year of tests and trials

As I noted above, the formal intention of the QCF tests and trials was to encourage a wide range of organisations to test out all aspects of the sequence of activities that would result in the award of credits to learners, and the accumulation and (possibly) transfer of credits towards the achievement of a qualification. The starting point for this sequence was the development of units based on the standard QCF format. During the first year of the tests and trials, and following the initial problems over contracting and the problems of securing LSC funding, it is perhaps unsurprising that a significant majority of projects remained focused on this initial stage of unit development in their test and trial activity throughout 2006-7.

Within the Working Specification for the QCF tests and trials, the required format for all QCF units is set out. The specification is identical to that used in the FfA consultation proposals and reflects almost exactly that used in the 2004 *Principles for a Credit Framework for England*. In fact, the same unit specification can be traced through numerous documents on credit right back to *ABC?*. Indeed, by the time NOCN adopted the specifications of the National Credit Framework in 1994, the unit specifications used in the working specification of 2006 are fixed and remain unchanged (though with some additional fields) through to the *Regulatory Arrangements for the QCF* of 2008 (Ofqual et al., 2008).

This simple specification of a unit, which identifies its title, learning outcomes, assessment criteria, credit value and level is the most stable, the most enduring and the most utilised aspect of credit systems over the past 15 years. Following its adoption by NOCN it has been used as the basis for all the units developed by all OCNs up to the present day. Each OCN maintains a database of such units and units are shared widely across OCNs. NOCN itself maintains a unit database, but this includes only the units that form part of NOCN qualifications, rather than the locally accredited programmes that lead to the award of OCN credits. Many OCNs also maintain a separate databank of those units that form part of an Access to HE Diploma. Collectively, these databases contain tens of thousands of units. Over the years, OCNs have developed hundreds of thousands of units in every conceivable subject and vocational area, and tens of thousands of practitioners across the 6,000 or so organisations that use or have used OCN accreditation over the years have been involved in the development and validation of these units.

Not only is there a wealth of experience about unit development within OCNs, but there is also a history of continuous improvement and refinement of units over time. Both within individual OCNs and (as we have referred to above) across NOCN, there has been a process in place over many years to improve unit quality. This has gradually produced a dispersed databank of units across OCNs, in which titles clearly reflect the content of units; learning outcomes are clearly set out; assessment criteria enable clear and consistent judgements about achievements to be made; and the levels and credit values of units are consistent and comparable across sector/subject areas and over time. The development of units is not a complex process, but over a period of 12 or more years this process has been refined within OCNs to the point where units of good quality are produced consistently across the whole national network.

Some of this experience was brought to bear on the QCF test-and-trial programme. A small number of projects based their activity on existing units and focused instead on the construction of qualifications from these units. People with previous experience of working within OCNs became involved in the development of units by awarding bodies and SSCs without previous experience of credit systems. However, the majority of test-and-trial projects focused on the process of unit development without drawing on this existing experience. Here the results of the first year of tests and trials were mixed. Some units of good quality were developed, but in other areas it became clear that people needed a lot of help and support in the production of good-quality units.

It was also clear that, despite the positive signals from government about the development of the QCF, a small number of test-and-trial projects used the programme to try and prove that the QCF would not, or could not, work. This rearguard action against the adoption of the FfA model as the preferred blueprint for the QCF continued into 2007. Bizarre units were developed within which page after page of learning outcomes were listed, or in which 30 or more assessment criteria were set out for each learning outcome. The 'additional information' section of the unit pro forma was used to reproduce verbatim the complete NVQ Code of Practice for each individual unit. The fields of the unit pro-forma were subdivided into 'Performance Criteria' and 'Underpinning Knowledge'. Units with credit values of 153, 51 and 47 were produced – albeit in draft – and unit titles covering two lines and referring to the qualification from which they were drawn were submitted. As all the units developed through test-and-trial projects passed through the QCF development team (as the managers of each project) before admission to the unit databank, there were some elements of control over this process. However, it was clear by the end of the first year of the tests and trials that, alongside perfectly good units produced by people with experience of working in credit systems, there were others that would not meet QCF quality criteria in the longer term.

This illustrates an interesting problem about the process through which the QCF was developed and the nature of its connection with the rich experience of developing units within credit systems established, nurtured and refined through OCNs over many years. In effect, there is plenty of experience of credit-based unit development in the post-school sector, but it is not in the places where the traditional development of qualifications has taken place. Most awarding bodies and nearly all sector bodies have set up processes for the development of qualifications over a number of years that have been cut off from this rich experience of unit development within a credit system. What has become second nature to the many practitioners working in credit systems in colleges, in adult and community learning centres, in commercial and voluntary sector training providers over the years, falls outside the scope of the expertise utilised by awarding bodies and sector bodies in the development of qualifications. Although the test-and-trial programme produced a few examples where this expertise was tapped, a great many more projects struggled with the process of unit development, and spent a great deal of time and resources during the first year of the tests and trials simply trying to develop units of sufficiently good quality to be able to offer to learners in the second year.

It would be unfair to characterise the first year of the test-and-trial programme as simply an exercise in unit development. Some projects did go beyond this stage; indeed, by Christmas 2006 the very first qualification had been awarded to a learner in the QCF – Natalie Battle from East Yorkshire. Significantly, though, it was subsequently discovered that, although a qualification was awarded to Natalie in December 2006, the awarding body concerned neglected to award her the credits on which the qualification was based. Despite the principle of credit accumulation that underpins the award of all qualifications in the QCF, it transpires that the very first learner to achieve a qualification actually by-passed this requirement. Natalie's credits were eventually entered into her Learner Record in February 2008 – in front of a conference celebrating 25 years since the award of the first credits in Manchester. So Natalie actually holds a double achievement record in the QCF: the first learner to achieve a qualification and the first learner to be awarded credit in her Learner Record – some 14 months later!

The test-and-trial programme also permitted some projects to test out the process of entering rules of combination into the QCA's web-based accreditation (WBA) system. Again, this proved problematic and caused a great deal of frustration for some projects. In terms of the working specification for the QCF tests and trials, there were no major problems. The format established for setting out rules of combinations for qualifications proved robust and was able to accommodate all the particular patterns of achievement that qualification developers wished to see in their qualifications (though, in truth, most rules entered at this stage of the test-and-trial programme were relatively straightforward and did not exploit the full potential flexibility of the rules of combination format developed for the QCF). However, the WBA system, which had been adapted to support the QCF tests and trials, was tested and found wanting in almost every case. It became clear as soon as awarding bodies started to enter information into the WBA system about the rules of combination for QCF qualifications that the system simply could not cope with the demands placed upon it.

This problem with the WBA system illustrates a particular issue about the process of reform and the difficulty of bringing about the radical change in the qualifications system that the Skills Strategy, Leitch and the government wished to see. As there was no decision in 2006 to proceed with implementation of the QCF, there was no budget allocated to the development of an ICT system to support the development of the new framework. Some aspects of this ICT system were established in prototype (for example, the Learner Record); others (for example, the rules-of-combination structure and the unit databank) were adapted from the existing NQF infrastructure. What the test-and-trial programme illustrated at an early stage was that the design logic of the NQF and the QCF were entirely different, and the WBA system, although adapted for the tests and trials, simply could not accommodate the very different design principles of the QCF. So, for example, as units in the NQF were defined as part of a qualification, there was no facility to enter units into the WBA separately from qualifications. Similarly, although in the QCF it was possible for qualifications to be shared by different awarding bodies (the first qualification to be submitted to the QCF was developed jointly by five awarding bodies), it was not possible within the WBA to copy the rules of combination between awarding bodies. In the example quoted, each individual awarding body had to enter the identical data itself into the WBA – that is, a fivefold increase in bureaucracy brought about by the inability of the WBA system to escape from its NQF roots. This issue of an ICT system that was not fit for purpose was a clear outcome of the first year of the test-and-trial programme and would continue to be a major issue in the eventual implementation of the QCF.

When the test-and-trial programme had been initially set up, it was agreed that an Interim Report on the outcomes of the first year of the programme would be presented both to the UKVQRP board and to the responsible ministers of the three UK jurisdictions. As the test-and-trial programme progressed and the 50 projects continued their work, it became clear that the so-called Interim Report would actually be important in securing the technical features of the QCF. Much work would remain to be done in the second year of the tests and trials to increase the capacity of organisations to develop units and qualifications for the new framework, and to ensure that supporting systems were developed so that users would have access to a functioning system of credit-based qualifications at the end of the tests and trials. However, the QCF development team was keen to ensure that the Working Specification (slightly amended) would form the basis of the future framework. Indeed, despite the difficulties of some projects in using the Working Specification, there was no evidence that it was not appropriate for the purpose of implementing the QCF. In retrospect, one might conclude that this was an inevitable outcome of the test-and-trial programme. How could a small number of projects, operating over a six- to eight-month period at best, produce contrary evidence to the tens of thousands of people who had utilised the same basic specification for up to 15 years? The fact is that the Working Specification did not need to be tested to see if it worked, it just needed to be tested by different people.

Accordingly, the Evaluation Report on the first year of the tests and trials (QCA et al., 2007) included the following key recommendations:

The general basis for developing the QCF as a unit-based qualifications framework, underpinned by the award, accumulation and transfer of credits, is reconfirmed as the appropriate model for continued development.

A standard unit format will be adopted as the building block for all qualifications in the QCF.

The Working Specification for framework tests and trials will be updated ... [and] ... will form part of the consultation on proposed regulatory criteria for the QCF.

(QCA et al., 2007, pp. 11–13)

In effect, the *Year 1 Report* on the tests and trials removed from further testing and trialling the basic design specifications of the QCF, and ensured that the second year of tests and trials did not seek to test these specifications further. Arguably, the first year of the tests and trials had done little to actually trial the working specification beyond the unit format, and the number of units actually produced within this format during the first year of the tests and trials was a tiny fraction of the hundreds of thousands of units that had been developed by OCNs over the previous 12 years using exactly the same format. However, it was also clear by the spring of 2007 that the testing of the design specifications of the QCF would not be the main outcome of the test-and-trial programme. More important by far would be the engagement of awarding bodies and sector bodies in the process of unit and qualification development, and developing the capacity of providers, assessors, guidance workers, exams officers and others to actually make use of the QCF once implemented. The modest, though positive, achievements of the first year of tests and trials signalled the need to boost the pace and scope of development of the QCF in 2007-8 if the framework was going to be sufficiently well established by September 2008 to begin the process of implementation.

The first year of the test-and-trial programme is perhaps not best seen as a proving ground for the design features of the QCF. Most of these design features had been tested, trialled, evaluated, refined, updated, adjusted and amended within existing credit systems long before the test-and-trial programme actually began. What the first year of the test-and-trial programme actually did was to cement the negotiated settlement between the reform partners and key stakeholders that resulted in the creation of the UKVQRP in November 2005. By engaging individuals and organisations in a wide range of developmental activities to take forward the development of the QCF, the qualifications regulators were able to demonstrate that it was capable of supporting practical development activity. Of course, the fact that the design specifications of the QCF had been supporting practical development activity for many years before the test-and-trial programme meant that this 'test' actually had no risk of failure.

By the time that the *Year 1 Report* was produced, the noise in the post-school system that had followed the FfA consultation had subsided and, for the most part, had been channelled into some part of the test-and-trial programme. Sometimes the process of development is more important than its outcome. Arguably, what was really tested in the first year of the QCF tests and trials was the willingness of some organisations to continue to oppose the development of the particular model of the QCF, contained in the 2006 Working Specification. The *Year 1 Report* - which was accepted positively by both the UKVQRP Board and the ministers of the three governments - effectively ended the lingering suggestions from some quarters that an alternative framework model might have been chosen. Not that such dissent disappeared overnight. Indeed, it is not clear that some dissenters actually appreciated the tactical objective of the *Year 1 Report* at all. In January 2008 a FAB speaker at a QCF event suggested that 'further testing' of the unit template was required. She was forcefully reminded by a QCA representative that the unit template had been agreed by ministers in July 2007 in their response to the *Year 1 Report*. Judging by the expression on her face, the fact that some aspects of the QCF were no longer being tested had completely passed her by.

It is fascinating to trace the development of the *Regulatory Arrangements* for the QCF back through the Working Specification for the tests and trials, through the *Framework for Achievement* proposal and the *Principles for a Credit Framework for England,* through LSDA's *2002 Report on Credit Developments* to the LSC, FEDA's *2020 Vision* document, NOCN's *National*

Credit Framework, FEDA's *A Framework for Credit* and the FEU's *A Basis for Credit?* and beyond, to the MOCF *Manifesto for Open College Federations.* Although the design features of the QCF are only part of the story of how credit systems have developed over the years, the emerging consistency of these design features over the past 15 years and their continual refinement through practice finds an apotheosis of some kind in the *Year 1 Report* on the QCF tests and trials – a final acceptance that the case for a credit system is proven and that from here on in the task is to make it work properly, and to finally conclude the long, long debate about what it should actually look like.

43

Credit: The missing test?

Before leaving behind the Working Specification for the tests and trials, it is worth noting one aspect of the design features of the QCF that was not subject to testing or trialling. Neither in the project brief issued by the QCA, nor in the evaluation reports produced by individual projects, nor in the overall evaluation of the 2006–7 test-and-trial programme (PricewaterhouseCoopers, 2007), is there any reference to the definition of credit. Given the importance of credit to the overall design of the QCF, this is perhaps surprising. Indeed, it is perhaps even more surprising when we consider that the precise definition of credit used in the QCF is a relatively new and untested feature of UK credit systems.

This is not to suggest that the process of establishing credit values in the QCF was untested, nor that some test-and-trial projects did not evaluate the process and report, sometimes negatively, on their experiences. All these reports were considered before moving forward to recommend adoption of the working specification. What no one addressed (nor were they invited to address) was the issue of whether a ten-hour basis for calculating credit value was an appropriate metric for delivering on the anticipated benefits of the QCF. As we have seen above, the definition of credit value itself took some time to emerge from the early development of credit systems. Definitions of credit value based on 60 hours, 50 hours and 25 hours were either proposed or used before the 30-hour basis for awarding credit within OCNs was agreed some 20 years ago. In recent years, and noting the progress towards the QCF, OCNs have changed the basis of their definition of credit value from 30 to ten hours. On the surface, it seems as though this definition is uncontentious, but this does not mean that it is without its problems. Did the qualifications regulators miss a trick in not subjecting the particular definition of credit to evaluation during the QCF tests and trials? Or is the basis for calculating credit values an arbitrary and therefore inconsequential feature of the framework? Where did the ten-hour basis for determining credit values actually come from?

As we have seen, it was an early ambition for the promoters of the concept of a credit framework that such a framework should be comprehensive in scope. One interpretation of this concept was that it should encompass achievements at all levels, including achievements in HE. During the time that the idea of a credit framework could be taken forward as a separate entity from a qualifications framework, this all-encompassing concept of credit continued to be espoused by those that wished to see all learner achievements brought into a single credit framework. This concept of a single credit framework began to be questioned following the publication of *Choosing to Change* (Robertson, 1994) and the clear messages within the report that credit systems in the UK in HE were fundamentally different in concept and design from those put forward in *ABC?*. Robertson characterised these differences by contrasting the 'compositional' nature of the *ABC?* proposals (that is, the idea that a credit system should be based on units) with the 'impositional' nature of HE credit systems (that is, the derivation of credit from size of an academic year). The rejection of Robertson's proposals to bring these different credit frameworks closer together in the future merely confirmed the profound nature of these differences.

In essence, the definition of credit in HE was derived backwards from a concept of the academic year. Thus a full-time learner was expected to study for 1,200 hours a year. (How true this actually was – especially in those older universities with shorter terms – used to be a matter of some debate within the HE sector, but the assumption of 1,200 hours was just that, an assumption.) A year of study was valued at 120 credits, therefore each individual credit had a value of ten. Credit was based neither on learning outcomes nor on units. Indeed, in many HEIs, credit was not (and is not) based on the recognition of learner achievement. It is a numerical value applied to a proportion of a year's programme of study. As individual universities had a variety of different ways of organising their curriculum offer during a year, dividing the curriculum offer into 120 credits proved extremely flexible, as 120 is divisible by two, three, four, five, six, eight, ten, 12, 15, 20, 24, 30, 40 and 60. Even the most arcane curriculum timetable can be made to fit somewhere into the overall measure of 120 credits as a full year of study.

This intimate connection between a measure of learner achievement and the organisation of the curriculum is a perfectly natural and straightforward one for a university. A university is both a provider of learning opportunities and the awarding body that recognises achievement through those same opportunities. The explicit separation of responsibilities between provision and certification that characterises the post-school sector, and is enshrined in the regulation of qualifications in the UK, is actually brought together in the university sector. In such circumstances the derivation of the concept of credit from the length of the academic year is perfectly reasonable. In the context of the QCF, however, it is simply unworkable. In effect, credit is 'built up' into qualifications in the QCF, whereas the academic year is 'broken down' to arrive at a concept of credit in HE. In the QCF, credit is an award made to a learner. In HE, it is 'a means of recognising and quantifying learning' (www.qaa.ac.uk/england/credit).

These acutely different concepts of credit are meaningful in a context where credit is defined as a currency of achievement. It is simply not possible to establish a single credit framework to support credit as a currency of achievement where two different definitions of credit operate. However, if credit is conceived as a mathematical construct that is simply a way of measuring and comparing achievement rather than the basis for a transferable currency, these different concepts are not so problematic. It is from this idea of a framework based on shared mathematical features that the idea emerges that a single definition of credit could be applied both inside and outside HE. This 'weak' concept of a framework began to inform credit developments in Wales at around the same time that the Robertson Report was highlighting the problems of bringing HE and FE credit frameworks together. The proposition was put forward that, as HE used a ten-hour unit of credit and OCNs used a 30-hour unit of credit, if OCNs simply divided the basis for their calculation of credit value by three, a single definition of credit value could be established across both credit systems. It is this concept of a single definition of credit that still informs the concepts of credit within both the SCQF and CQFW, and separates this definition from the one used in the QCF.

On the surface, the proposition that the 30-hour basis for calculating credit values should simply be divided by three seems sensible. OCNs had always accepted that the 30-hour unit was essentially an arbitrary figure. Why not simply change from 30 hours to ten hours so as to bring the National Credit Framework into line with credit in HE? Of course, if credit is conceived as a purely mathematical construct, such a position makes sense. If, however, credit is defined as an award made to a learner as it is in the QCF, the case for alignment with HE needs to be subjected to the much more important test of impact within the QCF itself. It is this test that has simply been missed in the development of the framework. The QCF will proceed on the basis of a ten-hour definition of credit value. However, the origin of this basis for calculating credit values comes, in large part, from the 'unitisation and credit-rating' concept of credit within the 'enabling' rather than the regulated model of a credit system. As an award made to a learner, the ten-hour unit of credit, though adopted in recent years (with significant constraints – of which more below) by OCNs, has not been fully tested as an appropriate basis for the calculation of all credit values in the QCF.

There are no examples in UK HE, or indeed anywhere else in the world, where a university makes an award made to a learner based on their achievements in ten hours of learning. Of course, there are many examples of universities making awards to learners that are expressed in a figure that is a division of 120 credits and a multiple of ten. Module certificates or transcript records have traditionally been issued by universities for completion of individual modules within a degree programme. Individual universities have (or had until fairly recently) many different relationships between modules and credits embedded within their credit systems. So, for example, universities in England operate (or have operated) credit systems based on modules with credit values of ten, 12, 15, 20, 24 and 30. Some allow for 'half modules' to be valued in their credit systems. But no university offers programmes leading to certification with a credit value of one. The ten-hour credit as an award made to a learner is completely missing from all HE credit systems in the UK and internationally. The argument that the QCF should adopt a ten-hour basis for determining credit values *that lead to the award of credit,* in order to ensure consistency with HE credit systems, is entirely misplaced.

Nevertheless, OCNs were eventually persuaded to adopt a ten-hour unit of credit, not because of any links to HE credit systems, but because of a more persuasive argument. The 30-hour unit of credit, it was argued, denies some learners the opportunity to have their achievements recognised because it is too large. If a ten-hour basis for calculating credit values was adopted, it was suggested, then smaller steps of achievement could be recognised and the credit system could become more inclusive. During the 1990s the advent of e-learning opportunities and the expansion of work-based training lent more power to this argument. If the basis for calculating credit values was arbitrary, did the 30-hour basis for determining credit values not arbitrarily exclude some achievements from recognition through the award of credit? This case, based as it was on both a clear definition of credit as an award and on the principle of widening access to recognition, rather than 'alignment with HE', proved to be much more persuasive. Notwithstanding the power of this argument in contrast to the single framework case, there was still hesitation within OCNs about moving to a ten-hour basis for calculating credit values. The relative merits of the 30-hour and ten-hour credit systems proved worthy of argument for some years prior to the shift to a ten-hour credit in the early twenty-first century. These arguments have important resonances for the QCF.

If credit is to be a genuine currency of achievement, then it has to have stability. In other words, the face value of the currency – the credit – has to be accepted by all users across the credit system. The award of credit is linked explicitly to the credit value of units, so stable and consistent credit values are an essential feature of good-quality units. In a paper on credit values I produced for the NOCN in the late 1990s, I quote one of the tenets of total quality management (TQM) to emphasise the importance of stable credit values: 'Quality assurance is the reduction of variation' (Wilson, 1998a, p. 2).

This is an interesting concept, and one which is helpful in thinking through the purpose of quality assurance in the QCF. In relation to the stability of unit credit values, I went on to propose a logical consequence of this principle: 'The smaller the unit of measurement in calculating credit values, the greater is the risk of variation in the determination of these values' (Wilson, 1998a, p. 2).

To illustrate this point, I used the example of the training videos used on the production line at Ford's Bridgend factory (still pre-e-learning). Each video was produced in multiples of 30-second clips. Some videos lasted a minute, one or two for 90 seconds, but most were based on a single 30-second clip. If we accepted that real learning took place in 30 seconds, why should we not base our currency of credit on a 30-second unit of time rather than a ten-hour unit? At the other end of the spectrum some HEIs assumed that the minimum length of time during which learning could be valued was 300 hours – that is, a unit of measurement 36,000 times greater than the Ford video clip. So a judgement about the amount of time it might take to learn something of value (the rationale behind the 50-hour basis for credit values adopted initially by the MOCF) could lead to huge differences in the definition of credit. However, a 30-second basis for calculating credit values would produce major problems for unit developers in 'the reduction of variation'. A 300-hour basis for such calculations would produce a very stable and consistent currency, but would exclude many learners from the opportunity to achieve credit for their learning.

This then is the key balance that has to be struck in deciding on a basis for determining credit values in a credit system based on awards to learners – between the stability of credits as a currency and the accessibility of credits to learners. In adopting ten hours as the basis for calculating credit values, the QCF has ensured that its credit system is accessible and responsive to the needs of learners undertaking short episodes of learning. However, in allowing the relative size of units to be represented by any multiple of this base credit value, the QCF may generate future problems of comparability between credit values and so undermine the stability of credit as a currency of achievement. This could lead to practical restrictions on the operation of credit accumulation and transfer across the framework, unless some mitigating measures are also taken. Here, once again, the experiences of OCNs may prove important.

The outcomes of the tests and trials began to illustrate these potential problems. Units now exist within the QCF databank with credit values from one to 22, and every number in between. Units of values higher than 22 also exist, up to 40 credits. (These numbers are bound to change prior to the publication of this book.) Through what process can a unit developer make a reasonable judgement that one unit should have a credit value of 18 and another of 19? How can we ensure the application of quality assurance processes has reduced variation to such an extent that the distinction between credit values of 18 and 19 is clear and incontrovertible? My personal view is that it is impossible to give such an assurance, a view confirmed by other credit systems in the UK (both the SCQF and HE credit systems place restrictions on the permitted range of credit values for individual units or modules) (SCQF,

2002) and internationally (New Zealand also places such restrictions on unit credit values).

This is where the experience of OCNs might be useful to the future development of the QCF. The argument about accessibility to the recognition of learner achievement was the key factor in persuading OCNs to shift from the 30-hour to the ten-hour unit of credit. However, this argument logically applies only to achievements which can be recognised in fewer than 30 hours. The accessibility case therefore does not apply to all multiples of credit value, but only to credit values based on ten hours or 20 hours (that is, on units leading to the award of one or two credits). This is the point at which the experience of other credit-based systems needs to be noted, as well as the facility to set rules within a regulated framework. What is needed, I suggest, is not a return to a 30-hour unit of credit, but an additional set of regulatory criteria for the QCF that limits the range of permitted credit values (in common with the SCQF and UK HE credit systems), and thereby creates an appropriate balance between the accessibility of credits to learners and the stability and consistency of credits as a currency of achievement.

Restricting the range of permitted credit values, and perhaps varying this range of permitted values by level, has been considered and rejected as an option in the process of developing the technical specifications of the QCF. Credit values of one, two, three, six, nine, 12 and 15 were proposed as part of the 2005 Seminar Series on the FfA, but were seen as too inflexible by some awarding bodies and by SSCs. Interestingly though, the one awarding body with long experience in this area – NOCN – does restrict unit credit values in this way. The flexibility demanded by unit developers in their own particular process may turn out to produce precisely the opposite quality from a learner's perspective in the future operation of credit transfer between qualifications.

An example perhaps best illustrates this problem. A learner with (say) ten credits in a particular vocational area may find it impossible to transfer those credits to another qualification because the relevant equivalent unit has a credit value of 11. If such an instance occurs, how will the developers of the two units justify to learners the difference in credit values? As I suggest above, it simply is not possible to make such fine distinctions between credit values of ten or 11. The same is not true for very small units. The experience of OCNs suggests that meaningful distinctions can be made between units with credit values of one, two and three. Above these 'prime' integers, confidence in the comparability and consistency of credit values declines rapidly. The experience of OCNs in 'blind testing' units (that is, in asking different groups of people to determine the credit values of units based on identical sets of learning outcomes and assessment criteria) suggests that even distinctions between credit values of four and five cannot be reliably established. Perhaps this blind-testing process might be useful to Ofqual in regulating the QCF in future.

Allowing any multiple of credit value for a unit therefore benefits unit developers rather than learners. Restricting credit values to a permitted range can still allow access to recognition for small steps of achievement, while balancing this against the stability of credit values and the future operation of credit accumulation and transfer. It remains to be seen how the QCF develops in this area, and whether Ofqual deploys this simple requirement in order to increase the comparability and consistency of credit values. My personal view is that the balance between accessibility and stability in the QCF is not yet established. Restricting unit credit values may seem on the surface to be an attack on the flexibility of the QCF. In fact, undermining the stability of credit values and creating future obstacles to the transferability of credits will actually be more damaging to flexibility in the longer term. Those responsible for developing units and establishing credit values are doing so without an imagined future in mind. Perhaps Ofqual and its partners can establish a principle of 'regulation with imagination' to create this balance in the future. We will see.

44

The final push: From development to implementation

Although the formal announcement of the government's decision to implement the QCF was made on 14 November 2008, it was clear by July 2007 that the QCF would be implemented. By this date, ministers in England, Wales and Northern Ireland had accepted the recommendations in the *Year 1 Report* that the design features of the framework would no longer be subject to testing and trialling, and that work should now proceed on a formal consultation on the regulatory arrangements that would support the QCF. Work on the new regulatory arrangements would be taken forward in England by the new Ofqual, which assumed responsibility for the regulation of qualifications in England in the spring of 2008. Once the design features of the QCF were fixed in the summer of 2007, the focus of development activity turned to engaging new organisations in the development of the framework and building the capacity of users to use it to full effect.

One of the other innovations of the summer of 2007 was the establishing of a 'fast track' mechanism to bring qualifications into the QCF. The concept of a fast track was aimed in part to engage in the development of the QCF those awarding bodies and sector bodies that had not been involved in the first year of development of the tests and trials. It had been agreed by the UKVQRP in 2006 that only awarding bodies involved in the tests and trials could submit qualifications for accreditation to the QCF. As I have shown above in Chapter 40, a combination of contracting delays and a lack of funding effectively restricted the scope of the year-one tests and trials to fairly modest numbers. In addition, the timetable for development of SQSs by SSCs also slipped during this same period, which meant that some awarding bodies could not secure SSC approval to begin work on redeveloping qualifications for submission to the QCF. The idea of a fast-track process was also meant to encourage SSCs to identify priority qualifications for submission to the QCF and support the process of development. The DIUS (recently assuming responsibility for the QCF from the divided DfES) was also concerned that the timetable for transition from the NQF to the QCF was starting to look challenging. The fast-track process was essentially a mechanism for accelerating the process of development beyond the self-imposed restrictions of the test-and-trial programme.

The concept of a fast-track process also hints at an interesting divide in viewpoint between DIUS officials and their counterparts in the Welsh Assembly government. The criteria for admission of qualifications to the QCF via the fast-track process were drawn very widely indeed. In essence, any vocational qualification identified as a priority for development by an SSC (without restrictions on the numbers that could be prioritised) could be submitted to the QCF via the fast-track arrangements. In effect, 'fast track' was implementation of the QCF during the tests and trials. It was the Welsh Assembly government that reminded the UKVQRP that no decision on implementation of the QCF could be made until the end of the test and trials in 2008. Although this was accepted as the formal position, the DIUS made it very clear (and David Lammy made it even clearer in his address to the FAB Conference in 2007) that the QCF would be implemented in England, irrespective of the formal position of the UKVQRP, and FAB members should act in accordance with this position. The importance of securing the technical specifications of the QCF through the *Year 1 Report* now became clear. It allowed the expansion of the scope of the 'implementation-by-any-other-name' of the QCF from September 2007, and the expansion of engagement of awarding bodies and sector bodies with the framework, in the confidence that the basic design features of the QCF would not change and that there was now no going back to the NQF.

In another signal of its commitment to the implementation of the QCF, and of the fact that its view of the QCF was different from its Welsh counterpart, the DIUS supported a particular strand of development activity in England from September 2007 that was designed to increase the engagement of employers with the QCF. Resources were ploughed into a process of promoting the opportunity for employers to become recognised as awarding bodies within the QCF and of supporting the process of recognition of employers by Ofqual. By the end of 2007, in a welter of publicity, it was announced that three employers – McDonalds, Flybe and Network Rail – had been duly recognised by Ofqual to offer qualifications in the QCF (a trio that the *Guardian* referred to as 'beyond parody') (*Guardian*, 2008). For a couple of days the front pages of national newspapers were full of 'McDonalds A levels', and it seemed that the QCF would be forever associated with McDonalds, but, after a few 'would you like some credits with that?' headlines, the unusual experience of seeing vocational qualifications on the front page of national newspapers began to recede. Of course, the DIUS' own publicity machine could not resist referring once more to these three employers at the formal launch of the QCF in November 2008,[1] but it is now pretty clear that few employers will seek to become awarding bodies in the QCF and that the QCF is perfectly well able to offer recognition for the achievements of employees on in-company training courses without the need for employers themselves to become awarding bodies.

The Employer Recognition Project also marks an interesting shift in government policy in relation both to the role of SSCs in the process of qualification approval and to the concept of rationalisation in the qualifications system. About a decade after Gillian Shephard mused publicly that, although she was opposed to the idea of one big awarding body, perhaps three was more than we really needed, one of her successors was prepared to commit public money to encouraging the development of more than the 120-plus awarding bodies then recognised in the NQF. And, once recognised, the process through which employers could submit qualifications for accreditation to the QCF effectively by-passed any approval by an SSC. Indeed, if the primary role of SSCs in a demand-led system was in effect to be the voice of aggregate employer demand for their sector, how could an SSC possibly oppose the direct engagement of this demand with the QCF through employer awarding bodies? During the second year of the QCF tests and trials, it was becoming clearer that the previous concerns of the DfES about the proliferation of qualifications were not necessarily shared by DIUS.

In some part, the negotiated agreement that led to the development of the QCF contributed to this shift in thinking. It will be recalled that the initial proposal in the FfA consultation was that all units in the FfA would be shared between all users of the framework. This, as I have shown, caused major problems for a number of awarding bodies, some of whom vociferously opposed this proposal. As part of the process of consensus building that led to the transition from the FfA to the QCF, it was agreed that the QCF would be built on a 'mixed economy' of units – some shared and some owned by awarding bodies. This consensus was effectively arbitrated by the DfES, in discussions with QCA and awarding bodies. By the end of the first year of the tests and trials of the QCF, it was starting to become clear that the decision to allow awarding bodies to own units would lead inevitably to a proliferation of both units and qualifications in the QCF. Thus, if three awarding bodies each decided to develop units in the same area then, if the units could not be shared between them, each qualification offered by those awarding bodies would be based on a different set of rules of combination and would therefore be classified as a different qualification from the other two. So, unit ownership produced three qualifications where unit sharing produced only one. Although some SSCs realised the implications of this and insisted that all units in qualifications approved for their sector should be shared, most SSCs simply did not appreciate the implications of allowing awarding bodies to own units. By the time the *Year 1 Report* was produced, it was clear that the mixed-economy model of unit ownership was not going to support the process of rationalisation.

Having proposed initially that all units should be shared, the QCA accepted in its *Year 1 Report* that this mixed economy of units should be continued into the second year of tests and trials. This was in part because the focus for rationalisation had now shifted away from the design features of the QCF itself to the role of SSCs and other sector bodies in controlling the content of units and qualifications in the QCF. Indeed, in some sectors (for example, in qualifications for IT users), SSCs had exercised their new responsibilities to introduce significant rationalisation of qualifications. It was also due in part to the fact that the tests and trials were beginning to show the potential of the design features of the framework itself to support and even to induce rationalisation as a long-term and voluntary process, rather than through imposed regulatory requirements. By insisting on a standard unit format, by requiring all rules of combination to be expressed in a similar standard format, by requiring all credits awarded to be recorded in a common Learner Record, and (most importantly) by requiring mutual recognition of credits by all awarding bodies the QCF was effectively setting in motion the development of a qualifications system with a series of 'self-rationalising' mechanisms. Although not entirely convinced by all these arguments in the *Year 1 Report*, DIUS was sufficiently persuaded of the rationalising merits of the QCF itself to shift from the previous position of the DfES on the need to reduce both the number of qualifications and the number of awarding bodies. Indeed, the formal announcement from DIUS of the implementation of the QCF in November 2008 focused on both the large number of qualifications accredited in the framework – 'over 1000 already' – and the new awarding bodies (the familiar trio of employers) being recognised.

It may not be the reason why some of us signed up, but the recognition of McDonalds as an Awarding Body is actually a subtle testimony to the power of the QCF to shift the focus of rationalisation away from a discussion about numbers (of awarding bodies, of qualifications or of units) and towards a more humane concept of rationalisation as the gradual development of units and qualifications in the QCF, with a shared set of design features that make them easily understood, more accessible and more 'systematic' in a literal sense than the traditional jungle of qualifications in the NQF that gave rise initially to the demand for rationalisation. We may also note in passing that this shift in the concept of rationalisation within DIUS made the fourth strand of the UKVQRP – the work of FAB/JCQ in reducing qualification numbers in the NQF – effectively redundant (though FAB and JCQ continued to pursue this strand of work with enthusiasm throughout the second year of the tests and trials). The *Year 1 Report* may have come half-way through the test-and-trial programme, but it marks the point of no return in the process of transition from the NQF to the QCF.

This is not to suggest that the second year of tests and trials, nor the parallel running of the fast-track arrangements, was a waste of time. By the second year of the programme the initial problems with the LSC funding were sorted out and the numbers of learners registered for a qualification in the QCF rose significantly from its very small base in 2006-7. Some new awarding bodies and SSCs became engaged through the fast-track process (though not nearly as many as had been anticipated), as well as significantly larger numbers of providers. The second year of the tests and trials also enabled some of the prototype ICT systems that supported the framework to be tested at scale, though how much these prototypes will influence the final form of the operational systems within the QCF remains to be seen. Notwithstanding these gains, it is now clear that most of the key design features of the QCF were secured at the end of the first year of tests and trials. Although the second year of tests and trials produced useful benefits, the key activity in preparing for implementation of the framework during 2007-8 was not the test-and-trial programme, but the establishing of the regulations that would govern the operation of the system of credit-based qualifications now clearly developing within the QCF.

Note

1 Indeed, the QCF 'animation' presentation developed by QCDA in late 2009 still features these same three organisations. By the end of 2009 each of them had one qualification accredited in the QCF.

45

Preparing for launch

Once the *Year 1 Report* on the QCF tests and trials had been accepted by the three relevant government departments in England, Wales and Northern Ireland, the focus of further development shifted towards the regulatory arrangements to support the QCF and of the capacity of organisations to use the new framework. The test-and-trial programme continued into its second year, the fast-track arrangements allowed some new organisations to join in the QCF development and the employer recognition project continued to stimulate the interests of employers in the QCF (if not in becoming an awarding body).

It should be recalled that the test-and-trial programme itself was a structure within which the previous tensions and disagreements between key actors in the process of development could be resolved over time. Without tests and trials there would have been continuing sniping from the sidelines of the development process and no three-country Framework. However, it soon became clear – again David Lammy's speech to the 2007 FAB conference encapsulates this position – that DIUS now wanted to make rapid progress on the further development of the QCF (www.awarding.org.uk/public/nationalconference). The second year of the test-and-trial programme became a brake on progress as far as DIUS was concerned. It also provided the opportunity for those opposed to the reform programme to continue to offer their critiques of the QCF, either through correspondence with DIUS and the QCA or through the more formal evaluative mechanisms of the continuing tests and trials and fast-track process. Nevertheless, DIUS accepted that the tests and trials had to run their course. There was also the problem that year one of the tests and trials had produced a great deal of testing of the design features of the QCF and very little trialling of the processes of assessment and certification of learners. In year two, the clear identification of QCF tests and trials as a priority for the LSC, and the subsequent earmarking of resources to support provision leading to QCF qualifications, meant that there was a significant increase in learner registrations on QCF-related provision in 2007–8 (an increase that continued in 2008–9) (LSC, 2009). Despite the desire of DIUS to move quickly to implementation of the QCF, there were still some sound reasons to continue trialling activity through 2007–8 prior to any formal launch of the new framework.

In the autumn of 2007 the newly 'separated but conjoined' Ofqual (still formally part of the QCA until the legislation establishing its independence was enacted) led, with its partner regulators (the term 'regulatory authorities' was now dropped), a formal consultation on the new arrangements for regulation of the QCF. The consultation document on the new regulations was launched in November 2007 and the process of consultation ended in February 2008, almost three years to the day from the conclusion of the formal consultation on the FfA. The consultation process was supported through a series of events held in different English regions and in Cardiff and Belfast during the winter of 2007–8.

In effect, the consultation process revealed the same support and the same concerns about the QCF that had been evident three years earlier in the FfA consultation. In some respects the debate had moved on – there was now an acceptance that the QCF would happen and that there was no point in trying to argue for a return to the NQF – and in others the issues remained depressingly familiar. So, for example, in the plenary sessions of nearly every event an awarding body representative asked a question about the standard unit format for the QCF. Why was such a standard format necessary? Why could not awarding bodies determine their own unit format? (Is it possible that these interventions were coordinated in some way?) In fact, of course, the issue of the QCF unit format was officially not an issue. The adoption of a standard format had been recommended to ministers in the *Year 1 Report* on the QCF and accepted in July 2007. There were no invitations in the regulatory consultation to comment on the standard unit format as there was no question that such a format would not be part of the QCF regulations. Yet the questions persisted – an indication perhaps that, even in 2008, some people were still hoping for a return to 2003.

Interestingly, and conversely, there were very few questions about possibly the most radical and certainly the most challenging feature of the QCF regulations: the proposition that all awarding bodies operating in the QCF should recognise the credits awarded by all other awarding bodies. This requirement – the basis of the system of credit accumulation and transfer that would underpin the QCF – was once again widely supported by respondents to the consultation and, indeed, was supported by a clear majority of awarding body respondents. Of course, the development of units to meet the QCF format was an issue that awarding bodies had dealt with from the outset of the test-and-trial programme. By the winter of 2007–8 there had been no single instance of the transfer of credits between awarding bodies in the tests and trials. To object to the requirement that all credits should be mutually recognised would require respondents to imagine a future when the QCF became fully functional. Perhaps this is the simplest explanation of why this particular proposal in the regulations received only a handful of objections in the consultation process.

The importance of regulation for the QCF should not be underestimated. Indeed, I would argue that the establishing of a credit system within a qualifications framework in which a large number of independent organisations operate is critically dependent on clear and active regulation. It would not be possible to guarantee to learners that their credits constituted a genuine currency of achievement if the ability to trade this currency was determined by the voluntary decisions of individual awarding bodies about whether to accept credits as a medium through which learners could 'save up' for the 'purchase' of a qualification. In effect, the regulators of the QCF act as the guarantors of credits as the currency of achievement in the framework. Without this guarantee, credits simply cannot function as a currency and the flexibility and responsiveness of the qualifications system anticipated through the UKVQRP could not be realised. Of course, this role of the regulators as the central bank of the credit system is a new one and perhaps one that the regulators themselves do not yet fully appreciate. Perhaps this is because the concept of credit as a currency of achievement is still not fully understood.

In a paper entitled 'The Unit of Credit and Statements of Competence', David Robertson first elaborated on the qualities of the credit as a currency of achievement (Robertson, 1988). These qualities were later refined in *Awarding Credit: The Principles of Quality Assurance*. In essence, successful currencies must have four key characteristics:

- Stability – the face value of the currency must be consistent in all circumstances
- Liquidity – it must be easily stored and easily moved
- Ubiquity – it must be available everywhere and to everyone
- Exchangeability – there must be goods of value that can be purchased with it.

(Wilson, 1993c, pp. 2–3)

If qualifications are conceived as the goods that can be 'purchased' through the accumulation of credits, then it can be seen that the accumulation and transfer of credits is essentially a process of 'saving' enough currency to exchange for a desired qualification.[1] The guarantee of stability in the currency is one important responsibility of the regulator – that is, the quality assurance of processes leading to the determination of unit credit values – but the regulators also have a responsibility to ensure that the currency of credit is ubiquitous – hence the importance of mutual recognition of credits by all awarding bodies in the QCF. The liquidity of the currency is supported by the requirement that all credits are recorded in a standard Learner Record, owned by the learner themselves, by all those organisations licensed by the regulators to issue the currency within the credit system. So when John Denham referred to credits as 'a currency of achievement', he probably thought he was using a metaphor. In fact, within the QCF, credits function as real, not metaphorical, currency.

The *Regulatory Arrangements for the Qualifications and Credit Framework* (Ofqual et al., 2008) were published in August 2008, and set out the essential connections between credits and qualifications that lie at the core of the new framework. The design features of the framework, previously set out in the working specification for tests and trials, were now integrated into the QCF regulations. For the first time, those carefully crafted definitions of units and credits that have been tested and refined over many years by many different people now find their way into a document with statutory force in the qualifications system. Indeed, the formalisation of the credit system exceeds even this exalted position. As part of the tidying up of legislation to support the introduction of the QCF, the government introduced some minor amendments to existing laws in the 2008 Education and Skills Act. One of these changes (Section 159) introduces a new statutory requirement on awarding bodies to award credits as well as qualifications (DIUS, 2008).

So, 27 years after the first reference to 'credit awards' outside HE in the City of Manchester Education Committee minutes (City of Manchester Education Committee, 1981), the requirement of awarding bodies to make such awards becomes a duty in law across England, Wales and Northern Ireland. The journey of credit reaches its present destination, albeit in one of the later clauses of an unspectacular piece of legislation, but, nevertheless, credit is now legal.[2]

The Education and Skills Act also corrected one of the unfortunate drafting errors in the 1997 Education Act, and confirmed that the qualifications regulators had the right to regulate awarding bodies (now referred to as 'awarding organisations') in the QCF and not just the qualifications that they offered within the framework. This change is technically important in that it actually gives the regulators some powers to require a change in or a cessation of the particular actions of an awarding organisation (rather than the suspension or withdrawal of its right to offer a particular qualification). More importantly, it also reflects a significant shift in the focus of regulation from the detailed scrutiny of qualifications to the quality assurance systems of awarding bodies. The Regulatory Arrangements for the QCF embody this shift of focus. The duty of the regulators to accredit qualifications is maintained and is essential if the duties of the regulators in relation to ubiquity and exchangeability of credits as a currency of achievement are to be effectively discharged. However, the QCF regulations focus very clearly on the responsibilities of the organisations that operate within the framework, rather than the qualifications that are placed within it. This reflects not only the objective of the QCF to reduce bureaucracy, it also illustrates the dynamic purpose of regulation in the new framework. Rather than regarding the accreditation of qualifications into the QCF as an end in itself (as was the case with the NQF), the regulations of the new framework set out a clear intent by the regulators to monitor, evaluate, report on and (if necessary) change the actions of awarding bodies offering credits and qualifications in the QCF. It must be remembered that (again, unlike the NQF) the QCF has been established with an explicit set of policy purposes in view. Regulation in this context does not simply mean the maintenance of confidence in standards; it also means the protection of the rights of individuals in this new marketplace of qualifications, and the regulation of this market to ensure that it offers to individuals qualifications that are inclusive, responsive, accessible and non-bureaucratic. It remains to be seen how the regulators (and, in particular, the newly established independent regulator in England) enact these responsibilities in taking forward the implementation of the QCF, but the scope and intent of regulation in this new context is dramatically and emphatically different from the accreditation of qualifications in the NQF.

The 2008 Education and Skills Act and the *Regulatory Arrangements for the QCF* also embody another significant change in the development of qualifications in the twenty-first century. The QCF regulations reflect this change by implication, in that they are a single set of regulatory arrangements that are applied through a standard set of procedures to all the qualifications accredited within the framework. In other words, in their initial iteration at least, the *Regulatory Arrangements for the QCF* include no reference to particular 'types' of qualification. In fact, the regulations will permit the future development of such types – if government policy directs the regulators to do so – but in their 2008 form no such types are established. In other words, there are no 'additional regulatory requirements that relate to a particular group of qualifications, over and above those set out in the regulatory arrangements themselves' (Ofqual et al., 2008, p. 18).

In a later chapter we consider the implications of this position in relation to the future development of 14–19 Diplomas, A levels and GCSEs within the QCF. However, the implication of this feature of the regulations for vocational qualifications is perhaps best illustrated by another tidying-up aspect of the Education and Skills Act. In several places the Act identifies within current legislation an explicit reference to 'National Vocational Qualifications' and consciously replaces such references with the more general term 'vocational qualifications'. This minor change again reflects the view of policymakers (and, indeed, reflects the views of a majority of respondents to the consultation on the regulatory arrangements for the QCF) that there should be no particular types of vocational qualification within the QCF. More explicitly, this means that there are no National Vocational Qualifications within the QCF and no mechanisms within the regulations for the framework to establish NVQs as a particular type of qualification. As can be imagined, this change has been welcomed by some, and not by others. Such is the significance of this change for the future development of vocational qualifications within the QCF that it is worthy of further consideration within these pages.

Notes

1 James Buchan's characterisation of money as 'frozen desire' captures neatly this process of accumulation (Buchan, 1998).

2 Notwithstanding this change in legislation, an exchange of views at the 2008 FAB conference – once again an interesting marker of awareness among 'the awarding community' – revealed that most awarding bodies believed that 'units' rather than 'credits' were what were awarded in the QCF. By November 2008 this view of credit as a number attached to a unit, rather than an award made to a learner, was not only mistaken, it was illegal.

46

Beyond NVQs

As I have shown in previous chapters, there were several attempts by OCNs in the late 1980s to integrate the development of their credit systems with the newly established NVQ Framework. I have also identified the important influence of some of the theoretical underpinnings of NVQs on the development of the National Credit Framework and, ultimately, on the design features of the QCF itself. Also recorded is the antipathy of NCVQ to credit systems and the intention that NVQs would, over a period of five years to 1993, replace all existing vocational qualifications. As we have seen, the incorporation of FE colleges and the establishing of the FEFC stimulated a dramatic increase in the number of vocational qualifications offered across the post-school sector, as well as a similarly dramatic increase in the spread of OCN credit systems. Even before 1993 it was clear that the intention that NVQs would replace all existing vocational qualifications would not be realised. By 1998 it was clear that NVQs would remain as a minority of vocational qualifications, even within the newly established NQF. This position of NVQs was formalised by establishing them as a particular type of qualification within the NQF (rather than the sole type that had been originally intended) with a set of regulatory arrangements, based on the NVQ Code of Practice (QCA et al., 2006a) that continued to set them apart from other vocational qualifications. In order to distinguish NVQs from these other vocational qualifications, the term 'vocationally related qualification' (VRQ) was coined. VRQs make a brief appearance as a type of qualification in the *2000 Statutory Regulations* for the NQF (QCA et al., 2000, p. 17). By the time the *2004 Statutory Regulations* were published (QCA et al., 2004), the term had disappeared from formal use. VRQs as a distinct type of qualification simply did not exist in the NQF from 2004, though many awarding bodies continue to use this term right up to the present day. Others have never used the term VRQ, maintaining a simpler and more accessible reference to 'vocational qualifications' throughout the 1990s and into the NQF.

NVQs always occupied a minority position within the NQF. At the time of the publication of the 2003 Skills Strategy White Paper, the LSC statistics showed that NVQs accounted for around 10 per cent of the total number of the LSC-funded learner registrations in England (LSC, 2003). NVQs were well established in some sectors at the outset of the qualifications reform programme, signalled in *21st Century Skills*. In other sectors they had made little impact. It is also important to note the level of public investment in the development of NVQs and their related National Occupational Standards (NOS). NVQs may have constituted a minority of registrations on vocational qualifications throughout the 1990s, but they also represented a significant investment of public funding in their development. Indeed, prior to the formal establishment of the UKVQRP, the development of NVQs and SVQs (and later of GNVQs) was, in effect, the public face of vocational qualifications reform in the UK.

Despite the commitment of some sectors to NVQs within the NQF, it was clear that the objectives of the QCF reform were, in part, an implied criticism of NVQs. Reform was needed to make vocational qualifications more inclusive, more flexible, more accessible and less bureaucratic, and it was possible to identify all these undesirable features of qualifications within the make-up of NVQs. It is possible to view the UKVQRP as a direct attack on NVQs, though, in fact, no explicit remit to get rid of NVQs has ever been part of the reform programme. Another view is that the UKVQRP simply continued a process of reform that had begun with the Beaumont Review of NVQs and continued within the context of the Skills Strategy and the Leitch Review. The advent of the QCF may have formally brought an end to NVQs as a type of qualification, but this was simply a logical consequence of a series of changes going back for nearly a decade. Once it was clear that NVQs were not going to be the only vocational qualifications on offer within the NQF, the rationale for continuing to support them as a distinct and separate type of vocational qualification was always going to be flimsy.

As we note above, another strand of the UKVQRP related to the role of SSCs and other sector bodies in the process of both identifying employer demands and approving qualifications for submission to the QCF to respond to these demands. SSCs were also expected to continue the work previously undertaken first by Industry Lead Bodies (ILBs), and later by National Training Organisations (NTOs), in the development, maintenance and updating of NOS. Within the framework of sector qualifications reform, the demands of employers were to be mediated through the development of appropriate occupational standards, and in turn these standards would form the basis of approved vocational qualifications. In approving a qualification for submission to the QCF, an SSC was effectively confirming that it was based sufficiently closely on NOS to satisfy the SSC that the aggregate demand of employers in that sector, as represented within a set of occupational standards, was being met through appropriate qualifications.

In effect, this concept of 'SSC approval' took the relationship between NVQs and NOS and extended it across all vocational qualifications. Although, initially, this relationship between NOS and NVQs had been direct and explicit (that is, the standards themselves were reproduced verbatim within the specifications of the qualification), ever since the Beaumont Review this relationship had not been a requirement of all NVQs. Although still based exclusively on NOS, some NVQs were based on an interpreted rather than a verbatim relationship to occupational standards: the NOS informed the development of the qualification, but were separate from it. This distancing of the relationship between NOS and NVQs was seen as a positive aspect of modernised occupational standards, which were capable of supporting a range of different uses (for example, the development of job descriptions, performance appraisal schemes or in-house training programmes), as well as the development of NVQs. This process of extending the uses of NOS had been undertaken in some sectors some time before the advent of the QCF. In other sectors the traditional verbatim relationship between NOS and NVQs continued unchanged.

In effect, the unit specifications of the QCF imposed an interpreted relationship between NOS and units of qualifications, and in so doing posed a direct design challenge to those sectors where the more traditional design specifications of NVQs had been maintained. It was in these sectors (for example, in engineering) that the development of the QCF presented the biggest challenges to existing practice. In other sectors (for example, in information technology) the transition to the QCF presented a minimal challenge to existing NVQs, as these had already undergone some reform within the NQF.

Another feature of the QCF tests and trials was that there was no requirement for awarding bodies to apply the NVQ Code of Practice in their qualifications. This not only meant that some of the more bureaucratic elements of the code were not enforced (for example, the requirement that ten weeks had to elapse between assessment and certification), but it also enabled awarding bodies to develop more flexible approaches to assessment. Indeed, it allowed some qualifications to be developed that were not based exclusively on NOS, but were built up from a combination of NOS-based units and other units based on, for example, literacy and numeracy skills, on enterprise and employability skills, or on personal and professional development. Once the increasingly artificial barriers between NVQs and VRQs were removed, those involved in the test and trials of the QCF immediately began to take advantage of the flexibilities offered by this innovation. The evaluation of the test-and-trial programme revealed some interesting views about the NVQ Code of Practice. For example: 'The freedom from existing codes of practice, in particular the NVQ code of practice, has been liberating... The suppression of the NVQ code of practice has enabled free thinking about the best method of assessing vocational competence' (PricewaterhouseCoopers, 2007, p. 62).

These views were duly noted by DIUS officers and, indeed, they informed the consultation on the regulatory arrangements for the QCF, which included no explicit reference to NVQs as a qualification type. This exclusion of any reference to NVQs in the consultation on the regulation of the QCF has been interpreted by some as an oversight on behalf of government, and led to subsequent accusations that NVQs were omitted from the QCF by mistake or by accident. The truth is very different. Unlike the pro-NVQ lobby, DIUS officers understood clearly the implications of agreeing that the regulatory consultation on the QCF should not include a question about NVQs. This, they realised, would lead to a single set of regulations, without an explicit NVQ type, and would contribute positively to rationalisation within the QCF based on a single, shared definition of a vocational qualification. Indeed, responses to the regulatory consultation from some SSCs and from many awarding bodies showed that such a position was understood and supported.

For other SSCs and awarding bodies, however, involvement in the QCF tests and trials (and, indeed, in the fast-track arrangements) provided an opportunity to defend the existing position of NVQs. It is perhaps not stretching a point too far to suggest that one or two SSCs took part in the QCF tests and trials in order to demonstrate that it was simply not possible to develop units based on NOS within the QCF, and therefore that the development of the framework was at odds with the demands of employers. Such views were always in a minority, and for every vociferous attack on the QCF by a defender of NVQs, there was an equally forthright defence of the new framework by a body operating in a different sector. What the tests and trials did demonstrate was that the traditional NVQ model, though favoured in some sectors, was not liked in others. In fact, as the QCF was based on a set of design features and was agnostic on both the content of qualifications and the methodology of assessment, it actually posed no threat at all to the development of qualifications based exclusively on NOS, assessed through performance in the workplace, and attesting to competence in an employment role. What it did propose was that such a model should not be imposed on qualifications design and delivery via a Code of Practice, and that other forms of relationship to standards and assessment were potentially of equal value within vocational qualifications. In effect, the QCF said: if you really like NVQs then you can reproduce everything you like about them in the new framework. And if you do not, you can do something different. This remains, in effect, the current position in the QCF regulations.

Of course, the QCF went beyond this simple enabling position in relation to NVQs and also said that, however a vocational qualification in the QCF was designed and assessed, it would be subject to the same set of regulatory requirements as any other vocational qualification. There was, therefore, no basis for calling one particular qualification an NVQ. Indeed, the very act of constructing such a type would logically have to be based on an additional set of regulations (perhaps embodied in a revised Code of Practice) 'over and above the common requirements for all recognised organisations and accredited qualifications' (Ofqual et al., 2008, p. 18). How could such a set of additional regulatory arrangements make the QCF more inclusive, more responsive, more accessible and less bureaucratic?

This illustrates the crux of the issue. The purpose of establishing NVQs was to make them different from existing qualifications because they were intended to replace them. The purpose of establishing the QCF was to ensure the maximum possible interconnection between qualifications through the credit system. The rationale for the establishment of NVQs is actually diametrically at odds with the rationale for establishing the QCF. As the two initiatives arise from two very different political and economic contexts, these differences are hardly surprising. The Leitch Review and the de Ville report belong to different eras. They may be separated by little more than 20 years, but the world has changed significantly in that time. Although there is still a need for occupational standards to be identified and for people to be able to attest to competent performance in the workplace through the award of credit, the NVQ model has clearly shown itself to be inappropriate in some sectors and in some employment roles. It is time to take the best elements of the NVQ model and move on. Indeed, a more considered view of the relationship between NVQs and the QCF might see one as a logical development from the other.

As we have shown above, the development of a learning outcomes approach to credit systems can be traced directly back to the influence of NVQs. Although the unit format of the QCF differs significantly from the original NVQ format, the principle that all qualifications should be unit based and that all units should have a standard format was part of the initial design of all NVQs. Indeed, all NVQ units were shared between awarding bodies too – another feature that has informed (or tried to inform) the development of the QCF. More subtly perhaps, the QCF inherits from NVQs a clear concern about assessment separate from any interest in programme delivery. That this assessment should be criterion-referenced and should be accessible to all those who wish to demonstrate their ability to perform to a given standard are again features of the QCF that can be traced back to the influence of NVQs. Thus, although the QCF might signal the end of NVQs as a type of qualification, it also portends the dramatic extension of some of the key design features of competence-based qualifications across a much wider range of vocational qualifications than were ever encompassed within the NVQ type.

Notwithstanding this positive view of the future of competence-based qualifications within the QCF, there remains some residual opposition to the implementation of the new framework from those most closely involved in the development and delivery of the old NVQs. In order to accommodate this residual opposition, a temporary facility has been created within the QCF to include the letters 'NVQ' in a qualification title. The purpose of this QCF titling convention is to allow those sectors that wish to indicate a connection to an NVQ in the NQF to do so, under certain given conditions. Thus the new boots of qualifications in the QCF can be made less shiny through the addition of some mud from the NQF. In time the mud can be washed off, but its familiarity to those used to working in the NVQ field is of some comfort in the new field of the QCF. As the QCF regulations make clear, the use of the letters 'NVQ' in a qualification title does not signify that such a qualification is a National Vocational Qualification, or even that it is an NVQ. It signifies that it is a different qualification with a connection to a previous NVQ. Those who welcome this temporary facility within the titling conventions of the QCF have either failed to appreciate the actual limitations on the use of 'NVQ', or are satisfied with a literally 'hollow' victory.

It is possible that both positions are held by those who still argue that NVQs should 'continue to exist' in the QCF. One of the reasons why it has been relatively easy to avoid the inclusion of NVQs in the QCF is that the opposition to this change, though vocal, coordinated and (at times) voiced by people in relatively influential positions, has actually been spectacularly misplaced. It seems that, throughout the whole period of consultation, tests, trials and further consultation, those involved in the defence of NVQs have either never realised or never accepted the simple fact that the QCF is a new framework. No qualifications 'continue' from the NQF to the QCF. No qualifications in the NQF can simply transfer to the QCF. All have to be respecified to meet the QCF requirements. In this context, arguing that NVQs should 'continue in the QCF' or 'become part of the QCF' is simply to deny reality. The case for NVQs was further undermined by the explicitly sector-based arguments assembled in their favour. It was as though opponents of the changes had forgotten the 'N' in NVQ. Not one strong case was put forward for the preservation of a type of qualification that set out explicitly to be 'national' rather than 'sectoral' in intent. The following defences are typical: 'Employers within our sector supported the NVQ as a type of qualification... During consultation on our sector qualifications strategy employers expressed serious concerns about the loss of the NVQ' (BESA, 2008, pp. 3-4).

Even when the draft QCF regulations were set out for consultation, arguments continued to be put at consultation events that NVQs should be 'included' within the QCF, as though somehow the remit from government to establish a 'new' framework could be ignored. At no time did anyone argue that a new type of qualification called an NVQ should be specified within the QCF and the current design features of NVQs should be adjusted to comply with this new type. Such a proposition might well have found some favour during the early stages of development of the QCF. Instead, opposition centred around 'preserving' NVQs, rather than changing them to meet the requirements of the QCF. In the event, the publication of the *Regulatory Arrangements for the QCF* in August 2008 simply ignored NVQs, consigning them to history via the act of omission rather than through direct confrontation.

Of course, there is no threat (despite dire warnings from some quarters) to the key design principles of NVQs within the QCF. If an SSC requires all its qualifications to be based exclusively on NOS, to be assessed through performance in the workplace, and to attest to competence in a particular occupational role, it is free to set such requirements in the QCF. What it cannot do (because other SSCs will not wish to set such requirements) is call such a qualification 'a National Vocational Qualification'. To do so would be to imply that other qualifications in the QCF were neither 'national' nor 'vocational' – a patent nonsense. The noise in the system about the loss of NVQs will no doubt rumble on for some time. Meanwhile, the QCF is being populated with new and updated vocational qualifications, designed to meet the new regulatory requirements, and will continue to do so without reference to NVQs.[1] The debate about 'the future of NVQs' in the QCF is gradually becoming a debate about the past.

It would be tempting to go back to those early meetings between the NCVQ and NOCN and to present the advent of the QCF and the demise of NVQs as a kind of hare and tortoise, or perhaps a David and Goliath, parable. In fact, as I have attempted to show above, the QCF takes significant design features from the principles that underpinned NVQs, as well as from the credit systems of OCNs. Indeed, one possible interpretation of the QCF is that it marks a significant extension of the scope of reforms begun by NVQs and now embedded into the development of all vocational qualifications. Whatever one's interpretation of this process, it would be a mistake to represent the QCF as a triumph of one world view over another. On second thoughts though, maybe this historical parity of world views is reason enough to permit a wry smile at the remembered demeanour of those who thought that NVQs would be the only form of vocational qualification on offer by 1993.

Note

1 At the time of writing, 11 qualifications out of some 1,400 have chosen to use the letters 'NVQ' in their title – including two qualifications unrelated to an NVQ in the NQF.

47

A truly comprehensive framework?

Although the various iterations and models of credit frameworks, or of credit and qualifications frameworks, examined in this paper have had distinct differences in both design features and purpose, they have all shared one aspiration; that they should be comprehensive in scope. There are no examples of credit systems in the UK, whether envisaged by OCNs, the FEU or FEDA, by *Choosing to Change* or in NICATS, CQFW or the SCQF, that have been established to recognise one particular type of achievement. In this respect the QCF, despite its origins, is no exception.

In effect, the QCF, through a process of evolving remits, carefully constructed consultations, popular sentiment and occasional technical subterfuge, has escaped from its origins within the Skills Strategy White Paper and fulfilled the expectations of early proponents of credit systems that it should be a potentially comprehensive framework, capable of recognising the achievements of learners at all levels and in any sector or subject. Whether this is what government ministers anticipated when they sanctioned a reference to an adult credit framework within a White Paper targeted at the development of workforce skills will probably never be known. The 'adult' nature of the original remit for development was soon lost. The division of responsibilities for taking forward different strands of work within the VQ Reform Programme freed QCA and its partners from the need to consider any particular type of content in developing the framework. Indeed, charging other organisations (for example, SSCs) with responsibility for determining what kinds of things should populate the QCF created an obligation on the framework design team to ensure that any kind of achievement could be recognised within it. The QCF therefore fulfils one clear previous aspiration for the characteristics of a credit framework in its design features.

Of course, the comprehensive nature of the QCF is not always acknowledged and is often obscured even by those who seek to support the framework. So, for example, long after the DfES agreed that the then Framework for Achievement would be an appropriate structure within which to take forward the development of the Foundation Learning Tier (later Foundation Learning), and therefore of awards offered to 14- to 19-year-olds, the FfA was being characterised in Wales as an 'adult framework'. A more recent description of the

QCF, produced by QAA, refers to the QCF as an 'adult skills framework' (Harris, 2008). When the implementation of the QCF was announced on the DIUS website, one might have been forgiven for assuming that the QCF was a mechanism for recognising employers who award qualifications (DIUS, 2008b). And the first communication to SSCs and awarding bodies following the implementation of the QCF from the Acting Chief Executive of Ofqual refers to the QCF as a 'new modular approach to the way vocational qualifications are awarded' (Nisbet, 2008, p. 1).

Notwithstanding this narrow perception in some quarters of the scope of the QCF, there is a clear expectation among users of the framework that, in time, it will become a comprehensive framework. This is a position that has been argued strongly by FAB, the AoC, NIACE and many others in the consultations leading up to the implementation of the QCF. Indeed, many people coming new to the QCF are surprised to find that, in 2009, A levels and GCSEs are not part of the framework and that no definite plans to bring them into the QCF have yet been agreed. Indeed, they are even more surprised to find that the new 14-19 Diplomas have been developed within QCA and QCDA over the past four years without reference to the QCF. Although the QCF has been able to escape from its policy roots, the makers of these policy roots cannot, it seems, escape from the original perception that the QCF is a framework for vocational qualifications offered to adults. The division of the DfES into two separate departments in 2007 and the change from DIUS to the Department for Business, Innovation and Skills (BIS) in 2009 has done nothing to broaden this perspective.

How then might the QCF realise its potential to become a comprehensive framework within which all achievements actually are, rather than could be, recognised? More explicitly, how might general qualifications, and in particular A levels, GCSEs and 14-19 Diplomas, be brought within the QCF in the future? Although there are technical difficulties that would need to be resolved - of which more later - the main obstacles to admitting general qualifications into the QCF are political, perceptual and philosophical. Although work is under way to prepare the ground for the admission of general qualifications into the QCF, it is by no means certain that this will actually happen and, if it does happen, under what conditions imposed by government.

In late 2009 the current government has something over six months to run before the last date at which a general election can be called. Received wisdom at this juncture suggests that this time will, indeed, run its course. If it wins this election, then a returned Labour government is committed to a further review of 14-19 qualifications in 2013, to ascertain whether or not reforms of A levels and GCSEs should be undertaken in the light of the success or failure of the 14-19 Diplomas. The outcomes of this review will not be able to bring about any changes to A levels or GCSEs within the accreditation cycles for these qualifications before the last date at which another general election must be called – in May 2015. It should be remembered that the review of 2013 is the one originally promised for 2008 and postponed for five years. The 2008 review was announced at the time that government rejected the recommendations of the Tomlinson Report and decided not to discontinue A levels and GCSEs in favour of new diplomas. The Conservative Party has no plans for the reform of A levels and GCSEs, though it is decidedly lukewarm about the long-term future of 14–19 Diplomas. In this context it seems that, even if a radical overhaul of A levels and GCSEs is announced following the 2013 review, implementation of any reforms will be dependent on the return of Labour to a fifth consecutive term in office. Well, would you put money on it?

It is now clear, and indeed those closely involved in the Tomlinson Review warned of exactly this eventuality, that the opportunity to bring about the radical reform of 14–19 qualifications, presented by the 2002 A level debacle and the subsequent Tomlinson Report, represented a once-in-a-generation opportunity that was spurned by the very same government that loved education so much they named it thrice. It now seems that the natural cycle of change in British politics might bring about the opportunity to reform A levels sometime after they pass their 75th birthday. How amazing that something should last so long. Or perhaps, how amazing that anyone believes that something first established in the early 1950s should be an appropriate way of measuring achievement in the twenty-first century. A levels belong to gentian violet and the nit nurse. They should have disappeared with gym bags and milk tablets. But a combination of political timidity and political opposition to change now looks set to guarantee them a life beyond any real expectation. A levels will live on, but what kind of quality of life can they have?

Combined with this political inertia about switching off life support for A levels, we have a toxic combination of philosophical conservatism and technical design that, unless challenged, should in theory ensure that A levels are still in place when the melting waters of the arctic lap around the atrium of Sanctuary Buildings. This philosophical conservatism is represented in one of the most potent constructs wheeled out to combat the threat of change in UK education – the maintenance of standards over time. This is in essence the Achilles heel of attempts by government to reform A levels. The accreditation cycle of an A level and the maximum life expectancy of a British government are identical. It is technically impossible for any government to announce and to complete the process of reforming A levels within any one term. And – which is where the nitrogen of maintaining standards meets the glycerine of norm-referenced qualifications in the crucible of sensitivity formed by the 2002 A level debacle – the reform of A levels is incompatible with the maintenance of standards over time.[1]

This apparent impossibility of changing A levels without undermining standards is brought about by the particular technical processes of assessment, marking and grade determination that go to ensure that A level standards are maintained over time. In fact, the received wisdom within those responsible for the design and development of A levels is that even the relatively minor changes brought about by the Curriculum 2000 reforms resulted in sufficient disruption to the processes of ensuring that standards were maintained over time to bring about the resignations of the Chief Executive of a major Awarding Body, the Chair of the QCA, and a Secretary of State for Education. The doctrine of 'maintenance of standards over time', now reinforced and honed by the experiences of 2002, says that, in essence, this year's A level has to be just like last year's A level, and if it is not then standards cannot be guaranteed. Of course, the reform of A levels is to be welcomed, as long as this umbilical connection between this year and last year is never broken.

It is in this context that the question of bringing A levels and GCSEs into the QCF needs to be considered. Can these qualifications be brought into the QCF while still maintaining standards over time? If they can't, then which brave government minister is going to stand before Parliament and say that it is the intention of government that A levels and GCSEs *should* be brought into the QCF, even though by doing so, standards over time cannot be maintained? This is the conundrum that confronts those charged with responsibility for preparing recommendations to government about the future development of general qualifications in the QCF. If the relatively modest reforms of Curriculum 2000 produced the trauma of 2002, how much greater might be the trauma if the regulatory requirements of the QCF are applied to GCSEs and A levels? And an initial assessment of the potential impact of these regulations on the existing structure of A levels and GCSEs, and – equally importantly – on the arrangements for assessment, marking and grading them, suggests that changes to the current qualifications would indeed be more radical than the Curriculum 2000 reforms. At which point the lack of any remit from government to change A levels and GCSEs becomes an impediment to making further progress.

In considering this issue, why should we be in the least bit surprised that bringing A levels and GCSEs into the QCF will result in major changes to these qualifications? The whole purpose of the QCF is to support a major reform of the qualifications system. If the application of the QCF regulations has a significant impact on some vocational qualifications developed five years ago in the NQF, why should anyone think that a 57-year-old qualification (here I refer to A levels rather than GCSEs) could be brought into the framework without change? Indeed, what would be the motivation to bring unreconstructed and unreformed general qualifications into the QCF? The desire for a comprehensive framework is strong, as is the predilection of governments for neat solutions. Nevertheless, the effects of bringing (or trying to bring) unreconstructed A levels and GCSEs into the QCF, without a clear and explicit remit from government that these qualifications should be reformed, is not only a danger to the stability of the QCF, it is an insult to its integrity. In this, I am at one with Lenin: 'Smaller but better' should be the watchword for the QCF at this stage of its development.

To illustrate the potential problem with bringing A levels and GCSEs into the QCF, consider the operation of 'compensatory assessment' within these qualifications. The functioning of 'compensatory assessment' within general qualifications means that, currently, not all learning outcomes in a unit have to be assessed; that a unit can be successfully completed even though not all the outcomes have been achieved, and that a qualification can be awarded even though some of the units within that qualification have not been successfully completed. It is technically possible to be awarded an A Level even if three of the four units in that A Level have been failed. No such facility to 'compensate' for failure in some areas through success in another exists within the QCF. So, in order to bring A levels and GCSEs into the QCF *and to maintain standards over time*, it would be necessary for units within these qualifications to be different from other units in the QCF; for the principle that credits are awarded for achievement to be suspended; and for qualifications to be awarded, even though the rules of combination for the qualification had not been met.

In this context, the concept of 'maintaining standards over time' needs to be applied not to general qualifications, but to the QCF itself. Bringing general qualifications into the QCF without reforming them would effectively destroy the technical integrity of units, credits and qualifications, as defined in the QCF regulations that were statutorily enforced from 1 December 2008. In effect, the QCF would be fatally compromised early in its existence in an attempt to accommodate the patently eccentric design features that accumulate from a series of technical fixes to a 57-year-old qualification. In such circumstances, I suggest we should keep some general qualifications out of the QCF until such time they have proved themselves to be worthy of inclusion in the new framework. In other words, what is needed is a clear remit from government that these qualifications should be respecified to meet the requirements of the QCF, in order to make them fit-for-purpose in the twenty-first century. Without such a remit, general qualifications have the potential to fatally undermine the rationale for the QCF. We have not travelled this road from Manchester in 1981 to see the basic design features of credit-based qualifications swept aside in the name of a comprehensive framework that includes all qualifications. As Michael Young has warned us (Young, 2003), such a 'weak' conception of a framework means it will fail as an instrument of change.

It will be perfectly feasible to develop new types of general qualification in the QCF that are subject-based, assessed (in whole or in part) through examination, and differentiate individual achievements through grades. The proposition that the QCF is a potentially comprehensive framework is not really harmed by the continuing absence of A levels and GCSEs from the framework, and its reputation is certainly not harmed by the continuing absence of 14–19 Diplomas. It can wait until a future government (perhaps one confronted by evidence of the success of the QCF in realising its antici- pated benefits) feels itself brave enough to announce a further review of 14– 19 qualifications that finally confronts the issues exposed by the Tomlinson Review and, rather than forcing inappropriate qualifications into the QCF, gives a clear remit that a future generation of general qualifications should be devel- oped that is explicitly designed to conform to the regulatory arrangements for the QCF. In so doing, it will serve learners of all ages much better than the enforced acceptance of A levels and GCSEs as currently constructed into a still new and still fragile framework. It may even save future governments from having to conduct endless reviews of general qualifications to ensure that they continue to be fit for purpose in the twenty-first century.

In this desire to keep A levels and GCSEs (as currently specified) out of the QCF in the immediate future, I am probably at one with the views of those currently responsible for policy in relation to these qualifications. The origins of the credit system that underpins the QCF spring very clearly from the needs of adult learners. The formal policy context within which the QCF has been developed remains 'vocational' in name and remit. The division of responsibilities between different government departments for 'skools and skills' makes a comprehensive framework even more complex to achieve. For once, it is to be perversely hoped that this combination of prejudice against the origins of the QCF and divided bureaucratic responsibilities affords suffi- cient protection against those perhaps over-zealous supporters of the frame- work, who wish to see its potential to be comprehensive realised immediately. For the foreseeable future, the critics of the QCF might protect it more assidu- ously than its supporters.

Note

1 For a fuller critique of this position, I recommend 'The Fluttering Standard', by Paul Bridges.

48

Credits and qualifications, peaches and cream

In 1997, shortly after the return of a Labour government, FEDA organised a conference on credit and invited Baroness Blackstone (newly appointed to the DfEE with a responsibility for Lifelong Learning) to give the keynote speech at the event. Of course, as is often the case at such gatherings, Blackstone herself was the real audience for the day, and a succession of speakers from the FE sector left her in little doubt about the enthusiasm for a credit system among college principals, the FE Funding Council and other senior figures, and the expectation that the new government would act decisively to introduce a national system of credit. Tony Tait played the master of ceremonies role at the event on behalf of FEDA. He reminded the Baroness of all the work that the FEU and FEDA had done in the previous five years to build on the original proposals in *ABC?* and paid tribute to all the local initiatives that had sprung up around the idea of a national credit framework, including the work of OCNs. The message was clear – FEDA had done all that it could do to support and promote this idea, and now it was up to central government to make the running. Tait's words sound plaintive in the light of what actually happened, but at the time they were intended as a direct invitation to Blackstone to take over the reins and put some serious muscle and resources into the development of a national credit system: 'We've come about as far as we can without a clear national commitment on credit' (Tait, 1997).

As we now know, no such clear commitment emerged for a further six years. What Tony Tait was referring to when he said 'We've come about as far as we can', was the need for a remit from government to convert FEDA's network of local initiatives into a formal national policy. His words proved, in part, to be accurate. Although OCNs continued to grow and local initiatives on credit continued to spring up after 1997, the feeling that 'we'd come about as far as we can' started to grow among the enthusiasts for a national credit system.

There is another interpretation of these words, reflected in the argument that, following the announcement of the NQF, the call for a national credit framework needed to be replaced with an argument in favour of the development of credit-based qualifications within the NQF. This alternative interpretation is that, in itself, a credit system can only deliver part of what is demanded by learners in recognition of their achievements. In order to fulfil the real potential of credit systems it is necessary to link them to qualifications. Perhaps by 1997 this was the truth that was beginning to dawn on those involved in the development of credit systems – that they had come about as far as they could without being integrated into a qualifications system. The proposal to develop an adult credit framework in *21st Century Skills* offered a last chance to make this essential connection – though as I have tried to show, the initial policy impetus in 2003 still regarded an adult credit framework and the reform of vocational qualifications as two different strands of policy. Uniting these different strands in the development of the QCF was an essential prerequisite of making a success of the reform programme and, if a little late, finally accepting Tony Tait's invitation to 'take it from here'.

This is the essential success factor in the QCF and one of the reasons why QCA so willingly gave up the term 'Framework for Achievement' in its negotiations with Welsh colleagues to establish a genuine three-country framework. From the perspective of policymakers, the QCF deliberately seeks to add in to the future development of qualifications the qualities of inclusion, responsiveness, accessibility and a lack of bureaucracy that characterised the development of credit systems for two decades prior to 2003. From the perspective of 'credit enthusiasts', the development of the QCF offers the opportunity to realise the full benefits of a credit system by establishing the critical connection with qualifications that was missing in 1997. Qualifications need credits, but credits also need qualifications.

Most of the arguments about the benefits of joining credits and qualifications in a single system have been made, quite naturally, by people charged with responsibility for taking forward government policy on the reform of qualifications. There is no government policy on the reform of credit and so the case for the QCF has been made, and continues to be made, from the perspective of 'bringing in' credit to support the reform of qualifications. Indeed, one of the illusions that continues to engage those unfamiliar with the operations of credit systems is that somehow a thing called 'credit' can be added to the existing NQF, and this will create a credit framework within the qualifications system. I have tried to show through these pages how such an idea grew, how seductive it can be, and how pointless it is in any genuine process of reform. The establishing of the QCF signals an end to this ersatz model of credit – 'credit-lite' as Mary Curnock Cook calls it – and confirms the central position of credit in the framework as a currency of learner achievement and not a set of numbers added to existing qualifications.

What exactly is this relationship between credits and qualifications in the QCF? And why do we need qualifications to realise the full potential of credits? The answer lies again in the concept of credit as a currency of achievement. One of the qualities of credit that enables it to fulfil this role as a currency is that it has a consistent value across all achievements. The award of credits to a learner signifies that a certain set of learning outcomes have been achieved. But the credit itself does not identify these outcomes, nor does it identify the exchange value of these particular outcomes in comparison to another set of outcomes. Indeed, as a currency, credits attest to the consistency of learner achievements across all subjects, sectors or vocational areas. The only additional information about the nature of the achievements that are recognised through the award of credit is the level at which the credits are awarded. So six credits at Level Three has a value equivalent to six credits at Level Three. No other representation of value is possible within a system based purely on credits. What makes credits so useful as a currency of achievement is precisely the same quality that makes them impossible to use as a way of distinguishing between the exchange value of credits in relation to real life ambitions or desires. Six credits at Level Three in keepy-uppy is equivalent to six credits at Level Three in financial advice. In their own right, credits – like any other ubiquitous currency – are incapable of distinguishing between the relative values of different kinds of achievement. In order to do this, an additional representation of value is required, and this additional representation is manifested through a qualification.

In effect, the QCF provides a structure within which it is possible to set out for individuals the particular numbers of credits that must be achieved through particular groups of units, in order to create a meaningful combination of achievements that can meet the requirements of an employer, a higher education institution, a professional body or, indeed, any other organisation that sets out required or desired achievement sets in order to enter or progress within that organisation. These meaningful combinations of credits are called 'qualifications'. Thus the core information contained in any qualification in the QCF are the 'rules of combination' for that qualification. These establish the particular pattern of credit achievement that will fulfil the requirements of the qualification, and in so doing these rules therefore offer a mechanism through which the currency of credits can be exchanged for the 'goods' of employment, career enhancement, progression or other desirable outcomes that individuals anticipate in agreeing to subject themselves to formal assessment leading to the recognition of their achievements.

Those of us involved in the development of credit systems through local OCNs will know well the entirely reasonable question from a learner when presented with their credits: 'What are they worth?' The answer to this question has usually been couched in terms of equivalent value rather than intrinsic value. In its simplest form, credits are identified at a particular level alongside examples of well-known qualifications at the same level. So, for example, credits at Level Three are deemed to be 'equivalent' to an A level. Such tables are familiar to all those involved in credit systems. Indeed, despite the wishes of the Manchester pioneers to find a way of expressing levels of achievement without comparing them to O levels and A levels, these representations of equivalence are to be found in *ABC?* itself, and in many FEU/FEDA and LSDA publications over the years, as well as in NOCN and local OCN documents. Establishing that credits awarded at Level Two are 'at the same level' as a GCSE (A* to C) is indeed a kind of equivalence, but it is not the answer to the question 'What are my credits worth?'.

The desire to answer this question of equivalence has also been a motivating factor in the drive to ascribe 'equivalent credit values', as well as 'equivalent levels' to these same familiar qualifications. So, for example, the CREDIS database informed enquirers in the 1990s that an A level (and here I translate for present day readers) was worth 54 credits at Level Three. Similar statements of equivalent value can be found in FEU/FEDA documents of the same period and on the current CQFW website. In effect, this credit equivalence (the term actually used in Wales) adds an additional dimension to the concept of 'equivalent level', but it still manifestly fails to answer the learner's question about the value of the credits that they hold in their hand. Of course, if you are not confronted with such questions – because there are no credits in the hands of learners – then perhaps the feeling of frustration at not being able to give a precise answer remains unknown.

As long as the concept of a credit framework remained separate from a qualifications framework, the only way in which the concept of relative value between different numbers of credits at different levels could be expressed to learners was through these equivalence tables with familiar qualifications. The QCF finally offers the opportunity to provide a real and full answer to these questions. The rules of combination for qualifications actually establish a purpose to the accumulation of credits. Indeed, within the QCF they actually define what 'credit accumulation' means. Learners may, if they so choose, select combinations of credit achievement that do not conform to the rules of combination for a qualification. Credits will still be awarded for the successful completion of units, and these credits will still be recorded in the Learner Record, but the process of putting these credits together will not be called 'credit accumulation'.

It is this facility to accumulate credits towards a qualification, and to transfer credits from one qualification and one awarding body to meet the rules of combination for another qualification offered by another awarding body, that is the really radical innovation at the heart of the QCF. These rules of combination effectively cement the award of credits into the process of achieving qualifications, and in so doing they dissolve the need to express the value of credits in terms of equivalence. Credit-based qualifications therefore free credits themselves from this unrealistic burden, and return them to their true status as a currency of achievement, devoid of exchange value in their own right. This facility to exchange credits for goods of value is, as I have tried to show, one of the four key attributes of a genuine currency. Thus the integration of credits and qualifications in the QCF enables credits to fulfil this fourth key quality of a currency – exchange value – that a credit framework of itself could never deliver. This is why I argue here that credits need qualifications just as much as qualifications need credits. Without this relationship, you can amass as many credits as you like, but you will never be able to answer the question 'What are they worth?' unless you can exchange them for goods of value, and only a credit-based qualification can provide the medium for this exchange.

Of course, one of the ironic things about the implementation of the QCF following two years of tests and trials is that the functioning of this system of credit accumulation and transfer through rules of combination remained completely untested. This is not to argue that the test-and-trial programme should have been longer, or that the tests and trials did not reveal some valuable lessons in their own right. The tests and trials provided the opportunity for a new group of people to rediscover within the context of a formal remit from government what was already known by others outside this context. Indeed, given the gradual tailing off of dynamism within the credit movement in the years prior to development of the QCF, the tests and trials also offered the opportunity to retrieve and regenerate a collective memory that was in danger of withering away (outside its OCN redoubts at least). What the tests and trials certainly did not do was to test or trial in any meaningful sense the actual operation of the system of credit accumulation and transfer that is intended to deliver the anticipated benefits of the QCF. Which just goes to show that sometimes the ambition for change and the concept of 'evidence-based policy-making' are simply not compatible.

By bringing together both credits and qualifications in a single, regulated system for recognising achievement, the QCF finally resolves the previously insoluble problem of credit systems by establishing the fourth essential characteristic of exchangeability that enables credit to fulfil its intended function as a currency of achievement. The desire to establish links between OCNs and NVQs; the proposals to BTEC and RSA that they should award qualifications based on OCN credits; the decision of NOCN to become an awarding body – all these acts can be seen as representative of an understanding within the credit movement that this fourth essential characteristic of a currency was missing.[1] In order to realise this full potential of credit as a currency of achievement, it has been necessary to create an internationally unique framework: the QCF. Notwithstanding that much of the formal critique of the new framework focuses on the undoubted benefits of credits to the development of the qualifications system, from the perspective of this author it is the successful, formal and systematic insertion of qualifications into the previous concept of a credit system that marks the truly elegant and meaningful triumph of the reform process.

Note

1 Indeed, John Sanders remembers the 'what are they worth?' question being asked by the very first learners that received MOCF credits in 1983.

49

Credit transfer, learner mobility and rationalisation

The absence of any real examples of credit accumulation and transfer within the QCF tests and trials might be seen as a major impediment to the implementation of the QCF. At the very least, it might be seen as a legitimate reason for awarding bodies and sector bodies to adopt a cautious approach to developing credit accumulation and transfer arrangements within the QCF as it is implemented. Some responses to the evaluation reports required of test-and-trial sites were sceptical about the benefits of credit accumulation and transfer, and questioned why an 'untried and untested' concept was being implemented based on faith in its potential benefits, rather than evidence that it would work. Others could see the potential benefits of credit accumulation and transfer within the QCF, but were unsure how it would operate in practice. So just how is credit accumulation and transfer going to operate within the QCF, and will it bring about the benefits anticipated for the new framework?

Although the terms 'credit accumulation' and 'credit transfer' are usually bound together in the concept of 'CAT', within the QCF they are best considered separately. In fact, the process of credit accumulatio – that is, the putting together of credits from particular combinations of units to meet the achievement requirements of a qualification, though a new process for most awarding bodies – does not challenge profoundly the existing operational models utilised by awarding bodies in the NQF. Although the process of credit accumulation may open up more flexible routes to achievement for learners, especially over time, the process also involves progress towards the achievement of a single qualification offered by one awarding organisation. Changes to current practices in relation to certification of learner achievement may need to be made, but basically the process of credit accumulation falls within the remit of a single awarding organisation to manage, without reference to the processes of any other organisation in the QCF. In considering the implications of the QCF for their future business models, awarding bodies are, by and large, fairly relaxed about credit accumulation.

Credit transfer – that is, 'the process of using a credit or credits awarded in the context of one qualification towards the achievement requirements of another qualification' (Ofqual et al., 2008, p. 40) is an altogether more challenging process for awarding bodies, especially when taken together with the QCF requirement that 'all awarding bodies must support credit transfer by agreeing to mutually recognise the credits awarded by all other awarding bodies recognised to operate within the framework' (Ofqual et al., 2008, p. 17).

I confess that this is my favourite line in the QCF regulations, but is it actually going to deliver on a system of credit transfer within the QCF? Or are those that say there is no evidence of demand for a system of credit transfer going to be proved correct?

Actually, there is a source of evidence that might be quoted by those unconvinced of the merits of credit transfer arrangements within the QCF, and that is *Choosing to Change*, although Robertson is very explicitly positive about the potential benefits of credit transfer in bringing about the development of a more accessible and individually responsive HE system. Nevertheless, he acknowledges that:

> demand for credit transfer is difficult to assess and some scepticism is often expressed concerning its scale and character ... most informed opinion appears doubtful that demand is ever likely to be substantial.
>
> (Robertson, 1994, pp. 86–7)

In his extensive research on credit systems, Robertson found little evidence (outside the Open University) that credit transfer systems actually operated in HE:

> From our investigations, credit transfer between HEIs in the same regional cluster or consortium appears to be minimal... There is no official data confirming the extent of student credit transfer between universities nationally.
>
> (Robertson, 1994, pp. 87–8)

It should be remembered that the HE sector in 1994 was somewhat different from that of today. Robertson notes that the sector 'remains heavily circumscribed by traditions, regulations and the absence of a culture of mobility and choice' (Robertson, 1994, p. 86).

Just how far the above is a valid description of HE in 2009 is a matter of opinion. Certainly, though, the intervening 15 years have brought about a considerable increase in the proportion of learners in HE who are studying part-time, as well as a significant growth in work-based approaches to learning, as well as the development of a wider range of qualifications at levels below and of sizes smaller than an undergraduate degree. Coupled with the recent changes to the funding of part-time HE in England (HEFCE, 2009), the establishing of the new HE Credit Framework for England (Universties UK et al., 2008) and the proposals for yet further reform of the HE Sector (King, 2008), it would be reasonable to assume that the HE system of the future will be more receptive to the operation of credit transfer, and that demand for credit transfer by learners will be greater than when *Choosing to Change* was published. Despite these assumptions, the lack of national data in 2009 about the extent of credit transfer between HEIs remains as problematic as it did 15 years ago. And, as we note elsewhere, the culture of credit within HE is arguably less strong in 2009 than it was in Robertson's day. I suggest that, if we want to defend the potential benefits of credit transfer and to anticipate the demand for credit transfer from learners within the QCF, we should not be looking to HE, even as it develops in the future, for evidence of such trends.

This is partly because of the different institutional context within which people learn in HE and outside it, partly because of the very different regulatory context of the QCF in comparison to HE, but mainly because of the different role played by awarding bodies in the QCF and in HE. So, for example, although there are some 140 HEIs offering learning opportunities in England, Wales and Northern Ireland, plus a similar number of other institutions (mainly FE colleges) offering HE programmes, there are far more places offering (or planning to offer) learning opportunities that lead to awards in the QCF. Especially in large urban conurbations, the opportunity to transfer credit between local providers is simply a more practically accessible opportunity for learners within the QCF than it is between HEIs. Coupled with this, the ability to enrol on short courses, to move from employer-based to college-based training, and (as is beginning to happen within still-significant constraints) to receive public funding to support learning leading to the award of credits (rather than a qualification), further enhances this accessibility to learners. In short, there are simply many more opportunities, and many more reasons, to want to transfer credits between providers offering awards in the QCF than there are in HE.

The regulatory basis of the QCF also creates a much clearer and more explicit offer of credit transfer opportunities to learners. In HE, most credit transfer opportunities are negotiated between institutions, based on individual requests from learners, and are subject to constraints imposed by the HEI itself, by a receiving faculty or school, or in some instances by the admissions officer for a particular course. Although the principle that credits may be transferred between HEIs is accepted across the HE sector, the actual transfer of credits is never presented in terms of a guarantee to learners. In contrast, opportunities for credit transfer within the QCF are made explicit to learners through the rules of combination for qualifications and are not subject to negotiation with the receiving awarding body, which is required by the regulators to accept credits for transfer within these rules. In summary, credit transfer in HE is an institutionally focused concept and is based on negotiation; in the QCF it is learner-focused and based on an exchangeable currency. We may anticipate that demand for credit transfer within the QCF in this context is likely to grow more quickly than in HE.

However, it is in the relationship between the delivery of learning opportunities and the awarding of credits and qualifications that the most significant difference in demand for credit transfer is going to develop between HE and the QCF. As a university is both a deliverer of learning programmes and an awarding organisation, it follows that credit transfer between HEIs is by definition an inter-institutional process. The concept of credit transfer *within* an HEI is meaningless. A learner wishing to transfer credit *between* HEIs will, in so doing, transfer their registration arrangements and their future programme of learning from one geographical location to another, perhaps distant, location. In contrast, a large, general FE college may offer awards within the QCF through a number of different awarding bodies. Some colleges report registrations with 60 or more awarding bodies across all areas of the curriculum. In such circumstances, demand for credit transfer, from both providers and from learners, is more likely to come from *within* a single institution, rather than *between* institutions. From a learner's perspective, being able to transfer credits between qualifications within the same provider or within the same locality, served by venues operating as recognised awarding body centres through that provider, is likely to produce far more demand for credit transfer than transfer between different and often distant geographical locations. In this crucial respect, credit transfer within the QCF is likely to develop into a very different phenomenon from the same concept in HE.

This does not necessarily mean that credit transfer will establish itself rapidly in the early years of QCF implementation. There will still be some awarding bodies and sector bodies that are sceptical of the benefits of credit transfer and seek to limit its operation within the qualifications that they offer or approve. The continuation of public funding arrangements linked to the achievement of qualifications, rather than the achievement of credits towards them, will also act as a depressant on this particular feature of the QCF. Nevertheless, as opportunities for credit transfer begin to grow, those awarding bodies that offer the greatest possible range of opportunities for learners to transfer credits into qualifications will, we may assume, become the most attractive organisations not only to learners themselves, but to the providers that seek to maximise learner success, and in so doing enhance their quality performance indicators and future levels of funding. Those awarding bodies that seek to limit opportunities for credit transfer may be able to protect their existing market position in the short term, but, if the qualifications market is to expand in the way government anticipates in the future, will increasingly lose out to competitors in terms of future market share in an increasingly flexible system.

There is also some evidence from BIS in its strategy for development of the QCF that the operation of a system of credit transfer is seen, at least in part, as a potentially important mechanism for rationalisation of the qualifications system. Although BIS, like DIUS and the DfES before it, retains a strategic interest in rationalisation as an explicit objective of qualification reform, the evidence from the Employer Recognition Project[1] suggests that rationalisation no longer means simply a reduction in the number of qualifications and the number of awarding bodies. This limited definition of rationalisation was still very much in evidence at the beginning of the QCF tests and trials, but had ameliorated significantly by the time the final report on these trials was submitted to the DIUS. This was due in part to the gradual appreciation by government that, if the QCF was to expand significantly into the 85 per cent of the qualifications marketplace not covered by the NQF, then simply measuring the number of qualifications available in the QCF would not provide a useful or comparable measure of this process of rationalisation. It was also due to the fact that, in part to stimulate this expansion beyond the boundaries of the NQF, DIUS has been subsidising employers to encourage them to become recognised as awarding bodies within the QCF. This financial encouragement is continuing through BIS during the first phase of QCF implementation, has already added new awarding bodies to those recognised in the NQF, and will continue to add (a few) more. In such circumstances, basing rationalisation on a reduction in the number of recognised awarding bodies is clearly not a tenable proposition.

In addition to both these processes, there is some evidence that the DIUS and its counterparts in Wales and Northern Ireland accept the proposition from the regulators that the operation of credit accumulation and transfer within the QCF can itself drive this process of rationalisation between qualifications and awarding bodies. If all credits are potentially transferable between all awarding bodies, then actually government does not need to worry about the number of awarding bodies operating in the system. Providing the system operates effectively (and here we may anticipate an acute interest from government in ensuring that credit transfer does, indeed, operate effectively) and that credit does become a genuine currency of achievement within a quality-assured system based on the regulation of the QCF, then government can assume with confidence that the number of awarding bodies offering awards within the framework can be sufficiently constrained by the operation of market forces, rather than by intervention from government itself, to limit the number of awarding bodies in the system.

In this context, awarding bodies may come to view the operation of credit transfer within the QCF as a way of securing their future place within the qualifications market, rather than as a threat to their existing position in that market. In other words, without the operation of the QCF credit system, awarding bodies may still be open to a much cruder interpretation of rationalisation within government policy than the one now apparently emerging with the implementation of the QCF. If, over time, awarding bodies seek to protect their current market position by thwarting attempts to develop credit transfer between qualifications, then not only could this encourage new organisations with more flexible approaches to seek recognition within the QCF, it may also lead to a return to a definition of rationalisation based on reducing the overall number of recognised awarding bodies. Not only do individual awarding bodies therefore have an interest in offering qualifications that maximise opportunities for credit transfer for learners, but awarding bodies also have a *collective* interest in ensuring that credit transfer operates effectively across the QCF as a way of guaranteeing that rationalisation remains a policy objective delivered through the operation of a qualifications market, rather than through direct intervention by government to reduce the number of qualifications or awarding bodies.

We should not anticipate the immediate delivery of this effective system of credit transfer within the QCF. Those who have sought to establish such a facility for learners in the past will be under no illusions about the potential limitations to this ambition. Nevertheless, with effective regulation in pursuit of the QCF's objectives, the development of funding arrangements capable of accommodating the operation of a credit transfer system and the operation of competition between awarding bodies in a context where rewards flow to those offering the greatest flexibility to learners, we can be confident that, despite the lack of current evidence to support this contention, there will be an increasing demand for credit transfer from learners, supported by providers, as the QCF expands. This will be accompanied by increasing evidence that the benefits of the QCF are linked in no small part to the effective operation of credit transfer across qualifications and awarding bodies in the framework.

Note

1 Now re-titled the Employer Engagement Project.

50

Transforming qualifications through credit

In Chapter 48, those who know me might well have been possessed by the occasional thought that I was over-egging the qualifications pudding to the detriment of credit systems. Having argued that the integration of credits and qualifications in a single framework finally allows credits to realise their full potential as a currency of achievement, one may be mistaken for thinking that all those pioneering achievements of the people who developed local credit systems, and who constructed a national credit framework separate from existing qualifications, were somehow misguided or deluded about the value of what they were doing. To these people (among whom I include myself) I apologise, for this is not my intention. To explain myself a little further, I want to return to a distinction I drew in Chapter 48 between 'exchange value' and 'intrinsic value'. The integration of credits and qualifications in a single framework enables this concept of 'exchange value' to be established, but 'intrinsic value' is something different.

The person who best captures this intrinsic value of credit systems in my own memory is Ray. Everyone who has ever worked in an OCN knows Ray. His gap-toothed grin is still there in the photograph of him receiving his OCN Credit Record at an evening awards ceremony, in a community centre in Leicester. Long before the government had ever thought of developing qualifications to recognise the achievements of adult learners on literacy and numeracy programmes, Ray proudly shows to the camera the Level One credits he has achieved on his 'Making sense of numbers' course. The light catches the sleeve of the startlingly shiny suit he wore that evening, though his shirt and tie are more like the crumpled Ray known to his tutors. Surrounding Ray are members of his family, his mum, aunt, brother and sisters, all smiling with the same puffed up pride you can detect in Ray himself. The photograph cannot capture the few words he said on receiving his credits, but again they are the words that everyone in an OCN has heard before: that it is the first time he (or indeed any member of his family) has ever received a certificate for his achievement, that he did not think he could do it when he first started the class, but, with the help of his wonderful teacher (she is in the picture too), he has succeeded and he cannot wait for next term so he can go on to another class and get some more credits for something else. This is what intrinsic value means. Ray is not the least bit interested in tables of equivalence. He knows the value of the credits to him, which is why his Credit Record sits on the mantelpiece of his living room for all to see.

Are we going to lose within the QCF some of this intrinsic value in the award of credit for achievement as worthy of recording in its own right? Will we find ourselves a few years down the line in the world of credit and qualifications, as envisaged by the QCA's press officer at the launch of the test-and-trial programme: 'Now people who cannot gain a qualification will be awarded credits for their achievement.'

He was trying to be positive, but it just came out wrong. There is, though, a danger that, in joining together credits and qualifications in a world dominated by qualifications, the potential benefits that we know a credit system can deliver will be thwarted by a concept among policymakers that credits are what you get for the partial achievement of a qualification. While there is a mindset about 'partial achievement' afoot, there is a danger to the intrinsic value of credits. Try telling Ray his credits are just for 'partial' achievement.

My personal view is that this will not happen. By integrating the award of credits and the achievement of qualifications in a single framework, and securing the place of credit as the currency of achievement in that framework, we are, I suggest, setting in motion a process of change that will gradually transform qualifications as they exist in the NQF. By transformation, I mean something more than simply changing qualifications to be more flexible, more inclusive and so on, though this will be an obvious benefit of the QCF that can already be seen in microcosm through the tests and trials and the initial year of implementation. In the longer term, I think the QCF will gradually transform the way in which we currently conceive of qualifications and that, providing policymakers do not intervene to stifle or divert the process of developing credit-based qualifications in response to demand, the gradual assertion of the intrinsic value of credit as a currency of achievement will grow as the QCF itself develops.

In order for this to happen the QCF itself needs to mature over time, and other features of the post-14 system also need to change to support the development of the new framework. Providing the four key benefits (more inclusive, more responsive, more accessible, less bureaucratic) of the QCF continue to inform policymakers, regulators and funding bodies, the future of credit within the QCF is secure. Indeed, achieving these benefits without continually enhancing the role of credit within the QCF will not be possible. However, as international comparisons remind us, the development of the QCF will take time (Coles, 2006). The QCF is still in its infancy. We should be confident that it will be able to deliver on some of the ambitions of the early pioneers of credit systems, but we need to be patient. Indeed, the implementation plan for the QCF itself envisages a timetable of development up to 2020 (though the later years of the plan are not exactly detailed) (QCA, 2008). I take this as a compliment to the potential of the QCF and as testimony to the seriousness with which those responsible for the QCF have undertaken their task. Personally, I would not have wanted to be involved in something that could deliver its promises in a couple of years.

The first task in implementing the QCF is simply to ensure that it works properly. The second task is to get people using it. These need to be the two priorities in the first phase of development of the framework. This initial phase is supposed to last until December 2010, by which time the accreditation of the last vocational qualifications in the NQF will have expired. Personally, I cannot see this target being met by the due date, but that is not my business. Whenever the process of transition from the NQF to the QCF is completed will mark the end of this first phase. During this period, the focus of development must be on simply populating the QCF and ensuring that all qualifications meet the technical requirements of the new framework. As a majority of NQF awarding bodies were not involved in the QCF tests and trials, there is work to be done with these organisations in developing new qualifications that meet the regulatory requirements of the QCF. For most awarding bodies that had been involved in the tests and trials, the majority of their qualifications still lay outside the QCF in 2009. And, of course, it is the expressed intention of government that more awarding bodies (employers in particular, but perhaps colleges and universities too) should be recognised within the new framework.

All the evidence from the tests and trials, and from work undertaken by both the LSC and the Learning and Skills Improvement Service (LSIS) as part of the QCF 'Readiness' programme, suggests that much work remains to be done in preparing providers to take advantage of the potential flexibilities of the QCF. Although almost every general FE college in England, Wales and Northern Ireland has some credit-based provision (accredited by an OCN) in its curriculum offer, this provision is often marginalised or separately organised from learning leading to vocational qualifications in the college. Of course, providers will be dependent to an extent on guidance from awarding bodies on utilising the design features of the QCF. We can assume it will take time for this guidance to begin to have a significant impact on provision in many vocational areas. In addition, there is a major task in briefing and training advice and guidance workers and learner support staff in making best use of the QCF. Again, this will take some time.

It must also be remembered that the ICT infrastructure to support the implementation of the QCF is not yet in place. Although the prototype Learner Record used in the tests and trials illustrated what a fully functioning record might look like, it is still some way from being delivered. We are promised the Learner Record will be fully functional by September 2010. Once it is available in something approaching its final format, we may anticipate that it will take some time for awarding-body record-keeping and reporting systems to be able to interoperate securely and speedily with it through what is termed the 'QCF Service Layer'. Ensuring that the ICT system for the QCF can support the Learner Record and its associated functions is bound to take time, and will further slow down the pace of change in delivering the benefits of the new framework.

It will also be necessary to make changes to both the funding arrangements for provision leading to awards in the QCF and the performance indicators of providers offering credit-based provision. If we are to escape from the concept of credit as 'partial achievement of a qualification', then the facility of providers to support learners aiming to achieve credits rather than qualifications must be supported both through funding arrangements and through success measures. The LSC is continuing to trial such changes during 2009–10, but for the foreseeable future we may anticipate that both funding arrangements and performance measures will continue to incentivise the achievement of whole qualifications rather than individual credits. The absence of a comprehensive set of funding arrangements that can support the potential flexibilities of the QCF is one more reason why we should not expect the new framework to deliver on its benefits during the first phase of its development.

For all these reasons, it is possible that, by December 2010 (or perhaps 2011), the QCF might look more like the NQF than perhaps was anticipated. It is certainly not going to deliver proof of benefits to the desk of a Secretary of State before the next general election. The influence of credit on the structure of many qualifications will be marginal. We may expect that, as awarding bodies get to grips with the design features of the QCF, and as the pressure to respecify NQF qualifications in the QCF begins to grow as December 2010 (or whenever) approaches, the temptation for many qualification designers will be to reproduce as closely as possible in the QCF the qualifications that already exist in the NQF. This generalisation is perhaps unfair to those individuals and organisations that have used the transition from the NQF to the QCF to review their current qualification offer and make significant changes to it. Nevertheless, if the priority is to get things into the QCF and to get people used to its design features, reproducing current qualifications as closely as possible in the first instance must be seen as a legitimate pursuit of these aims.

The implication of this for the QCF credit system is that, in this first phase of development, learner choices of routes to achievement within rules of combination may be limited. Opportunities for credit transfer between qualifications may also be limited and may be severely restricted between awarding bodies. Many qualifications will make no use of the facility to grant exemption from credit achievement on the basis of an equivalent qualification or certificate outside the QCF. The opportunity to claim credit through the recognition of prior learning (RPL) may be restricted to certain centres and certain award-ing bodies. The number of learners achieving a qualification may constitute a high proportion of those achieving credits. Those learners actively choosing to achieve credits as an alternative to qualifications may be a small minority of the total number of learners registered with awarding bodies. Those doing so through provision funded by the public purse may be a very small minority indeed. I suggest that all these are things that we will have to put up with dur-ing this initial phase of populating the QCF. By gradually extending the scope of the QCF and by involving an increasing number of awarding bodies and providers in the framework as it expands, we not only increase the mutual confidence of users in the stability of the QCF and the credit system that oper-ates within it, we also create the necessary range and volume of achievements in different sectors and subject areas that can make the process of credit accu-mulation and transfer practically useful to users.

If we conceptualise the QCF credit system as a new bit of innovative tech-nology that can improve the responsiveness of our qualifications system to individual demands, we can perhaps see the functional necessity of populating the QCF with a sufficiently large number of credit-based qualifications before the benefits of this technology start to be realised. If credits were mobile phones, the benefits of a credit system would not be immediately obvious if only 10 per cent of people had a mobile phone. By the time 50 per cent of people have access to a mobile phone, the benefits start to become more tan-gible and the shift from 50 per cent to 100 per cent takes place in a relatively short space of time. Similarly, it is not until a sufficiently large number of credit-based qualifications actually exist within the QCF that users can see the benefits of building into the design of qualifications opportunities for learners to transfer credits from neighbouring qualifications. Once this process does start to happen, the QCF can move into its second phase of development.

This second phase of development will, I suggest, be characterised by a sig-nificant expansion of what Ofqual currently terms 'the qualifications market'. In fact, this market will become increasingly a 'qualifications and credit market' and expansion will be driven in part by the ability of individual learners to achieve credits, rather than qualifications. Indeed, if the QCF is going to sup-port this expansion into the 85 per cent of the qualifications iceberg that cur-rently sits outside the NQF, and is going to ensure that the system remains responsive to individual needs and is easily accessible and non-bureaucratic, then extending the use of credit as a currency of achievement is the key to this expansion. Whatever the interpretation of rationalisation of qualifications might be in the future, the process of bringing these tens of thousands of cur-rently unregulated qualifications into the QCF cannot be conceived as a process of simply adding them to those already regulated. In many instances, the award of credit in itself, and the ability to accumulate credits towards a larger qualification, will meet the purpose of many of these 'qualifications'. Extending the reach of the credit system, rather than adding more and more qualifications into the system, is the only practical way of managing this anticipated expansion. To prepare the ground for this, credits will need to become more and more recognised as an achievement in their own right, even if they are never exchanged for a qualification.

In these 'second generation' QCF qualifications, we might anticipate that the regulators, having supported the process of population by simply ensuring that qualifications conformed to the technical specifications of the QCF, begin to exercise their powers in more consciously regulating the QCF in pursuit of its four key objectives. Having used this initial phase to ensure that the QCF worked properly and that people became familiar with its design features and requirements, the regulators might intervene more proactively in the re-accreditation of qualifications to enforce opportunities for credit transfer and exemption within these second-generation rules of combination. It remains to be seen whether Ofqual and its partner regulators will adopt such an approach to ratcheting up the flexibility of the QCF through the process of accreditation, to ensure maximum interconnection between qualifications over time through the operation of credit accumulation and transfer between them.

Of course, in many instances the regulators may not need to exercise these powers. We may anticipate that many awarding bodies will seek to develop qualifications that offer the maximum range of opportunities for learners to transfer credits from qualifications offered by other awarding bodies. In so doing, they will maximise the opportunities for previous achievements to be counted towards their qualifications, which, we may surmise, will give them a market advantage over less-responsive awarding bodies in the eyes of both learners and providers of programmes leading to awards in the QCF. If we envisage a context in which increasingly large numbers of learners aim to achieve credits rather than qualifications through small episodes of learning (a facility already hinted at in the use of the LSC funding in England to offer some individual units leading to credit within the QCF), then the ability to count these credits towards a qualification becomes an important added value feature of the framework.

During this second phase of development of the QCF, not all awarding bodies will utilise the full range of flexibilities in the framework. Some will be able to preserve their niche market positions by continuing to offer qualifications based on rules of combination that do not offer opportunities for credit transfer or exemption. This will be their choice, and the QCF can continue to expand even if some awarding bodies do not themselves pursue a policy of maximum flexibility in qualifications design. The role of the regulators in this context will be to ensure that those awarding bodies that make maximum use of the potential flexibilities of the QCF are those that are rewarded through an increased share in an expanded 'qualifications and credit' market. Similarly, it will be the role of funding agencies to ensure that those providers that offer to learners the widest possible range of choices in their routes to achievement of credits and qualifications in the QCF are given incentives to do so through the funding system. Once these market-based mechanisms are in place and functioning effectively, the QCF can move into the third phase of its development. In moving from this second to the third phase of QCF development, I am shifting from educated guesswork to optimistic speculation. This change of tone is, I think, worthy of a separate chapter.

Before anticipating these potential future benefits, however, I want to return to the question of who is actually going to benefit from the QCF and how. The above examples try to show how a virtuous cycle of change can be kick-started within the QCF once the framework itself matures and the supporting mechanisms of funding, performance measures and policy targets are aligned with the objectives of the QCF. The gradual exertion of the power of credits as a currency of achievement that is recognised in its own right, rather than needing to be mediated through the goods of qualifications, is, I suggest, a necessary feature of a successful framework (that is, one that fulfils its anticipated benefits for government) and one that, once established with sufficient traction, will gradually lead to the reassertion of the credit system itself, rather than credits accumulated towards qualifications, as the essential mechanism through which learner achievement will be recognised. But which learners? And what achievements?

51

A credit system for all

During the second year of the test-and-trial programme for the QCF, the LSC released its annual statistical return confirming that, for the second year running, huge numbers of publicly-funded learning opportunities for adult learners had been lost. Particularly savagely hit by this 're-alignment of priorities' (the onset of recession seems to have made it once again acceptable to refer to 'cuts') were OCN-accredited programmes at Entry Level and Level One. I was part of a team running seminars for new organisations coming into the second phase of tests and trials at the time, and I was reminded of these figures by a participant in one seminar. I agreed with her pessimistic analysis and said that I could not imagine a worse year than 2007 to be introducing the QCF reforms. 'That's because', she said, 'you haven't lived through 2008 yet'. I'm sure she would say the same thing about 2009.

In early 2009, I attended another meeting at which a participant made a spectacularly miscalculated claim that getting rid of NVQs would lead to a 'collapse of training for skilled jobs' in his sector. It occurred to me at the time that this is probably a good time for a government to make brave decisions about implementing the QCF. The collapse of training for skilled jobs in a number of sectors is already becoming a reality and will remain so for some time to come. Pinning an argument to that particular mast in the current climate is simply not a good idea. Effectively, all previous bets are off, all comparisons are insidious, all indicators are skewed and all criticisms are compromised by this wider context of recession. The evidence available suggests we can anticipate a significant downturn in employer demand for training and development for some time to come (Bewick, 2009). So where does that leave the QCF, and how far will the difficult first years of its implementation make it a more or less inclusive, accessible and flexible framework within which all achievements might be recognised?

The decision to implement the QCF in November 2008 was taken at a time when the view of its potential benefits was probably at its most limited and its most instrumental in the eyes of government. Even in the five years between the 2003 Skills Strategy White Paper and implementation in 2008, the conception of purpose in reforming qualifications, and the anticipation of benefits from the QCF, have noticeably diminished in scope. Kennedy, Fryer and the

Learning Age belong both literally and symbolically to a different millennium. The concept of lifelong learning hardly survived into the twenty-first century. The creation of a comprehensive 'learning and skills sector' lasted little more than a decade before a (redefined) FE sector was restored. The combination of Train to Gain funding, with the increasingly closer strategic relationship between the LSC and SSCs, has produced (in England at least) an amalgam of detailed planning (though the 'p' word is still not used – 'modelling' is the preferred LSC term) allied to inefficient delivery mechanisms (the Skills Broker system has been widely criticised), based on the concept of a 'demand-led' system that is witnessing a rapid decline in demand. This has removed opportunities for learning from hundreds of thousands of adult learners who wish to learn on 'non-priority' provision. The complex and bureaucratic reforms to the machinery of government promised in 2010 – one of the most depressing documents produced for many a long year – will simply serve to make things worse.[1]

In this context, the QCF is coming to be seen by both government and its agencies such as LSC (soon to become the Skills Funding Agency (SFA) – though the term 'Agency' seems to have gone missing recently) and the UK Commission on Employment and Skills as a way in which 'unsuitable' qualifications, for which there is insufficient demand, can be removed from the qualifications system and therefore from the burden of the public purse, enabling resources to be targeted at those qualifications that recognise the skills that will be needed in the future – as identified by SSCs through their planning mechanisms. The gradual solidification of the concept of the QCF as a 'new' framework, requiring new regulations and a decisive break with the NQF, has been essential in securing the critical operational features of credit accumulation and transfer in the qualifications system. At the same time it has handed this most instrumental of governments, and its agencies such as the LSC/SFA, a gold-plated opportunity to erect new eligibility gateways for qualifications approval, and the funding of learning opportunities as new qualifications are designed to meet QCF requirements.

As NIACE's own work reveals, the main victims of this realignment have been the hundreds of thousands of adult learners for whom opportunities to learn have disappeared in the past three years. Current estimates are that 1.3 million places were lost from 2005 to 2008 and more will be lost in 2009. This does not just mean that fewer people are offered learning opportunities; it means that in some areas whole services are shattered or venues (often those most distant from a college and therefore most accessible to a particular community) closed down. Many of these learning opportunities have been lost in 'unaccredited' provision, but ironically the most savage cuts have taken place in 'locally accredited' provision outside the NQF, as provider budgets are aligned ever more closely with the LSC targets, themselves framed in terms of achievement of qualifications. In the run-up to implementing the QCF, the LSC suggested it was compelled to fund provision leading to qualifications in the NQF that were not 'fit for purpose'. We may therefore safely assume (though of course this has never been said) that the opposite is also true – that is, that the LSC has ceased to fund provision that *is* fit for purpose but lies outside the NQF.

Of course, locally accredited provision in this context is primarily OCN-accredited provision. How ironic that these local systems of OCNs, built up over so many years, are being dismantled at such an alarming rate, just as the framework is being created that will legitimise these local credit systems by integrating them – after many years of effort – within a genuinely national framework of qualifications. OCNs should have been at the forefront of populating the QCF, bringing new learners and new areas of achievement into the framework, and ensuring that their wealth of collective expertise was shared widely across the QCF. Instead, both NOCN and OCNs have been struggling to maintain their credit systems, and with them the learning opportunities of tens of thousands of learners, at the very moment when the QCF needed them most. For OCNs, the QCF is being implemented several years too late.

The rationale for this strategy of savage attacks on the locally accredited adult learning opportunities, that were gradually built up through the expansion of the 1990s, is built on an assumed logic that neatly encapsulates the narrow instrumentalism of recent government policy in this area. In order to remain internationally competitive, the skills of the UK workforce need to be improved. These skills are represented through qualifications, and the identification of which qualifications are needed in order to ensure an appropriate balance of skills for the future needs of 'UK plc' (another term that always makes me distrust the user) rests with SSCs. SSCs represent the aggregate demand of employers for skills in the future and therefore resources must be devoted to the delivery of these skills (measured through the achievement of qualifications) in order for us to remain internationally competitive. Learning that leads to these qualifications is therefore prioritised, and funding is gradually (perhaps not so gradually) removed from learning that does not lead to these qualifications. In order to demonstrate that the UK is on course to remain internationally competitive in this context, government sets targets for the achievement of qualifications that will recognise these future skills, and the system of developing, delivering and funding the skill system is linked to achievement of these qualifications.

The rationale for creating and maintaining a skilled workforce, able to sustain UK competitiveness and prosperity in the twenty-first century, is perhaps most clearly set out in the final report of the Leitch Review. Few commentators have challenged Leitch's critique of the impact of both globalisation and technological change on the UK economy and the UK workforce. However, the response to this critique, and the actions that government and its agencies have taken to implement 'the Leitch agenda', has been subject to more widespread criticism (Keep, 2007; Unwin, 2007). It is worth noting here that there is no 'Leitch Implementation Plan' for Wales. In essence, the government's response to the challenge of Leitch is still trapped in a central planning culture, driven by corporatist structures inherited from the reforms of the New Training Initiative. Although the linguistic trappings of a 'demand-led' system have been incorporated into the rationale for current policy, the forward planning of this demand-led system is as detailed and restrictive as the NTI was in 1981. In this 'command-led' system, the QCF is clearly going to struggle to realise its anticipated benefits of greater inclusiveness, responsiveness and accessibility, and reduced bureaucracy.

It is also likely that the QCF will continue to be implemented on a shoestring budget (in comparison to the resources that were made available to implement NVQs, or the initial NQF, for example). The continuing responsibility of the newly created Qualifications and Curriculum Development Agency (QCDA) for the implementation of the QCF will surely be a short-term one. Budgets for other agencies involved in QCF implementation (for example, LSIS) are also not secure. I suggest that, with one exception, such reductions in budgets to support the implementation of the QCF should not alarm us too much. The framework is in place, the initial process of recognising organisations to operate within it will soon be complete, and the great majority of vocational qualifications will have been re-specified in the QCF by the end of 2010. For all the frustrations about the slow rate of progress since 2003, the QCF is now no longer 'a project', but simply part of the furniture of the education and training system. Indeed, there are some who may say that, now the design features of the QCF are in place, the best way of realising the benefits of the framework are to let it develop organically through the actions of users, rather than bureaucratically through a government-led 'implementation plan'.

From the perspective of 2009, there is a fine balance to be struck between these two approaches. The QCF is still in its infancy. In theory, a new independent regulator for England could make some far-reaching changes to the regulations that support the QCF (if minded to do so). There is still much noise in the system about the costs of re-specifying qualifications to meet the 2010 target for transition from the NQF, and much uncertainty about the future relationship of the QCF to general qualifications. Set against this is the proven ability of credit systems to survive and prosper – given supportive conditions to do so – without central investment by government, and the continuing commitment of a majority of stakeholders to the principle of reform based on a credit system. Perhaps a little more nurturing of the QCF by government is necessary before it too can be 'set free' from its own implementation plan.

I referred above to an exception to this sanguine approach to a reduction in government support for the implementation of the QCF. This exception is the delivery of a fully functioning Learner Record to support the new framework. Such a record is promised for September 2010 as part of the delivery of the QCF Service Layer, but in the current climate of reductions in budgets this must seem like a tempting target for cuts. Of course, it would be possible to deliver a Learner Record without other aspects of the Service Layer, but the danger is that all features of this system will either be curtailed or delayed by broader financial strategies. The Learner Record is an essential tool for supporting the operation of the system of credit accumulation and transfer that underpins credit-based qualifications. Without a Learner Record – that is, a single electronic facility, owned by the individual learner, within which credits can be recorded, stored, accumulated, transferred and exchanged for qualifications – the QCF will not be able to break out of the 'qualifications-based' mindset that still runs through many awarding bodies, and regards the process of recognising achievement as a 'business process' rather than an entitlement of all learners in a regulated system. There are many benefits that can be realised through the QCF without the continuing support of government, but these benefits are dependent on the availability of a fully functioning Learner Record.

We should not be too dismayed by the difficulties posed by beginning to implement the QCF in this context. Even in much more favourable circumstances, it would have taken many years to begin to realise the full benefits of the credit system that will drive change through the QCF. It may be that these benefits will take a little longer to materialise, but we should have confidence that they will be realised. A future government with a different agenda that accepts the critique offered by Leitch, but responds in a more appropriate way, will find in the QCF a ready-made instrument that can support a more genuinely demand-led system within which individual learners are seen as the source of this demand, rather than the dubiously representative intermediaries of the interests of employers. The experiences of the current recession will surely accelerate the shift away from these current models.

The rational response to the critique offered by Leitch, of increasing uncertainty in capital markets, rapid shifts in production outputs between countries, increasing competition in service industries and more rapid change brought about by technical innovation, is actually to plan less rather than more. A genuinely 'demand-led' system would abandon current skills planning structures and accept that ignorance about the future is the only safe assumption that can be made about investment in the UK workforce. Of course, basing a developmental strategy on the principle that we have no idea what skills are going to be needed in the future is an impossible basis on which governments of any hue can be expected to act. Perhaps a little more humility in the accuracy of the predictive powers of government is the most that can be expected in the foreseeable future. Again, the current recession, which has effectively junked in a few short months enough financial advice about investment opportunities over the past decade to reach to the moon and back, will surely induce greater scepticism in the power of planning to meet the future skills needs of the UK workforce.

In this context we can see that, just as the LSC is about to be transformed into the SFA, the realisation is dawning on government that most of the assumptions about skills needs contained in SSC plans will need to be dramatically rethought or scrapped altogether. Planning for future skills needs just got even more difficult, and the manifestation of 'demand' through the current Train to Gain arrangements is going to prove that demand, as mediated through employers, is not going to sustain the process of improving skills across the UK workforce. To misquote both Napoleon and Studs Terkel: 'Work is too important to leave to employers.'

How then can government best prepare people for this 'unplannable' future, in which the actual jobs that will be done will continue to change rapidly and significantly during a (potentially longer) working life? The answer is simply to make them good learners – that is, to develop in people both the motivation to keep on learning and the skills necessary to be effective learners in a technology-driven learning environment. Of course, the best way to ensure that people are motivated to learn things is to let them learn whatever they want to learn. In other words, the whole culture of planning and skills development that began with NTI and continues a generation later is now clearly no longer fit for purpose in the twenty-first century, and the longer it takes to escape from this culture, the more ill-suited the UK workforce is going to be able to sustain UK prosperity in an increasingly competitive global economy. In order to realise the benefits of the QCF, we need to understand how focal the development of a qualifications-led approach to funding, performance measures and target setting has been to this culture, and how radically we need to change the UK qualifications system to meet these future challenges.

The QCF is unlike any previous qualification reform in this respect. For the first time the object of the reform process has not been the development of a particular group of qualifications (for example, 14–19 Diplomas) or qualification type (for example, NVQs). The QCF aims to establish a new set of design features for all qualifications, rather than develop a new set of qualifications, and to ensure that these design features are capable of accommodating the kind of rapid, sustained and radical changes that we can anticipate will be needed in any qualifications fit for the twenty-first century. In fact, the QCF aims to go beyond this static concept of a framework and to influence directly the operation of the systems through which achievements are recognised within this new framework. As the QCF makes no assumptions about the content of the qualifications that will populate it, it is capable of accommodating the kind of changes we can anticipate in future years without the need to change its basic design features. In this sense, the QCF mirrors the characteristics of US credit systems about which Rothblatt was so dismissive. Cementing together these 'tiny fragments of experience' into a whole system has actually created a rock-solid foundation capable of withstanding future changes in demand for recognition of achievement, however unpredictable these might be in 2009.

If Leitch's critique of the need for change by 2020 is accepted and the logical shift to a system through which individual demands for learning rather than employers' 'mediated aggregate demand' for skills drives forward change, then we can anticipate a gradual evolving of the systems for recognising achievement in the QCF that will actually be much closer in ethos to the original manifesto for OCNs than to the corporate planning culture of the NTI and its successors. As individual demand for learning and for the recognition of achievements based on this learning increases, so the variety and breadth of learning outcomes recognised through the QCF credit system will grow. At the same time the value of credits as a currency of achievement will become increasingly well established, and the ability of qualifications to predict or capture the particular combinations of credit achievement that will be demanded by individual learners will diminish. In such circumstances, individuals, employers, HE institutions and other users of the QCF will progressively shift the focus of their confidence, trust and ambitions in the system away from qualifications and towards credits as valuable representations of achievement in their own right.

In this possible future, the fourth characteristic of credit as a currency of achievement – exchangeability – gradually begins to be realised without reference to qualifications. Opportunities for employment, for career and personal development, and for progression to further learning opportunities, are increasingly expressed in terms of credits themselves, at particular levels, in particular combinations, through particular units, without reference to a qualification. In establishing their value in such circumstances, credits will simply be reflecting the experience of other successful currencies within which confidence is well established – that is, the purchasing power of the credit as a currency will gradually be extended so that it no longer has to work through the medium of a qualification (though, of course, in many instances it will continue to do so), but may be exchanged directly for access or progression to each individual's personal goal.

In this context, a future historian of credit systems might view the establishing of the QCF and the development of an integrated system of credits and qualifications as an interim stage in the development of credit systems that permitted credits to be incorporated into the regulatory arrangements that were previously reserved solely for qualifications. The QCF might come to be viewed as a framework that first legitimised credits as the currency of achievement and then gradually extended the reach and power of this currency, as the previously necessary but increasingly redundant shells of qualifications were discarded in response to the ever-increasing diversity of demands for recognition of achievement from people living and working in a modern, twenty-first century democracy. If at some point in the future it is deemed necessary to reform the QCF, then surely it will be to diminish the importance of the 'Q' and reassert the primacy of the 'C' as the real and meaningful representation of learner achievement in the third millennium. How important then will be the vision of the pioneers who built the first credit systems in the UK without reference to qualifications?

At this stage, I crave the reader's forgiveness for exercising the privilege of all soothsayers who prey on our collective ignorance about the distant future. Turning Borges' torch forward rather than backward, to shine on imagined rather than real events, is a temptation that needs to be resisted after a few initial flashes (Borges, 1999). Nevertheless, a less distant and more considered assessment of the development of the QCF over the course of the next decade seems to be an appropriate way to conclude this publication. In Chapter 50, I have referred to the first and second phases of the development of the QCF, before taking this detour into the realms of critique (and speculative critique) of current and future government policy on qualifications reform. It is now time to envisage how the third phase of development of the QCF might unfold.

Note

1 Assuming that they are implemented. We may assume that an incoming Conservative government will not be enthusiastic about many of these changes. Indeed, even a Labour government faced with severe deficits in public spending may be tempted into a minor conflagration of quangos in 2010.

52

Rediscovering credit

I want to conclude this story by envisaging a mature QCF as we approach the year 2020. Just as this story started with Borges' perspective of history illuminated by the light of the present (see Preface), so the easiest way to envisage what the QCF might be like as it approaches the end of this third phase of development is to do the same thing. Rather than think forward to 2020, I choose to place myself in that year and imagine how a light shone backwards to 2009 might illuminate some of the characteristics of the QCF. As Borges himself might have said, it is a fabulous conceit, and one that allows for a positive view of history untrammelled by the need for actual, rather than fabricated, evidence. I hope the reader of this final chapter will forgive me this device as I revert to my known default position of indefatigable optimism.

In 2020 the marketplace for credit and qualifications has expanded dramatically from the old NQF (though there are still many qualifications offered – particularly by professional bodies and associations – outside the QCF). The obsessions of previous governments in measuring improving skills and productivity through the achievement of qualifications has disappeared. A primary cause of this shift in policy was because the precise measurement of qualifications achievement over a period of some 12 or 15 years, during which time the UK slipped down all the international league tables related to economic performance and improved workforce skills, demonstrated conclusively by about 2013 that there was no meaningful connection between qualifications achievement and the competitiveness of the UK economy. There are still performance measures in place of course (accountability for best use of the public purse is still important), but gradually the use of credits achieved at different levels of the QCF has become more and more important as a performance measure, as the use of qualifications as such a measure has declined.

This use of credit achievement to measure performance is of course one of the advantages of establishing credits as a currency of achievement. Within the QCF, all achievements lead to the award of credit, so the measure is both uniform and comprehensive across the whole system – something that was never true of qualifications. The credit success measure is also, of course, much more sensitive, capturing the myriad of small steps of achievement and improvement in skills and knowledge that actually contribute both to economic improvement and to the human capital of the UK. The decision of the Scottish government in 2015 to adopt the design features of the QCF in a revised SCQF has already started to produce concrete examples of cross-border sharing of skills and knowledge that proved so difficult to accomplish in the previous relationship between the two frameworks.

Another shift in public policy that can be attributed to the QCF is the return to a wider and richer concept of lifelong learning, rather than the narrower focus on skills that characterised the early years of the framework. As the QCF expanded and as more learners began to earn credits within the framework across a wide spectrum of sectors and subjects, it gradually became clear that the progression of people (especially adults, of course) through learning was actually less predictable and more varied than had previously been thought. Given the freedom to choose units leading to the award of credit that met immediate employment, career or personal needs, people chose an ever increasing range of achievable targets with greater frequency as the number of unit options within the QCF continued to expand. The exercise of this choice not only had no apparently negative effects on productivity and workforce skill levels; in some sectors and employment roles, the ability to select units leading to the award of credits, rather than qualifications, has led to an increase in workplace performance levels. It seems as though, given the freedom to choose to earn credits rather than qualifications, people generally make rational and informed choices that not only benefit themselves, but also contribute positively to workforce skills and employer demand.

The QCF has helped to demonstrate (by providing reliable and comparable evidence to support the case) that, in fact, it was *learning* and not *skills* that were really important in improving both workforce development and social cohesion. Given the continuing rapid churn of employment patterns in the UK workforce, the impact of technological changes and the dramatic shifts in inward and outward investment brought about by the globalisation of financial services following the 2008-10 recession, it is more obvious than ever that the future skills requirements of the UK workforce cannot be predicted with any certainty over anything more than the short term. In such circumstances, creating a culture of learning in the UK workforce is proving to be a better protection against future changes than training in a particular skill. Being an effective, efficient and engaged learner is the best preparation for future employment, and supporting people to continue to be active learners has gradually become an acceptable aim of government policy over the preceding decade. The QCF has helped to support this change by demonstrating that what people learn is actually of less importance in meeting workforce needs than the act of learning itself. It is this gradual development of a genuine culture of learning, supported by recognition of achievements in this learning, that is now seen as critically important for the future development of both the UK workforce and its social cohesion. As several million people have achieved credits in all manner of subjects and sectors within the QCF in recent years, evidence is now available to prove conclusively that supporting people to learn whatever they want within the QCF, rather than compelling them to select certain qualifications in certain skill areas, is actually a better way of meeting both the immediate demands of employers and the longer-term needs of the workforce and society. As this evidence has accumulated, so the variety of units within the QCF has increased as people demand that their achievements in learning should lead to recognition through the award of credit.

Some of this variety has resulted from the development of new qualifications in the QCF outside the original vocational qualifications that were first offered within the framework. The decision to abandon diplomas and reform A levels in 2013 can be seen in retrospect as the critical moment in bringing about this change, together with the decision to extend the scope of the Foundation Learning programme to Level Two and to phase out GCSEs. The flexibility of the original Foundation Learning programme (the term has simply withered away over time) has proved equally successful in engaging learners at Level Two, and the raising of the age of entitlement to full-time education or training to 18 simply left GCSEs without a clear purpose. The process of bringing revised A levels into the QCF from 2013 to 2018 was protracted and technically challenging. Nevertheless, it proved feasible to establish an assessment regime for these new qualifications that reassured the Department of Education that the standard of these new qualifications could be maintained in comparison to previous A levels, while still conforming to the unit design specifications of the QCF. When offered within A levels or as part of a Level Two qualification in schools, these units are of course still subject to particular assessment requirements. At A level, these are linked to grading criteria. What is interesting to note is that units from these qualifications are already beginning to be used in other qualifications – many of them without grading criteria – either in combination with more explicitly vocational units, or as options within broad-based qualifications designed to prepare people for progression to higher level skills. Indeed, in some of the more academic subjects, units from the new A levels, shorn of grading arrangements but still leading to the award of credit, have proved popular as stand-alone courses for adult learners. Already there are suggestions from the Department that, in future, units from vocational qualifications may be offered within (some) A levels, just as Foundation Learning enables combinations of subject-based and vocational units to be offered at lower levels of achievement within schools.

Of course, none of this ability to exercise choice in selecting individual units leading to the award of credit, rather than qualifications, would have been possible without the development of flexible funding arrangements to support the development of this genuinely demand-led system. Initially, the benefits of the QCF proved more difficult to realise as, despite the best efforts of the LSC before its demise in 2010, the then separate BIS still insisted on funding arrangements and performance measures that incentivised people to achieve whole qualifications. With the creation of the short-lived SFA though, this position began to change as evidence from the final year of the LSC trials of unit-based funding began to demonstrate how popular this facility was proving to be with employers, particularly in the context of Train to Gain. The decision of SFA to establish a direct connection between the value of Skills Accounts and the credit value of an individual learner's programme of study also helped to move these arrangements forward. However, the really critical change came about as learners who had achieved credit in one qualification re-registered for a further qualification in the QCF, and transferred some credits forward from their previous qualification. BIS realised that, in the context of credit transfer between qualifications, continuing to fund and measure performance through qualifications achievement could lead to 'double-funding' of some achievements, as well as creating perverse incentives to maximise credit transfer opportunities to meet qualification success targets, rather than meet learner or employer needs. Even before BIS disappeared in 2011, the shift to a credit-based funding method was already underway in England.

The gradual easing of restrictions on funding individual units, coupled with the definitive switch from guided learning hours to credit value as the basis for calculating funding allocations, created the flexible and responsive funding arrangements of the Tertiary Funding Agency that were essential to the realisation of the benefits of the QCF during the third phase of its development. In the first instance, this shift had the most significant impact at lower levels of achievement, as the ability to create individual programmes of learning based on credit achievement, rather than qualifications, helped to improve success and progression rates for learners at Entry level and Level One of the QCF. However, as the end of 2020 approaches, it is now clear that this facility to create (and to fund – perhaps only in part) individual pathways to achievement, based on the award of credit, is being utilised in all areas of provision at all levels of the QCF.

Alongside this gradual development of more flexible approaches to funding has gone the development of a new generation of teachers, assessors, guidance workers and curriculum managers, who understand how the QCF works and how to support learners to get the best out of the framework. As with the development of the first OCNs and the creation of the credit movement of the 1990s, this new generation has produced its own enthusiasts and experts. In the third phase of its development, a sufficiently large and sufficiently knowledgeable group of people were able to influence the design of units and qualifications in the QCF that utilised its potential to the maximum benefits of learners. The currency of credit really has become ubiquitous in this third phase of development, and finally there is evidence from users of the framework that the benefits anticipated by those who designed the QCF in the early years of the twenty-first century are being realised. Some of this evidence from the recent Garrett review of the QCF reveals just how far the effect of the credit system has transformed qualifications since 2008.

One of the interesting statistics revealed by this recent review of the QCF is that there are actually fewer awarding bodies (the term 'awarding organisation' never really caught on) in the QCF in 2020 than there were in the final days of the NQF. In the first phase of development of the QCF, there was actually an increase in the number of awarding bodies – stimulated in part by continuing subsidy by government for employers and providers to become recognised as awarding bodies within the new framework. Numbers reached a peak of almost 200 at the point at which the transition from the NQF to the QCF was completed in 2011, held steady for a time, and has continued to fall each year for the last five years to the current number of 84. This decline is due in part to the demise of some smaller awarding bodies that simply failed to adapt their business models to the demands of the QCF; partly to the realisation by others – particularly professional bodies – that their interests can be well protected by becoming recognised to develop and submit units to the QCF databank, rather than by continuing investment into the costs of maintaining the quality systems demanded of awarding bodies; and partly by the gradual withdrawal of the employer- and provider-based awarding bodies created through the 'policy stimulus' of 2007-9.

Comparing the list of 130 awarding bodies recognised in the NQF at the beginning of the implementation of the QCF with the 84 at the end of this third phase of development, we can see that over half these current awarding bodies did not exist in 2008. Of course, some of these names have been changed through the process of mergers and acquisitions of smaller awarding bodies by larger ones as the development of the QCF challenged some business models, but a number of new awarding bodies have appeared, several of them built from consortia or associations of providers (including – interestingly – a number that trace their history back to an OCN). Also in evidence are a number of universities that have chosen to become awarding bodies, as well as the UK arms of some European associations and organisations.

Of course, one of the changes brought about by the QCF was the ability for an organisation to become recognised to develop and submit units to the QCF databank. Such organisations still have to meet quality standards set by the regulators and are subject to monitoring, reporting and (as has happened on a few occasions since 2008) sanctions. In the first instance, most of the organisations that became recognised to submit units to the QCF were Sector Skills Councils (the precursors of today's Workforce Learning Partnerships), but even in the initial phase of development, other organisations also started to become recognised. Thus universities, professional bodies, charitable trusts, some FE colleges and a small number of employers started to become recognised to submit units to the databank. These numbers have continued to grow over the years, especially as the funding arrangements and performance measures for the QCF began to become more flexible in phase three of its development.

Today, over 300 organisations are recognised to submit units to the QCF databank (including 75 of the 84 awarding bodies). This means that, effectively, the QCF is able to draw on a massive range of expertise and experience in developing and updating the units that form the building blocks of qualifications in the framework. The regulators continue to monitor and evaluate unit quality, working in partnership with the Unit Databank Management Group, a representative body of all recognised unit-submitting organisations that works to improve unit quality and to encourage the widest possible use of the databank. Indeed, it was the establishing of this group and the development of its Memorandum of Understanding with the regulators in 2011 that led directly to the critical switch in unit-funding methodology (in England) from guided learning hours to credit values. Thus the essential function of the regulators in ensuring the stability of credits as a currency, mediated through representation from unit developers, became sufficiently well established through the second phase of QCF development to provide both the Tertiary Funding Agency and government with the reassurances they sought that linking the allocation of public funds to the credit value of units (and to the credits actually achieved by learners) constituted a sufficiently low level of risk to abandon the previously restrictive methodology based on guided learning hours.

This shift to a credit-based funding methodology began to produce immediate benefits for users during phase three of the QCF's development. The funding of work-based provision leading to the award of credit became more straightforward. There were noticeable increases in the numbers of learners utilising e-learning and e-assessment opportunities leading to the award of credit. Project-based and activity-based learning leading to the award of credit could also be funded. Even more traditional modes of provision benefited as colleges and training providers made more imaginative use of technology, learning centres, projects and self-directed study alongside classroom-based learning. Throughout phase three of its development there is evidence that the facility to gain credits within the QCF is enabling new forms of provision to be developed, to meet the needs of new and different learners across all areas of the framework. By releasing providers from the requirement to record guided learning hours, the credit-based funding methodology of the QCF has not only established more creative and innovative curriculum offers to learners; it has also improved success rates by focusing funding arrangements around the achievement of credit, rather than a particular form of delivery of learning opportunities.

The benefits of all these processes are reflected in some of the statistical evidence from the review. Sometime in 2020 the millionth unit will be entered into the QCF databank. Of course, many of these units are no longer active – some of them have been updated or replaced several times since the first units were developed in the QCF tests and trials of 2006. Although there was a steady increase in the number of units entered into the databank throughout the first two phases of development of the QCF, the beginning of the third phase saw the steepest increase in numbers, as more organisations became recognised to submit units to the databank and the number of units at higher levels began to grow more rapidly. Evidence from the most recent years suggests this explosion of unit development activity is now past its peak, and that the focus of most unit developers is on improving and updating existing units rather than creating new ones. The other interesting aspect of the review is the tiny fraction of units in the databank that are restricted in their use to one or a few awarding bodies. Although the QCF continues to permit the assertion of ownership over units, the number of awarding bodies exercising this right is now very small: most units are now made freely available to all users of the QCF. Indeed, units from the databank are becoming widely used in HE and, following the recent reform of the SCQF, are being used in many qualifications in Scotland. Units are also being used in other parts of the world, particularly in Eastern Europe, the far east and Australasia, as other countries adopt the basic QCF model for their own national frameworks. The launch of the European Credit and Qualifications Framework in 2018 gave further impetus to this extension of the QCF model, which is now recognised internationally as the essential blueprint for qualifications reform. An international unit databank will soon be launched, linking some 20 nationally-based databanks into a rich global resource, freely available through Web3.0.

Another interesting finding of the recent review is that the number of qualifications available to learners in the QCF is now decreasing. There are actually far more people achieving qualifications in the QCF than there ever were in the NQF and, indeed, there are as many qualifications available as there were at the point of transition from the NQF to the QCF (though it seems the current decline in numbers will continue as qualification accreditations run out and are simply not renewed or replaced). However, in comparison to the NQF, the QCF supports a hugely expanded market of qualifications and credits, with over three times as many learners registered for a QCF award in 2018–19 as the highest number in the NQF. How has this come about? How could such a significant expansion of this market take place without a concomitant rise in the number of qualifications available? The answer, of course, lies in the increasing acceptability of credits, rather than qualifications, as the currency of achievement.

This expansion of the role of credit takes several forms. As the review of the QCF shows us, there has been a significant increase in recent years in the number of people choosing simply to achieve credits rather than qualifications, and being able to secure funding of some kind from the public purse to support this choice. In fact, the proportion of people in any one year that achieves a qualification within the QCF, in comparison with those that achieve credits (including credits that contribute to a qualification), has fallen steadily in every year of the QCF's life. In recent years it has fallen even more dramatically, so that now fewer than 30 per cent of people who achieve credits in the QCF also achieve a qualification in the same year. For adult learners the figure is closer to 25 per cent. Of course, these figures are explained in part by the fact that many more people now choose to accumulate credits towards a qualification over longer periods of time (and are able to do so without being penalised by government targets on qualification completion rates). A significant proportion is also accounted for by people who gain some credits for a short episode of learning and then, for whatever reason, choose not to continue with the process of credit accumulation. In fact, longer-term evidence shows that significant numbers of people gaining a small number of credits in any one year do intend to add to these credits over time to achieve a qualification. As the review shows, more people achieve a qualification in the QCF than ever did in the NQF, but many of them take a considerable time to do so.

There are other inter-related and very interesting phenomena that have become apparent in the last two or three years, that are also contributing to this reduction in the number of qualifications in the QCF. For example:

- There has been a reduction in the number of qualifications of all sizes offered at Entry level and Level One of the QCF. As none of these qualifications actually constitutes a specific requirement for employment or licence to practise, and as very few qualifications at Level Two set any specific entry requirements in terms of previous qualifications, the rationale for offering qualifications at these levels of the QCF is starting to weaken. In some curriculum areas, a single qualification is offered by an awarding body at each stage of Entry level that includes within it a huge range of units, supported by very open rules of combination. In effect, the qualification becomes a holding framework for units and learners put together individual programmes of learning at this level that may or may not conform to these rules. The qualification itself becomes a set of model rules of combination, around which guidance workers and tutors construct individual programmes that lead to the award of credit, but which may never actually meet the requirements of the qualification. Learners demonstrate their capability to progress to the next level of achievement through the award of credits, and the qualification itself becomes a secondary goal, sometimes achieved, sometimes not. Evidence from the review suggests that the QCF is being successful in supporting learners to progress through Entry level and Level One achievements, even though fewer qualifications are available and only a minority of learners actually achieve a qualification.

- At all levels of the QCF, the number of small qualifications has started to decline in recent years. The evidence from the early years of development of the QCF was that awarding bodies continued to develop many small qualifications in order that these could be achieved relatively easily, and thereby contribute positively to qualification success rates and related performance indicators. Once the connection to these performance measures was broken and replaced with more sensitive measures based on credit achievement, the necessity to measure relatively small achievements through a qualification, rather than through the award of credits, gradually disappeared. During phase three of the QCF development, some awarding bodies have simply not applied for re-accreditation of some awards, where these form part of a suite of qualifications including certificates and/or diplomas. As learners become more familiar with the credit system and more aware of the acceptability of credits as a currency of achievement, demand for small qualifications begins to weaken further. Indeed, in some cases where an awarding body continues to offer an award as a stepping stone to a certificate, there is a noticeable decline in recent years in the number of learners bothering to claim the intermediate award – the award of credit in the Learner Record is sufficient to satisfy the demand that their achievements should be recognised.

- Of course, this appreciation of the value of credits as a currency of achievement has also been enhanced in recent years by the number of employers presenting opportunities for employment or progression, both publicly and in-house, based on the achievement of credits rather than qualifications. The TUC Learning Academy's 'Quid Pro Quo' campaign has also produced significant results in this area. Basically, the TUC argued that if an employer was prepared to support employees to achieve credits through individual units, rather than full qualifications, trade unionists would support this position if the employer then advertised employment and promotion opportunities that were also based on the achievement of credit, rather than whole qualifications. In many areas of work, qualifications remain an essential prerequisite for employment in a particular job role. But in many other areas, employers are happy to accept that the recent achievement of credits at a particular level, perhaps in a particular subject or vocational area, is sufficient evidence of an employee's commitment to learning to meet employment or progression opportunities. In such cases, demand from both employers and individuals for qualifications falls dramatically.

- A similar trend can be detected in HE, and in particular in that majority of provision in HE that is now offered outside the traditional structure of a full-time, three-year degree programme. There are now numerous examples to be found in university prospectuses and student handbooks of admission requirements to many courses being expressed in terms of qualifications or credits, and others where a combination of qualifications and credits is an acceptable trigger for admission to HE. Of course, the establishment of a single credit and qualifications framework for HE in England in 2015, and the involvement of many universities in the QCF itself, has enhanced both the real and the perceived value of credits in recent years. Indeed, some universities themselves are offering a number of qualifications in the QCF, giving rise to some speculation that a 'fourth phase' of development of the QCF might yet extend the framework to encompass Higher Education.

Taken together, these trends point to an inexorable process through which the acceptable format in which learner achievements are recognised is moving from qualifications to credits. As familiarity with the credit system grows and the public acceptability of credits as a currency of achievement penetrates popular consciousness, a shift in the discourse through which learners themselves, as well as other users of the QCF, describe their achievements is perceptible. The language of credit achievement, credit accumulation and credit transfer is beginning to replace the previous discourse about qualifications. We should have expected it to do so – just as the introduction of coins gradually replaced bags of salt. Thus the bringing together of credits and qualifications in the QCF in 2008 marked the start of a process through which credits began to reassert their power as a currency, just as they had done during the 1990s. Far from burying credits within a qualifications system, the process of credit accumulation and transfer that underpins all QCF qualifications sets in train an inexorable logic through which credits begin to replace measurements of achievement, previously the preserve of qualifications.

Clearly, this is gratifying to those who designed the QCF. However, it seems this trend is also welcomed by those who continue to promote the value of particular qualifications. By the time of the end of the NQF, it was abundantly clear that we were expecting too much from our qualifications system (a process that had been unfolding for a number of years and set the UK apart from most other modern democracies). In effect, the function of qualifications had expanded beyond the literal meaning of the term that signifies that someone is qualified to do something. Qualifications were also expected to signal that someone was ready to proceed to further learning (even though they were not qualified to do anything). Then qualifications became used as a proxy measure for the quality of the programmes that led to them, and from there it was a short step for qualifications to become also a proxy for value for money in the distribution of the public purse. In the final years of the NQF, the burden of expectations on the qualification system was extended further to the measurement of progress in achieving national prosperity and competitiveness in a global economy. Even without the advent of the QCF, such burdens would have eventually proven both too onerous and too restrictive on our qualifications system.

Some of these pressures have been relieved through changes in government policy, others because the evidence they produced seemed to mark a decline in international competitiveness and productivity, rather than an improvement. However, some of them still remain in place, particularly in relation to progression, quality and value for money. In each of these areas, as the review of the QCF demonstrates, the use of credits rather than qualifications to produce the required evidence effectively relieves further the pressure on qualifications themselves. What we are beginning to witness in this third phase of the QCF development is a return to the more literal meaning of a qualification that existed prior to the creation of a concept of a 'national qualifications system'. Within the QCF, qualifications can once again come to mean 'qualified', and the importance of being qualified to perform any number of important roles and tasks is undiminished by the process of achieving such a qualification through the accumulation and (possibly) transfer of credits. For all other purposes, credits themselves can and – as the evidence from the review is beginning to show – will suffice.

This is actually fairly close to the vision of the Manchester pioneers of credit systems nearly 40 years ago. From the perspective of 2020, the QCF appears as a kind of transformative prism through which the long march of credit systems had to pass, in order to realise the ambitions of those who set off on the journey in 1980. Subsuming these ambitions in the conscious synthesis of credit and qualifications cultures that forged the QCF in 2008 seemed at the time like a huge risk – a risk that Gordon Conquest's 'good idea that people liked' would be lost as a minor feature of a largely unreformed qualifications system. In the end, though, credit proved a sufficiently powerful concept to protect itself from this risk. Having stripped itself of the value systems in which it was created and refined in order to engineer this engagement with qualifications, the credit system of OCNs proved technically robust enough not only to survive and prosper, but gradually to allow the reconnection to these original values – inclusion, accessibility, responsiveness and the primacy of the learner – that, in its third phase of development, the QCF is finally beginning to realise.

To those early pioneers in Manchester, with the vision to imagine a future in which all learners had the right for their achievements to be recognised within a single system of credits, we offer the QCF in 2020 as a work in progress that is beginning to demonstrate its potential to deliver on this vision.

To those who struggled to implement the QCF in such difficult circumstances in its initial phase from 2008, we validate your belief that the framework would be resilient enough to survive the conditions of its inception. To all others, we confirm that the QCF is a good idea and people like it.

Bibliography

AfC et al. (1994). *Post-compulsory Education and Training: A Joint Statement*. London: AfC.

AoC et al. (1998). *Qualifying for Success, Unitisation and Credit. A Joint Statement from AoC et al*. London: FEDA.

Ball, C. (1989). *Aiming Higher: Widening Access to Higher Education*. London: RSA.

Beaumont, G. (1995). *Review of 100 NVQs and SVQs*. London: DfEE.

BESA (2008, 5 November). Built Environment Skills Alliance. *Minutes of an Extraordinary Meeting on NVQs*. London: BESA.

Bewick, T. (2009). *UK employment and skills in a global recession*. London: LSN.

BIS (2009). Apprenticeships, Children, Skills and Learning Act. London: HMSO.

Bjornevold, J. and Coles, M. (2006). *Governing Education and Training; the case of qualifications frameworks*. Thessaloniki: Cedefop.

Black, A. (1982). *The Development of the Manchester Open College Federation*. London: FEU.

Bloom, B. (1956). *Taxonomy of Educational Objectives*. Boston, USA: Allyn and Bacon.

Borges, J. L. (1999). Kafka and his Precursors. In J. L. Borges, *Everything and Nothing*. New York: New Directions.

Boston, K. (2004, March). Welcome speech on the publication of 'Principles for a Credit Framework for England'. London: QCA.

Boston, K. (2005). Putting the Learner First: Creating a 14–90 future from the 14–19 White Paper. *Association of Learning Providers Annual Conference*. London: QCA.

Boston, K. (2005a, 9 June). Letter to Phil Hope. London: QCA/LSC/SfB.

Bridges, P. H. (1996). *The Fluttering Standard: How should Higher Education approach academic standards in the 21st century*. University of Derby.

Browning, D. (1988, 28 October). A Provisional Map of Development. Manchester: UDACE.

Browning, D. (1988a). *NCVQ and Open College Networks: A contribution to the discussion*. Manchester: NOCN.

Buchan, J. (1998). *Frozen Desire*. London: Picador.

Cabinet Office (2002). *Quinquennial Review of QCA*. London: Cabinet Office.

Capey, J. (1996). *Review of GNVQ assessment*. London: NCVQ.

City of Manchester Education Committee (1981). *Progress Report of the Working Party on Alternative Entry to Higher Education*. Manchester: City of Manchester Education Committee.

City of Manchester Education Committee (1981a). *Report of the Continuing Education Sub-Committee*. Manchester: City Council.

CNAA (1989). *The Credit Accumulation and Transfer Scheme: Regulations*. London: CNAA.

Coles, M. (2008). The EQF – a platform for collaboration, integration and reform. *EQF UK Launch Conference*. Birmingham: QCA.

Conquest, G. (2008). Speech at NIACE Conference on 'Celebrating Achievement'. Manchester.

CQFW (2003). *Implementation Plan for the Credit and Qualifications Framework for Wales*. Cardiff: CQFW.

CQFW (2006). *Credit Common Accord*. Cardiff: CQFW.

DCSF (2008). *Promoting Achievement, valuing success: a strategy for 14-19 qualifications*. London: DCSF.

Dearing, R. (1996). *Review of Qualifications for 16-19 year-olds*. Hayes, Middlesex: SCAA.

Dearing, R. (1997). *Report of the National Committee of Enquiry into Higher Education*. London: HMSO.

Department of Education Northern Ireland (1999). *Report of the Northern Ireland Credit Accumulation and Transfer System (NICATS) Project*. Belfast: DENI.

Derbyshire Regional Network (1993). Derbyshire Regional Network. *The credit framework and the credit accumulation and transfer system*. Derby: University of Derby.

DES (1973). *Adult Education: A plan for development*. HMSO.

DES (1978). *Higher Education into the 1980s: a discussion document*. HMSO.

DES (1978a). Special courses in preparation for entry to higher education. *Letter to Chief Education Officers*. London: DES.

DES (1987). *Higher Education: Meeting the challenge*. London: HMSO.

DES/DE/WO (1991). *Education and Training for the 21st Century*. London: HMSO.

DfEE (1997). *Education Act*. London: HMSO.

DfEE (1998). *The Learning Age: a renaissance for a new Britain*. London: DfEE.

DfEE (1998a). Blackstone announces A Level improvements. Press release. London: DfEE.

DfEE (1999). *Learning to Succeed.* London: HMSO.

DfES (2002). *Success for All - reforming further education and training.* London: DfES.

DfES (2002a). *Success for All.* London: DfES.

DfES et al. (2003). *21st Century Skills: Realising Our Potential.* London: TSO.

DfES et al. (2005). *Getting on in business, getting on at work.* London: SO.

DfES (2007). *Implementing the Leitch Review of Skills in England.* London: DfES.

DIUS (2008). Education and Skills Act. *Education and Skills Act Part 5 Chapter 2 159-163.* London: HMSO.

DIUS (2008). VQRP e-News. *Launch of the Qualifications and Credit Framework.* London: DIUS.

Ensor, P. (2003). The National Qualifications Framework and Higher Education in South Africa. *Journal of Education and Work Vol 16 No 3,* pp. 325–46.

European Commission (2005). *Towards a European Qualifications Framework for Lifelong Learning.* Brussels: European Commission.

FEDA (1995). Framework Guidelines 2. *Learning outcomes, units and modules.* London: FEDA.

FEDA (1995a, 14 August). CAT Network National Update. London: FEDA.

FEDA (1996). *FEDA's 2020 Vision: Why we need a credit-based qualifications system.* London: FEDA.

FEDA (1998). *Qualifying for Success: Implementing the Post-16 Framework.* London: FEDA.

FEDA (2000). *Qualifications for the Future.* London: FEDA.

Federation of Awarding Bodies (2003). *Development of a Credit Framework in England.* London: FAB.

FEFC (1993). *Funding learning.* Coventry: FEFC.

FEFC (1998). *Student numbers, inyear retention, achievements and destinations at colleges in the further education sector and external institutions in England 1996-97.* Coventry: FEFC.

FEU (1992). *A Basis for Credit?* London: FEU.

FEU (1992a). *Joint ULEAC/FEU Project 9RP768.* London: FEU.

FEU (1993). The CATalyst. *Newsletter of the FEU CAT Network.* London: FEU.

FEU (1995). *A Framework for Credit.* London: FEU.

FEU (1995a). Framework Guidelines 1. *Levels, credit value and the award of credits.* London: FEU.

Finegold, D. et al. (1990). *A British Baccalaureate: Overcoming divisions between education and training.* London: Institute for Public Policy Research.

Freeston, M. (1996, December). *Open College Networks: An investigation into their historical development.* MA Thesis. London: Institute of Education.

Fryer, B. (1997). *Learning for the Twenty-First Century.* London: NAGCELL.

Gallagher, J. et al. (2005). *Evaluation of the Impact of the Scottish Credit and Qualifications Framework (SCQF)*. Glasgow: The Scottish Office Central Research Unit.

Gosling, D. (2001). *Lost opportunity: What a credit framework would have added to the National Qualifications Framework*. London: SEEC.

Grugulis, I. (2002). *Skills and Qualifications: The contribution of NVQs to raising skill levels*. University of Warwick: SKOPE.

Guardian (2008, 28 January). Burger bar A Level for staff at McDonalds. *The Guardian*.

Harris, N. (2008). Presentation to South East London LLN Seminar on Credit 17 June 2008. *The QCF: Implications for FE and HE*. London: QAA.

Hart, J. (2002). *Introducing the SCQF*. London: QCA.

HEFCE (2009, May). Part time First Degree Study: Entry and completion. *2009/18*. Bristol: HEFCE.

HEQC (1995). *Leicestershire Open College Network: Authorised Validating Agency's Periodic Review*. London: HEQC.

HMI (1990). *Access Courses to Higher Education*. London: HMSO.

Hodgson, A. and Spours, K. (1997). *Dearing and Beyond*. London: Kogan Page.

Hope, P. (2005, 18 July). Letter to Ken Boston. London: DfES.

House of Commons (1991, 26 June). Employment Committee Minutes of Evidence. *Vocational Training*. London: HMSO.

Houston, T. and Bellamy, A. (2002). *Establishing the feasibility of applying a level and size to NVQ units*. London: Unpublished QCA report.

Jessup, G. (1991). *Outcomes: NVQs and the Emerging Model of Education and Training*. London: Falmer Press.

Joint Council for Qualifications (2005). *Delivering a new credit and qualifications framework for England Wales and Northern Ireland*. London: JCQ.

Keating, J. (2003). Qualifications Frameworks in Australia. *Journal of Education and Work Vol 16 No 3*, pp. 271–88.

Keep, E. (2007, 6 March). The Leitch Review: Does it make sense? *National Skills Forum Seminar Paper*. London: National Skills Forum.

Kennedy, H. (1997). *Learning Works: Widening Participation in Further Education*. Coventry: FEFC.

Kerton, B. (1993). *Widening access to National Vocational Qualifications through Open College networks*. London: FEU.

King, C. (2008). *Part time studies in Higher Education (Report to DIUS)*. Stoke-on-Trent: University of Staffordshire.

Leitch, L. (2005). *Skills in the UK: The Long Term Challenge*. London: DfES.

Leitch, L. (2007). *World Class Skills*. London: DfES.

Lillis, F. and Stott, C. (2005). *Learning from experience – implementing credit*. Derby: Credit Works.

LSC (2002). *Workforce Development Strategy*. Coventry: LSC.

LSC (2002a). *The Learning and Skills Council: Report on Credit.* Coventry: LSC.

LSC (2003, 23 July). Statistical First Release. *ISR/SFR25.* Coventry: LSC.

LSC (2009). *Qualifications and Credit Framework Policy Update Issue 2.* Coventry: LSC.

Manchester Open College Federation (1983?). *A Manifesto for Open Colleges.* Manchester: MOCF.

McNamara, J. (2003). Speech to the FAB Annual Conference. Coventry: FAB.

McNamara, J. (2005, 30 September). Letter to Ken Boston. JCQ & FAB.

MerOCF (1988). *The unit of credit and statements of competence.* Liverpool: MerOCF.

Miliband, D. (2002, 1 August). Letter to Sir William Stubbs. London: DfES.

Miliband, D. (2002a, 1 August). Letter to Bryan Sanderson. London: DfES.

MSC (1981). *A New Training Initiative: Agenda for Action.* London: HMSO.

MSC and DES (1986). *Review of vocational qualifications in England and Wales.* London: HMSO.

NCVQ (1988). Developing a National System of Credit Accumulation and Transfer. *NCVQ INformation Note No. 1.* NCVQ.

NICATs (1999). *A Credit Framework as a Vehicle for Lifelong Learning in Northern Ireland.* Belfast: NICATS.

NICATS. (2002, 8 October). *UK Credit Equivalence Project.* Retrieved from NICATS: www.nicats.ac.uk/using/ukcep.htm

Nisbet, I. (2008, 4 December). Open Letter to SSCs and AOs on the regulatory expectations for developing qualifications for inclusion in the QCF. Coventry: Ofqual.

NOCN (1990). *Commonality Working Party: Proposals and Recommendations.* Sheffield: NOCN.

NOCN (1990a). Credit accumulation and transfer agreement. NOCN.

NOCN (1994). The National Credit Framework. NOCN.

NOCN (1998). *Annual Report 1997-98.* Derby: NOCN.

NOCN (2003). *Annual Review.* Derby: NOCN.

OECD (2007). *Qualifications Systems; Bridges to Lifelong Learning.* Paris: OECD.

Ofqual et al. (2008, August). *Regulatory arrangements for the Qualifications and Credit Framework.* Coventry: Ofqual.

Percy, K. (1980). *The Open College of the North West.* Coombe Lodge: Further Education Staff College.

Peters, T. (1992). *Liberation Management.* New York: Alfred A Knopf Inc.

Philips, D. (2003). Lessons from New Zealand's National Qualifications Framework. *Journal of Education and Work Vol 16 No 3,* pp. 289-324.

PIU (2001). *In Demand: Adult Skills in the 21st century Part i.* London: Cabinet Office.

PIU (2002). *The role of credits in the qualification system*. London: Cabinet Office.

Pricewaterhouse Coopers (2007). *Qualifications and Credit Framework Evaluation Project 2006/07*. London: PwC.

QAA (2005). *Principles and Criteria for the Licensing of Authorised Validating Agencies*. Gloucester: QAA.

QCA (1999). *Unitisation and Credit in the National Qualifications Framework*. London: QCA.

QCA (1999a). *Flexibility for Adult Learners: Report on Outcomes of Consultation*. London: QCA.

QCA (2002). *Report on unitised and credit-based qualifications*. London: QCA.

QCA (2004). *A framework for achievement: Recognising qualifications and skills in the 21st century*. London: QCA.

QCA (2005). *The Framework for Achievement: Report to the DfES on the outcomes of the stakeholder consultation*. London: QCA.

QCA (2008). *Qualifications and Credit Framework Outline Business Case*. London: QCA.

QCA and LSC (2004). *Principles for a Credit Framework for England*. London: QCA.

QCA et al. (2000). *Arrangements for the Statutory Regulation of external qualifications in England, Wales and Northern Ireland*. London: QCA, ACCAC & CCEA.

QCA et al. (2004). *The statutory regulation of external qualifications*. London: QCA.

QCA et al. (2006). *Support Pack for the Qualifications and Credit Framework tests and trials*. London: QCA.

QCA et al. (2006a). *NVQ Code of Practice. Revised 2006*. London: QCA.

QCA et al. (2007). *Evaluating the Qualifications and Credit Framework: Year 1 report*. London: QCA.

Robbins, L. (1963). *Report of the Committee on Higher Education*. HMSO.

Robertson, D. (1988). *The Unit of credit and statements of competence*. Liverpool: Merseyside Open College Federation.

Robertson, D. (1993, June). Speech to FEU Conference on 'Credit Frameworks'. London.

Robertson, D. (1994). *Choosing to Change: Extending access, mobility and choice in higher education*. London: HEQC.

Rothblatt, S. (1991). The American Modular System. In R. E. Berdahl, *Quality and Access in Higher Education*. London: SRHE.

Sanders, J. (2009, June). E-mail to the author. Manchester.

Sanders, J. and Whaley, P. (2007). *Celebrating Achievement. 25 Years of Open College Networks*. Leicester and Derby. NIACE and NOCN.

SCQF (2002, December). SCQF: National Plan for Implementation of the Framework. Glasgow: SCQF.

SCQF (2002). *The Scottish Credit and Qualifications Framework: National Plan for Implementation of the Framework.* Glasgow: SCQF.

Smithers, R. (2002, 15 June). Government report condemns shoddy exam board standards. *The Guardian.*

SQA (1999). *Adding Value to Learning.* Glasgow: SQA.

Stanton, G. (1997). Unitization: Develping a common language for describing achievement. In Hodgson, A. and Spours, K, *Dearing and Beyond* (pp. 121–34). London: Kogan Page.

Sterne, M. (2008). Speech to NIACE Conference on 'Recognising Achievement'. Manchester.

Stott, C. (1993). *From Authorised Validating Agency to Open College Network.* London: FEU.

Strategy Unit (2002). *In Demand: Adult Skills in the 21st century – Part 2.* London: Cabinet Office.

SYOCF (1987). *The accumulation of credits towards a National Vocational Qualification. A response to the NCVQ consultative paper.* Sheffield: SYOCF.

SYOCF (1989). *Exploration of the Feasibility of relating Open College Federation Awards with National Vocational Qualifications. Proposal for a WRFE Development Fund Research and Demonstration Project.* Rotherham: SYOCF.

SYOCF (1989a). *Developing a Comprehensive Local Credit Framework.* Sheffield: SYOCF.

Tait, T. (1997). Speech to FEDA Conference on 'A National Credit Framework'. London: FEDA.

Tait, T. (2002). *Further Education and Credit Developments: a report to the Learning and Skills Council.* London: LSDA.

Tait, T. (2003). *Credit Systems for Learning and Skills.* London: LSDA.

The Independent (2002, 3 October). The A-level debacle and the accountabiity of ministers. *The Independent.*

The Independent (2003, 15 April). Government to blame for A-level fiasco, rules enquiry. *The Independent.*

Torrance, H. (2005). *The impact of different modes of assessment on achievement and progress in the learning and skills sector.* London: LSDA.

Toyne, P. (1979). *Educational Credit transfer: feasibility study.* DES.

UDACE (1990). *Developing Open College Networks.* Leicester: NIACE.

ULEAC (1993). *FEU Research Project 768.* London: ULEAC.

Universties UK et al. (2008). *Higher Education Credit Framework for England.* London: UUK et al.

Unwin, L. (2007, 8 May). Why don't we question the Leitch report more? *The Guardian.*

Williams, J. V. (2005, 6 September). Meeting of Awarding Bodies and Regulatory Authorities – 7 September. *Letter to Ken Boston et al.* Cardiff: ACCAC.

Wilson, P. (1987). *Current Developments in Credit Accumulation and Transfer.* Sheffield: City of Sheffield Education Committee.

Wilson, P. (1988). Modularisation and Credit Accumulation and Transfer: A Framework for Development. *Further Education Staff College Seminar Paper.*

Wilson, P. (1988a). *A NOCN Study Passport? A proposal.* Sheffield: SYOCF.

Wilson, P. (1993). *Levels within the Credit Framework.* London: FEU (unpublished paper).

Wilson, P. (1993a). Beyond 'A Basis for Credit?' – developing technical specifications for a national credit framework. *Unpublished consultation paper.* London: FEU.

Wilson, P. (1993b). Developing a Post-16 CAT Framework: the technical specifications. In FEU, *Discussing Credit.* London: FEU.

Wilson, P. (1993c). *Awarding Credit: Principles of Quality Assurance.* London: Unpublished FEU Report.

Wilson, P. (1995). Lasers in the Jungle. *University of Warwick Centre for Education and Industry.* Coventry: University of Warwick.

Wilson, P. (1998). From credit framework to credit-based qualifications. *Unpublished internal document.* Derby: NOCN.

Wilson, P. (1998a). Angels and Pinheads: Does size really matter? *NOCN Discussion paper.* Derby: NOCN.

Wilson, P. (1999). It's credit Jim, but not as we know it. *Adults Learning,* October, pp. 23-4.

Wilson, P. (1999a). *Lifelong Qualifications.* Leicester: NIACE.

Wilson, P. (2004). *Devilish Details: Developing the new Framework for Achievement.* Leicester: NIACE.

Wilson, P. (2005). *Learning from learning from experience.* London: QCA.

Withers, W. D. (2006). *Intellectual Property in a Digital Age.* London: IPPR.

Wolf, A. (1996). The cost of the NVQ programme. In P. Robinson, *Rhetoric and Reality: Britain's New Vocational Qualifications.* London: London School of Economics.

Working Group on 14-19 Reform (2004). *14-19 Curriculum and Qualifications Reform: Final Report.* London: DfES.

Yeo, S. (1998, Winter). The pre-history and theory of credit. *Journal of Access and Credit Studies,* pp. 53-69.

Young, M. (2003). National Qualifications Frameworks as a Global Phenomenon: a Comparative Perspective. *Journal of Education and Work,* Vol 16 No. 3, 223-37.

Young, M. (1997). The Dearing Review of Qualifications: A step towards a unified system? In Hodgson, A. and Spours, K, *Dearing and Beyond* (pp. 25-39). London: Kogan Page.

Index